BLAZES ALONG A
DIPLOMATIC TRAIL

A Memoir of Four Posts in
the Canadian Foreign Service

J.C. GORDON BROWN

Canadian Cataloguing in Publication Data

Brown, J. C. Gordon (John Clemence Gordon), 1922–
  Blazes along a diplomatic trail

  Includes index.
  ISBN 1-55212-524-6

  1. Brown, J. C. Gordon (John Clemence Gordon), 1922–
2. Diplomats--Canada--Biography. 3. Diplomatic and consular service, Canadian--Anecdotes. I. Title.
FC601.B77A3 2000   327.71'0092   C00-911370-3
F1034.3.B77A3 2000

F
1034.3
.B77
A3
2000

TRAFFORD

This book was published *on-demand* **in cooperation with Trafford Publishing.**
On-demand publishing is a unique process and service of making a book available for retail sale to the public taking advantage of on-demand manufacturing and Internet marketing.
On-demand publishing includes promotions, retail sales, manufacturing, order fulfilment, accounting and collecting royalties on behalf of the author.

Suite 6E, 2333 Government St., Victoria, B.C. V8T 4P4, CANADA
Phone   250-383-6864   Toll-free   1-888-232-4444 (Canada & US)
Fax   250-383-6804   E-mail   sales@trafford.com
Web site   www.trafford.com   TRAFFORD PUBLISHING IS A DIVISION OF TRAFFORD HOLDINGS LTD.
Trafford Catalogue #00-0189   www.trafford.com/robots/00-0189.html

10   9   8   7   6   5   4

CONTENTS

PREFACE

My time in the Canadian Foreign Service lasted 32 years, from 1947 to 1979. Of those years, the most rewarding were almost a dozen that formed the middle period of my career. From mid-1958 to the beginning of 1970, I served abroad in South Africa, the Soviet Union, the Democratic Republic of the Congo and Cyprus, with only a two-year stint in the sixties at headquarters in Ottawa. During my days in each of the four countries troubling events took place, and they faced uncertain futures. Their situations were of international concern and impinged on Canadian interests. Their problems and the unfolding of our bilateral relations provided me, as a Canadian diplomat, with challenges and great job satisfaction.

The years marked great changes universally. A rocket lifted the chirping *Sputnik* into orbit a few months after I arrived in South Africa. Gagarin became the first man to travel into space. By the end of the 1960s, rocketry would land man on the moon. The wide-bodied jet aircraft superseded the ocean liner, transforming the journey to a foreign post from a period of thoughtful reflection into a physical and spiritual jolt. Colonial powers rushed to rid themselves of empires and, for many former colonies, independence was soon to be tarnished by corruption, ethnic hatred and worse. The nuclear arms race and rocketry development steadily intensified the peril to civilization. Everywhere the Cold War diminished the freedoms that most of my generation of diplomatic practitioners had served in war to defend.

From 1958 to 1970, each of the three very different men who were prime ministers of Canada reacted in very different ways to foreign affairs and the conduct of foreign policy. All three enter into this story. Seen from South Africa, John Diefenbaker's deep respect for human rights appeared as the motor of both his condemnation of the regime that had brought on the Sharpeville massacre of 1960 and his role in the departure of that country from the Commonwealth. There was some truth in his suspicion that we were "Pearson's old gang", although he was off base in that as a general assessment. L.B. Pearson's hand at the helm was usually — but not always — comforting to the professionals serving in the Soviet Union. His decency would be evident during my Congo years as was his determination when Canada's existence was under attack at home and from abroad. The last year of the sixties exposed the Department of External Affairs to the intellectual arrogance of Pierre Trudeau and his declared preference for the views of *The New York Times* to those of Canada's diplomats.

This is a "working" biography, a description of how one foreign service officer functioned on behalf of his country in various capacities, with increasing responsibility, in a variety of situations. It also relates family events and experiences along the trail that created boredom and excitement, frustration and satisfaction, sadness and joy, tension and togetherness. But my recollections do not adequately reflect the extra difficulties that my wife and daughters faced as they accompanied and supported me, especially when they could not always know about or share the allure of my work, but still had to put up with the challenges of foreign, often hostile, environments. My first wife, Wynne, was an active partner throughout my career despite the heart condition that interrupted her enjoyment of life and, eventually, caused her death.

My career covered the last decades of elegance in diplomatic style and practice. They were also the last years when our country, like others, relied on the initiative of its representatives abroad and respected their sound judgement to protect and promote national interests.

With the transition to the electronic age of instant communications, the diplomat abroad has a negligible role in the formulation of national positions. Staccato exchanges via satellite between Ottawa and posts precipitate instant solutions by those at headquarters and demand immediate compliance. Judgement, at either end, has been reduced to that of the driver of a vehicle, cellphone in hand, engaging in a conversation while making a turn at a busy intersection. May the pages that follow suggest to the reader that much has surely been lost in the transition from more thoughtful times.

While my oath of secrecy restrained the frankness with which I wrote privately about events when they happened, I have been able since to amplify those sources drawing on despatches that I wrote from posts to headquarters and comments that were made then on my reports and proposals.

I should like to acknowledge both the valuable assistance that I enjoyed from Pauline Dozois of the National Archives of Canada in leading me along the paper trail of my days in these posts and the unfailing encouragement in this enterprise of my colleague and the department's historian of my days, Arthur Blanchette. I wish to thank E.A. Kelly of the Department of Foreign Affairs and International Trade for steering my manuscript past the shoals of official clearance and offering useful comments. Parts or the whole of the manuscript were read by Rosemary Bauchman, Charles King and James Langley, who offered helpful criticism.

Special recognition is due to Terry Linford of Ottawa for designing the cover, and Patricia Brown of Ottawa, who prepared the book layout.

I acknowledge the kindness of McGill-Queen's University Press, on behalf of Carleton University Press, in granting me permission to include the chapter "Closing a Mission", which first appeared in the Carleton Press book of 1996 entitled *Special Trust and Confidence*, edited by David Reece.

Finally, my gratitude goes to my wife Francine for her patience and support during the many hours that I "played" at my word processor to recall some of the blazes that marked my diplomatic trail.

CHAPTER I

POSTING TO
SOUTH AFRICA:
THE FIRST YEAR

Winter was about to begin when the *African Endeavor* arrived at Cape Town harbour on the morning of 16 June 1958, the 18-day voyage from New York ended. The posting to South Africa that would last 45 months began for me and for my wife, Wynne, and daughters, Jane and Patricia, respectively 10 and 7-years-old.

It was a time of rain and gales. So strong was the wind that it was almost impossible to walk up Adderley Street, the broad main avenue of department stores and office buildings that led from the dock area to a tree-lined mall running up past the Houses of Parliament towards the old residential suburb of Oranjezicht. All was dominated by Table Mountain wearing its thickest tablecloth.

Our posting to South Africa had been in the books since the beginning of the year. I had corresponded about housing and other personal matters with Arthur Blanchette, whom I was replacing as First Secretary, and had learned from the Trade Commissioner, M.R.M. ("Mac") Dale, that a house had been leased for three months from our arrival. "Mouillé Grange" was a large, handsome building on the seafront at Mouillé Point on Table Bay. Though totally walled in, it had views of the sea and of the nearby lighthouse, known locally as the "Mouillé Cow" for the long, lowing sound of its horn on foggy nights. We learned only on our arrival that the landlady lived in an apartment in the house and that we would share a houseboy with her while taking over her Cape Coloured cook.

The arrangement was far from perfect: it reminded us that on our first posting in Switzerland we had shared a house with a landlady. And, we were unhappy to have to settle into, in essence, a very large entrance hall two storeys high — which had been set up as a reception room — a very large dining room, a billiards room, a few smaller rooms in which to live and sleep, and a tennis court. Moreover, along with other residents: a dog and cat and a cage of budgerigars, we had acquired a host of sand fleas which not only made the lives of our children miserable but also ruled out the quiet enjoyment of the beach across the road. Yet some found the house enchanting: after his visit to Cape Town with the Imperial Defence College, a foreign service colleague would write to thank us for an evening at our "Max Reinhardt palace".

The house was located about four kilometres from the office which was on the sixth floor of Norwich House on the Foreshore at the foot of Adderley Street near the docks. The front entrance faced a statue of the founder of the Dutch East Indies colony of the Cape of Good Hope, Jan van Riebeeck, on land that had once marked the gates to the port before new docks had been built across the edge of the former tidal flats. There were still few buildings on the Foreshore in 1958, but construction had begun of a new railway station and roads had been laid out across the flat land. The Norwich House office was the permanent quarters of one of the two Canadian Trade Commissioners in South Africa, the senior one being based in Johannesburg, 1450 kilometres to the north-east in Transvaal Province, close to the administrative capital Pretoria.

Arthur Blanchette arrived from Pretoria the morning after we had docked and we had several chats about the office and its personalities as well as the South African political scene before he left for his next posting, to Cambodia. A few days later the High Commissioner, J.J. Hurley and his staff, including Ross Francis the Second Secretary,[1] made the trek to Cape Town for the parliamentary session. By this time, we had settled in, having arranged for the schooling of our daughters at St. Cyprian's School on Belmont Avenue in Oranjezicht and taken delivery of our car and household goods.

My boss, James Joseph Hurley, was approaching his 60th birthday. He had served in the First World War from the age of 18, and was active in the militia between the wars while employed in the family printing firm in Brantford, Ontario. In the Second World War, he was commissioned as a Lieutenant-Colonel and, six years later, after various instructional roles in the United Kingdom, was discharged as a Colonel with an OBE and the Order of Orange-Nassau.

In 1947, Hurley's Liberal Party connections brought him an appointment as an Administrative Officer in External Affairs and an immediate assignment to the Canadian Military Mission in Berlin. A year later, he was made Consul General in Detroit, a post that he held for three-and-a-half years. There followed a stint in Ottawa as head of the Supplies and Properties Division at headquarters and, in mid-1953, he was appointed High Commissioner to Ceylon. He held that post until he was moved to South Africa, three months before my arrival.

I had received a great deal of intelligence from friends in the service about Hurley before I met him, for the first time, in Cape Town. Though not considered a heavyweight intellectually, he was regarded by all as a friendly man who craved the friendship of others. He was "Gentleman Jim", a sobriquet that flowed from his favourite introductory response of "Call me Jim", often abbreviated to CMJ. Golf was his passion, as well as the conviction that goodwill would conquer all. Perhaps this was a consequence of a lifetime of association with service clubs and involvement with the Moral Rearmament Group. His background made him an easy mark for the members of the Afrikaner Nationalist Government and a difficulty, often an embarrassment, for the members of his staff and for the Department in Ottawa when he propounded his simplistic political philosophy in public.

Before the first week was out, there was such an occasion when the High Commissioner was the guest speaker at the first meeting of Mac Dale's new creation, the Canadian-South African Businessmen's Association report of the speech in Cape Town's leading Afrikaaner daily *Die Burger* read in translation:

> Mr. Hurley stated that it was... his desire to give Canadians a better idea of South Africa. He had not been in the country very long, but it appeared to him that the two countries do not enjoy very good press relations. Too much emphasis is laid on the sensational... Only through mutual understanding of one another can the peoples of the two countries really learn to know one another. Because of that, Mr. Hurley wants to make sure that the more favourable aspects of South Africa appear in the Canadian press.

Reading that, I knew that I was in for rough weather.

There was another disturbing side to Jim Hurley. Although he was not a profound person, he considered himself a thinking man and a judge of character. If he found another person's point of view reasonable, he accepted it as honest. In reports to Ottawa, he based his own remarks on the opinions that were expressed to him. I learned from John Dougan, who had worked for Mr. Hurley in Colombo, that he had the habit of showing his drafts to his juniors before sending them to the Department. It appeared that he was seeking praise. John wrote:

> Do not, repeat not, make any changes, grammatical or otherwise, in any political draft he may give to you for comment. He is very touchy on this and the results can be dynamite.

Yet Hurley was, in John Dougan's words — which I quickly found to be true — a "kind, helpful and considerate boss" who went out of his way to make the office run without friction and who was always solicitous towards the staff. Hurley and I were to have our differences in the office, but it was to be he who made the greater effort to ensure that our personal good relations survived the problems that arose. However, I had to learn how to present a range of opinions in reports to Ottawa and have Hurley sign them even when they offended his view of the South African scene. Also, I sought to educate him in the intricacies of the Union's politics by bringing him into contact with individuals and groups who opposed the National Party's programme of separate development or *apartheid*. In this I failed, but I had a lot of satisfaction in trying.

Hurley valued his growing connections with Nationalist cabinet ministers and some might have thought that he was using them to argue quietly for changes in the application of the system of apartheid. Those that he cultivated were keen golfers, though not especially high in the pecking order of power within the ruling party. Neither Prime Minister J.G. Strijdom nor his successor Dr. Verwoerd, the Minister of Native Affairs, were in his group of friends. Nor was the Minister of External Affairs, Eric Louw. But, on the golf courses of Cape Town and Pretoria, Jim Hurley listened to the case of the Afrikaner Nationalists, who accounted for 60 percent of the white population. He became convinced of the need for the blacks to live separately from the whites. He accepted as legitimate the goal of the Nationalists to achieve their "rightful" place in the running of the country, free of the domination of the English South Africans and their Afrikaans-speaking allies, known pejoratively as "Loyal Dutch" by the Nationalists..

So as to demonstrate his sincerity and sympathy to his Nationalist friends, Hurley took up the study of the Afrikaans language soon after arriving in South Africa and encouraged others on the staff to follow his example. He was not the first Canadian diplomat to do so: Ross Francis had already achieved some scholarly proficiency. In Cape Town that winter, five of us took lessons from Sarah Goldblatt, once the secretary of an Afrikaner named Langenhoven who had done much to codify the Low Dutch *tael* of the Boers and obtain for it equal status with High Dutch as an official language along with English. At the beginning of August, our linguistic endeavour was recorded in a front-page article in the *Cape Argus*[2] accompanied by a photo of a happy Sarah sitting amongst her pupils. Afrikaners may have been pleased with our efforts but the Argus was, after all, an English-language paper, and we probably did not win the hearts of many Capetonians.

I did not pursue my studies to the point of fluency in Afrikaans but I learned most of the simple grammar of this undeclined language and enough words to appreciate the elements that had been fused into its creation, elements from Dutch, Portuguese, French, Malay and Hottentot, seldom from English. I learned how to say Good Morning — *Goeie More*, and How are You? — *Hoe gaan dit?* The terms for hill, farmer and foreigner — *koppie*, *boer* and *uitlander* — were familiar: indeed, as a result of the Boer Wars, they were already embodied in the English language. I learned how to pronounce *apartheid*, not as apart-hide, as most of its opponents abroad intoned it, but as apart-ate. The double negative *"nie ... nie"*, a relic of the French of the Huguenot settlers, amused me. I wondered why Sarah and Langenhoven had chosen to transliterate the ugly North American term "dead-end street" as *straat loop dood* (street runs dead) rather than employ the gentler French *and* English *cul-de-sac*. Perhaps their motivation was like that of the language exarchs of Quebec who, for traffic signs, refused to accept the French word *"stop"* for the English "stop" and ordained that *arrêt* be used.

The parliamentary session began on 20 June 1958 and the High Commissioner left Cape Town on home leave in Canada on 6 August, returning to Pretoria towards the end of September. Hurley spent a few days in Ottawa on consultations in the Department and I conspired with friends to ensure that he be reminded of the Canadian distaste of the racial policies of the government of Prime Minister Strijdom.

During the High Commissioner's absence, I was in charge of the post: it was my first and last stint of duty in South Africa as Acting High Commissioner. As the head, albeit temporary, of a diplomatic mission, I was involved in all of the formality and circumstance that occupied the Ambassadors and High Commissioners. There were receptions for national days and functions for departing Heads of Mission. A farewell lunch given by Eric Louw for Sir Percivale Liesching, the departing British High Commissioner, took me to the House of Assembly restaurant while a dinner honouring the new South African Ambassador to the United States, W.C. du Plessis, was held in the historical Castle of the Dutch East Indies Company. But the most memorable experience for me was to take part, on 27 August, in the funeral service for Prime Minister Strijdom[3] at the *Groote Kerk* — the oldest church of the Dutch Reformed Church in South Africa — and afterwards to walk in the funeral procession behind the body down Adderley Street to the station in one of the front rows of official mourners between lines of cadets of the Navy Gymnasium and thousands of quiet members of the public. I was not mournful over Strijdom's death but taking part in the pomp and circumstance of the occasion revealed to me a side of my job that I had not contemplated.

Strijdom was succeeded by Dr. Hendrik Frensch Verwoerd who had provided much of the philosophical basis of the grand apartheid — the separation of the races into their own homelands — that was to dominate his years as Prime Minister. As Minister of Native Affairs, Verwoerd had already established himself as the high priest of the National Party. On 9 September, when I called on him briefly to convey the congratulations of the Canadian Government on his new position, I was conscious of the steely determination behind the smiling graciousness of this quiet-spoken man.

When I arrived in South Africa, the National Party (NP) — to a man, in Parliament, Afrikaners — had been in power for almost a decade. It had taken the Afrikaners almost a half-century to reverse the defeat of the South African War by seizing power from the English South Africans and the "Loyal Dutch". Now the NP was engaged in asserting white domination, *baaskaap*, over the other, non-white, elements of the South African population: the majority of the people of the country who were playing a bigger part than ever before in the economy, especially in manufacturing, and were settling in ever-increasing numbers in the cities where their labour was needed by industry. When the Afrikaner nationalists came to power in 1948, they began a legislative programme of restrictions on the non-white peoples — Africans, Cape Coloured, Indians and Chinese — which created the system of racial discrimination or apartheid. It was this codification of racial discrimination that was to bring down the wrath of the international community on South Africa.

The keystone of apartheid was the Group Areas Act of 1950 under which people were separated into three categories: White (often known as "European"), Native (called "African" by the liberal-minded, "Bantu" by later theologians of apartheid and "Kaffir" by white racists) and Coloured, they being sub-divided into Indians, Chinese and Malay, the latter the description of the Cape Coloured. At the time that the Group Areas Act was passed, the Afrikaner Nationalists openly declared that its goal was to maintain white supremacy. (The population statistics reinforced the concern of the whites who numbered only three million in a country approaching 15 million. The blacks accounted for almost 10 million, Coloured 1.36 million and Asians 440,000.) When I came to South Africa, the rationale was more sophisticated: the Act was said to be necessary to eliminate friction among the races by separating them and enabling each community to conduct its own affairs and preserve its own culture and identity. It was a justification that appealed to many white South Africans, including the more conservative of the United Party Opposition — and to J.J. Hurley.

Although the Group Areas Act was central to the introduction of official apartheid, it was not the first legislation of the Nationalists after their election in 1948. That distinction was given to the subject of sex. In 1949, the Prohibition of Mixed Marriages Act prohibited marriages between whites and blacks and whites and Coloured or Asians, but not amongst blacks, Coloured or Asians. Thus the law made formal one of the discriminatory conventions by which white South Africans were insulated from the rest of the population: the law was designed to protect the Europeans, not to prevent miscegenation generally. Following the ban on mixed marriages, another was imposed on sexual relations by means of the extension of the Immorality Act of 1927, prohibiting "carnal intercourse between Europeans and Natives and other acts in relation thereto", to such relations between Europeans and Coloured.

The Population Registration Act of 1950 established a national register in which everyone was classified according to race. Sir de Villiers Graaff, later the Leader of the Opposition, termed it "a human stud book". The Act laid the foundation for the Group Areas Act and other apartheid legislation because it provided that, eventually, everyone in the country would carry an identity document stating his race. The Reservation of Separate Amenities Act, 1953, separated the facilities used by Europeans and non-Europeans — buses, benches, beaches, hospitals, swimming pools, entrances to public buildings, railway coaches and so on and on — and added up to legalised prevention of social contact. The Bantu Education Act of 1953 centralized the education of Blacks under the Ministry of Native Affairs and eliminated most of the country's mission schools by withdrawing financial support from them; only the Roman Catholic mission schools remained open. The Government's attack on the university system stirred up fierce opposition in the mid-1950s. Its objective of closing the doors of "white" universities to "others" was not achieved until 1959. The principal targets were the "English" universities of Cape Town and Witwatersrand.

As the decade progressed, the volume of apartheid legislation proliferated. Multi-racial trade unions were forbidden and the existing ban on strikes by Africans was reinforced. On the political side, the National Party moved to disenfranchise non-whites and new measures were adopted to deal with public emergencies and civil disobedience. More, much more, was to follow during my four years in the country.

Despite the limitations that were being put into place on the freedom of the African and Coloured peoples, Cape Town was still a relatively relaxed city in 1958. The central city and its southern suburbs had not

7

yet been zoned to separate the races residentially under the Group Areas Act and there was still a thriving Cape Coloured community just a mile up the valley from the city centre. Buses had only just been segregated. Relations between whites and Coloured people seemed reasonably good. But the story was different in respect of the blacks whose labour had assumed an importance, especially in the Cape Town Docks, that was recognized neither by the local whites nor the Government when it came to the right of the blacks to reside in the Cape with their wives and families and to be properly housed. In the country as a whole, one in four of the blacks lived in the cities. This did not include the migrant mine workers. I had my first brush with group areas when, through the State Information Office, I made a visit to three black townships near Cape Town: Windermere, Matroosfontein and Nyanga. The visit impressed on me the rigid segregation of races that the white South Africans imposed, the futility of the effort to control the influx of blacks to the cities and the condescending paternalism of the white officials of the Department of Native Affairs who administered the rules. When I returned to my home in Cape Town, I found it difficult to accommodate to the contrast in living conditions that I had seen that day.

I spent much of my time in those first months on calls on people to establish contacts useful to my understanding of the situation in the Union. Apart from fellow diplomats, I made it a priority to meet members of the press, calling on the editors of the major Cape Town newspapers: Morris Broughton of the *Cape Argus*, Victor Norton of the *Cape Times*, and Phil Weber and Piet Cillié of the Afrikaans-language *Die Burger*. I was then able to turn to the other journalistic lights, above all in the Press Gallery of Parliament. At various events, I met parliamentarians. Indeed, one of the first South Africans with whom I became acquainted was Sir de Villiers Graaff, the Leader of the United Party (UP), the party of the legendary Jan Smuts which was now the Official Opposition. I was given honorary membership in the Civil Service Club; established in 1858, it was the oldest club in the Union. Its location on Church Square, only a block from Parliament, provided me with a convenient, pleasant and inexpensive way to entertain my new acquaintances. More senior diplomats were given membership in the City Club on Queen Victoria Street and I was often taken there as a guest. There was an Afrikaner club, the *Here Sewentien* ("Seventeen Gentlemen", formed only in 1956) which I saw occasionally as a guest of the editors of *Die Burger*.

There were other, less serious, duties in those first few months which we engaged in to learn about the country and to meet people. In August, my wife and I went on a tour of the Cape Town docks arranged by a new friend in the South African Broadcasting Corporation; we lunched at the Master Mariners Club and went aboard a ship of the whaling fleet. Later in the month, we visited Paarl, inland from the Cape, for a day at the wineries of the KWV (Ko-operatieve Wijnbouwers Vereniging or Co-operative Winegrowers Association). There was a lunch on board the *Thorshope* of the Christensen-Canadian African Lines, a Norwegian merchant ship that plied between southern Africa and the Canadian east coast, and a visit to the Royal Navy submarine *Alaric* at Simonstown Docks.

In our first week in the Cape, we had met our first South African friends, Jim and Maureen Turner, over the garden wall at Mouillé Grange; through them we came to know an ever-widening circle of Capetonians. At the end of July, we held our first cocktail party and prided ourselves that there were almost 50 diplomats and locals present. In August, we added variety to our entertaining by having a Sunday tennis party and a Friday evening showing of Canadian films. In September, we gave a dinner party. We entertained a half dozen sailors, including three Canadians, from the *Alaric* along with the staff and South African friends at a dance on a Saturday night, making good use of the marble-floored hall of Mouillé Grange. A few days later, one of the sailors was seriously injured in a car accident and had to be left behind at Wynberg military hospital when the sub sailed. I recalled, when I visited him, that a friend in England had told me about his convalescence at the same hospital during the Anglo-Boer War.

By the time we left for Pretoria, we were well into the world of South African politics, the bureaucracy, the media and academia and the Cape business community. We had also become close friends of several diplomats with whom I was in regular touch on developments in the Union. Lunch at the Civil Service Club was our usual venue. Waldemar B. ("Waldo") Campbell, a First Secretary of the United States Embassy, had been in South Africa for a year when I arrived, but his knowledge of the country pre-dated his posting by several years. His doctoral thesis at the University of California, Berkeley, had been on the expansion of the South African frontier from 1865 to 1885;[4] research for it had brought him to the country a decade earlier. Waldo and his wife, Mary, became fast friends. At the British mission, Eleanor Emery, First Secretary — who had been raised in Calgary, Canada — and John Baines ("Jack") Johnston, Deputy High Commissioner, were close and fruitful sources for most of my posting as well as congenial colleagues.

Hurley did not return to the Cape: his home leave extended for a month beyond the move of the office to Pretoria at the end of the parliamentary session early in October. At this point, the Canadian staff consisted of two FSOs, Ross Francis and myself, two foreign service secretaries, Jean Smith and Mae Edwards, and an administrative clerk, Maureen Pepper. Jean, my secretary in Ottawa a few months before, had succeeded the popular Winnie Anderson as the High Commisioner's secretary. There was no communicator: for confidential exchanges with Ottawa and other posts, we — the Canadian staff — had to use book cypher and one-time pads, a process that accounted for untold hours of dedication and unpaid overtime.

Wynne and I had been encouraged by friends to drive to Pretoria by way of the long coastal road, known as the "Garden Route", and I planned a nine-day trip which was a mixture of business and pleasure. Leaving Jane and Tricia as boarders at St. Cyprian's School, and feeling like very bad parents because Jane's 11th birthday was the next day, we set out on Saturday, 11 October. The first day took us along 450 km of magnificent coastal scenery to the village of Wilderness, beyond Mossel Bay and George, the Outeniqua Mountains flanking the coast just inland. The next morning we continued past Knysna — another beauty spot famous also for its forest of stinkwood, which the South Africans used for their fine furniture — to Cape Seal and Plettenberg Bay and on to Cape Recife and the city of Port Elizabeth. We were now 640 km due east of Cape Town on Latitude 34 South.

In Port Elizabeth, I visited the General Motors automobile plant, where North American models were assembled using parts imported from Canada, and called on John Sutherland, the editor of the *Evening Post*, to learn a little about the importance of the city's Asian population in the political equation. Sutherland brought in B.B. Ramjee, a prominent member of the Indian community, for my meeting. That Monday afternoon, we drove on to Grahamstown, where we had dinner with Mr. and Mrs. Edward Sherwood of Rhodes University and spent the night at the comfortable Stone Crescent Hotel. In the morning, we visited Rhodes, one of the four English-speaking universities in the country, lunching with E.H. Wild, the Acting Vice-Chancellor, and meeting members of the faculty whose views challenged the actions of the government as well as some of my own half-formed opinions. Rhodes served as the "examiner" for our next point of call, the non-European university college of Fort Hare where, of the student body of close to 400, two-thirds were training as teachers.

Before reaching Fort Hare, we crossed the Great Fish River and turned inland towards Alice, stopping for the night at the Hogsback Hotel, a famous inn situated in a dramatic setting high up in the rolling countryside of the eastern Cape Province.

The Principal of Fort Hare College was Professor H.R. Burrows, a white who had replaced Dr. Z.K. Matthews, the celebrated African prominent in the liberation movement for over a decade. In December 1956, Matthews had been arrested, along with 156 others of all races, for treason under the Suppression of Communism Act; the "Treason Trial", as it was known, had begun in August 1958 and was to grind on well into my posting. During my visit, I met, amongst others, Professor L. Blackwell of Law, Mrs. Z.K. Matthews, two other Africans, Professors Mzamame and S.B. Ngcobo, and a Canadian, Fred Sass, who had taught at Fort Hare for a couple of years but was on the point of leaving. The college had been the scene of a major protest against apartheid in 1955 and was about to pay the price of dissent. In 1959, the connection with Rhodes University was severed and Fort Hare became a Bantu University College, the student body restricted to Africans, under the aegis of the Bantu Education Department and affiliated to the University of South Africa for examination purposes. The imminence of this fate cast a pall on the faculty members during my visit. Many of them were to resign when the blow fell; Professor Burrows was replaced as Principal by Professor J.J. Ross of the University of the Free State in Bloemfontein, an Afrikaner despite his name.

The remainder of the trip was devoted to sightseeing. After an overnight stay in East London at the Hotel Dolphin on Nahoon Beach, we drove through the Transkei Native Reserve, stopping at Umtata for a brief call on officials before going on to Port St. Johns where we put up at the Needles Hotel. On Friday, 17 October, we drove the final 430 km along the coast to Durban. We stayed at the Park View Hotel and had dinner with the American Consul, John Bentley, and his wife, with whom we had travelled to South Africa in the *African Endeavor*. Saturday saw us in Fort Mistake near Harrismith and we finished the 2688 km trip from the Cape the next afternoon when we arrived in Pretoria.

It was full spring in the city, which seemed to be covered with a veil of mauve by the blossoms of the jacaranda trees that lined the boulevards. We took a small suite at the Assembly Hotel on Van der Walt Street, in the city centre next door to the State Model Schools where 60 British officers, Winston Churchill among them, were held as prisoners of war in 1899. After a short search, we found a house at 29 Victoria Street at the top of Crown Avenue in the attractive Waterkloof area. By the end of the month we were installed there and had held our first dinner party.

The rent for 29 Victoria, partly furnished, was 75 pounds monthly. The house was very nicely located. The grounds were on a hillside looking north over the broad valley, where the eastern suburbs of the city lay, to *Meintjies Koppie*, the ridge running east from the Union Buildings and ending at Steubens Fort, one of the remaining Boer defensive positions around the erstwhile capital of the South African Republic of Boer days. About six km due north of our house was the High Commissioner's residence, "Canada *Koppie*", on top of the ridge in the suburb of Colbyn.

A small swimming pool was located below a terrace in front of the house and a metal slide afforded a quick way of going for a dip. Below the pool were more terraces of flowers and bushes and a steep driveway led up to the house on the west side to the carport adjacent to the house and a parking area for three or four cars. In the grounds behind the house was a small hut with two tiny rooms and a primitive bathroom which functioned as the quarters for our two servants, a man and a woman. The male servant was a Nyasa named Daison. When he decamped a few months later, we hired Dickson Chirente, a very loyal man who had served in the King's East African Rifles in Burma during the war. We were most fortunate with the female servant, Josephine, who was the wife of the second driver at the High Commission, Simon Maseromulu. She was to remain with us for over two years.

The house at 29 Victoria Street was to be our Pretoria base for the remainder of our posting. On 12 December, the girls arrived by air from Cape Town to spend the Christmas break with us, looking overfed and unkempt. One of their teachers at St. Cyprian's had written in mid-November to tell us that both had adapted remarkably well to their new environment. She said that Jane was working well and "was very good indeed to her little sister" who had been "a great success as a Bluebird in a boarders' entertainment, bringing the house down." Wynne and I had been relieved by this news for we were especially concerned that Tricia was not even eight years old when she entered the school.

The chancery in Pretoria was kept in operation during our time in Cape Town by a few local staff who tended to matters such as film distribution and consular enquiries. The office was located in Suite 66 of the Kerry Building, an unpretentious edifice on Vermeulen Street, a commercial street which ran parallel to and a block north of Church Street and was close to Church Square, the heart of the city where

Oom Paul Kruger's statue reminded all of the proud independence that the Boers of the Transvaal had once enjoyed.

Once we had settled into the office, we began to make new acquaintances in Pretoria and Johannesburg. I joined the Pretoria Club which was similar in style and cost to the Civil Service Club in the Cape. But I was not to use it as much, partly because the pace of work in Pretoria, lacking the focus on politics that the parliament gave to Cape Town, was not as intense and partly because there were simply not that many interesting people in the administrative capital. Wynne and I became members of the Pretoria Country Club which was just a couple of blocks away from our house. There we played golf, badly, and enjoyed the club's facilities for entertaining and being entertained. Our path to society was eased by helpful colleagues in the diplomatic corps as well as Ross and Ardath Francis of the High Commission and C.R. (Chuck") Gallow, the Canadian Trade Commissioner in Johannesburg and his wife, Gwen. Our progress was also assisted by the fact that I was still Acting High Commissioner for the first weeks in Pretoria and benefited from invitations at the head of mission level. Wynne was the first to cash in on this factor when, in company with the wives of other heads of mission, she was received by the Prime Minister's wife at the official residence, *Libertas*, in Bryntirion, the suburb where the state-provided houses of all cabinet ministers were located.

I made my first excursion to Johannesburg on 24 October to meet Quintin Whyte, the director of the South Africa Institute of Race Relations (SAIRR) and members of his staff, notable among them Miss Muriel Horrell, a research officer who was responsible for many of the Institute's publications. While in Cape Town, I had called on the head of the Institute's regional office for the Cape, but my visit to the central office and its library in Johannesburg was to convince me of the importance of the SAIRR to my own activity in South Africa.

Founded in 1929, the Institute of Race Relations had been established to further, in the words of its statement of aims, "inter-racial peace, harmony and co-operation in South Africa by seeking the truth in all inter-racial situations and making it known, whether it be popular or unpopular with any Government or party or group." Membership was multi-racial and was to remain resolutely so in the years to come. About the only concession that the Institute made to soften the disfavour in which it was held by the NP Government was to drop the final defiant clause in the statement of objectives. Every year, the Institute published *A Survey of Race Relations*. Edited by Muriel Horrell, the *Survey* was an encyclopedic review of developments affecting the racial question in all its aspects and a most valuable source for diplomats and all who followed the South African scene.

My contact with the SAIRR became closer early in 1959 when I attended its annual Council meeting in Cape Town. The official opening ceremony, held in Hiddingh Hall at the University of Cape Town with a multi-racial audience, was addressed by the former Chief Justice, the Honourable A. van der Sandt Centlivres, who had very little good to say for the Nationalist Government. He was followed by the president of the Institute, Donald A. Molteno, who gave a careful, scholarly dissertation on the theme of the conference, the possible constitutional forms that a multi-racial South Africa might take. I attended the Council meetings for the next three days and noted in my diary how refreshing it was to hear Africans taking part in discussions. One was Professor Ngcobo whom I had met at Fort Hare. Also taking part was B.B. Ramjee to whom I had been introduced in Port Elizabeth; his contribution was in the discussion — initiated by Muriel Horrell — of the Group Areas Act. Besides renewing these contacts, I made a number of others during the sessions which were rewarding in themselves. It was gratifying to hear the participants take a cool, thoughtful approach to racial problems and speak of a brighter future. But it was also somewhat depressing because no one saw an early end to the the National Party Government. I gained a deep respect for the work of the Institute and remarked in a letter that its continued existence was one of the few bright facts on the South African scene. I added:

> It can be useful even to the Nationalists: Quintin Whyte told me with some self-satisfaction that the SABRA [South African Bureau of Racial Affairs] people, whose executive members are now on a Union-wide tour to meet African intellectuals in order to sell apartheid, had to ask the Institute to arrange the meetings.[5]

SAIRR envisaged a South Africa in which all peoples would be part of the governance of the country. At the end of March 1959, I experienced the other side of the Union's coin of racial "solutions" when I attended the annual conference in Durban of SABRA. I travelled to Durban by air, my first flight in South Africa taking me there via Port Elizabeth in four-and-a-half hours. It was hot and muggy, so hot that a swim in the Indian Ocean did nothing to cool me off. But I was comfortably lodged at Claridge's Hotel on the waterfront. I had dinner on my first evening with Tom Karis, a Second Secretary of the United States Embassy, and Milton Bracher of *The New York Times* who was on a six-month tour of east and southern Africa; I was to meet him again in May in Windhoek in South

West Africa. We went on to the Wesley Hall to hear the Minister of External Affairs give the opening speech with a mediocre dissertation on the Union's policy towards the rest of the continent of Africa, which was the theme of the four-day conference. The proceedings were in Afrikaans but diplomats and the few others who did not understand the language were given simultaneous translation in English.

SABRA was wedded to a theoretical version of apartheid that was far in advance of that practised by the National Party and Government and had a moral basis which appealed to many Afrikaners whose religious convictions were troubled by the naked racism of some of the laws that had been enacted since 1948. To the intellectuals of the organization, racial separateness was in the interest of the non-whites as much as it was necessary for the whites. It was essential for the Africans, above all, to have their own homeland in order that they might preserve and foster their own culture. Hence *total* apartheid was needed.

The Bureau was established at Stellenbosch, the most liberal of the Afrikaans-language universities in 1950, two years after the National Party gained power. There I had my first contact with the organization on a visit in October 1958 to meet Nick Olivier and Professor Sadie, two of its leading theoreticians. By this stage in the affairs of the country, both had become doubtful that SABRA's ideas would work and were sceptical that the Government would live up to its pledge to provide the Blacks with a viable homeland. The creation of "Bantustans" with non-contiguous territory scattered around the country did not meet the SABRA ideal. Moreover, Olivier and Sadie and their associates at Stellenbosch were unhappy with the isolation of the Coloured people from the Whites under the Group Areas Act.

It was evident at the Durban conference that there was no solid support for either SABRA's doctrine or the policies of the Afrikaner Government, although lip service was paid to them by all the speakers. As for the official theme of the conference, the delegates' endorsement of the foreign policy objective of developing contacts with other African states gave no indication of the disappointment among the Stellenbosch group at the failure of the Government to make much headway towards this goal.

The Durban meeting gave me the opportunity to get to know some of the parliamentarians who were there, especially three young United Party MPs — Colin Eglin of Cape Town, Zach de Beer of Johannesburg and Ray Swart of Durban — and J. duP. ("Japie") Basson, a National Party member from Windhoek. On the third afternoon of the conference, I played hookey to visit the Indian market of Durban with Japie and Bob Cunningham of the U.S. Consulate-General in Cape Town. I wrote in my diary:[6]

> As we were driving through the Indian quarter, Japie asked 'How would you
> unscramble this omelette?', a reference to the Group Areas shemozzle here.
> Bob answered: 'Call in the troops and clear the Indians out!' After a
> thoughtful moment, Japie responded 'Perhaps we'd better forget it exists.'

The SAIRR and SABRA meetings helped to round out my education
on the subject of apartheid. But before they took place, I had seen other
facets of the South African diamond in those first 10 weeks in Pretoria.
I spent an afternoon at the Old Synagogue to get a taste of the Treason
Trial of which I learned much more from an evening with the two principal defence attorneys in the case, I.A. Maisels and Sidney Kentridge, at
dinner at Tom Karis's. In Johannesburg, I visited the office of the lively
and courageous magazine *Drum* which was now being edited by Tom
Hopkinson of *Picture Post* fame in England a decade earlier. In the late forties, *Drum* had been launched by Jim Bailey, the son of the press baron Sir
Abe Bailey. With Anthony Sampson as its editor from 1950 to 1954, it
became an authentic urban African voice. At the office, I met some of the
astonishing team of black writers and photographers whose investigative
journalism had made the publication a thorn in the side of
Afrikanerdom.

Another visit during that stay in Pretoria was to the Leuwkop Prison
Farm where the Director of Prisons sought to impress on us the excellent
conditions in which convicted Africans were held. After an earlier visit to
Kingston Penitentiary in Canada, I could not find much to quarrel with
in what little we saw of the treatment of the prisoners.

Relatively few members of the civil service left Pretoria for Cape Town
during sessions of Parliament. This was true of the Department of
External Affairs and so, during this time, I came to know a large number
of its officers. In the High Commissioner's absence, I had some dealings
with the Secretary (the top civil servant) of the Department and I called
on the Assistant Secretaries and met the staffs of divisions, all diplomatic
officers who were on home postings. These meetings stood me in good
stead during the rest of my time in South Africa.

We enjoyed the house during the late spring and early summer and,
with the girls, even accepted the heat and the consequent destruction of
the Santa Claus myth at that first Christmas in the Southern Hemisphere.
The small swimming pool and the slide were a joy that season. When the
New Year came, we turned our thoughts to the move back to Cape Town.

We left Pretoria earlier than the rest of the office in order to attend
the SAIRR council meeting in Cape Town. Our route was the direct one

on the national road through Bloemfontein and Beaufort West, a distance of 1600 km for which we were allowed two nights lodging en route. The first day's drive, on 6 January, to Bloemfontein — the Union's judicial capital because the Supreme Court was located there — was uneventful. That evening, we walked along the streets of the city and rested on a bench in the central park; it was a benefit which we enjoyed together with other Whites in consequence of a nine o'clock curfew that confined the Blacks to their "area". In the morning, we visited the nearby "Women's Monument" commemorating the great numbers of Boer women and children, as many as 26,000 when the entire population of the Boer republics was less than a million, who died of typhoid fever in the camps where they were brought together or "concentrated" — a term that would become repugnant — by the British during the second Anglo-Boer War. Near the monument was the grave of Emily Hobhouse, an English woman who chose to work for the Boer cause. The museum at the site, not surprisingly, seemed dedicated to the inculcation of hatred for the "Brits" and their *concentration* camps.

The next day, we drove under a blazing sun across the arid Karroo from Colesberg to Beaufort West. The scrub-covered plateau that was the Karroo seemed beautiful on this first encounter with its mesa-like *koppies* rising in isolation from the flat landscape. But it was a semi-desert and there were more dust-devils to be seen than bushes or cactuses. That night in our room at the Wagon Wheel Motel at Beaufort West, we discovered a monkey spider, a large creature at least 15 cms broad, and Jane and I found another floating on the pool early the next morning when we went for a swim before setting out on the final leg of our journey. At that hour, most of our fellow travellers were already on the road to escape the heat, having been awakened shortly after five o'clock by the servant who delivered tea to the rooms; we were a little slower, getting away only at 8:15. We stopped for coffee near the Hex River Pass, lunched at Worcester and had a leisurely drive down the Du Toit's Kloof Pass to Paarl and on to Milnerton, across Table Bay from Cape Town. On Alamein Road, we took over *Vrede Vlei* — "Peace Pond" — the house that we had leased in October for the parliamentary session from its owner, Major General F.H. Theron.

The setting of *Vrede Vlei* was most pleasant. We were close to the Milnerton Lagoon and a smaller body of water known as *Riet Vlei* which was a stream in summer but became a lagoon in winter when Atlantic storms dammed its entrance with silt. The beach nearby was perfect for swimming and, when we tired of it, we had only a short drive to make to the salt-water pool at Sea Point or the surf at Muizenberg. We were surrounded by flowers, mostly indigenous Cape varieties that tolerated the sandy soil. Had we not had to endure a maid who could not resist the bottle, *Vrede Vlei* would have been idyllic for the Therons had indeed been imaginative in creating their retirement home.

It was easy to settle back into the routine of following political developments by means of calls on the players and business lunches, three a week on average and most of them at the Civil Service Club. I made it a habit to go on to the House of Assembly after lunch and watch the proceedings from the vantage point of the diplomatic gallery, looking down on the backs of the Government members and exchanging nods with my friends on the Opposition benches. Wynne soon had *Vrede Vlei* organized for entertaining and, during the session, was the hostess at a half dozen memorable occasions.

The Nationalist Government used the 1959 parliamentary session to push through the university apartheid bill, which had been stalled for a couple of years, and the legislation by which the foundations were laid for the creation of quasi-independent states, dubbed Bantustans by the Opposition, out of the Native Reserves. A law was also passed to establish a decimal currency replacing pounds, shillings and pence, a move seen by the increasingly beleaguered English-speaking Whites as cutting another tie with the British tradition.

I could now claim to have a group of very useful South African friends to guide me through the political scene, some in the Assembly. Zach de Beer was a UP member who, along with several other younger MPs of that party, had become unhappy with the leadership of De Villiers Graaff and his tendency to move to the centre — even to the right of centre, too close to the Nationalists. Unlike those whites in the Liberal Party who were ready to accept a multi-racial state, de Beer favoured a concept of power-sharing with non-whites. We were to hear more of Zach and his like-minded colleagues in the UP before the year was out.

Japie Basson had been at the SABRA conference in Durban with me but that was after I had lunched with him at the Civil Service Club and we had had him and his stunningly attractive wife, Clarence, to dinner at *Vrede Vlei*. Japie was squirming under the excesses of apartheid and, above all, the isolation of the Coloured people from the Whites. I saw Japie frequently that session before and during my trip to South West Africa, his parliamentary turf. Unlike most of his fellow-Nationalists, he had a conscience and was not prepared to see the country die because of rigid white Afrikaner racism; I formed a deep respect for his courage.

Stanley Uys was the parliamentary correspondent of the *Sunday Times* of Johannesburg. He was a thorn in the side of the Government, questioning everything that the National Party stood for at this time in the Union's history. It did not seem to faze Stan, an Afrikaner himself, that he would be considered a traitor by the governing Afrikaners, even more perfidious than those Afrikaners who were simply "Loyal Dutch". His reports and comments on political developments were at once thoughtful, incisive and totally to the point. His manner was studious but there was no mistaking where he stood when he summed things up, usually ending his comments with a humorous tag added with a meaningful smile. He had no equals in the press gallery during my time in South Africa.

Patrick Duncan was already a legend, despised if not hated by most Whites and held in esteem by politically conscious non-whites. The son of a former Governor-General of the Union of South Africa, Patrick had served in Basutoland as a district commissioner in the early fifties. In November 1952, he quit the colonial service and moved back to South Africa where he farmed and ran a mail-order bookshop. He was by now completely opposed to the direction in which race relations were being taken by the Nationalists and decided to throw his energy into the Defiance Campaign that had been launched by the African National Congress (ANC) in opposition to the Pass Laws, feeling that it was imperative that the blacks should see that there were whites who shared their aspirations for freedom. On 2 December 1952, he and six other whites joined 32 Indians — one of them Manilal Gandhi, the son of the Mahatma — to take part with members of the ANC in a peaceful demonstration at Germiston Location outside Johannesburg. They were arrested and Patrick spent two weeks in jail before appearing later that month at the annual meeting of the ANC where he was hailed as a guest of honour. (It was at that meeting of the ANC that Chief Albert J. Luthuli was elected president.)

When I met Patrick Duncan, he was prominent in the Liberal Party and working in Cape Town as Editor of the magazine *Contact*, the Liberal organ, whose masthead read "South Africa's Non-Racial Fortnightly". Pat suspected that his office, which was located close to the Civil Service Club, was being watched by the police and that his staff, mostly non-white, were being harassed. He was having difficulty obtaining a new passport and lived under the threat of one or other of the many sanctions that were available to the authorities if they wished to silence him and his publication. I and other diplomats valued him as a source and it was apparent that he considered that this relationship provided him with a shield against the Special Branch of the police.

There were others whose friendship was important that session. I had met the distinguished historian and Liberal, Leo Marquard, at the SAIRR meeting; his 1952 book *The Peoples and Policies of South Africa*[7] was a valuable political and social commentary on the country. Hilgard Muller of Pretoria was a useful contact in the National Party. Though not one with whom it was possible to argue a point frankly, he was more civilized than most other NP backbenchers, perhaps because he had been to Oxford as a Rhodes Scholar. Margaret Ballinger was the leader of the Liberal Party and one of the three whites who represented the African population in the Assembly. A fearless critic of the Nationalists, Mrs. Ballinger was to lose her seat in Parliament in 1960, eliminated under the "Promotion of Bantu Self-Government Act, 1959". Her colleague as a Native representative, Walter Stanford, was also worthwhile knowing.

Given that the High Commissioner was in regular touch with National Party opinion, my time and that of Ross Francis was better spent among those South Africans whose thinking was directed at finding ways out of the bog of apartheid. However, I continued to make calls on senior officials such as the Commissioner of Coloured Affairs and the Commissioner of Police, both thoroughly inflexible protectors of white purity and privilege. Socially we got on well with the Minister of Agriculture, P.K. LeRoux, and his wife, though conversations with them never counted for much. We also had many acquaintances among the less liberal UP politicians whose views were generally close to those of most of our purely social friends and neighbours.

Throughout the 1959 session, I pursued the goal of rounding out Jim Hurley's picture of the South African political scene. We held dinner parties at which we exposed him to people such as Leo Marquard and Margaret Ballinger; he liked them but squirmed at their comments about Verwoerd and his policies. After the SABRA conference, I thought that I had at last found a way of making him begin to question the rectitude of the Government's course. At my suggestion, Professor Sadie of SABRA invited the High Commissioner to its headquarters at Stellenbosch for a dialogue on the Bureau's aims and activities. Ross Francis and I accompanied him. Sadie introduced us to the others who included Dr. Gericke, the Vice-Principal of Stellenbosch University, and Professors Schuler, Weiss and Germishuys, the latter the secretary of the Bureau.

Ross and I listened, fascinated, while the SABRA group outlined their position on race relations, intimated how it differed from that of the Government and, by implication, set out their quarrel with the Prime

Minister himself. When all this did not go completely over Hurley's head, he reacted coldly, especially to the veiled criticism of Dr. Verwoerd. At length, he could not contain himself and blurted: "There is only one thing I want to know: do you or don't you support Dr. Verwoerd and the policy of apartheid?" The SABRA hosts glanced at each other in shocked disbelief but eventually one of them conceded that they did, indeed, *support* the Prime Minister.

It was all Jim Hurley wanted to hear. Smiling, he thanked the SABRA people for their hospitality and we got into the car and pulled down the tree-lined driveway from the Cedarwood Hotel where we had lunched. When we were out of sight, Hurley turned to me to comment that the SABRA admission on Verwoerd and apartheid meant that I had been misleading him about the position of the organization. As we sped towards Cape Town, I tried without success to persuade him that their attitude was not as simple as all that. He would have none of my explanation and, when he repeated his charge of my misleading him, I lost my temper and told him to write his own despatches. Silence reigned between us for the rest of the trip and until the next day in the office when life resumed its normal smiling course. It was the last time that I tried to educate Jim Hurley.

From 6–16 May, I made a visit to South West Africa, the first of several journeys to remote parts of southern Africa during the posting. It was great tourism and satisfying to my sense of adventure as well as improving my knowledge of the area and its politics. The official reason for my journey was to attend the opening of a new government building in the territory. A fellow passenger on the flight from Cape Town was Japie Basson, also on his way to attend the ceremony in Windhoek — and with better reason because he was the member of parliament for Namib. Japie was met by his wife and they gave me a lift to my hotel, the Thuringer Hof, on Kaiserstrasse; I was to see the Bassons often during my visit.

After dinner that evening, I went out to look at the city:

I walked along Kaiserstrasse and Bulowstrasse and Bahnhofstrasse — all the streets seem still to have their German names. Goeringstrasse is near the hotel, named after Hermann's father who was an early governor here.[8]

And the next morning, I continued my reconnaissance:

Ascension Day holiday. Went for a 2-hour walk... and wasn't very impressed with the dusty streets that Dr. van Rhijn, the former cabinet minister, said he preferred to those of London where he went at the end of '58 as High Commissioner. But the grounds of the administrative building, the Tintenpalast, are green and pretty and the horseman monument to the

21

Herero War of 1904–7 is handsome. I came across two other monuments: one to German soldiers killed in the 1892–94 war with the Namas and the other to Union soldiers who died in the Ovambo campaign of 1917.[9]

The official opening of Suidwes Afrika Haus, a cultural centre, was performed by the Minister of Justice of the Union, C.F. ("Blackie") Swart. Harry Oppenheimer was a major participant as head of the Consolidated Diamond Mining Corporation and De Beers, the major producers of the territory's wealth, and a benefactor of the Haus. That evening, as one of 250 guests, I attended an official dinner. Thanks to Japie, I met a number of prominent local businessmen and politicians, one of whom invited me afterwards for champagne at his house — a fort in German colonial days — with some of the other dinner guests, including Oppenheimer. It was not the last evening that I spent in the company of local whites and my days passed in calls on many of them at their banks, businesses and government offices.

The German colonization of South West Africa had lasted from 1883 to 1915 when South African troops occupied the territory during the First World War. The Treaty of Versailles conferred South West Africa on South Africa as a Mandate to be administered by the Union as an integral part of its territory. Between the wars there was criticism in the League of Nations of the manner in which South Africa was exercising its mandate; clearly, the territory was run for the benefit of the whites who accounted for about one-eighth of the population. When the United Nations was established after the Second World War, South Africa asked to be allowed to incorporate the territory into the Union. The UN refused this request and voted to bring South West Africa under the trusteeship system. The Union frustrated this course. After the National Party gained power, legislation was passed to incorporate the territory and give it much the same powers as those of the four provinces of the Union and similar representation in the Union parliament. When I visited South West Africa, this was the *de facto* situation. However, only the National Party hard-liners considered that the matter was settled.

My contact with the non-white population was essentially nil although I came across members of the Kung (Bushman), Nama (Hottentot), Baster ("Coloured") and Herero peoples every day in Windhoek. There were few Ovambos in the city. The largest nation, the Ovambos lived in the northern third of the territory and there were already stirrings of an independence movement among them. The chief of police and his security branch lieutenant told me that the situation was quiet but that the

African National Congress was active and the possibility of subversion was not to be ruled out.

How seriously the police regarded opposition among the Europeans was illustrated just after I returned to Cape Town. On my last evening, I gave a party for new friends at the Thuringer Hof and included Milton Bracher of *The New York Times* who had just arrived in Windhoek. A few days later, Bracher was arrested and fined for having gone to the Windhoek "location" — the black township — without a permit. A security branch lieutenant, the one I had met, spent almost three hours going through the reporter's notes and the Administrator of the territory delivered a homily in the press on the malign interference of foreigners. The touchiness of the white officials suggested that not all was well, an inference that was borne out at the end of 1959 when a protest by residents of the Windhoek location resulted in a police crack-down and the death of several blacks.

From Windhoek, I did a side-trip to Walvis Bay in a Piper Apache whose pilot made his way under a fog-bank across the Namib desert, flying so low that the journey was like a roller-coaster ride as he pulled up and over seemingly endless dunes. I was fascinated at the idea of setting foot in this enclave of South Africa which had been part of the Cape Colony when South West Africa was German, became South African at the time of the formation of the Union and remained a part of the Cape Province while serving as the most important seaport of the territory. Apart from relishing that romantic bit of historical trivia, I was not impressed:

> A town of 5000 whites and 8000 blacks (mostly Ovambo contract labour), Walvis Bay must be the most unattractive place I have ever seen. The town is blocked off from the sea by the fish factories and the docks and behind it is the Namib Desert. [There are] few gardens and the houses are dirty from sandstorms and sulphur eruptions.[10]

Yet, the town was booming as four million pounds were being spent on harbour improvements and a railhead. The water supply had been assured and was being piped to Swakopmund, 32 km to the north, for its brewery.

Japie Basson used the trip to Windhoek to sound out his supporters — and his father, Senator Basson — on his opposition to the Bantu Self-Government Bill on which a debate was due later in the month. On Sunday, 10 May, I had lunch with the Bassons and the Senator and, when I left, I told Clarence that I hoped to see more of them in Cape Town. In a clear allusion to Japie's trouble with the National Party, she replied that there might be no need for them to go to Cape Town for the next session of parliament.

Japie drove me back to the hotel and we sat in his car outside the front entrance for more than an hour talking over his predicament. He said that he had not yet decided how to play his opposition to the Bill but would definitely speak out against it and expected to be penalized by the caucus. Others in the Party understood his stand and some sympathized with it. But, he went on, Dr. Verwoerd would not tolerate it: the Prime Minister was not the cool person of the popular image but was easily rattled. Japie asked for my advice and I could only agree with him that he would not retain his credibility if he did not follow through even if it meant that he might have to leave the National Party. Our conversation was the only important event, politically, of my trip to South West Africa.

In our exchanges that warm afternoon, Japie had described the Bantu Self-Government Bill as camouflage for the removal from parliament of the whites who represented blacks, Margaret Ballinger above all, who were among the government's most effective critics. His comment reminded me that much of the apartheid legislation of the fifties bore titles that were the antithesis of their apparent purpose. In the case of the Extension of Bantu Education Act, whose stated purpose was to improve the educational facilities available to blacks, the real objective was to remove black students in mission schools from the liberal influence of the churches and so cut their ability to proselytize the African people spiritually or politically.

Two days after my return to Cape Town, the debate on the Bantustan Bill, as it was now called in the opposition press, started in earnest under the shadow of the guillotine. Japie Basson spoke against the legislation but, in the vote on the second reading, sided with the government; this he did despite a taunt from the Prime Minister that his conscience should not allow him to vote affirmatively after declaring his opposition in principle. I wrote in my diary that Japie was through as a Nationalist MP. When the bill became law, he was expelled from the National Party and crossed the floor to sit as an independent.

There were numerous bitter clashes between the Nationalists and the Opposition which made excellent theatre for the diplomats who followed the proceedings. One evening in May, Wynne and I went on from a cocktail party to the Assembly, then debating the Bantustan bill in committee so heatedly that Harry Lawrence and another member of the United Party were thrown out by the chairman, prompting a dozen more UP members to leave. Japie Basson spotted us in the gallery and invited us down to the members' lounge where we stayed long after the evening sitting had ended, at 10:45, regaled by a post-mortem of the debate by him and other members.

Although it had its way over the Bantustan legislation, the government was now clearly concerned at the outcry that ensued. It was much more concerned at the repercussions abroad, so much so that, at the beginning of June Eric Louw told the assembled heads of diplomatic missions that they should acquaint themselves with all aspects of the government's Bantu policy before coming to conclusions. "All we ask for", he went on, "is an open mind and a readiness to see both sides of South Africa's racial problems."

Louw and the National Party — indeed most whites — seldom hesitated to counterattack countries that were critical of South African racial policies, turning up instances of discrimination whenever they could. The Soviet Union and the Third World were easy targets but the South Africans were much more concerned with placing western countries on the defensive. The United States was vulnerable: civil rights were still denied to blacks in the South, school integration had yet to come and there were parallel towns, black and white, in many parts of the country. Four years were to pass before Martin Luther King made his defining speech, "I have a dream". In this era, the American diplomats who exhorted South African whites to be more brotherly towards the rest of the population operated under a serious handicap: they could not turn arguments simply by arguing that racial discrimination in the USA was not institutionalized as it now was in the Union.

Official South Africa considered that Canada, too, was vulnerable. The new South African High Commissioner in Ottawa delivered a speech in May in which he suggested that Canadians should understand the policy of apartheid because they practised it themselves in respect of Indians and Eskimos. Not amused, Prime Minister Diefenbaker delivered a stern rebuke. The South Africans responded by protesting the treatment of their policies in a film, *Black and White in South Africa*, which was one of a series on the Commonwealth prepared by Edgar McInnes of the Canadian Institute of International Affairs. The stage was being set for the show-down between South Africa and the Commonwealth.

Although the parliamentary session was to go on until the beginning of July, Wynne and the girls and I left Cape Town on 16 June to return to Pretoria. There was sadness in leaving the Cape, especially for Jane and Tricia who had spent a year at St. Cyprian's and made many friends. One of Tricia's pals, Ann Gray, had asked me as I drove her home from a day at our house why "Pat" had to go away. "She's my best friend", Ann went on: "In fact, my only friend." I noted that there were many things that we had not yet seen or done in the Cape and that we would miss the sea and the mountain. But it was already likely that we would not be in the Cape as a family in 1960 because the Department had approved our proposal not to move the office from Pretoria for the next parliamentary session.

On the 16th, we drove to Beaufort West via Matjiesfontein, a Boer War rest camp with a row of Victorian houses facing the railway station, and Laingsburg. The second day took us past the Three Sisters, one of the Karoo's most distinctive features, Victoria West, Britstown and Hopetown. We had our picnic lunch near the bridge over the Orange River and arrived at Kimberley to check into the Grand Hotel where Labran, the American engineer who had designed the "Big Gun" used to defend Kimberley, was killed by a Boer shell.

As a family, we went to the Consolidated Diamond Mining Corporation — De Beers — and were taken by a PRO to see diamonds being sorted; it was a surprise to see them yellow, brown and blue as well as white and also the imperfects mottled with carbon. From there we went to the Big Hole, really an astonishing sight, from which had come the first wealth of the diamond pipe. Next morning, we were taken to a disused area, where the girls were thrilled to pick up garnets and olivites, and then to the milling plant, ending up with a look at diamonds on the grease tables. We looked at the day's take: 2600 carats weighing less than a kilogram that had come from the milling of 15,000 tons of "blue ground". We were shown the hostels where the African workers lived, never leaving the compound during their six-month contracts. Despite this, I recorded that the conditions in the hostel were "excellent" and found little objectionable in the capabilities of the 80 Alsatians that we saw in the kennels, the guard dogs of De Beers.

We continued on to Pretoria that afternoon through Warrenton, Wolmaranstad, Klerlsdorp, Potchefstroom and Johannesburg, arriving at 29 Victoria Street after nine o'clock. Josephine and Dickson were on hand to welcome us back.

Our first year in South Africa was over. The moves between the Cape and Pretoria with their concommitant problems of housing and education had been demanding but life was comfortable and the climate was easy to take. My work had been highly satisfying and, for the first time abroad, I felt that I was performing the role that my training had prepared me for.

There was another reason for satisfaction: 1959 was the first year in over a decade in which I had kept a diary, begun because I wanted to have a record of my travels in southern Africa. From then on, I had a daily journal of my years in the foreign service and, within the restrictions imposed by the Official Secrets Act, a wealth of evidence to review and condense into a chronicle in my retirement.

Life in Pretoria was more relaxed and more "social" than in Cape Town. The city was also duller as we found when we tried to have a coffee after a movie and were swept out of the restaurant at 10:45. Politics was not a subject for discussion at dinner parties in most Pretoria homes. We gardened and golfed and played tennis. Jane and Tricia enrolled in the St. Mary's Diocesan School for Girls as day pupils, looking smart in the brown D.S.G. uniform and school tie. There was time to plan trips and, when the school term ended, we set out to see more of southern Africa.

CHAPTER 2

VERWOERDIAN TUMULT

Towards the end of the South African winter of 1959, Dr. Hendrik Verwoerd had been Prime Minister for just over a year. With his first parliamentary session behind him, he had established full control of the National Party, even though some of its members including a few cabinet ministers found him excessively rigid and doctrinaire. Everything pointed to a busy session in 1960. The Doctor was expected to cross more of the t's and dot more of the i's of the litany of Apartheid and there were rumours that he would lead South Africa closer to the temple of true Afrikanerdom that the Volk and its secret society, the Broederbond,[11] ached for. He knew that there would be little problem in obtaining parliamentary approval for his legislation especially as the opposition United Party was on the verge of losing some of its younger, more enlightened members to a new grouping on the left of the old parties.

What Dr. Verwoerd did not take account of was the tremendous growth of political consciousness among black Africans and of their ability to play an effective role, albeit extra-parliamentary and disruptive, in the affairs of the country. The Prime Minister's evident conviction that he knew what was best for all the people of South Africa was a major cause of the turmoil that wracked the country from 1960 onward.

The split in the United Party (UP) resulted from the growing unhappiness of those within the party who considered that instead of being an English mirror of the racial policies of the centre-left of the Afrikaner National Party (NP), the UP should move towards an accommodation with the non-white peoples of the country, thus offering an alternative to what seemed to be the inevitability of black domination. The annual congress of the United Party for 1959 was held in August. Conservatives within the party who opposed the addition of further land to the Native Reserves, simply because it meant removing land from white control, found their views challenged by the more liberal wing. At the end of the congress, it was reported that seven members of the parliamentary caucus would resign from the party and that another half-dozen were thinking of leaving. I noted that my best contacts in the Opposition were among them: Zach de Beer, Colin Eglin, Clive van Ryneveld, Helen Suzman, Ray Swart and Boris Wilson.

Shortly after the UP congress, the dissidents established themselves as the "Progressive Group" under the leadership of Dr. Jan Steytler. In November 1959, they met in Johannesburg to set up a formal political party. Of great importance to the Progressives was the moral and financial support of Harry Oppenheimer, the head of the Anglo-American Corporation who, after announcing that he had quit the UP, was present at the founding congress. Zach de Beer, who was active in the preparations for the convention, invited four diplomats to the convention: Eleanor Emery of the United Kingdom High Commission, Lionel Phillips of the Australian mission, Charles Whitehouse of the United States Embassy and myself. We were to have fascinating insights into the establishment of a consensus among the delegates and often found that we were being used as sounding boards by those who were concerned about the image that the party would project abroad.

There were difficult moments at the congress. The first threat of schism came over the resolution on the question of the republic. By proposing opposition to the Verwoerdian republic but an open mind towards the eventual adoption of a republican form of government, the steering committee had sought to satisfy both republicans and monarchists. While the latter, found mainly among the Natal delegates led by Ray Swart, were mollified, an important Afrikaner MP, Professor I.S. ("Sakkie") Fourie, was not. He left the Progressives to sit as an independent in parliament. The second occasion when the unity of the new party seemed imperilled was during the discussion of a resolution which revealed the gulf between those who were willing to accept the social and residential integration of Africans and those who had not fully shed the United Party belief in "just but firm white leadership". A compromise was inevitable if the Progressives were to win votes among the all-white electorate. Sympathy was expressed for traditional South African conventions and obeisance was paid to "the maintenance and extension of the values of Western civilization". That said, the statement of principles and policies then asserted the notion of a multi-racial society in which "no citizen... shall be debarred on grounds of race, religion, language or sex, from making the contribution to our national life of which he or she may be capable."

With 12 members in the House of Assembly,[12] the Progressive Party would bring a new spirit to the debates of parliament in the session of 1960, challenging the concept of white domination to which the NP and UP both clung. Thus the Progressives began to serve the purpose which Harry Oppenheimer had foreseen when I spoke with him soon after the founding congress. While he was not too optimistic about the prospects of the party, and was especially realistic on the electoral difficulties that it would face, he hoped that it would at least condition the public to the idea of multi-racialism.

Apart from the emergence of the Progressives, there was little going on that cut into the enjoyment of life in Pretoria with its rounds of parties and golf. True, there was to be an inspection of the High Commission's operations and those of the Trade Commissioners in Johannesburg and Cape Town in October by a team from Ottawa, but we were not worried that we would be found wanting. I looked forward to the visit because my successor as head of the Establishment and Organization Division, Pierre Asselin, and my adversary of those days, the Chief Treasury Officer, Eric Beach, were members of the team. They brought welcome news of the Ottawa scene to us.

Though things seemed to be quiet, or what masqueraded as calm in South Africa, there were reminders from time to time that we were living in an unhappy country. The touchiness of the South African Government had been demonstrated anew in September when it expelled a television reporter, a United Kingdom national, for "false reports". The editor of the liberal publication *Africa South* was banned from attending public meetings for five years under the Suppression of Communism Act, the Government's favourite instrument for the suppression of disturbing ideas. There were signs of unrest in Pondoland and other tribal areas between Natal and the Eastern Cape and the white farmers who lived amongst scattered black reserves were nervous. Barely a week went by without a protest against apartheid by the "Black Sash", a movement of white women, mostly from the well-off and better-educated of the English-speaking population. There were manifestations of resentment at the Fort Hare University College as the liberal members of the teaching staff were rusticated, deprived of their pensions, and refractory students were expelled. The churches kept up their pressure on the Government. At a Remembrance Day service at the Anglican cathedral in Pretoria, the Reverend Mark Nye spoke of his profound shame at events in South Africa; his comment did not go unnoticed by the police.

There was also evidence of difficulty ahead for South Africa in the outside world. In September, the Canadian Labour Congress demanded the expulsion of South Africa from the Commonwealth and there were mounting calls for the imposition of boycotts. In September, the All African Trade Union Federation proposed that markets be closed to South African goods and, early in January 1960, the All Africa Peoples Conference in Tunis and the Pan-African Federation meeting in Addis Ababa voted for commercial, diplomatic and political sanctions against South Africa. But the spark had not yet been struck which would ignite passionate responses to these calls.

On 17 November, the United Nations General Assembly adopted a resolution voicing "deep regret and concern" that South Africa had not responded to earlier appeals that it reconsider those of its policies that denied fundamental rights and freedoms to all races. The resolution made it clear that the Assembly considered racial discrimination to be prejudicial to international harmony and, for this reason, was convinced that the Union's discriminatory policy was not simply a matter of domestic jurisdiction but an international subject of the utmost importance. The vote was 62 to three (Britain, France and Portugal) with seven abstentions, including Canada. A week earlier, when Canada had also abstained at the committee stage of the resolution, I had shocked a senior friend in the local External Affairs Department by regretting that we had not voted with the majority as the United States had done. I recalled with some amusement that a year before, when we had voted in favour of a similar resolution, my High Commissioner had felt constrained to apologize to the Foreign Minister.

I expanded my circle of acquaintances during the Pretoria winter and spring of that second half of 1959 and got to know many businessmen and academics as well as most of the middle-grade and senior levels of the South African diplomatic service. There were government-arranged tours of the Centre for Scientific and Industrial Research — the counterpart of Canada's National Research Council — and of SASOL, the government's oil-from-coal operation located on top of the vast lignite deposits of the Orange Free State. A 10-day visit to Basutoland in December added to my growing knowledge of southern Africa.

Save for parties, Christmas and the New Year were an uneventful time for the Brown family. There was an incident in the evening on Christmas Day that illustrated the South African version of the Christmas message by its very violence and pathos. A number of servants who had gathered in the servants' quarters of a house to the west of ours on Victoria Street had drunk too much and begun to fight amongst themselves. Tribal differences surfaced and one man was set upon by the others. He ran, pursued by his assailants; he was exhausted and bleeding from knife wounds and lacerations from the barbed wire that protected the yards of our suburb when he came to our fence.

Hearing the commotion, our office driver and our gardener pulled the victim into our yard and persuaded the pursuers to go back to their party. We were called and brought the man into the kitchen where Wynne bandaged his wounds which seemed to require attention at a hospital. Our employees dissuaded us from this course, saying that the man would be turned over to the police and, at best, sent back to his reserve. They told us that the man's brother was the "head boy" at a house a few streets away and wondered if we could drive him there. We carried him to the car and drove down the hill to one of the suburb's largest houses where an Afrikaner widow lived with her middle-aged daughter. After seeing that the man had been put in the charge of his brother at the servants' quarters which were located on the roadway at the side of the house, I went to the front door, introduced myself and explained what had happened.

The two women were reluctant to have him remain on their property and wanted me to take him away. I appealed for their sympathy but got nowhere. At length, I pulled out all stops and asked them if, on this Christmas Day, the man's brother could be his keeper. That did it. Before the women could change their minds, I was on my way home.

On 11 January 1960, Wynne and I set out for Cape Town by road, arriving on the 13th. We were to stay for 16 days and then return to Pretoria, leaving only the High Commissioner and a stenographer in the Cape for the parliamentary session. The decision not to move the entire office to Cape Town in 1960 was based on a long-held perception that it was unnecessary, as well as costly and disruptive, to keep all services together throughout the year. Before the 1959 session ended, we proposed to Ottawa that we should experiment with a split office. The Department gave us its blessing and we decided to put the scheme into effect in 1960. Mr. and Mrs. Hurley and one foreign service secretary would stay for the session, living in hotels. Ross Francis and I would travel down for short periods, alternating as needed. Events were to demonstrate that we could not have chosen a worse year to monkey with the old routine.

At the outset of 1960, all seemed to go well. For the first time since the Nationalists had taken power in 1948, no new apartheid legislation was proposed in the Speech from the Throne. The only contentious measures appeared to concern the white population alone, dealing with education and Senate reform. When the debate on the Speech was opened by the Leader of the Opposition, the session looked as if it would be extraordinarily sterile. I wrote in my diary on 19 January:

> Went to the House of Assembly for question period and the opening of the throne speech debate. Sir de Villiers Graaff was in good form and, with a purged United Party behind him, was able to stand for eternal white leadership, attack the government for the economic and political impracticableness of the Bantustan concept and, at the same time, indirectly attack boycotts, saying that South African problems must be solved by South Africans without outside interference.

If Sir de Villiers thought that he was setting the tone for the session, he was proved wrong the next day.

For months there had been speculation that the Prime Minister would set South Africa on the road to republican status. Yet he took the Assembly and the country by surprise on 20 January when he introduced legislation for a referendum on the issue. Two months were to pass before the debate began and before other events were to underline that the question was not as simple as it seemed. Almost certainly, what prompted Dr. Verwoerd to table the bill when he did was the imminent visit to South Africa of Prime Minister Harold Macmillan of Britain at the conclusion of a momentous journey through Africa.

At the end of January, I was back in Pretoria, pleased with what I had done in the 16 days in Cape Town but sorry that I would miss the Macmillan visit.

On 3 February, Mr. Macmillan addressed the South African parliament. He did not mince his words. The most striking impression that he had formed during his African trip, he said, was of the strength of African national consciousness. It took different forms in different places, he said, but it was happening everywhere for "the wind of change" was blowing throughout the continent. After setting this fact against the struggle between East and West for the minds of men, Mr. Macmillan implicitly rejected the South African stand that its racial policies were a domestic matter by declaring that, in a shrinking world, the internal policies of one nation might have effects on others. Britain believed in raising societies in which "individual merit and individual merit alone is the criterion for a man's advancement whether political or economic." In countries with peoples of several races, he continued, "it has been our aim to find means by which the community can become more of a community and fellowship can be fostered between its various parts." He added, bluntly: "We reject the idea of any inherent superiority of one race over another."

Mr. Macmillan said that he was well aware of the peculiar nature of the problems that faced the Union and that Britain, as a fellow member of the Commonwealth, would always try to give South Africa its support and encouragement. "But," he went on, "I hope you won't mind my saying frankly that there are some aspects of your policies which make it impossible for us to do this without being false to our own deep convictions about the political destinies of free men."

Dr. Verwoerd replied politely that day but was to return to the Macmillan speech a fortnight later when he charged that the West was prepared to abandon the whites in Africa. He did not accept "that the White inhabitants must be satisfied as a minority in a multi-racial country to compete with the Black masses on an equal basis, which in the long run can only mean a Black government."[13]

The "wind of change" speech was to have a more dramatic effect on the aspirations of Africans to the north of South Africa, who could see independence in the offing, than in the Union itself. However, it was not without impact in the country where it was delivered. Commenting soon afterwards, Leo Marquard, the historian and Liberal Afrikaner, wrote:[14]

> Mr. Macmillan was widely interpreted as having served friendly but firm notice to South Africa that her racial policies were not acceptable to the West, and that, if the West had to choose between the friendship of two hundred million blacks and a few million whites, the whites would be 'thrown to the wolves'. The conclusion drawn from this by the Nationalist Party Press was that the whites should unite to defend their right to a separate and independent existence. The Opposition Press, and the non-white leaders, drew a different conclusion: that South Africa should modify her racial policies. Mr. Macmillan's speech, coming from such a source and so urbanely expressed, had a profound impact on South Africa. It is too early to speak with confidence, but it is possible that the speech may have shaken the strong belief in the validity of apartheid. If so, it will have assisted the process of loosening the rigid ties that characterize party-political divisions — a process that had begun before Mr. Macmillan's visit.

Thirty years later, it would be possible to say *Amen* to that, but the process had taken most of the three decades.

I had been back in Pretoria only a week when I decided that I should return to the Cape on 14 February for a dozen days. There was little work to do when significant reports required the High Commissioner's signature and, I confided to my diary, "some of JJH's reports show that he needs help."

I was in my element back in Cape Town from 14 to 26 February, spending almost every lunchtime and many evenings with my contacts, shepherding Canadian visitors and dropping frequently in on the Assembly to watch the proceedings from the gallery or chat with members over tea. There were many small stories to report to Ottawa: the formation of Japie Basson's "National Union" Party, a forlorn hope which placed Japie well towards the Progressives; the rumours of disaffection within the National Party; the debate on Senate reform.

That debate was more acrimonious than was expected, probably because the legislation was basically a measure to pad the NP strength in the upper chamber well beyond the two-thirds majority — the majority needed for consitutional reform — which the Party had been able to deliver since the last Senate reform act of 1955. The Opposition did not take kindly to being made even more impotent. In the future Senate, there were to be 54 members, 11 of them nominated and 43 elected under a system of proportional representation by electoral colleges made up of the members of the House of Assembly and the provincial council in each province.

The dean of Canadian historians, Professor A.R.M. Lower, was in Cape Town that February during a round-the-world tour on a Canada Council senior fellowship for study and research into the English language. The linguistic aspect of the South African political situation fascinated him.[15] Among those whom we put him in touch with was Piet Cillié, the liberal-minded editor of *Die Burger*, who found Arthur Lower altogether too crusty and broadcast his exasperation at all such visitors in the column which he wrote under a pseudonym.[16] This visitor, he said, had come "to look us over with an eye to a book" and the conversation (with a mythical "colleague") had gone like this:

> *Visitor:* I find no spirit of compromise here... for example on this question of a republic.
>
> *Colleague:* Well, the choice lies between a monarchy and a republic. I don't know of a third form of government on which we could compromise. What would you suggest?
>
> *Visitor:* I can't see that the matter is that serious.
>
> *Colleague:* In other words, you would like us to remain a monarchy?
>
> *Visitor:* You stand for Afrikaner domination ..."

Cillié concluded the column with an appeal to diplomats not to bring "such obtuse foreigners" to his office.

When this article appeared, I showed it to Professor Lower who thought that Cillié might have had his interview in mind. A week later I had lunch with Cillié. After mentioning that Lower was really quite sympathetic towards South Africa, I asked him about the origins of the article. He acknowledged that it was indeed based on the conversation with Lower. I told the Professor this in a letter, adding:

> I then chided him that he had obviously not been in a good mood and Cillié eventually apologized for the article and said that he hoped that you did not take it too seriously.

Professor Lower wrote to me later[17] about his "vivid and valuable visit" to remark that "the South Africa we see reflected is entirely all black, with no case for the defence ever being put." He went on:

> That is just the tragedy, or an important aspect of it, that the Afrikaner Nationalists, if they had a somewhat different mentality and if it were reflected in their conduct, would have quite a good case in many respects. But whom the gods wish to destroy they first make mad.

Lower's words were written after the pivotal events in South Africa of March and April 1960 which slowly began to dissipate the cuckooland cloud that, for most whites in the country, hid the reality of the political scene.

The demonstration of protest by Africans that took place on 21 March 1960 was planned by the Pan-Africanist Congress (PAC) well in advance. The PAC had been established in April 1959 after Robert Sobukwe, a lecturer in Bantu Studies at Witwatersrand University in Johannesburg, had broken away from the older African National Congress (ANC) because he opposed the multi-racial basis of the ANC and its close ties to the South African Communist Party whose role in the ANC was often decisive. Sobukwe was also deeply committed to non-violence and, although he believed in government of the Africans, by the Africans and for the Africans, he denied that the PAC meant to confront white racism with black racism.

In December 1959, the ANC had decided that, on 31 March 1960, they would start a campaign of resistance to the pass laws which required every African to carry at all times an identity book in which his right to live in a given area was recorded. The PAC, which had grown dramatically in numbers to the point where it was almost equal to the ANC, determined to steal the initiative by launching a campaign 10 days earlier. To Sobukwe this was to be the beginning of a resistance movement whose goal was the achievement of freedom and independence for South African blacks by 1963. On 18 March, the PAC issued instructions to its members: on the morning of 21 March, they were to leave their pass-books at home and go to police stations to submit themselves without violence to arrest for having broken the pass laws. The ANC informed Sobukwe that it would not support the PAC campaign.

At police stations in African townships throughout the country, the 21st of March saw thousands of Africans present themselves for arrest. Almost everywhere the demonstrations went off peacefully with the police obliging by arresting the protesters or taking their names; in a few places, the police simply told the crowds to go home and they did. At the Sharpeville Township outside Vereeniging, 50 miles south of Johannesburg, and at Langa Township near Cape Town, the crowds were large, noisy and excitable and the police lost their discipline and reacted with brutality. At Langa, the casualties were two killed and 26 wounded and the scene was ugly as baton charges by police and the stoning of cars on the nearby highway by blacks provoked violence by both sides. At Sharpeville there was a disaster. Some police fired into the crowd without warning and without permission. Others joined in the shooting as the crowd fled. Sixty-seven Africans died and 186 were wounded. The day would go into history as the day of the massacre at Sharpeville.

In South Africa and abroad, reactions to the events of the 21st of March were vehement. On the black side, the atmosphere of the days that followed was electric as scattered clashes with police continued and large numbers of Africans stayed away from work. The ANC joined the fray by declaring a day of mourning for the 28th. There was fear among the white population: immigration enquiries swamped the resources of our office, an unknown woman called to implore us to take her children under our protection and false rumours were spread that calls were being broad-cast for white women and children to stay off the streets. My daughter, Jane, reported that at her Anglican-run school they were praying that the Government would "get some sense into its head". But Dr. Verwoerd declared that the situation was under control and the police regrouped to prepare for a crack-down.

The United States condemned the police action and Prime Minister Diefenbaker announced that he would raise the subject of South Africa's racial policies at the next meeting of Commonwealth heads of govern-ment. A special session was convened of the Security Council which, for the first time, would demand an end to the policy of apartheid. The governing white South Africans seem not to have understood that the repression of the 21st of March created a shockwave of anti-apartheid sentiment in the United States in spite of the preoccupation of many Americans with the contemporaneous racial clashes in Montgomery, Alabama.

Worst of all from the standpoint of a government that detested prying by outsiders into its conduct was the rapid descent on South Africa of scores of the world's best foreign correspondents that was made possible by new technology. For, as the first crisis in a far land at the outset of the era of the commercial jet, Sharpeville became an instant and heavily-covered international news story.

The High Commissioner phoned me on the morning of the 24th to tell me that he had received a telegram from Ottawa asking for more reports on the situation. I volunteered to go down to Cape Town and caught a flight alone that evening. (The flight was held up overnight at Bloemfontein because of fog at Cape Town and it was mid-morning the next day before I arrived.) It was announced on Friday the 25th that legislation to ban both the ANC and the PAC would be introduced after the weekend. On the Saturday, the police said that they would stop arresting Africans for pass offences; Chief Luthuli of the ANC chose to interpret this as a sign that the hated passes would be abolished and immediately burned his book and instructed his followers to do the same.

Monday the 28th was the day of mourning that Chief Luthuli had called for. Cape Town was very quiet that morning. At the Grand Hotel, where I roomed when I was at the Cape, service was slow because all of the 90 black employees had obeyed the ANC. The work stoppage would have been complete at the docks and on construction sites had the Coloureds joined in, but most of them ignored the ANC appeal. The situation was similar throughout the country that day and for the rest of the week as the black labour force largely remained at home.

I went to the Assembly on Tuesday afternoon to listen to the debate on the second reading of the bill to ban the two congresses. Called "The Unlawful Organizations Act", it incorporated many of the provisions of the notorious "Suppression of Communism Act" of 1950. The Minister of Justice, F.C. Erasmus, led off with a speech whose theme was *Hulle will ons land* — They want our country. Charging both the ANC and the PAC with advocating violence, intimidating "law-abiding Bantu", threatening murder and arson and taking hostages, Erasmus declaimed that the Government had decided:

> to call a halt to the reign of terror which the Pan-Africanist Congress and the African National Congress have been conducting recently among the Bantu peoples of South Africa, to call a halt to the activities of the

terrorists, White and Non-White, who act as instigators behind the scenes without taking an active part themselves.[18]

The Leader of the Opposition agreed that law and order had to be restored and said that the UP would support the bill. Only the Progressives rejected it.

Wednesday the 30th was another dramatic day, memorable for the proclamation of a State of Emergency, massive detentions and what proved to be the last great African hurrah of the crisis. I wrote in my diary:

> Impressive show of African strength took place in Cape Town at noon when up to 40,000 men marched from Langa towards the city and 15,000 gathered in Caledon Square in front of the police station. I saw police armoured cars and troop carriers arrive at the Castle and an air force helicopter fly about reporting on the situation. As I walked towards parliament at 1:45, two armoured cars arrived at each end of Parliament St. and blocked the road, guns trained along the road. In parliament, [I] heard the Minister of Justice announce proclamation of state of emergency in 40 main cities. The PM announced position completely under control! Over 150 Liberals etc. arrested including our GP, Dr. Colin Lang in Pretoria and the head of the Tumelong [Anglican] Mission [School], Miss Hannah Stanton.

At the head of the African marchers was a young student, Mr. Philip Kgosana of the PAC. When the column reached Caledon Square, Kgosana addressed the people and asked for silence. The police deputy commissioner was on the scene and Kgosana told him that he wished to see the Minister of Justice. On receiving what he took to be the agreement of the police officer and in turn agreeing to a police request that the crowd disperse, Kgosana spoke to the people again, asking them to leave. They did and then the police broke their word and detained Kgosana. My diary entry the next day described this as "a double-cross reminiscent of Budapest in Nov. 1956."

The emergency regulations were comprehensive and harsh. They made it an offence, inter alia, to disclose the name of anyone detained, to hold gatherings (divine worship was permitted as were the funerals of persons except those who had died from causes related to the emergency!), or to make any statement which was calculated or likely to have the effect of subverting the government or engendering feelings of hostility or "weakening the confidence of the public in the successful termination of the state of emergency."

My luncheon engagement the next day was with Patrick Duncan of *Contact*. I noted that the luncheon fell through "when Patrick was either arrested... or skipped the country." A few days later, Waldo Campbell of the U.S. Embassy phoned me to say that Pat was well and happy at home. The day after that, I saw him at his office and found him in a state of great agitation. He thought that there was no hope for South Africa unless the United Nations came in and ran the country for a long period.

Other liberal-minded whites were also concerned at the possibility of arrest. On 6 April, Ross Francis informed me from Pretoria that Wynne had been asked if she would house two women from the Tumelong Mission. I was inclined at first to agree but decided to check with Newman Robinson of the *Johannesburg Star*, whose wife was close to the Mission. Newman pointed out that there were many people who would normally give haven to the women. He thought, therefore, that the request was a bid for asylum at a diplomatic household to avoid detention... and gently suggested that we should not get involved. As the women were not even Canadian, Newman's cautious advice was wise.

Throughout the country, African townships and compounds were now cordoned off by heavily armed police and military units who conducted raids and searches for "terrorists" and weapons. Several black civilians were killed and three black policemen, the only fatal casualties on the government side during the emergency. Little by little, during the first full week of April, order was being restored, workers began to return to their jobs and the yoke of the police state settled on the country.

In spite of the troubles, there were dinners to go to almost every evening. On the 5th, I was invited to dinner by Stan and Edna Uys in the company of a large number of overseas newsmen. The group included Norman Phillips of the Toronto *Star*, with whom I had lunched the day before,[19] Stephen Barber of the London *News Chronicle*, Viscount Lambton of the *Evening Standard*, and correspondents whose names I do not remember from the *Christian Science Monitor*, the United Press and German News Agency. All characterized the situation as shocking. As the workload eased, I began to think of going back to Pretoria. On Friday the 8th, I wrote that it was a relatively easy day at the office after the events of the fortnight since I had flown down to the Cape. The High Commissioner had been in Johannesburg all week at the Rand Show, an annual agricultural exhibition, and Ross Francis was due to spend Saturday there with him. On that Friday evening I was at a dinner at the Grand Hotel as the guest of the Clerk of the House of Assembly. All at the table were Afrikaner Nationalists: all were confident that things were returning to normal.

On Saturday morning, when I went to the Norwich Union Building to check whether there were any messages that might require action,

I expected to spend no more than a half-hour in the office. I was mistaken: at 9:45 a phone call came that turned the routine morning into a frenzy of extraordinary activity.

The caller was Donald Gordon of CBC-TV who was at the Edward Hotel in Durban where he had learned that Norman Phillips had been taken from the hotel by the security police, presumably to the Durban jail.

I phoned Frikkie Botha[20] at External Affairs and asked him to confirm the report about Phillips. I remarked that I could not understand what the authorities had in mind in detaining Phillips and added that his arrest seemed to me an extraordinarily effective way of causing trouble for South Africa in Canada. Frikkie undertook to make immediate enquiries and, within a half hour, I received a call from the Chief of Protocol asking me to see the Minister of External Affairs at 11:30 a.m. Meanwhile, I had notified Ottawa and, through Ross Francis, the High Commissioner in Johannesburg.

I walked up to Parliament for my appointment with Mr. Louw at his office in the government building opposite the Houses of Parliament. It was a brief meeting. He told me that the arrest had been made under section four of the Emergency Regulations[21] as the result of a despatch that Phillips had filed at the Post Office telegraph office the day before, but which the police had held up. Louw went on to say that because, in the opinion of the South African Government, the despatch would have done serious damage to South African-Canadian relations, it had not been released. He did not show a copy to me. Almost apologetically, he volunteered that he had been unaware until the morning that a Canadian was involved[22] and he did not demur when I said that we would want to have access to Phillips. There was little for me to do but say that I would notify my government and the High Commissioner immediately.

Once back in my office, I sent an emergency message to Ottawa relating what the Minister had said. I added that I had informed Hurley, suggesting that he return to Cape Town, and had instructed Ross Francis to go to Durban to see Phillips in jail. Hurley called back in mid-afternoon to tell me that he would be arriving in Cape Town in the morning and to ask that I arrange an interview for him with Eric Louw at noon at which he would demand the release of Phillips.

By now the press were on to the story. Confirmation of the arrest had been obtained from the Minister of Justice who gave permission for the press to publish Phillips's name and identity; without this permission, an offence would have been committed under the regulations. In the afternoon *Cape Argus*, I was quoted as saying that the Canadian

High Commission had been officially informed of the arrest and that we were notifying our government and considering what further action must be taken.

I returned to the Grand Hotel to change for dinner and had just got to the lobby when there was a call for me from a journalist telling me that an attempt had just been made on the life of Prime Minister Verwoerd at the Rand Show. My reaction was similar to that of many others: I asked about the race of the assailant and then expressed relief that it had been a white man.[23] Dr. Verwoerd had been shot twice in the face and was severely, but not critically, wounded. He was to remain out of the public eye until the end of May.

That evening, when I went to a dinner given by the Secretary of Forestry, I found myself alone again among a group of Afrikaners, solidly Nationalist. Not surprisingly, the attempted assassination was the main topic of conversation and there was some difference of opinion over who would be acting Prime Minister. That issue was to be divisive at a meeting of the National Party caucus when it met after the weekend and it was only half-solved by the designation of a senior minister as "acting for the Prime Minister."

When I went to the office on Sunday morning, I found a telegram[24] from the Department in Ottawa with the highest ("emergency") priority. It contained the text of a press release that had already been issued in the name of Prime Minister Diefenbaker and instructed us to take immediately the action indicated in the release and to report back. After relating the gist of my report on the meeting with Eric Louw and the action that I had taken subsequently, the telegram went on:

> Instructions from the Prime Minister have been sent to the Canadian High Commissioner to inform the South African Government that the arrest and detention of Mr. Phillips cannot but add to the widespread public indignation already felt in Canada at the measures which have given rise to the recent violence and loss of life in South Africa. The High Commissioner has been instructed to make the strongest representations to the South African Government with a view to securing Mr. Phillips' release from custody.

We issued the press release to newsmen in Cape Town who used it to reveal that overseas press censorship was in effect. Protests from the presidents of the Canadian Press and the Canadian Daily Newspapers Association followed. The Canadian Press message described the arrest as "a startling negation of freedom of reporting as generally understood within the Commonwealth of Nations." Both protests were reported in South African newspapers.

The High Commissioner arrived from Johannesburg at 11:40 on Sunday morning, the 10th April. I met him at D.F. Malan Airport and we drove straight to Mr. Louw's official residence in the Rondebosch suburb of Cape Town. Mr. Hurley first presented official regrets at the shooting of Dr. Verwoerd and then turned to the instructions that he had received from Ottawa. There followed, I recorded later in my diary, "a discursive and at times stormy discussion of our representations on Phillips." The Minister "thought" that Phillips would be questioned that day, released on Monday and allowed to leave the country; but all he would say officially was that he would communicate the representations to the Minister of Justice. Again and again, the High Commissioner returned to the demand for the immediate release of Phillips and reiterated the view that the detention had caused very serious harm to Canadian-South African relations.

Jim Hurley's normal bonhomie was totally absent: his language became less and less diplomatic. There was no doubt that the Foreign Minister was his least favourite South African cabinet minister. At one point, both men were standing up, their faces only inches apart and voices raised and threatening. Hurley became so heated that he grabbed Louw's coat by the lapels and the taller South African shouted "Get your hands off me." I watched in amazement, delighted to hear Hurley give Louw a lecture on the freedom of the press and the conduct of foreign relations — and wondering whether I would have to separate them. The meeting lasted for an hour. The courtesies on our departure were uttered rather stiffly.

At the beginning of the day, I had spoken to Ross Francis in Durban and told him to go ahead with an interview with Norman Phillips at Durban Gaol. What followed was described later by Phillips in his book on his South African experience:[25]

> Ross Francis then arrived and I was marched into the Governor's office to meet him. Col. McLachlan and his deputy sat at their desks. 'Go ahead and talk to him,' the colonel told Mr. Francis, 'but remember you may discuss only family affairs. There must be no discussion of Mr. Phillip's arrest.' Francis stared coldly at the colonel and rose to leave. If this was the way in which the South African Government honoured its word to Canada, he would have no part of it. The Canadian Government had been promised a private interview with Mr. Phillips, with no conditions attached. The flustered governor said he would have to seek new instructions from Pretoria, four hundred miles away. I was led back to my cell. When the new instructions came, Francis and I were allowed to talk in private, and I

learned for the first time of Mr. Louw's theory that I was being held for questioning. It was a considerable relief to learn what was being done to secure my release.

Ross reported to me that Phillips was well, that the arrest had been carried out in an unexceptionable manner and that he was in a cell with two other political detainees. Ross visited him again in the afternoon without any difficulty being placed in his way by the prison authorities.

Mr. Hurley approved a telegram reporting on his conversation with the Minister and I spent much of the rest of the Sunday afternoon answering telephone calls from the press: "the whole raft," I exclaimed in my diary note, "AP, UP, NY Times, Daily Chronicle, Express, Reuters, Observer as well as the local papers."

On Monday, 11 April, I decided that I should return to Pretoria while Ross Francis should travel from Durban to Cape Town for a short stint with Mr. Hurley. Eric Louw informed Mr. Hurley at 12:45 that Phillips would be released as soon as he had been questioned; it was implicit that he would leave South Africa shortly after his release. At a press conferemce, Mr. Louw told foreign correspondents that Phillips had not been arrested but merely detained for questioning. He repeated this line in a reply to the protest of the Canadian Daily Newspapers Association, adding that Phillips would be "released in due course on condition he returns to Canada immediately."

The *Pretoria News* was not amused by Mr. Louw's remarks: in an editorial of 12 April, the paper took up his observation that this was the first time a news despatch from South Africa had been stopped by the Post Office and expressed the hope that it would be the last. "It is plain," the editorial continued, "that we are now entering a period of active censorship and that the emergency powers are being used for purposes that go well beyond the requirements of the emergency itself." The editorial went on:

> In the case of Mr. Phillips they are being used because he was allegedly harming relations between the Union and Canada. The first reaction to this essay in public relations was that the Prime Minister of Canada broke his silence to utter a condemnation of South African policies.

Back in Pretoria, I spent Tuesday morning on the phone to Ross Francis in Durban and the High Commissioner in Cape Town. In the early afternoon, I learned that Phillips had been returned to the Edwards Hotel by one of the same officers who had arrested him, and released to Ross's custody. Ross put him on the plane to Johannesburg in the early evening. My wife and I met him on the tarmac at Jan Smuts Airport when he arrived just after nine o'clock and brought him to our house where he could avoid interviews.

When we walked into the concourse, we were surrounded by a jostle of inquisitive newsmen and flash-popping cameramen. Phillips did well in handling questions, avoiding controversy as he cracked jokes about his three days in jail while we made our way to the car. We were soon out of the airport but had a flat tire on our way home. Phillips got his first exercise in days when he did most of the work of changing the wheel. Before bed, we talked for a couple of hours about his experience in jail. In the morning, Phillips drafted a statement to the *Star* on his release. He said that the stand taken by the Canadian Government to secure his release made him feel proud to be a Canadian; that pride was increased by the statements of the presidents of the two press associations. While Phillips was busy on his story, I read through the despatches that he had filed from South Africa and noted in my diary that, while they were not written in the External Affairs style, they did not seem to have been the "grossly inaccurate reporting" that Eric Louw had complained about. In the afternoon I took Phillips back to the Jan Smuts airport and saw him off on the Sabena Boeing 707 at 4:45 to Brussels and London; the occasion was all the more memorable because this was my first view of a 707. Back at the office, I sent a wire to Ottawa informing the Department of Phillips's departure and another to his newspaper transmitting the story that he had written in the morning.

On his way to London that evening, Phillips wrote a column for the *Sunday Times* of Johannesburg which appeared in that paper on 17 April. Entitled "Things I'll always remember about my visit to South Africa", the article expressed his belief that South Africans had become immune to assaults on civil liberties:

> Scarcely a day passed during my three weeks in the Union when I did not witness something that filled me with revulsion, something I have been brought up to believe an affront to human dignity. I am no shrinking violet or bleeding heart. In Canada I consider myself an ordinary citizen with ordinary reactions, but it seems to me that White South Africans have become so accustomed to the rights of the Native population being curbed that they have failed to notice the erosion to their own liberties.

I returned to Cape Town a week after Phillips had left to be on hand for the debates on the votes of the Department of External Affairs and the Information Service for which Mr. Eric Louw was also responsible. On the eve of the External Affairs debate in the Assembly, Mr. Louw made it known that he had been selected to represent South Africa at the meeting in London in May of Commonwealth Heads of Government. The debates in the House that week illustrated how bad that selection might be. My diary entry for 21 April read:

> Went to the House in p.m. for debate on Information Service vote which Louw used to vent his spleen on the press. Much of his main speech was an account of the Norman Phillips case and he revealed that he had been consulted about the arrest the day before it took place. He read the intercepted despatch and extracts from other Phillips stories and [those of] other reporters and his tone of voice suggested that none of the things they reported had ever happened. Scored heavily, however, by reading Toronto Star telegram to Phillips asking him to send 'blood and guts' stories.

Winding up his speech, the Minister said that he was convinced that if there were a similar state of emergency in Canada, the Canadian authorities would act similarly against foreign journalists who sent prejudiced and distorted reports abroad "for the express purpose of damaging Canada's name."

In its issue of 22 April, *The Times* of London reported fully on the External Affairs Minister's speech and used it as the basis for an unusually long leading article. Entitled "Big White Brother", the editorial warned the South African Government that "the evil of apartheid" would not last and that: "The longer its perpetrators manage to keep it going the more ugly will be the final reckoning." Louw's outburst had provided the key to this warning as these words showed:

> Encouraged by the success of shock tactics, [the present rulers of South Africa] have gone over to the attack, accusing the United Nations, the foreign correspondents, the liberals in their midst of having combined to delude world opinion with a false picture of apartheid and its architects.... World opinion is not deluded. The leaders of the starkly extreme end of the National Party should be under no illusion. They should be aware, before the Commonwealth Conference meets, of the charges that are almost universally brought against them.

The editorial had started with the assertion that nothing could better suit the book of the rulers of South Africa than that what they were doing should fade out of the news. On that very day the Assembly was trying to do exactly that as it dealt with proposals to limit the debate on the bills providing for the referendum on the republic and for reform of the Senate. I wrote in my diary that evening that it was amazing how the House was getting back to "normal" and discussing only those things which promoted the interests of the section of the white minority represented by the Government. A few days earlier this had seemed out of the question, especially when the Minister of Lands, Paul Sauer, from the more humane Cape wing of the party, had made a speech on 19 April in which he advocated a new deal for Africans including representative political bodies in the urban "locations", accelerated development of the reserves and softer administration of the reference book system. But he had been rebuked by Eric Louw who, by declaring that only the Prime Minister could make policy changes, confirmed the belief of most of us in the diplomatic corps that there would be no concessions to the blacks and Coloureds.

On 6 May, I returned to Pretoria. The parliamentary session still had two weeks to run but the Commonwealth conference overshadowed its work and the continued absence of the convalescing Prime Minister was an assurance that nothing important would happen in the time remaining.

The state of emergency was to remain in force until the end of August when the last of the 1600 detainees were released. That would not mark a return to status quo ante Sharpeville: the situation was now totally different. The ANC and PAC were illegal organizations and their leaders were in prison or banned from taking part in political life or had gone underground or had fled the country. Chief Albert Luthuli had been fined for burning his reference book and restricted in his activity when he had been given a suspended sentence. Oliver Tambo had escaped abroad. Nelson Mandela was in hiding and would not begin his long imprisonment until after he was caught in late 1963. The three ANC leaders were far luckier than Robert Sobukwe of the PAC who was convicted, with 18 of his associates, of inciting others to support a campaign for the repeal of the pass laws. He was given three years in prison, a sentence which was tantamount to life for, when he was due to be freed, the government adopted a law extending the confinement of a prisoner year by year at its whim. Close to a nervous breakdown, Sobukwe was finally released in 1969, but he was banned from attending gatherings and forced to live in an area where he knew nobody. In 1978, at 53 years of age, he died, still banned.

Police surveillance of the African townships had increased dramatically. In the months after Sharpeville, there were over 18,000 arrests for rioting, incitement, possession of weapons and for statutory offences, mostly related to the pass laws. Trials continued until the closing months of 1960, well after the lifting of the emergency.

For most of that Transvaal winter, we were free to enjoy the Pretoria house and garden. Pleasure was added to life by news from Ottawa of my promotion to the foreign service officer grade five: that meant a change in my title from First Secretary to the more prestigious appellation of Counsellor — and a significant salary increase which together with a large cost-of-living raise for all civil servants took my pay to over $10,000 a year. To celebrate my new dignity and be properly dressed among my new peers, I ordered a chancery jacket and striped trousers which I wore for the first time at the High Commissioner's "Canada Day" reception.

Events in the Belgian Congo were now attracting attention and the storm that erupted in that country after it became independent on 30 June would affect the thinking of white South Africans for a long time to come. The most immediate impact was to offer them justification for the crackdown on the black political movements after Sharpeville and for the strengthening of the laager against the threat of Black Africa. The white exodus from the Congo had begun in early June and South Africa withdrew its consulates after one week of Congolese independence because the new government refused to allow the South Africans to stay without granting reciprocity to the new black country. On 11 July, I wrote in my diary about the debacle in the Congo, noting that the *Force Publique* had mutinied and that one-fifth of the whites had fled and adding:

> The very understandable attitude here is that of 'I told you so'— irresponsible Africans in the Congo cannot run a country as big as that. The mines have closed down, communications are almost non-existent and the Katanga province is on point of seceding. It will be interesting to see if other independent African states have enough statesmanship to co-operate in keeping the Congo afloat — by agreeing to UN intervention.

Two days later, I saw Hewitson at the Department of External Affairs, a week after he had ceased to be the South African Consul General in Leopoldville. He minced no words about the Congo's Prime Minister, Patrice Lumumba, describing him as "a shifty, vacillating, incompetent, indecisive person" who had brought about the mutiny of the *Force Publique* by fanning anti-white sentiment one day, and the next day begging the Belgian experts to stay. On the 17th I wrote that the chaos in the Congo was complete except in Katanga where Moise Tshombé was co-operating with the Belgians. Perhaps influenced by the sombre slant given by the South Africans to the events, I wondered about the impact on the world at large:

> The Congo situation plus the U.S.-Cuban dispute make it seem doubtful that peace can be maintained for long.

Appropriately perhaps, I visited at the end of that week the factory of the African Explosives Limited at Modderfontein, then said to be the largest explosives plant in the world. Holidays and travels from Pretoria served well in putting distance between the crisis of Sharpeville and its immediate aftermath, and the beginning of the years in which the total repression of the African political movements at home was matched by the growth of the country's isolation from the outside world. Sharpeville had come at the halfway point in my South African posting: the second half would be easier because of the contacts that I had made and the knowledge of the local scene that I had acquired in the pre-Sharpeville era.

Prime Minister Verwoerd's first appearance after he recovered from his wounds was at the celebration in Bloemfontein of the 50th anniversary of the Union of South Africa. When he finished his speech, he tossed a dove into the air as a symbol of peace. There was a deathly hush when the bird nose-dived into the ground in front of the stand. The omen was fateful: few of those at the Union Festival that day would live to see peace take wing in South Africa.

CHAPTER 3

FROM UNION TO REPUBLIC — AND OUT OF THE COMMONWEALTH

The final 18 months of my South African posting began with the holding of the referendum on the establishment of a republic which led to the proclamation, on 31 May 1961, of the Republic of South Africa, no longer a country in the Commonwealth. Throughout this period the South African Government devoted steadily increasing resources to bolstering the country's internal security. The suppression of dissent in the country extended beyond the radical African, Asian and Coloured political movements, even beyond the liberal whites, to encompass moderate elements among the entire population. Sharpeville had already given new meaning to the country's standing as an international pariah. As the daily *Die Burger* of Cape Town expressed it, the country had become "the polecat of the western world". But the debate over the republic and Commonwealth membership was to add intensity to that unpopularity and to deepen the isolation of South Africa.

The announcement that a referendum would be held on the establishment of a republic had been made by Prime Minister Verwoerd at the beginning of the parliamentary session in January 1960. Only the white voters would take part and a simple majority would decide the issue. Dr. Verwoerd promised that there would be no radical change in the country's parliamentary institutions and that the monarch would be replaced by a president who would be outside the political arena. Moreover, the Government would declare itself before the referendum on the question of continued membership of the Commonwealth.

Two months later, on the very day that violence erupted at Sharpeville and Langa, the Prime Minister reiterated to the House of Assembly that a majority of votes would be adequate to determine the question: if a favourable result was not obtained, then a decision would be taken by a majority in parliament. On membership in the Commonwealth, he said that the Government believed "that on sober common-sense grounds, the

Commonwealth is of value to us today". He added, however, that it was of little help in connection with South Africa's colour policy.

In opposing the call for a referendum, the official opposition United Party risked offending its marginal Afrikaner support, but the issue also placed stress on the conservative English-speaking wing of the party from Natal, monarchists to a man. In the debate, the UP took the line that the Coloured voters should be included and that some means should be found to consult African opinion. The Progressives and Liberals went further, insisting that the Asian and African populations be given the opportunity to present their views. The Nationalists responded to these arguments by asserting that "White South Africa" was the guardian of the non-whites and the sole arbiter in the matter.

The wounds that Prime Minister Verwoerd sustained in an attempt on his life on 9 April were serious enough to remove him from the political scene for several weeks. The cabinet decided that Minister Eric Louw should represent South Africa at the meeting of Commonwealth Heads of Government which would take place in London in May. Frikkie Botha of External Affairs told me that he would accompany the Minister and did not relish the assignment.[26] My boss J.J. Hurley was upset at the cabinet's choice for he considered Louw the worst possible advocate of the South African case in the Commonwealth forum.

During the Commonwealth meeting, most reports in the South African press from London emphasized the clashes between Louw and nearly every other participant, especially Prime Minister Diefenbaker. The final communiqué of the conference made it clear that apartheid had loomed large in the discussions and that the South Africans had been reminded that the Commonwealth was "a multi-racial association". As we had foreseen in our reporting, South Africa failed to obtain approval of its continued membership in the Commonwealth in advance of the establishment of a republic. That issue was put off for another year in the communiqué:

> In the event of South Africa deciding to become a republic and if the desire was subsequently expressed to remain a member of the Commonwealth, the meeting suggested that the South African Government should then ask for the consent of the other Commonwealth Governments.

On his return from London, Frikkie Botha gave me an account of the conflict of views between Louw and Diefenbaker. Botha opined that during the informal meetings of the two, Diefenbaker showed little understanding of the South African situation and seemed preoccupied with problems over a wheat deal with India. Louw's pre-conference press statement in London had provoked the other Commonwealth leaders by declaiming that South Africa would neither modify its policies nor admit liability for the crisis that had developed. This did not deter him on his return to South Africa from making the incredible assertion that no Commonwealth leader had suggested changes in South Africa's policies.

The *Cape Times* had already given the lie to Eric Louw's fulminations and to the indignation of many white South Africans, including some Opposition politicians, who had believed that the country's membership in the Commonwealth could not be contested. An editorial of 6 May argued that all the reasons for the diplomatic failure of South Africa were exposed by Mr. Louw's words and concluded:

> Our diplomacy will continue to fail as long as we fail to realize (1) there is no support for White men only because they are White; (2) that the world loathes the principle of race discrimination; (3) that an exclusive minority cannot claim to speak for an unrepresented majority; (4) that in fact we run a country which would be a pastoral backwater without the non-White contribution.

Uncertainty over the assumption that a republic would continue to enjoy a place in the Commonwealth was to become an important factor in the public debate on the establishment of the republic as the referendum neared. It was not until early August that the vote was set for 5 October.

At the High Commission, Ross Francis and I were well aware of the post's duty to provide Ottawa with analyses of the thinking of South Africans of all colours and political persuasions on the issues of the campaign. We also knew that Mr. Hurley had already decided that South Africa should be permitted to remain in the Commonwealth. Moreover, he told us categorically that he would not sign reports which gave credence to views that were contrary to this conclusion.

Ross and I were equally determined to get the High Commissioner's signature even if that meant that our letters and telegrams lacked the usual concluding paragraphs summing up the views of the post. To this end, we adopted the stratagem of verbatim reporting of statements of South African thinking. At first, the High Commissioner objected when we asked him to sign any communication that broadcast calls for the rascals to be thrown out of the Commonwealth. When we responded that the views were not ours but so-and-so's, he gave in and we redoubled our efforts to turn up direct quotations from scores of prominent South Africans. Unfortunately but perforce, this technique was to characterize the post's reporting through to the Commonwealth Conference of March 1961.

One of our earliest reports was on the views volunteered to me by Frikkie Botha on 28 July when I called on him at the Union Buildings in Pretoria to enquire about the then imminent, but soon to be postponed, visit of the Secretary General of the United Nations, Dag Hammarskjold. Frikkie said that he was having serious misgivings on political grounds about continued Commonwealth membership. He was disturbed that the old "club rule" of one member not publicly criticizing another had been violated. He regretted that non-interference in the domestic affairs of members, which had been the rule in the United Nations as well as in the Commonwealth, seemed no longer to apply. Moreover, he argued, Commonwealth membership exposed South Africa to more attacks than if it were not a member of the organization. Finally, Frikkie pointed out that Britain, "the fountainhead of the Commonwealth", was the home of the bitterest critics of apartheid: the press, the Anglican Church and the Labour Party. Hurley signed this with reluctance.

At the end of September, I drafted a telegram for the High Commissioner's approval setting forward what might be the programme of the South African Government after the expected victory of the republican side in the referendum. I thought that there would be a leisurely approach to the establishment of the republic with enabling legislation presented to the parliament at the beginning of the 1961 session and the matter of Commonwealth membership submitted at a Prime Ministers' conference in the second quarter of the year. Hedging on the prediction of a win for the republicans, I emphasized that the Government would not take defeat as final: while the Cape Nationalists would prefer another referendum, the northerners would prefer gaining a mandate by means of a general election. In any case, there would be an election in 1961 which the National Party would win, and Dr. Verwoerd's position would be unaffected.

The closing thought of the telegram was that we did not foresee any legislation in 1961 to improve the political position of non-whites or serve to reduce international distaste for South Africa's policies. Hence, we pointed out, the South African Government was not going to make it easier for us to make a decision on its continued membership in the Commonwealth.

A few days before the referendum, Dickson Chirente, the Nyasa gardener at our Pretoria home, provided thoughts on the referendum on a day when he and I worked together on a terrace at our Pretoria house. He wondered why the Afrikaners did not want the Queen and thought that there would fighting between them and the English. When I questioned that this would happen and suggested that there might be a black-white conflict, he derided the notion, pointing out that the blacks had no guns.

Referendum day passed quietly in Pretoria. On my way to work, I stopped at a local polling station and was surprised to see how many party workers and placards were there. The anti-republicans (mostly women) were lined up on the right and the republicans (mostly men) on the left of the path leading to the returning officer's staff and the polling booths.

In the wee hours of the next morning, I got out of bed to listen to the results on the radio. The vote against the republic at that point was 150,000 votes but, because that reflected most of the urban results, the computers were already predicting a majority for the republic of 80,000. I took a transistor radio to the office and listened to the returns through-out the day. The majority against was slowly whittled down hour by hour until at six in the evening the pro votes finally dominated.[27] In percentage terms, the yes vote was 52.3 and the noes 47.7. It was a narrow victory for the Afrikaner whites, themselves only one-tenth of the country's people.

After the referendum, the English-language press urged that the anti-republicans would have to accept the result. But that was advice too facile for many to follow. When an English-speaking friend was asked at a reception by a cabinet minister what diplomatic mission she belonged to, she riposted that she was one of the 47.7 percent of white South Africans whom he did not know. The bitterness was especially intense in Natal where support for the republic was less than one-quarter of that province's electorate. Ironic indeed to those who had voted "No" was Prime Minister Verwoerd's suggestion, made during a ceremony of thanksgiving for the outcome of the referendum, that the country be renamed The Republic of Good Hope after the original Dutch settle-ment. In my diary that evening I recalled *Die Burger*'s description of South Africa earlier in the year and wondered: "Would a polecat by any other name still not stink?"

In mid-October, I drafted a three-page despatch[28] to Ottawa which was a summary of many conversations with diplomats and others on the ques-tion of South Africa's continued membership; most important of these was a long lunchtime review of the matter with the Australian High Commissioner, Owen Davis, and the U.K. Deputy High Commissioner, Jack Johnston. Not just to obtain Mr. Hurley's signature, I tried to pres-ent both sides of every argument and above all to deal with what the United Kingdom was now employing as its main case for the retention of South Africa, the non-white case.

The despatch began by suggesting that the U.K. would be largely motivated in its effort to achieve South Africa's continued membership by considerations important to it such as the presence in the Union of a million people of British origin, trade, investments, defence and the High Commission Territories. However, because these considerations were not necessarily of importance to the other Commonwealth members, the U.K. was privately advancing a case which differentiated between the country and the people on the one hand and the South African Government on the other hand:

> This U.K. case is based on the premise that the Union Government is not representative of the people of South Africa, is merely the Government of the day and will not retain power forever. Essentially it is a 'non-white case' for South Africa's continued membership in the Commonwealth.

There were three principal arguments in favour of the "non-white case": (a) The South African Government could be more easily influenced to ameliorate its racial policies if it remained within the Commonwealth; (b) Expulsion would mean the abandonment of the inarticulate non-white majority; (c) The Nationalists would eventually be replaced by a government favouring a multi-racial constitution.

On the first argument, the despatch asserted that everything that had gone on under the Nationalists made it extremely difficult to believe that they could be better influenced to mend their ways if they remained in the Commonwealth. Foreign prescriptions for the ills of the country had never been accepted by the Nationalists but there were many instances in which they had contemptuously rejected those remedies in favour of their own brand of medicine. Other members of the Commonwealth deluded themselves if they believed that keeping South Africa in would make the Nationalists amenable to accepting outside advice or following the example of others on human rights. However, it was true that South African membership exposed them to more criticism than if they were on their own and it was also true that liberals and non-whites took heart from this outside interest which could conceivably hasten a showdown in the Union.

The despatch was equally sceptical in dealing with the second point:

> The argument that to expel the Union from the Commonwealth would be to abandon the inarticulate 80 percent of the inhabitants of this country has more force. The vast majority of South Africans have no voice in the formulation of policy and were not permitted to record their views in the referendum on the republic. The Union Government would not, however, accept the argument that the interests of the non-whites make the

continued Commonwealth membership of South Africa desirable. Nor would any government dedicated to white supremacy permit the rest of the Commonwealth to intervene on behalf of the non-whites. It is a moot point whether the non-whites would consider themselves abandoned if South Africa were to be refused continued membership. It is also a moot point whether they would not feel abandoned if continued membership were granted without it being made clear that this was being done in the interest of the non-whites.

Taking the third point — that there would eventually be change in South Africa to a government which would establish a multi-racial, contemporary state — the despatch rejected the thesis of peaceful change because the minority position of the whites made it almost impossible for them to contemplate sharing power with the black majority and, further, there was little if any hope of an electoral shift from the conservative to the moderate whites *within a reasonable time*. As long as the whites could keep physical control of the country, there would be a government devoted to the maintenance of white supremacy. The end of white control, the despatch postulated:

> may come only by non-white rebellion or by outside intervention or a combination of both. If it is assumed that the end of white supremacy government in South Africa is only a matter of a few years, there is reason to accept the argument that the Commonwealth link be maintained in spite of the policies of the present Government. It would be more important then to be in a position to influence and help a multi-racial South African government. But it is highly questionable whether the cataclysm is so close: on the contrary, there is every indication that the whites can keep control for a decade at the very least, barring foreign military intervention.

The conclusion of the despatch was that it would be a long time before the U.K. "non-white case" became valid. During that waiting period, the presence of South Africa inside the Commonwealth would subject the organization to severe stresses: the question had to be answered whether, for the members of the Commonwealth, the resultant strains might be considered of more or less consequence than the interests of the 12 million non-whites of South Africa.

Although the despatch had brought the High Commission very close to advocating South Africa's departure from the Commonwealth, in the end we did not take sides, and Mr. Hurley found it possible to sign the communication with this ending:

> It is not our intention to conclude this letter by saying that the doubtful merits of the "non-white case" for South Africa's continued membership in

the Commonwealth make support of that membership impossible. I am personally sure that other considerations will be more telling.

On 25 October, I went to Cape Town for three days, primarily to look for a house for the next parliamentary session but using the opportunity to catch up on the post-referendum views of some of my friends there. On two of the three days, I had lunch at the Civil Service Club with Sir de Villiers Graaff who was planning a trip to the United Kingdom and possibly to Canada to gain support for continued Commonwealth membership. On the first occasion, "Div" (as he by now insisted that I call him) was accompanied by Jack Connan, the United Party MP for Cape Gardens and, on the second, by his two chief lieutenants, Marais Steyn and Frans Cronje. Members for two Transvaal constituencies, they had come to the Cape to help in the drafting of a statement on the eve of their leader's departure.

At the first meeting, Graaff sounded me out on the usefulness of a visit by him to Ottawa. While I cautioned him that the publicly-expressed views of most Canadians seemed unfavourable to his quest, the Government had not stated a position one way or the other on the issue of membership and his position would command attention. At the second lunch, Graaff said that he had made up his mind to go to Ottawa and would write to me asking that we arrange meetings for him there. The case that he proposed to make was essentially that his Party had never given up hope of regaining power and that, when it did, it would move to make South Africa's policies at once more humane and more palatable to the international community. I could not demur, but it seemed to me that, given the electoral weakness of the United Party, this case was not based on a realistic premise.

I had formed a great liking for de Villiers Graaff and wrote in my diary after the second meeting:

> I am very impressed by his easy charm, conviviality and common sense. He is almost courtly in his courtesy; quiet spoken, imperturbable — but does not draw easily.

Just before leaving for Europe the next morning, Graaff issued a statement in which he came out for the integration of Indians in the political life of the country, the representation of Coloureds by Coloureds in the parliament and acceptance of the permanency of the urban Africans whose emerging middle class must be given representation in parliament.

Graaff's visit was not, in the event, arranged through the High Commission. On returning to South Africa at the beginning of January, he wrote to me in Pretoria to apologize for failing to go through our office in setting up his schedule in Ottawa. The "very heavy pressure of work at the time" had made this impossible but "your Mr. Heeney in Washington very kindly fixed everything up for me." I knew, of course, that he meant that he did not want to risk Hurley's hindrance to his mission. The letter continued:

> There is... much that I would like to discuss with you so I would appreciate it if you would be kind enough to contact me the moment you get to Cape Town.

While I had had doubts that Sir de Villiers would get very far in Ottawa, I was pleased to hear when I spoke to him in Cape Town that he felt he had had a sympathetic hearing from Prime Minister Diefenbaker whom he had seen on 20 December.[29] Later, when he had me to lunch at Parliament on 1 February, he added that Mr. Diefenbaker was "fully acquainted" with South African affairs. However, Graaff told me that he had not appreciated beforehand the depth of anti-South African feeling abroad, particularly in Canada; the Canadian attitude on the membership issue worried him. He said that he was sure that Dr. Verwoerd did not realize that continued membership in the Commonwealth was by no means a certainty. Graaff gave me the impression that in his own mind he had become reconciled to the loss of membership for he commented that "it would be impossible to re-enter the Commonwealth if South Africa were expelled or withdrew." There would be conditions attached, he added, which not even a United Party government could accept.

Another visitor to Canada that December was Colin Eglin of the Progressive Party who also told me when he came back that feeling against South Africa seemed to be running high.

The terms of the "Republic of South Africa Constitution Act", which had been made known in December, were essentially what Dr. Verwoerd had promised before the referendum. As of 31 May 1961, the country's name was to be changed from Union to Republic with the head of state to be known by the old Boer title of State President and elected by an electoral college made up of the members of the Senate and House of Assembly. The flag and national anthem remained the same and the equality of Afrikaans and English as the country's official languages was restated. The bill was introduced in the Assembly on 23 January and opposed by the United Party, which proposed that it be deferred until Commonwealth membership was certain and by the Progressives who wanted a rigid constitution with guarantees for all groups.

A week later I was in the Assembly to hear Dr. Verwoerd move the second reading of the Constitution bill. The attainment of the republic, he said, was a "long-cherished ambition" of the Afrikaners; they were really not interested in the Commonwealth. Yet he knew that this was an ardent desire of the English-speaking people and so he vowed to put the case for continued membership "sincerely" and "honestly". The Prime Minister repeated this pledge in a radio broadcast but went on to warn that the solution to South Africa's race problems was for the Union alone to find and must not be tied to the question of membership:

> It must be understood that South Africa will not be prepared to pay the price for this of allowing interference in her domestic policies, of sacrificing principles on which her Government has been repeatedly elected since 1948 or of submitting to any reflection on her sovereignty or her national honour.

If there had been any hope previously that the Prime Minister might offer concessions to the non-whites as a means of providing the Commonwealth critics with a sign that change might occur, this statement closed the book on the subject.

The United Party proposal that the Coloureds be given direct representation in parliament was not just a cynical tactic to persuade the world that there could be movement in South Africa. The notion that the Coloureds ought to be brought on the side of the whites was also strongly held among the moderate Nationalists of the Cape; *Die Burger* had been advocating this on its editorial page. Dr. Verwoerd would not countenance any deviation from the party line: the National Party had to stand like a granite wall on its colour policy lest there be biological assimilation. In a policy statement of 23 January 1961, the federal council of the NP echoed this position and denounced *Die Burger*.

Just over a week later, I had lunch with the newspaper's editor, P.J. Cillié. He had hard words for Dr. Verwoerd, describing him as a "madman"; Cillié was equally disdainful of the party council which, he predicted, would "eat its words bit by bit over the next five years." While he did not think that Dr. Verwoerd would be considered a great hero in the country if he secured the continued membership of South Africa in the Commonwealth, rejection of the Union's application would play into the hands of both white and black extremists and polarize the racial conflict. The task of moderate Afrikaner Nationalists like himself, he said ruefully, would be made extremely difficult.[30]

The clock was now ticking down quickly to the gathering of Commonwealth Heads of Government in London which was set for the week of 13 March. As in May 1960, Frikkie Botha was again to be an adviser to the South African team which this time was to be led by Dr. Verwoerd. At lunch on 21 February, Frikkie told me that he was saddened by the deterioration of relations between Canada and South Africa; it did not console him when I responded that the problem was that there could be no common ground on the policy of apartheid.

There was plenty of evidence of resentment amongst Afrikaners and many conservative English-speaking people at Canadian criticism of apartheid which was widely reported in the local press. Incapable of ignoring foreign attacks on its policies, the South African Government was equally unable to resist countering them either by listing the racial sins of the critics' countries or by sponsoring trips to the Union by sympathetic politicians, journalists and others. The latter technique led to the appearance of one of the most bizarre Canadian visitors to inflict himself on us and to provide badly-needed comic relief during the 1961 parliamentary session.

John Selfe of External Affairs in Pretoria phoned me on 25 February to tell me, tongue-in-cheek, that a Mr. Sydney A. Williams, the executive secretary of the Canadian Asssociation for the Advancement of Coloured People, had arrived in South Africa for a visit under the auspices of the South African State Information Service. Although that suggested to me that Williams was a dupe, he shook the South Africans a couple of days later by asking to see Robert Sobukwe, the jailed PAC leader.

Ross Francis met Williams at the Cape Town airport at the end of his first week in the country and we brought him under our wing for a few days. Wynne and I held a dinner party for him and I recorded in my diary that he was a real character. I wrote:

> 95% bombast and 5% fact. We had Stan (Sun. Times) and Edna Uys, John Brook (Australia), Colin Eglin (Prog. MP), Dr. R.E. van der Ross and Mr. and Mrs. Taylor, (all 3 Coloured) and the company baited Williams all evening. His worst misconception was that the moderate Nat[ionalist]s would displace the extremists. We couldn't make Williams out.[31]

Despite his apparent misunderstanding of the South African scene, Williams confided to me that the 10 articles that he had contracted to write for the Toronto *Telegram* would be stronger in condemning apartheid than those of Norman Phillips. Given what he had said during the evening, I found that hard to believe.

He went on his way in the care of the South African Information Service and we heard nothing more about him until his departure from Johannesburg on 23 March when he had an altercation with a policeman at Jan Smuts Airport. Unkindly, we suspected that he had staged it to make copy.

We were not the only ones who were bamboozled by Sidney Williams. His later published views turned out to be as extremely critical of South Africa as he had confided to me that they would be, and quite different from those that he had seemed to espouse. Colin Eglin twitted Eric Louw in the Assembly on the day of the debate on the External Affairs vote about the use of public funds on such a visitor. Louw acknowledged the gaffe, saying that Williams had "grossly deceived" the South African High Commissioner in Ottawa by presenting himself as a personage of importance who was sympathetic to South African racial policy.

Just over three months before Williams's visit, the Toronto *Telegram* had sent Peter Worthington to South Africa. He was put in touch with me after he had arrived by Stanley Uys of the *Sunday Times* of Johannesburg. The *Telegram* subsequently took a strong stand against South Africa's continued membership in the Commonwealth in company with most Canadian dailies including its Toronto rivals, the *Globe and Mail* and *The Star*.

By the end of February, a fortnight before the Commonwealth Conference began, we completed our reporting of views and news on the South African issue. We were not surprised that we had seldom been pressed by Ottawa for reports — we were more aware of the Hurley factor than Ottawa seemed to be — but took satisfaction nonetheless in the depth and quality of our contribution to the enlightenment of headquarters. Now we sat back and awaited the outcome. My diary entries for the three crucial days of the London meeting tell the story as, relying on the press and radio, I saw it unfold:

Monday 13 March:
First day of PM Conference discussion of SA's continued membership in the Commonwealth. The meeting refused to treat it as formality & strong attacks were reported to have been made on apartheid. Verwoerd spoke for 85 minutes, a record at Comm. PMs meetings.

Tuesday 14 March:
Lunch with John Brook (Australia). Second day of PMs' discussion of SA's membership in the Commonwealth & tension mounted through the afternoon as no news of a decision came... [After dinner out with Stanley and Edna Uys] We returned to 'Flattop', the Uys's house, to find out about the membership question. The 2nd day apparently ended with no agreement on wording of a communiqué on the subject. Hope seems to be fading that SA will stay in.

Wednesday 15 March:
Another day of tension. At the Assembly at 2:15 I heard from an Argus correspondent that a SAPA [South African Press Agency] flash from London

said SA was 'in'. Walked back to the office where another correspondent phoned me at 2:45 to say the SAPA report had been cancelled. Other rumours followed & finally shortly after 8 p.m. came the news that Dr. Verwoerd had announced the withdrawal of SA's application... Dr. V. added that this was the beginning of the end of the Commonwealth.

With the Canadian role in all this in mind, I wondered "what sort of reaction there will be from our friends."

South African whites were split down the middle the following day, the division almost totally on linguistic lines. The English press condemned Dr. Verwoerd and *Die Transvaler* was joined by other hard-line Afrikaans organs jubilantly hailing his action. The scene in the House of Assembly that afternoon described it all: the Opposition members quiet and worried and the Nationalist backbenchers cocky to the point of arrogance, pouring scorn on Sir de Villiers Graaff when he moved that a debate take place on Dr. Verwoerd's "ill-considered action" and the Speaker rejected the motion. As was inevitable among my white friends, a joke soon illustrated the division: a prudish South African group decides that its women members should wear panties with Union Jack designs, the advantage being that no English-speaking South African would haul them down and no "Dutchman" would think of touching them.

It was not long before the role of Prime Minister Diefenbaker in the drama of the Ides of March surfaced as the central factor in the Canadian-South African relationship and put us on the defensive at the High Commission. As soon as the news broke, Patrick Duncan phoned to tell me that the next issue of his fortnightly, *Contact*, would feature Mr. Diefenbaker on the cover; obviously that would not please the South African Government. To newsmen who asked why Canada had "kicked South Africa out", we restricted ourselves to observing that nobody had done any kicking: South Africa had withdrawn.

At the end of the week we received the full text of Mr. Diefenbaker's statement to the House of Commons in Ottawa and circulated it widely. The Prime Minister had said that everything humanly possible had been done at the conference to find a solution but there was no corresponding readiness on the part of Dr. Verwoerd. Mr. Diefenbaker went on to describe the result as inevitable because it had become clear beyond doubt that, if the Commonwealth was to be a force for good, there was general agreement that discrimination in respect of race and colour should not take place. De Villiers Graaff called to tell me that the statement was "most useful".

Like Mr. Diefenbaker, Prime Minister Macmillan of the U.K. placed the blame for the result of the meeting squarely on Dr. Verwoerd. In the House of Commons on 22 March, he said that had the South African shown:

> the slightest move towards an understanding of the views of his Commonwealth colleagues, or made any concession, had he given us anything to hold on to or any grounds for hope, I still think that the Conference would have looked beyond the immediate difficulties to the possibilities of the future. For, after all, our Commonwealth is not a treaty-making league of governments; it is an association of peoples...

The tone of Prime Minister Verwoerd's version was quite different. Speaking in London before returning home, he said that he had withdrawn the application for continued membership because the Canadians and the Afro-Asian members wanted to interfere in South Africa's domestic affairs and he had not wanted to place "our friends and particularly the United Kingdom" in the invidious position of having to choose between South Africa and the others. South Africa, he went on, would now be able to develop friendship with the U.K. "and other old friends" unimpaired by any embarrassment on racial policy. And the U.K. could try to hold the changed Commonwealth together "if it can".

Dr. Verwoerd returned to Cape Town on 21 March to make a short statement on the Commonwealth meeting and announce that a full debate would be held two days later. Two sets of demonstrators crowded Parliament Street, one of Nationalists, mostly students from Stellenbosch University, and the other of anti-apartheid Liberals and the Coloured Peoples Congress; it was a peaceful event because, ironically, both favoured what had happened in London. When I came out of the Assembly, the Stellenbosch students were leaving. The police formed ranks to leave and as they marched off a Coloured demonstrator blew a whistle and his friends called "Left, left, left, *Right, Right*" — a neat summary of their approval of South Africa's departure from the Commonwealth.

On the 23rd, I spent the entire afternoon at Parliament, first at lunch as the guest of Hymie Miller, the UP member for Bezuidenhout, and:

> Afterwards to the gallery to endure a two-hour speech by Verwoerd, a one hour speech by Graaff, 45 minutes from Eric Louw and a good, snappy 15 minutes from Steytler. Verwoerd was not even plausible today and looked ill at ease during Graaff's fairly powerful speech. Eric Louw accused Diefenbaker of lying on the question of who introduced the discussion of apartheid at London and described [the] attitude of [the] New Zealand PM as shilly-shallying. 'One more friend gone', a UP backbencher quipped.

There was more tension in April and May than there had been since 1960. On a Sunday afternoon in mid-April, I went to the Grand Parade, the square by the Castle in Cape Town to observe a meeting organized by the Liberal Party, the Congress Movement and the Coloured Convention which attracted a relatively small crowd of 3000 cheerful and intelligent blacks and Coloureds. The purpose of the rally was to prepare for the three-day general strike and the demonstrations that the organizers hoped would take place on the 31st of May when the republic would be inaugurated. The reaction of the Government was swift. The biggest police raids in the country's history were conducted early in the morning of 3 May during which the homes of all those considered as leaders of the three-day demonstration were raided and documents seized. Intimidation seemed as much an objective as evidence-gathering.

Legislation was introduced on 5 May under the title of the General Law Amendment Act 1961 which, amongst other things, widened the power of the police to detain people without charge, added murder and arson to the offences that could be tried without jury, and placed further prohibitions on public gatherings. By mid-May the legislation had been rushed through Parliament and proclaimed.

But even that did not satisfy the nervous Nationalists that all the holes in the republican dike were plugged. On 19 May, the Government issued a proclamation under the Suppression of Communism Act of 1950 prohibiting all gatherings for the next five weeks. The only gatherings that were exempted from the decree were church services, funerals, movie shows, educational classes and business and trade union meetings. To prove its determination to launch the republic in a time of tranquility, the Government cancelled all police leave and called up reserve army units. More massive police raids were conducted on 24 May in an effort to catch the leaders of the demonstrations but these met with little success because most of the targets had gone underground.

At eight in the morning on 29 May, I drove around to see what was happening. I wrote in my diary that Africans were at work at garages and on milk deliveries. My survey went on:

> Later in the morning I drove about 30 miles through Woodstock, Athlone, past Langa and Nyanga to D.F. Malan Airport, Elsie's River and back to the city. Numerous police vans about, some soldiers guarding essential services and petrol dumps and up to half the shops in the Coloured townships shut and shuttered.

No diplomats planned to entertain during the three days lest they find themselves with guests but servant-less. But the stay-at-home was a failure: no protesters risked the consequences of defying the ban on gatherings and the security forces ensured that all was "normal" when the republic dawned.

On 31 May 1961 the Commonwealth connection was at last broken at a ceremony in Pretoria when the Republic of South Africa was proclaimed and the State President was inducted. These rites of Afrikaner atavism were the only celebration marking the passing of the Union. The transition caused no joy among the black, Asian and Coloureds of the country and was an occasion for mourning among many whites, especially in Natal and the Cape.

Thus the birth of the Republic was inauspicious. Terry MacDermot, who had served in South Africa as the Canadian head of post, had sensed the dark mood. He wrote to me that day from Canberra where he was High Commissioner:

> This is Republic Day — Vive la République! — and I see that your and my friend Hendrik together with another old friend Erasmus the Just have managed by filling the gaols to empty the market-place. I would suspect too that the communists, natives and other human trash of which you seem to have such hosts in that country are pretty despondent about the failure of the strike. However God will be happy. After all, his lords and masters the Nats are preserving one of the pillars of civilization. The other was pulled down when Hitler, that mad modern Sampson, brought down Nazi Germany about his ears.

There were numerous contemporary commentaries on the establishment of the Republic that addressed the question of whether it would ever be possible for South Africa to return to the Commonwealth. The United Party was to find it expedient to declare that this would not be possible because the Commonwealth would set conditions that even the UP could not accept. Patrick Duncan's *Contact* looked forward to the day when a non-racial government came to power and was invited back into the fold. This was the attitude of Albert Luthuli who wrote after the Prime Ministers' Conference:

> ... we [do not] desire the isolation of our country. But the progressive isolation of the men who live by the apartheid creed is desirable, if only because they are sick with a loathsome disease. The outcome of the Commonwealth Prime Ministers' Conference gladdens us, primarily because of the stand made there for the things we believe in. Had there been an attempt to accommodate Dr. Verwoerd's wild dream, the end of the Commonwealth would have been in sight because of a basic betrayal of the things the Commonwealth stands for. Now it is strong in a world shaken by the myths of Hitler, Mussolini and other despots. I do not doubt but that we shall return when South Africa is differently ordered.[32]

A third of a century later, Luthuli's prophecy was fulfilled.

For our diplomatic mission, the republic meant that we ceased to be the Office of the High Commissioner for Canada and became the Canadian Embassy. Apart from that — and putting aside the effect of the atmospherics between the two countries at the London meeting on our diplomatic activities — the breach of the Commonwealth link made little immediate difference to the relationship between Canada and South Africa. The South African Assembly had passed a standstill bill in May which left in effect the provisions of all laws relating to Commonwealth relations. On the Canadian side there was an equal disposition to leave arrangements as they were including trade preferences, immigration and arms exports.[33] Although Ghana, India and others had initiated sanctions against South Africa and entry inconveniences were encountered by South African travellers to a number of countries, it would be a while before Canada joined in adding to the isolation of the Republic.

On 30 May 1986 *The Star* of Johannesburg marked the 25th anniversary of the establishment of the Republic with an editorial that deserves to be remembered. Under the title "Republic: the dream and the reality", the editor wrote:

> If Afrikaner Nationalists believed the arrival of the Republic on May 31 1961 was going to be Paradise Regained, then the turbulent events of the Republic's first 25 years will have produced a more sober assessment. Escaping from the hated British connection may have been emotionally therapeutic for those with deep-seated memories of the past, but life in isolation — accelerated by the Nationalists' own political and ideological choices — has been an unpleasant by-product. Perhaps the coming of the Republic helped to bury obsolete Boer-Brit animosities (and for that we should all be grateful), thereby enabling the country to concentrate on its real problems in the fields of race relations, human rights, and economic opportunity.

> For much of its life the Republic saw intensified efforts to segregate society racially; not only did the experiment heighten racial tensions, but in the end it also conclusively demonstrated that apartheid was unworkable in practice. At the same time, the independence of African states to the north, the overthrow of the Portuguese empire and the fall of white Rhodesia began to bring home the prescience of Harold Macmillan's comment in 1960 that the wind of change was blowing 'throughout the continent'.

> Today South Africa stands at once both better and worse off than a quarter of a century ago. Better, because time has proved the apartheid policy a

failure, spurring an effort at last to come to terms with legitimate black aspirations and demands. Worse, because racial polarisation has advanced so far that white offers of compromise and negotiation are being confidently rejected by blacks seeking a straight transfer of power.

South Africa, in reaching another milestone in its history, now knows the Republic created in 1961 will have to look very different from what it is if it is ultimately to provide a climate of welfare and prosperity to equal its undoubted potential.

The commentary of *The Star* has, for me, an uncanny ring for I knew members of the paper's editorial staff in 1961 who then, for future publication, could have set forward the same observations and only been wrong in guessing the right dates. They would not have had to consult tea-leaves or the stars because the fate of the Republic was predictable from its inception.

My tale of South Africa's departure from the Commonwealth would be incomplete if I did not mention a conversation with the Under Secretary of State for External Affairs, Norman Robertson, during a courtesy call I paid on him when I returned to Ottawa a year later. Deploring what he called the "expulsion" of South Africa, he was optimistic that the Nationalists would have modified their policies if spoken to softly and left alone to work out their own problems. I responded that few South Africans believed that the Nationalists would have come around soon enough with policies acceptable to most of the Commonwealth. Robertson considered this view defeatist. He told me that he had been impressed by Sir de Villiers Graaff. I agreed that Div was a nice person but went on to say that he was not to be reckoned as a force in South Africa. Robertson was visibly upset by that remark and our discussion ended.

It was many years before I learned how deeply Robertson had been hurt by the snubs of Diefenbaker and by having to stand aside while the Secretary to the Cabinet, Bob Bryce, was allowed by the Prime Minister to play a leading — one may even say sinister — role in the Commonwealth meetings at which South Africa's goose was cooked. I firmly believe that the Commonwealth made the right — the only possible decision on South Africa — but I wish I had known about Bryce's role before I called on Norman Robertson that day in 1962.

CHAPTER 4

TOTSIENS! SUID AFRIKA

There was more to our lives in South Africa in the last half of our posting than the issue of the membership of the Republic in the Commonwealth. Important as that was, it was only part of the quilt of events that was being woven in the country and whose political, economic, trade and administrative threads occupied us in the office. The business of diplomacy spilled over into many evenings spent at receptions and dinners but there was still time for the unfolding of family affairs and for travel and holidays.

In the last quarter of 1960, I had travelled to Cape Town on a house-hunting quest and Wynne and I had spent a week in Basutoland. At the end of the year, I had finally given up on my ambition to round out my travels in southern Africa with a visit to Angola. Two Canadian mission-aries stationed in the Portuguese colony, with whom I had been in touch and who knew of my plans, came to Pretoria on holiday. They and the other Canadians in Angola had close contacts among aspiring African politicians and their advice for me was that I should forget about making the journey because it was "too late". They were well informed: the revolt against the Portuguese was to begin early in 1961.

Ross Francis was notified in December that he would be leaving South Africa in mid-1961 and would be succeeded by David Miller. David was a 28-year-old graduate of the University of British Columbia. Born in Srinigar in Kashmir, he was Swahili-speaking in consequence of having been raised in East Africa.

The referendum on the establishment of a republic had occupied us in the latter part of 1960 but, with it out of the way, the only event of importance, before we would leave Pretoria for the Cape and the 1961 parliamentary session, was the visit of Dag Hammarskjold, the Secretary-General of the United Nations. This visit had its origins in the resolution of the Security Council in April 1960 deploring the situation in South

Africa after the events at Sharpeville; the Secretary-General was requested to act, in consultation with the Union Government, to uphold the purposes and principles of the UN Charter. The crisis in the Congo delayed the event.

On 2 January 1961, Frikkie Botha of the foreign ministry filled me in on the visit which seemed to have been designed by both sides to exclude the local diplomats. My diary entry read:

> Frikkie said that the South African Government is not putting Hammarskjold in touch with Opposition leaders or non-whites other than the Coloured Advisory Council (an unpopular group with most Coloureds) and Botha Sigcau, the head chief in the Transkei who has a revolt on his hands in Pondoland where military and police operations are now going on behind a curtain of secrecy.

On the 6th, I noted that the Secretary-General had arrived at Waterklook military airport in Pretoria and was staying at the Union Hotel. He had been greeted by a crowd of a few hundred, mostly Africans, who had "produced placards when he arrived (the placards had been hidden under coats) welcoming him to the police state, asking him if he had his pass and referring to Pondoland". The following day, I wrote that Hammarskjold "had a 2 1/2 hr. talk at the Union Bldgs with Dr. Verwoerd & later left for Cape Town". My last diary note on the visit was on 12 January when I recorded that the Secretary-General had left South Africa "saying he had learned much and still had more to learn".

I was at the House of Assembly in Cape Town on 23 January when Dr. Verwoerd reported on the Hammarskjold visit. The Prime Minister claimed that no obstacles had been placed in the way of the Secretary-General meeting whomever he wished because the Government had considered that misunderstanding might be avoided if he "acquainted himself personally" with the South African scene. The talks had been useful and constructive, Verwoerd said, and the Government had invited Hammarskjold to visit South Africa again in order to continue the contact.

The Secretary-General made a similar report to the Security Council, saying that he looked forward to continuing the talks. That was not to be: on 18 September 1961, he died in a crash near Ndola, Northern Rhodesia, where he was to meet Premier Tshombé of Katanga about the war then going on between the secessionist Congolese province and a United Nations Force.

Unlike 1960, the entire office went to Cape Town for the 1961 session. Though the experiment in the year of Sharpeville had convinced us and Ottawa that it was impractical to split our small operation, the annual trek was clearly disruptive. On Wednesday 11 January I wrote:

> The trek to Cape Town is now general. Some diplomats usually leave before Xmas and from the first week of January to about the 16th, the move goes on. The Americans went the first half of this week, the Australians a week ago and the U.K. and ourselves will all be down by Sunday. It's all a ridiculous waste of manpower and money that began in 1910 as a compromise which made Union possible in South Africa.

We left on Friday afternoon with the girls and Bruno the dog to drive to Parys on the Vaal River where we spent the first night of the trip. Next morning we were away just after six o'clock and drove 880 km through Winburg, Bloemfontein and Colesberg, arriving at the familiar Wagon Wheels Motel at Beaufort West at seven in the evening. It had been a hot day, the temperature in the car had been at 40 degrees Celsius for several hours. We were thankful for the swimming pool at the Wagon Wheels and the cool night air of the Karroo. The third day was easier: again we were on the road early and completed the last 480 km to Cape Town by noon.

Our residence for the session was "Umdoni", an imposing two-storey Georgian house in the pleasant suburb of Bishopscourt which we rented from Paul and Cathy Mincher. (Cathy Mincher was the adopted daughter of General Jan Christian Smuts, the legendary Boer general who later became Prime Minister.) The grounds were beautiful and we found that the location offered a different climate from Mouillé Point and Milnerton where we had previously lived in Cape Town. When there was a stiff southeaster downtown — the wind known as the "Cape Doctor" — Bishopscourt got little wind but was under the cloud that formed on the rear of Table Mountain and spilt over the city side to form the celebrated tablecloth, and then dissipated leaving the city in brilliant sunshine. Our friends Molly and Stanley Wilson lived nearby and we were always welcome to use their pool.[34] Tricia flew back to Pretoria at the end of January to continue her schooling at the St. Mary's Diocesan School for Girls. Jane began to attend Herschel School in Cape Town as a day pupil, but it was an unhappy choice for her and in April she moved on to the Bergvliet High School where our friend Joan Ribbink was a teacher.

We spent the entire parliamentary session of 1961 in Cape Town, not venturing on official or private trips beyond the Cape peninsula. At the office the onset of the republic and the question of its continued membership in the Commonwealth dominated our agenda but there were diversions. My new diplomatic rank of counsellor seemed to open doors more easily and we enjoyed the extra income that the promotion and general civil service pay increases provided.[35]

I always enjoyed renewing contact with my Cape friends, some of whom were much more than contacts because they were direct participants in the political drama that played on in the country and was nowhere more a matter of national theatre than in the Cape. Friends in Parliament were important to me but three non-parliamentary personalities had become sources and close friends. Nearing retirement was Leo Marquard of the Oxford University Press: he could always be counted on for calm and sound advice that came from his encyclopedic knowledge of the country and his liberal views. Stanley Uys was one of the most highly respected English-language journalists in South Africa: he was always as willing to bounce ideas off his diplomatic acquaintances as they were to extract his pithy and pregnant commentaries on the local scene. Patrick Duncan was the gadfly of the trio. Visionary and impulsive, feisty and courageous, his brushes with the authorities were to mount in frequency and gravity during the rest of my stay in South Africa.

During the brief October 1960 house-hunting visit to Cape Town, I had seen all three of these friends. When Stanley Uys and I lunched on 26 October with Patrick Duncan, he was only two days out of jail for refusing to reveal the source of an article in *Contact* on communism; he looked thin after 20 days on prison diet but was as unrepentant as ever in condemning the Nationalist regime. He believed that the Government would never be able to restore order to the Pondoland and Tembuland without resorting to armed force and predicted that there would soon be trouble in Ovamboland in South West Africa. Next day, I mentioned my conversation with Duncan when I called on Leo Marquard at his office at the Press. He was clearly troubled by some of Patrick's activities and volunteered the candid admission that he had remained "with misgivings".in the Liberal Party, rather than joining the Progressives, in order to exercise a moderating influence on the younger man.

The battle between Duncan and the authorities was now seriously joined, with the security wing of the police apparently less inhibited than before by the fact that Patrick's father had been the first South African Governor-General of the country. In March 1961 Patrick was served with an order under the Suppression of Communism Act banning him from attending meetings for a period of five years. That did not prevent him from working or from meeting his friends in numbers below the maximum permitted under the banning order; just a week afterwards I took him to lunch at the Civil Service Club. Nor did the official disapproval of Duncan and *Contact* deter diplomats from visiting the periodical's office. I was a frequent caller because *Contact* was just down the street from

Parliament, conveniently located on the fourth floor of the turn-of-the-century Parliament Chambers which housed offices and boutiques. It was always useful to find out what was on Pat's mind or try out ideas on him.

Across the atrium within Parliament Chambers, *Contact's* fourth floor neighbour was a millinery which was patronized by the wives of members of Parliament and especially those on the Government benches. South African white women were still in the Edwardian era of hats which served the dual purpose of protection from the elements and from the threat that the sun posed to their racial purity. Theirs were not the simple bonnets that had satisfied their foremothers but shining fezzes, garish turbans or towering canopies from which cascaded hanging gardens of flowers and cornucopias of fruit.

One of the millinery's clients was the wife of the Minister of Agricultural Technical Services and Water Affairs, a tall, ample woman whose reputation for monumental hats had to be maintained by regular visits to the shop. I had turned my attention in the second half of my posting to the Nationalist benches and had become acquainted socially with the Minister and his wife. On a few visits to Parliament Chambers, she and I travelled in the elevator cage together to the fourth floor and I detected a certain coolness in her when she saw me turn towards the *Contact* office. At the farewell party that the High Commissioner gave on my departure from South Africa, the Minister's wife professed her deep friendship for my wife and me and then confessed that she had been troubled when she had seen me with "that terrible man Patrick Duncan".

It was not only Afrikaners who had difficulty with the political views of Duncan and his associates on *Contact*: conservative English-speakers were equally troubled by them and sometimes reacted drastically. Tim Holmes, a young white assistant editor on the fortnightly's staff, had escaped arrest in 1960 by fleeing to Swaziland. In that colonial backwater, at a Commonwealth Society dinner held at the local hotel, he had made the mistake of refusing to join in a toast to the Queen. The wife of the hotel manager was infuriated and, to calm her, the manager had to promise to "fix" Holmes. This he did: when Holmes left the hotel to make a clandestine trip into the Republic, the manager phoned the South African Police who picked Holmes up at the border crossing.

The pressure on Duncan became more intense in 1962. He wanted to travel overseas but his passport was withdrawn even though he gave an undertaking that, while abroad, he would give no interviews, address no meetings and refrain from any public political activities. His movements were confined to the Cape peninsula. Later in 1962, the banning order against him under the Suppression of Communism Act was extended to prohibit the publication of any of his speeches or writing. (He was in good company for also on the list were Albert Luthuli, Oliver Tambo and Walter Sisulu; Nelson Mandela was added towards the end of the year.) By this time, Duncan had probably decided to leave the Liberal Party and throw in his lot with the Pan-Africanist Congress (PAC) which he favoured over the Communist-backed ANC. Imprisonment was now a very real prospect: only by getting out of the country could he continue the freedom fight.

Shortly after our return to Canada on home posting, Duncan made his way to Quthing in Basutoland from where he sent me a change-of-address postcard in October by which he informed his friends that "on 3rd May he left Cape Town".and, with typical defiance of the South African authorities and optimism about the future of the country, added:

> He does not expect to return in the immediate future, but is confident that he will be back before long.

In 1963, he was forced to leave Basutoland on being banned by the British Government from the High Commission Territories. He moved on to Europe and worked as an emissary of the PAC.

At the end of August 1963, Duncan spent a weekend at our home in Ottawa; the visit is worth a footnote here. Pat had been in the United States for three months lobbying on behalf of the PAC. He told me that the Congress had 200 members in training in North African countries as saboteurs and predicted that hit-and-run raids by them across the northern border of Transvaal would begin in 1964. According to him, the PAC still had strength inside South Africa while the ANC was moribund; he admitted, however, that the ANC was better organized abroad because of its Communist backing. My wife thought that Pat was unbalanced; I wrote in my diary:

> He may be. Certainly he has a martyr complex. He repeatedly referred to his belief that he will die in the cause of a free South Africa and mentioned that he was liable to [the] death sentence if caught in SA.[36]

The October 1963 issue of the respectable and authoritative American publication *Foreign Affairs* carried an appeal by Duncan for international intervention under United States leadership in the situation in South Africa. The article was also written to gain support for the PAC over the ANC: Duncan stated that he was a member of the PAC and asserted that it was the leading and more effective of the two African parties with "particular support among the more militant and the students".[37] His case for intervention was powerfully simple:

> Two facts are generally overlooked by those who hold that time should be
> afforded to the South Africa authorities to solve the problem themselves,
> and that interference from outside merely aggravates the situation by mak-
> ing the supporters of apartheid more militant and unified. The first is that
> developments in South Africa are going the wrong way: where there were
> rights, these have been taken away; where there was a little integration, it has
> been abolished; where there was some hope in the minds of the ruled, it has
> given away to despair. The second is that there is no longer any effective
> opposition to apartheid within the South African electorate... Thus the ini-
> tiative has already passed irrevocably away from the whites to the voteless,
> and to their friends and allies. For all these reasons, it is difficult to see how
> intervention can make matters worse than they are.

Patrick's battle for freedom in his own country was not to last much
longer. In 1964, when he was working for a relief agency in Algiers,
Pretoria deprived him of his citizenship. He died of natural causes in a
London hospital on 4 June 1967 at 48 years of age. In the London
Observer of 11 June 1967, Cyril Dunn concluded a tribute, under the
heading "Warrior against Apartheid", with these words:

> Patrick Duncan lived under a tyranny to which, after all, nobody has yet
> found an effective answer. He was without doubt one of the Heroes of
> that war.

During the 1961 session, the Treason Trial ended in Pretoria. Almost
six years had passed since the event that gave rise to the trial. It was
in June 1955 that the ANC had joined with other extra-parliamentary
political movements — the Indian Congress, the National Council of
Coloured Peoples, the Congress of Democrats whose members were
white communists, and the Congress of Trade Unions — to form the
"Congress of the People" and adopt the "Freedom Charter". The
Charter opened with these cadenced words:

> We, the people of South Africa, declare for all our country and the world
> to know: that South Africa belongs to all who live in it, black and white,
> and that no Government can justly claim authority unless it is based on the
> will of all the people ...

For a thousand more words the Charter went on to set forward the belief
in human dignity under the headings:

> The people shall govern.
> All national groups shall have equal rights.
> The people shall share the country's wealth.

The land shall be shared among those who work it.
All shall be equal before the law.
All shall enjoy equal human rights.
There shall be work and security.
The doors of learning and of culture shall be opened.
There shall be houses, security and comfort.
There shall be peace and friendship.

The meeting was broken up by the police who searched and recorded the identities of its participants. From the 3000 present that day, 140 were selected for punishment and arrested in middle-of-the-night raids throughout the country on 5 December 1956. Eventually 155 appeared in court to undergo preparatory examination which led to charges of high treason against 91 of them. The trial had opened at the Old Synagogue in Pretoria on 1 August 1958, just six weeks after my arrival in South Africa. Three months later, the original indictment was suddenly withdrawn by Oswald Pirow, the leader of the Crown team. A new indictment was framed with the charge being conspiracy to overthrow the state by violence and replace it with a communist regime or some other form of government; this indictment was presented on 19 January 1959 with only 30 of the 91 defendants charged.

In 1959, I met Hoexter of the Prosecutor's Office and I. A. Maisels QC, the defence leader, and saw them frequently on the Pretoria circuit in the latter part of that year as the trial droned on. Pirow died in October that year, an event which prompted Hoexter to comment lugubriously to me in respect of Professor Murray, an elderly witness giving lengthy testimony for the Crown, that Murray would be in the stand for another fortnight "if he lasted". (He did!) One day in February 1960 I spent a half-hour at the Synagogue and noted:

> Three scarlet-robed judges busily working on documents while an African detective read extracts from notes he had taken 4 or 5 years ago at ANC meetings. The Court Clerk, below the judges, read a paperback & the accused occupied themselves with books, newspapers, letters and filling in stubs of a book of lottery tickets (lotteries being illegal in SA!). The Treason Trial Defence Fund is running short now & after so long it is difficult to collect money.[38]

Hence, it seems that I assumed, the illegal lottery.

When the State of Emergency was imposed after the Sharpeville disturbances, the trial ran into difficulties. The accused, who had been out on bail, were detained; witnesses might have been arrested, because under emergency regulations, their testimony might be deemed subversive.

Maisels argued that it was improper for the case to continue in view of the fact that the Government, in supporting its decision to impose the State of Emergency, had made statements about the issues that amounted to a prejudgment. Shortly afterwards the defendants dismissed their counsel and it was not until August that the defence team resumed the case. The Crown argument took from November until March and the defence argument was barely underway when the presiding judge adjourned the hearing. Two days later, on 29 March 1961, he announced that the accused were acquitted and discharged. The cornerstone of the case for the prosecution, he said, was the alleged policy of violence attributable to the ANC; if that case failed, it must also fail against the other organizations involved. Although the organizations had been working to replace the existing form of state with a radically changed one, it had not been proved that form of state would be a communist one. Finally, it was not possible for the judges to come to the conclusion that the policy of the ANC was to overthrow the state by violence.

There could be no appeal by the Crown against this verdict because it was based on questions of fact and not points of law. And so the drama that had gone on at a measured pace for over two-and-a-half years at the Great Synagogue ended without regret for all concerned except the junior and middle-grade diplomats in Pretoria who, for so long, had used the Treason Trial as a place of entertainment and a haven from serious work.

The republic had been inaugurated by the time we began to pack up to leave Cape Town, near the end of the 1961 parliamentary session. "Umdoni" had been a nice residence but we looked forward as usual to getting back among our own possessions in Pretoria. We left Jane in Cape Town as a boarder with friends who lived close to the school in Bergvliet that she was attending. Our dog threw our 22 June departure off schedule when he disappeared early that morning and was found by our neighbour only at four in the afternoon lying exhausted among a pack of dogs outside a house where a bitch was in heat. An hour later we were on the road north and at 10:30 p.m. we checked into the Wagon Wheels Motel at Beaufort West. An early start the next morning made it possible to do a record day's drive of over 960 km, through Victoria West, Kimberley, Klerksdorp, Potchefstroom and Krugersdorp. At eight in the evening, 27 hours from Umdoni, we pulled up the driveway at 29 Victoria Street in Pretoria.

Settling back into the Pretoria house and office took longer that June because Ross Francis had left the post and David Miller had not yet arrived. Not until the Ambassador's July-the-First reception was out of the way did we get down to a steady schedule of reporting again. The reception itself provided the first subject because the South African Government decided to demonstrate its coolness towards Canada at this early opportunity after the ending of the Commonwealth connection by sending as its official representative one of the most junior and certainly the least likeable cabinet minister, Dr. Albert Hertzog. His presence and the perfunctory manner in which he proposed the toast on this national day disgusted most of those present and dismayed Jim Hurley who later made sure that his true friends in the cabinet knew what he thought of Hertzog. The 200 days of our last Pretoria interlude were relatively quiet at the office but busy on the road as I made official trips, some with Wynne, to all three High Commission Territories, Natal and the Northern Transvaal. With Tricia, we also spent a holiday in Mozambique. (Tricia remained in St. Mary's D.S.G. as a boarder until the beginning of August when the mid-winter term ended.) In October, I also travelled to Cape Town for discussions with the architect of the new African Life Centre in which we had signed a lease for the thirteenth floor. A common purpose of the official trips was to present to universities and colleges sets of books from the Canada Council.

As my diary entry for 10 August reveals, the Canada Council book scheme had merit:

> Went with David Miller... to call on the rector of Pretoria University, Prof. Rautenbach, and present him with the... Canada Council books. Our 3rd presentation — Turfloop and Moeng were the first. David will go to Potchefstroom on Monday to make the 4th. A good scheme which permits us to get around to the universities and colleges. There are 11 more to visit: Roma in Basutoland, a teachers' college in Swaziland, Wit[watersrand], OFS [Orange Free State University], Natal, the new Indian College in Durban, Ngoya (Zululand), Fort Hare, Rhodes, UCT [University of Cape Town] and Bellville, the new Coloured university college.

Wynne accompanied me on the July visit to the new Bantu University College of the North at Turfloop, an isolated spot in the hilly country-side 30 km east of Pietersburg, surrounded by koppies that were covered with aloes in bloom and other sub-tropical plants amidst the thorn bushes. It was my first look at one of the four colleges that had been created under the apartheid legislation of recent years which was designed to remove Africans, Asians and Coloureds from the "white" universities. Construction of teaching blocks, dormitories and other facilities was still going on (we were welcomed in the first ceremony to be held in the Council Chamber) but the infrastructure of the college hardly seemed to justify the appelation "university". Like all but one of his counterparts at the new colleges, the rector was an Afrikaner and a Nationalist. He differed from the Government only in believing that it was not going ahead fast enough with territorial apartheid. I noted that he seemed sincere in his determination to make a real university college at Turfloop even though at this stage the staff numbered barely 40 and the student population was at just a quarter of the goal of 500.

Later in the year, I visited two of the new colleges in Natal: that for Indians on Salisbury Island, Durban, and the college for Zululand at Ngoye. The rector of the Salisbury Island college was Professor S.T. Olivier who had previously taught at Cape Town. He acknowledged that there was some resistance to the new college within the Indian community but believed that, in time, the college could take the place of the non-European wing of the University of Natal. This view was contested by the principal of the University of Natal, Dr. E.G. Malherbe, who was opposed to the separation of college facilities on a racial basis. He remarked to me that African students would be hard pressed to afford the tuition and boarding fees at the remote campus of Ngoye whereas in Durban they could find jobs in their spare time to put themselves through Natal University. The rector of the University College of Zululand was Dr. Peter Cook who had been Under-Secretary for Bantu Education before taking on this lesser position. In its second year of operation, the college had only 51 students of whom less than half were in degree courses. Cook would not comment on the pace of expansion but hoped it would be slow so that resources could be directed to developing high standards. His pragmatism was encouraging but the isolated and segregated institution at Ngoye was a depressing sight.

At the beginning of August 1961, Dr. Verwoerd had called a general election for 18 October. Though a full 18 months early, it came as no surprise: rumours had circulated ever since the referendum on the republic that with that issue and the Commonwealth out of the way, the Nationalists would go to the polls. As the Progressives well knew, one of the objectives of the ruling party was to eliminate them from Parliament where they were the only liberal voices. The Nationalist leadership was also intent on purging its own ranks of anti-Verwoerd elements. When these two goals were achieved and continued Nationalists rule assured, the Government would be better placed to weather the economic difficulties that seemed to be in store for the country and to deal with impunity with the extra-parliamentary opposition. The best formula for election success was the issue of white supremacy without pain: the platform paid lip service and little more to the Bantu "separate development".which satisfied NP supporters that they would not have to give sweat and tears to the Bantustan chimera.

Another angle that the Prime Minister was working on was indicated by him in the debate on the Address of the newly-installed State President when he opened the first session of the republican parliament. Speaking in the House on 8 June, Dr. Verwoerd said:

> Everything points to the necessity for us to get together, because what is our problem in the future? It is to ensure that this White Republic of South Africa remains White. From now onwards it is our common white heritage that counts above all else.

The emphasis on white unity, and its reverse image the "Non-White question", was confirmed as the major thrust of Nationalist strategy when the theme of the annual conference of SABRA was announced. SABRA had intended to devote the meeting, held in September in Bloemfontein, to a discussion of the place of the Cape Coloureds in political life, a subject considered timely by the moderate Cape wing of the party including the Stellenbosch intellectuals and *Die Burger*. But Dr. Verwoerd vetoed this and SABRA was directed to examine the relations between English- and Afrikaans-speaking South Africans in the aftermath of the debates over the republic and Commonwealth membership.

I noted in my diary for 25 September:

> In the coming election there are two English-speaking candidates running as Independent Republicans — really Nats — but they have been nominated in constituencies impossible for Nats to win. Dr. V. could have given them safe Nat seats in areas such as Pretoria East which have significant English minorities but his idea of national unity apparently doesn't run to this.

Not only the Progressives but the United Party was threatened by the election. To save resources, the UP did not run candidates in 49 safe NP seats; the Nationalists were equally realistic and left the UP unopposed in 20 constituencies. The UP was confident that it could regain the Progressive Party seats which had indeed been won for the UP in 1958 and was more concerned about its right flank. To protect this, the Party made an election pact with the tiny National Union Party of Japie Basson and Judge H.A. Fagan by accepting their notion of "race federation". Although the UP spurned an offer by the Progressives for a deal, the Progressives decided not to enter into any three-way contests in which the Nationalists might benefit from a split of the opposition vote. In fulfilment of this decision, Ray Swart, the sitting Progressive for the Natal constituency of Zululand, withdrew from the contest in order to ensure the victory of the

UP candidate. At the High Commission, we gave the Progressives little hope of retaining their parliamentary foothold in the election.

We predicted that the Nationalists would win with little change from the outcome of the 1958 election, before the Progressives split from the UP. Our forecast was 105 NP, 50 UP and one National Union. We were wrong by one, a seat held by a Progressive which we thought the UP would take. It was not a remarkable feat to come this close to perfection in our estimate: at this stage in South African politics, the political loyalties of the white voters were rooted in language, religion, old nationalisms and current perceptions of race relations, and defections were rare. The changes in party standings in the Assembly that had taken place since the Nationalists obtained power had not been caused by voters crossing party lines. Rather, they were the result of revisions in the boundaries of constituencies, of gerrymandering which increased the number of seats in the Afrikaner backveld, the sparsely populated rural areas of the Transvaal and Orange Free State.

The seat that the Progressives retained in 1961 was Houghton, an affuent constituency in Johannesburg whose member was Helen Suzman. One of the most remarkable South African politicians of the second half of the century, Suzman was to be the sole Progressive in the Assembly for the next 13 years until a handful of her colleagues, some of them members of the founding group like Colin Eglin and Zach de Beer, joined her in providing the only meaningful opposition to the Nationalists. Through the years when Dr. Verwoerd was spinning the mad web of apartheid and his successor, John Vorster, erected walls of state security, she alone could be credited with keeping the conscience of white South Africa out of the gutter and with offering hope for everyone in South Africa.

While I was happy after the election that Helen Suzman had made it back, I regretted the disappearance of my other Progressive friends from the Assembly, though I was to see some of them again in Cape Town. Ray Swart told me in November that to ease Helen's burden, she was to have a panel of advisers made up of Harry Lawrence, Zach de Beer and Colin Eglin, who would form the permanent core, and Walter Stanford, Donald Molteno and Swart himself who would join the others once a month.

During my three-day visit to Cape Town shortly after the election, the announcement was made of the award of the Nobel Peace Prize to ex-Chief Albert Luthuli, the former president of the banned African National Congress. In my diary that day (24 October, United Nations Day) I noted that it was "a real shock to most whites and a slap at the

Nationalist Government to have Luthuli so honoured at a time when he is banished to his home district of Groutville near Stanger, Natal." The day was made extra bad for the South African Government because in New York, the United States delegate in the special political committee of the UN calmly and completely denounced the policy of apartheid.

These events were to be high on the agenda of a curious meeting in which I took part the next day back in Pretoria. My Ambassador gave a luncheon for four Canadian businessmen from Johannesburg, representatives of a community that found little to quarrel with in the policies of the South African Government. The four were members of a Canada-South Africa committee of the South African Foundation, a creation of the Government whose aim was to create a climate of confidence in South Africa abroad. The committee wanted Mr. Hurley's advice on their proposal to improve the image of the Republic in Canada by presenting "facts" untainted by politics. It was an idea to which my boss had given much attention in the past and, although I was beginning to suspect that he now doubted that anything the South Africans might say would wash abroad, he gave the four a sympathetic hearing. In my diary entry after the luncheon, two words of comment summed up my reaction to the proposal: "Hopelessly naive".

I decided to go to Natal to see Chief Luthuli and, after the arrangements had been made on my behalf by Ray Swart, visited him on 15 November. Because it would have been necessary for me to obtain a permit from the Bantu Affairs Department to go to his home at Groutville in a native reserve, we met in Stanger in the back room of the office of an Indian lawyer, E.V. Mohamed. I was greatly impressed by Chief Luthuli, noting in my diary afterwards that he had: "a kind almost noble face; highly expressive, modulated voice".

After I conveyed the Canadian Government's congratulations to him on the Nobel honour and passed on greetings from those of his friends whom I had already seen on the journey to Stanger, our conversation turned to the state of South Africa. Luthuli was clearly greatly concerned at the events of the past two years. Though he reaffirmed his belief in moderation and his faith in non-violence, he went on to warn that the Government's ruthlessness would lead to further trouble and described the situation as worse than it seemed.

Harry Rasky, a free lancer on contract to the Canadian Broadcasting Corporation, was waiting outside when my interview was over and we agreed to meet later for lunch. Rasky told me then that the Chief was the most impressive African he had seen so far on his tour of the continent, the quality of his personality far higher than that of Julius Nyerere of Tanganyika.

In December, Chief Luthuli was allowed to go to Oslo to receive his prize: the Government, declaring that it could not understand or support the award, tried to save face by issuing him with a passport *valid for 10 days*. Luthuli's speech of acceptance reaffirmed his belief in peaceful protest but he asserted the legitimacy of the use of armed force in responding to "the adamancy of white rule" and repeated the demands of the ANC for sanctions and other external pressure on South Africa. The speech set the stage for the first acts of terrorism by the ANC which occurred a few days later, at about the same time that Luthuli returned from the dignified setting in Oslo to the odious confinement to the Lower Tugela district of Natal.

Professionally, the trip to Natal had already been valuable before I met Chief Luthuli. At Kloof, amidst green hills and rich soil, I had called on Alan Paton whose first book was *Cry the Beloved Country*, an international success that made his reputation as a white South African writer who cared deeply for all the people of his country. At his house I met his wife and Peter Brown, the chairman of the Liberal Party. I brought with me a copy of Paton's short book on the role of the Liberal Party entitled *Hope for South Africa*[39] which I asked him to autograph. "Did I suggest there was hope for South Africa?", he asked rhetorically, going on to say that three years later he would not have used that as the title.

When we talked about the political situation, Paton commented on the apparent stability of the Government in the past year and remarked that motions of censure at the United Nations were like injecting more drugs into a man who was already unconscious. He was deeply pessimistic on the possiblity of a change of mind by the Nationalists. When I asked him about the progress on his latest book, a biography of Jan Hofmeyr, the successor to Smuts as the leader of the United Party, his gloom disappeared and he began talking about the man whom he clearly believed would have been able to save South Africa had he lived. He compared him in stature with John Stuart Mills, another child prodigy.

In Durban I went to the office of the Liberal Party to meet Joseph Ngubane; Peter Brown was also present. Ngubane had recently been convicted for activity in the Continuation Committee of the South African Churches' Conferences, a body set up in 1960 to plan interracial consultations among the leaders of churches with a view to seeking means of promoting reconciliation among them. The committee had met in December 1960 and issued a statement — called the Cottesloe Declaration after the residence at the University of Witwatersrand where the meeting took place — asserting the scriptural grounds for opposition to some aspects of apartheid and calling for the creation of a South African Conference of members of the World Council of Churches to study and deal with local matters. These conclusions were not supported by the three Afrikaner churches that had taken part in the consultations. They reiterated their belief in the scriptural basis for separate racial development but in 1961 were to have to deal with the "heretical" views of some of their enlightened ministers.[40]

Ngubane was appealing his conviction to the Supreme Court. He observed that as the area for legal opposition was reduced by legislation, the chances of non-violent change also became smaller.

Ray Swart had also put me in touch with the Indian community in Durban which was then divided between those of the South African Indian Congress, who favoured a non-racial country, and the South African Indian Organization which supported the recent creation of the Department of Indian Affairs by the Government. The Congress was led by Dr. G.M. Naicker and the Organization by Mr. A.M. Moolla. I saw them on successive evenings at their respective homes.

Dr. Naicker, a white-haired man of 55 who resembled Nehru, lived in a large, comfortable house on Percy Osborn Road in Durban in a neighbourhood that was scheduled to become "white" under the Group Areas Act. He was holding out against moving voluntarily in the hope that the Government would fall before he was forced to relocate to an Indian township. The Natal Indian Congress, with 34,000 paid-up members, could claim to have mass following; it was also the oldest of all the congress parties in the country having been founded by no less a person than Mahatma Gandhi in 1894. Dr. Naicker had become the Natal party's head in 1946 and had taken over the leadership of the country-wide South Africa Indian Congress only in 1961. Considered a young radical himself only a few years before, Dr. Naicker said that he was concerned that the younger members of Congress, along with other non-whites, would resort to violence against the Nationalist regime; he favoured non-violent means in the economic field to bring about a multi-racial state. The party co-operated closely, he said, with the African National Congress and Luthuli's Nobel Prize had had a "tremendous" effect on the morale of his people.

The next evening I was invited to dinner at the home of A.M. Moolla, a wealthy businessman who was the head of the Indian Organization. I was accompanied by the aging academic and author, G.H. Calpin, who reduced the usefulness of the evening by talking too much. There was little, however, to draw from Moolla whose political strategy was to work within the system imposed by the Government and seek to get the best deals possible for the Indian community. I noted later that he felt that the Nationalists would modify apartheid in the face of world opinion and was "the only person who has said that to me recently".[41]

On the drive down to the coast and back, I saw more of the places that figured so importantly in the history of Zulu and Boer and Brit. Outside Dundee was Blood River, where the Voortrekkers, the Boer pioneers, took their revenge on 16 December 1838 on Dingaan and the Zulus for the slaughter a year earlier of another trek party led by Piet Retief. That battle later became central to the mythology of the Afrikaner: the vow to observe their victory as a day of thanksgiving that the victors are said to have sworn on the eve of the battle led three decades later to the establishment of the 16th of December as the Day of the Covenant and, a century after the battle, to the consecration of the massive grey granite Voortrekker Monument in Pretoria.

A short distance downstream, the Blood River joins the Buffalo. To the south-east is the battlefield of Isandhlwana where, on 22 January 1879, the army of the still vibrant Zulus surprised and savaged a column of 4000 troops of the most powerful nation on earth. To the south is a ford called Rorke's Drift which was held the next day by a tiny British force against two impis of victorious Zulu warriors. A simple cenotaph marks that stand and records the names of the 17 British troopers of the 24th Regiment who died. Behind the memorial is the old Swedish Evangelical Mission Church where British wounded lay. The Zulus lost 350 men before they gave up at dawn on the 24th. Withdrawing from Rorke's Drift and Isandhlwana, they were pursued to the heart of their land and crushed in a battle at Ulundi in July 1879, never again to pose a threat to the whites.

My third visit that day was to the little Anglican church of St. James in Dundee. There I saw the grave of Major-General Sir William Penn Symons who died on 20 October 1899 when his force stumbled on a Boer column of equal strength at Talana in the first major engagement of the second South African War. In a few hours in that small area, I had come across reminders of three of the seminal events of South African history.

In late November, Bruce Williams, then High Commissioner to Ghana, spent five days with Wynne and me before flying to Dar-es-Salaam where he represented Canada at the inauguration of Tanganyika's independence. Bruce had become intensely attached to pan-Africanism in

Accra; although he was impressed by the low-rent housing for blacks in the Atteridgeville township west of Pretoria, which we visited during his stay, he was naturally appalled by the political and social restrictions on black South Africans. While some of his observations seemed extreme, they served to remind me that three years in South Africa had probably distorted my own judgment.

A few weeks later, I had another reminder when David Miller and I and our wives joined a number of American diplomats for a tour of the Daveyton Township near the city of Benoni, 50 km south of Pretoria. We were shown around the township by the director of the city's Non-European Affairs Department, an official who seemed to me to be level-headed, imaginative and decent, obviously sympathetic to Africans and trying to make Daveyton a good community. That he was unusual among such officials was demonstrated when we attended a meeting of the Bantu Advisory Board, the "municipal council" of the township. The director gave the Board free rein: we found ourselves listening to speeches by two of the African members in which they heatedly criticized the subjection of Africans by "the so-called democratic government of South Africa". It was an example of political interaction between blacks and whites and of dissent by the disenfranchised in an institutional forum rarely glimpsed in South Africa.

We said goodbye to Pretoria early in January 1962 after selling the Chevrolet Biscayne and handing 29 Victoria back to its owners. The family had been together for Christmas as Jane had arrived from the Cape early in December; the family was indeed an extended one because Jane was accompanied by a close school friend from Bergvliet School who stayed with us for a month. On the first day of the year, we gave a party for our Pretoria friends, an occasion graced by the presence of two Rolls Royces and a Bentley at the foot of our driveway. We packed for the move back to Canada, all but our clothes and a few books and bric-a-brac going into storage until then. On the 9th, we moved into the Continental Hotel, smuggling Bruno into our rooms, and said goodbye to our ever-loyal, Nyasa servant, Dickson Chirente. Two mornings later, we boarded the train for Johannesburg where we transferred to the Blue Train for the trip to Cape Town.

The Blue Train was still the most elegant means of travel between the Rand to the Cape. Bedrooms were very comfortable, there was a splendidly furnished lounge car and the restaurant was as good as that of a four star hotel. Only the view of the passing countryside and the swaying of the coaches caused by the narrow gauge tracks reminded us that we were on a train. Several fellow diplomats were on board and we played cards in the lounge between dinnertime and a midnight stop at De Aar Junction in the Karroo, the halfway point in the journey. At De Aar, John Dunrossil of the British Embassy persuaded the engineer of a diesel locomotive to let us climb up into his cab for a demonstration of the controls and we barely made it back to our train in time for its departure. When we woke up in the morning, we were at Laingsburg. The train pulled into Cape Town station at two in the afternoon; our exit was impeded by the security precautions that were already in place for the arrival of the State President in the official South African Government train, appropriately called the White Train.

We stayed at the Arthur's Seat Hotel in Sea Point for the first eight days in Cape Town before moving into the house at 8 Sunningdale Road in Kenilworth which we had rented for our last three months from friends. An attractive bungalow with ample space for entertaining and three bedrooms, the house was within walking distance of the Main Road where Jane would catch the bus to Bergvliet School and only five blocks from Tricia's new school, Wynberg Girls' School. Our new car, a red Austin 850 that we would take back to Canada, was landed in Cape Town on the 17th, the same day that we delivered Bruno to his new master, a friend at the British Embassy. The move into the new office in the African Life Centre occupied two days and the parliamentary session had begun before Wynne and the girls and I settled into the house in Kenilworth.

In the office, we hoped that there might be a quieter time than we had had in the previous two parliamentary sessions. We assumed that the achievement of the republic might be followed by a period of calm retrenchment and reflection. This was not to be. Although the general election had almost eliminated all of its erstwhile opponents from parliament, the Government was still not satisfied and was to move on several fronts in 1962 to silence what dissent remained and further strengthen the laager — the circle of wagons — against all dangers. In security terms, there was reason to do so. A handbill had been circulated in December promising violence to complement the actions of "the established national liberation movements"; this would be the task of Umkonto we Sizwe, the "Spear of the Nation", described as a new independent body formed by Africans. On 15 and 16 December 1961, plastic bombs exploded harmlessly in Durban, Port Elizabeth and Johannesburg. We were to learn later that these explosions were the beginning of the campaign of the military wing of the ANC. Although the reaction of the whites was generally disdainful, the authorities took the threat seriously and from this time on, police and military guard were stationed at key points.

The onset of terrorism was to spur the Government to draft yet another General Law Amendment Bill which it introduced in May, a month after I left South Africa. It was to be the harshest and most repressive instrument that the Nationalists had forged and its passage in June 1962 was marked by protests from jurists, the churches, the women of the Black Sash movement and a wide segment of the white population. This was all in the future and after my time: although the opening of the parliamentary session was marked by the highest level of security up to that time in South African history, with police sharpshooters conspicuous on roof tops around Parliament Square, the proceedings of the Assembly began with an emphasis on matters which ignored the dangers and only added to the image of unreality of Dr. Verwoerd and his government.

I was not as assiduous as in previous sessions in keeping up my old practice of visiting the House almost every day to watch its proceedings and to chat with members. My sympathies were with neither the truculent racists on the Government benches nor the jaded members of the Official Opposition, who had failed to offer change for South Africa. It was just as well that I would soon be leaving the country.

The State President's Address at the opening of parliament on 19 January was, I wrote in my diary, "a long complaint against the UN and the rest of the world and an apologia for apartheid — the only realistic policy". On the 23rd, the first day of the no-confidence debate, there was no room left in the gallery when I got to the Assembly. I had to content myself with reading a copy of Dr. Verwoerd's speech announcing that self-government would soon come to the Transkei native reserve and thus the day of "grand" apartheid had arrived. Discussions, he said, would be held between South Africa and the future Transkei Government to prepare for "an association on Commonwealth lines". The next day I wrote in my diary:

> The scheme for the Transkei — if Dr. Verwoerd means what he says about eventual independence — signals the balkanization of South Africa and does not solve the problem of the urban Africans who outnumber all other racial groups in the so-called 'white' areas. Dr. V. said the step was being taken under pressure from the outside world.

I noted that the Transkei was the most populous and compact of the Bantu homelands and that the others, even Zululand, were broken up by enclaves of white farms. How they could become independent states, I wrote, was hard to imagine.

The English-language press, which was blamed by the Government as much as its parliamentary critics for the stigmas on the South African body politic, was exposed to new attacks early in February 1962. During the 1961 parliamentary session, the Government had introduced the "Undesirable Publications Bill" which provided that any publication could be deemed undesirable if, amongst other things, it was "prejudicial to the safety of the State, the general welfare or the peace and good order of the country". Before its second reading, the Bill was sent to a special committee and the association of newspaper proprietors set about to head off the legislative threat by drawing up its own code to be enforced by a board of reference. Although the proposal was seen by many as a danger to press freedom equal to that of the Bill, the move satisfied the Government which agreed to shelve action on the legislation in order to give the self-disciplinary approach time to prove that it would work.

That the dangers faced by the English-language press were not just those that might be legislated was illustrated by the case of Anthony Delius, whose privileges in the Press Gallery were suspended by the Speaker of the Assembly early in February. Delius had written a satirical piece in his column in the *Cape Times* in which he poked fun at the Nationalists for retaining vestiges of the monarchy in their republican House. The Speaker, Henning J. ("Hennie") Klopper, a founding member of the Broederbond and one of the most narrow-minded of the verkrampte Nationalists, ordered that Delius be expelled from the Gallery for a year. Barred from his place in the Gallery, Delius spent his spare time writing an amusing novel about the secession of Natal from the Republic[42] which made more fun of the Nationalists than they would have suffered had they permitted him to continue decrying the parliamentary scene from the Gallery.

At lunch on 9 February, Stanley Uys commented to me that as the offending article itself did not seem to warrant so severe a sentence, it was obvious that the Nationalists had been gunning for Delius and awaiting a pretext to silence him. Piet Cillié of *Die Burger* remarked to me that he was "depressed" by the severity of the Speaker's action. The affair was not over. After the *Sunday Times* had referred sardonically to the matter in an editorial column, the Clerk of the Assembly called in Stanley Uys to notify him that the Gallery privileges of the newspaper were withdrawn. On the 7th, I wrote in my diary:

> Dropped in on Stanley and Edna Uys on the way to work to extend com-
> miseration at his expulsion from the press gallery. As they are leaving a
> month today on a long holiday in Europe, Stan is not too unhappy. An

amusing facet is that the Sunday Times is one of few papers giving outright support to the UP. This may influence Sir de Villiers Graaff to institute a move in parliament to have the Speaker's ruling reversed or amended. The editor, Joel Mervis, is flying from Jo'burg to C.T. tomorrow to see Klopper, the Speaker — not, according to Stan, to present abject apologies.

Next day, Wynne and I were in the parliamentary dining room for lunch as guests of the UP deputy leader, Marais Steyn. Also dining nearby was de Villiers Graaff whom I saw later in the day. I wrote:

> De Villiers Graaff had a party incl. Victor Norton of the C. Times & Joel Mervis of the Sunday Times to discuss the Speaker's withdrawal of privileges of the latter. Mervis had an interview with the Speaker earlier & said afterwards that old Klopper got quite apoplectic. UP is considering asking for establishment of a committee of rules & procedure in the Assembly to deal with such matters in future.

Shortly afterwards, two Afrikaans newspapers urged the Speaker to reconsider the ban on the *Sunday Times*. This set the ground for an apology from Joel Mervis and the restoration of the newspaper's facilities in the Gallery by Hennie Klopper. Only Tony Delius remained unpardoned — and free to continue writing about the day that Natal took off.

In early February, I went to Belleville to present the last of the sets of Canada Council books to the University College of the Western Cape, the tribal institution for the Coloureds. The rector was Dr. Meiring whose better-known brother, Piet, was the head of the Department of Information and unloved by the press and diplomats alike. I found the rector "a bit of a school-marm" and it was difficult to imagine academic success for a college which was then housed in a former primary school building and was about to move to its permanent campus amidst the sand dunes of the Cape Flats on the road from Bellville to the Cape Town airport. The student enrolment was 400 of whom only 40 percent were on degree courses; the target five years ahead was a thousand students. None enjoyed government bursaries and instruction was mainly in Afrikaans.

Discipline seemed relaxed at Western Cape with the students going about their lives like students everywhere. I did not detect anything that day of the resentment that Coloured politicians had expressed to me at the exclusion of their sons and daughters from the University of Cape Town under the infamous "Extension of University Education Act, 1959". But it must have been there.

Our departure from South Africa had by now been fixed: we were to sail from Cape Town on the Transvaal Castle on Friday, 13 April. Other diplomats who had long been with us at the post were also leaving and there was a change of guard in the press gallery. As the old colleagues and contacts went and our own departure came closer, it was not easy to pick up new friends amongst their replacements. But some fitted in better than others: among the journalists, we saw a lot then of Allister Sparks of the *Rand Daily Mail* and his wife, Mary.

Friends were overwhelmingly kind to Wynne and me in those final weeks, entertaining us at dinners and cocktail parties or just having us over for tea or a family meal to say *Totsiens*, farewell. It reminded us that we had lived some of the most important years of our lives in South Africa and had established close bonds with scores of people. Some were diplomatic wanderers like ourselves but most — those who lived in Pretoria, the Cape and so many corners of Southern Africa — would remain there. And that alone would keep our thoughts riveted to the region's troubled future for the rest of our lives.

On Monday, 9 April, Jim and Vera Hurley gave a farewell reception for us at the Mount Nelson Hotel. It was a nostalgic affair attended by well over 100 of our diplomatic and local friends, a fact that made it impossible to say much more than "hail and farewell". Just as it touched us to see friends for the last time, it flattered us that among those who came was a cabinet minister, the permanent head of the South African foreign ministry, and a half dozen ambassadors including Sir John Maud of the U.K. and the new American, Joseph Satterthwaite. As the era had not yet come to South Africa when multi-racial parties were given by the diplomatic corps, the reception was an all-white affair. Save for the definition of race under the Population Register Act, only the cabinet minister — a swarthy Transvaal Afrikaner of typical trekboer ancestry with some genes of indigenous origin — might not have been permitted in the hotel as a guest.

Next morning, after I had taken a photograph of our two trunks and 12 pieces of hand luggage on the front porch, we left 8 Sunningdale to go on board the Transvaal Castle which, I noted in my diary, would be "our hotel for the next three days and transportation after that".

Though we were afloat, we were not yet free from farewells. Wynne saw Nancy, our maid, on the train for Pretoria on Wednesday morning and went to lunch with Maureen Turner, our first South African acquaintance at Mouillé Grange almost four years back. That evening, at dinner at Milnerton on Table Bay, a diversion among the guests was the sight of our ship ablaze with light in the harbour across the bay. Thursday was our last full day in South Africa and my diary entry attests that it was full indeed:

To the office in the morning to clean up the desk — completely this time. Lunch at Maxim's with Stan and Molly Wilson of Mobil Oil. Wynne was presented with [a] fish server by counsellors' wives in [the] morning and in the afternoon she showed Michael and Jonathan Rolfe around the boat. I went to Foreign Affairs to say goodbye to John Enderman (Chief of Protocol), Frikkie Botha — busy on the negotiations with the UN Committee on SWA — and Boy Viljoen, still occupied with [the South African] departure from the Commonwealth. Dropped into Parliament for a half hour to listen to Dr. Verwoerd speaking, the last time and the last look. Crossed the road to the British Embassy to say goodbye to some of the chaps. Back to the ship where Joan and Mrs. Ribbink spent 6–7 p.m. with us. Wynne and I drove at 8:15 to 8 Sunningdale to talk to Sandy and Joan Little [the owners of the house that we had rented] and then went on to the Owen Davises' (Australian Ambassador) dance, his farewell party and 50th birthday. Left at 12:30 and Colin and Joyce Eglin came back to the ship with us to look it over. Bed at 2:30 a.m.

Until the ship was pulled away from the dock, the day that we sailed was equally hectic. We were late rising but in time for a farewell call on board by Maeve Steward of the British Embassy after which I went to the office for the final vale. The Hurleys returned to the ship with me for drinks and then the rush of friends was on us until the time came for visitors to leave and streamers to be thrown to those, among them school-mates of Jane's, who stayed on the dock and watched us go. And, out of the harbour and past Mouillé Point and Sea Point, we went to our cabin and slept.

CHAPTER 5

A TASTE OF THE
SOVIET UNION:
POSTING TO MOSCOW

From the first day to the last of the Moscow assignment, my wife and I were constantly transforming our preconceived two-dimensional images of the Union of Soviet Socialist Republics into the three-dimensional world of reality. All the advice that we had received from foreign service friends who had been there earlier, all that we had read in books and on the files and seen in films and photographs — and salted and spiced with our prejudices and misconceptions — could not prepare us for the reality that we would experience in Moscow.

The assignment as the second officer of the Canadian Embassy was daunting. The Soviet Union was currently the world's second superpower, vying for global leadership with the United States of America. Territorially, the USSR was larger than the land mass of all of the countries of the North Atlantic Treaty Organization combined. Soviet industrial output had grown massively in the two decades since the Second World War and the country was challenging the USA in many areas — not least in military power and space exploration, and not without success.

The assignment was daunting also because the Soviet Union was an adversary and seemed to pose a threat to world peace and to stability in the West. That threat brought its own challenges to my work as number two of the Canadian Embassy, placing demands on me in a variety of roles. These included the pursuit of improvements where these were possible, or accommodations if not, in Soviet-Canadian relations; the cultivation of contacts and sources, especially amongst the elite band of diplomats and foreign journalists but also within the Soviet bureaucracy; the welfare and protection of the Canadian Embassy staff from the mercies of the Soviet intelligence agencies and the miseries of daily living in the peoples' paradise.

All household and educational preparations completed, Wynne and I flew with our daughters Jane and Tricia from London to Moscow on a direct flight of a Comet 4B of British European Airways on Friday, 17 July 1964. Just before landing at Sheremetyevo Airport, Moscow's new international gateway from the West, we looked down on the rows of large apartment blocks of a Moscow suburb. The airport seemed only recently to have been hacked out of the forest but already its buildings showed signs of dilapidation.

The Embassy's First Secretary, Godfrey Hearn, and the Administrative Officer, Arthur Haggins, were at the foot of the Comet's steps to greet us and lead us through the customs and immigration formalities. On the drive to the Embassy compound at Starokonyushenny Pereoluk 23 (No. 23 Old Stables Lane) Godfrey filled me in on personalities and problems within the office. I rode in his Volga car, the model that I had ordered, something like a Chevrolet of the mid-forties, high up in the air and uncomfortably sprung. Wynne and the girls travelled with Arthur in a Canadian-built stationwagon. I noticed that the streets of Moscow were wide but traffic was sparse, consisting mostly of battered trucks of an uneconomic size.

We were delivered to our quarters. Flat "A" was located on the court-yard at the rear of a pre-Revolutionary sugar merchant's mansion which served as both the Ambassador's residence and the chancery. Flat "A" was in a two-storeyed, ochre-stuccoed, log house, a *domik* built shortly after Napoleon and the Grand Army had burnt this quarter of the city — the Arbat — before they left Moscow and died in the Russian snows on the retreat towards France. We had two entrances: the formal doorway that faced the driveway from the street where the militiaman's sentry-box was located, and a doorway from the living room to the courtyard which we used most often, so as to deny the sentry visual knowledge of our comings and goings to and from the chancery.[44] Our accommodation occupied most of the ground floor and about half of the second floor, the other half providing an apartment for the embassy's communicator and his wife.

Little time was wasted that weekend in getting to meet other members of the staff and to begin unpacking. We both knew Ambassador Robert Ford and his wife Thereza from the brief months in 1954 when I worked under his direction in European Division in the Department. They came to the flat to greet us soon after we had arrived and, the following day, had us over, with Jane and Tricia, to a luncheon served with the elegance for which Thereza was renowned. We made our first excursions from the compound. We visited the Naval Attaché and his wife, John and Joan

Bovey, whose apartment was located beyond Gorky Park in a building reserved for diplomats at Leninsky Prospekt 45. We went to see Godfrey and Joan Hearn in their flat in another diplomatic ghetto at Kutuzovsky Prospekt 19. Their building was just across the Moscow River to the west of the Embassy and near the Ukraine Hotel, one of the seven mock-Gothic skyscrapers in Moscow which were better known as "Stalin's wedding cakes".

On our first Sunday evening, Wynne and I went for a walk in the neighbourhood of the compound. Across the road from the Embassy was a school which, during holidays, served as a *Pioneerski Lager*, a camp for the boys and girls of the young Pioneers, the Soviet equivalent of the Cubs and Brownies of the Scouting movement in the West. The Embassy was flanked by two eight-storey apartment blocks that overlooked our court-yard at the rear. Barely a block away was a street of picturesque log and clapboard houses, the homes of the workers of a century past that had survived along with the grander stuccoed residences of the rich merchants and the ugly apartment blocks of more recent decades. During our second summer, these houses were to be the backdrop for a Soviet film; the front of one of them was given a neon sign identifying it as "Cooper's Bar" for the production of what seems to have been an anti-Western "western".

At the end of Starokonyushenny Pereoluk was the Arbat, then the main shopping street of old Moscow. Shabby now, but still wearing the charm of faded and chipped nineteenth century stucco flourishes, many of the Arbat's shops — above all the pharmacy — would have qualified in the West for inclusion in a heritage village. The general goods stores were evocative of African trading posts with their goods stacked unappealingly on austere shelves; condescendingly, we found prices ridiculously high and the window displays laughably primitive. But Wynne was pleased to discover the "Commission Shop", a state-run second-hand store to which needy descendants of the once-prosperous brought pre-revolutionary antiques. She was to become a regular visitor to this shop on the Arbat and some of the ornaments of the Russian past became hers.

What we saw in that evening's walk confirmed what we had been told about the decadence of the Soviet urban landscape. There were potholes in the sidewalks and no guard-rails protected pedestrians from the apertures for basement windows. Vomit from drunks was another hazard. Greyness and decrepitude were pervasive along our walking route and we were glad to return to the colour and comfort of the flat.

A drive next day around Moscow with Art Haggins revealed that there were attractive areas in the city, especially near the river, but drabness remained the predominant impression of the Soviet capital in our first days. It was an impression that would be deepened during the short, cold days of the bleak winter that was to come so soon.

In the office, the first days were spent in getting to know the other members of the staff and in probing the limits of my own authority as the most senior officer after the Ambassador. This was not a one-way street for the staff were also keen on finding what made me tick and the Ambassador wanted to assert his concept of the second-in-command job on me.

A highly respected member of the Canadian foreign service, Robert Ford was a Sovietologist of distinction whose three postings in Moscow had provided a wealth of experience matched by few other diplomats. On top of his experience and knowledge was a fluency in the Russian language that qualified him to become a successful translator of Russian poetry. This enormous advantage did not prevent Robert Ford from being petty. But most of that pettiness could be attributed to Thereza, his wife who, in her defence and promotion of her physically-handicapped husband, often went beyond the acceptable bounds of that cause. His affection for her sometimes led him to take decisions in administrative matters which were contrary to policy and directives and against the interests of the staff of the Embassy.

It was Thereza who caused my first quarrel with Ford. On the advice of my predecessor, I had arranged for the financing of the construction of a second floor bathroom in Flat "A", my predecessor having warned me that I would soon tire of nocturnal promenades of 59 steps down to the only complete facilities. When I arrived in Moscow, I was informed that the Ambasador had already converted the money authorized for the bathroom into new drapes for the ambassadorial bedroom. It was a switch that I refused to suffer and I wrote over my own signature to ask Ottawa to re-instate the funds that had been diverted. Ottawa readily obliged, to Ford's chagrin.

Within weeks, there was another confrontation. In March 1964, the Ambassador had obtained washer-dryer laundry equipment of high efficiency for the compound on the understanding that it was to be available to all Canadian families. Accordingly, when we left Ottawa, we placed our washer and dryer in storage there. When we arrived and found that the use of the laundry equipment was denied, I brought the issue out into the open by asking Ottawa to take mine out of storage and ship it to me;

I placed a copy of my letter on the circulating diary to be seen by the Ambassador. The atmosphere in the office cooled but, not without irony, the showdown in our relations came only after Ford had been ordered back to Moscow on the fall of Khrushchev. By then, it was too late in the game for him to try to defend his lost cause, or for me to threaten him again with my early departure. We had a good relationship from this time except for the occasional contretemps instigated by Thereza.

Despite my view of Ford's administrative failings, I knew when I frequented the meetings of the political counsellors of the NATO embassies or those of the Commonwealth missions that my opinions were regarded as worth listening to because they might reflect Ford's.

Carried on in the homes of the participants, the NATO "tea parties", as the meetings were known, did not deal with matters that were confidential except in circumstances when one or more of us wanted the Russians to hear, through their microphones, comments that would have been undiplomatic to state to their faces. However, the gatherings provided a regular opportunity for exchanges of information gleaned from the Soviet media that one or other of us might have been alone in noticing.

In addition to these gatherings, the Canadian number two took part in a more select NATO group whose membership was limited to those embassies that possessed "safe-speech rooms" where conversations were physically and electronically protected from eavesdropping by the Russians. At these meetings it was possible to exchange classified information and to discuss the activities of Soviet intelligence and counter-intelligence agencies. Both forums, however, were serious affairs where there was seldom any of the light-hearted gaiety that characterized exchanges among diplomats on the other side of the Iron Curtain. The quality of the participants was also superior to that of colleagues in easier posts: several of those with whom I drank tea or huddled next to in safe-speech rooms were to go on to the highest levels of their services.

In addition to the staff of the Embassy, there were a handful of Canadian journalists in Moscow at this time. Last and least among them was William Devine, the correspondent of the great Canadian newspaper, the organ of the Communist Party of Canada, the *Canadian Tribune* — or so our hosts the Soviets would have us believe. We saw him seldom. But, at Easter 1965, the Second Secretary of the Embassy, Bill Warden, took him to the service at the Orthodox Cathedral and reported to me that Devine should be worth cultivating because he was shaky on his communist ideology.

The senior Canadian correspondent during my time was Jack Best of the Canadian Press. Very steady, competent and hard-working, Best was an asset to the Embassy, sharing his experiences with us and prepared to seek and act upon advice. The fact that he and Warden played hockey together was beneficial both to Best and the Embassy. Jack's use of the Associated Press telex link became a subject necessitating the Embassy's successful intervention on his behalf with the Foreign Ministry in June and July 1965, when I was Chargé d'Affaires.

Less steady and less reliable was the correspondent of the Canadian Broadcasting Corporation (CBC), David Levy. A fluent Russian-speaker who had studied at the School of Slavic Studies at the University of British Columbia, Levy had been in the Soviet Union briefly in 1963 and had given the Embassy cause for concern during that visit. Next year, he arrived in Moscow on 17 October, two days after Khrushchev was deposed. That evening, accompanied by Eric de Maunay, the correspondent of the British Broadcasting Corporation, Levy came to the *domik* for a drink. He told me that he had just taken part in a London-Bonn-Paris-Washington-Toronto panel which analyzed the Soviet change of government for the CBC audience. It seemed to me to be a remarkable achievement for someone who had been in the Soviet Union for less than six hours.

It was Levy who instigated the attempt of Premier Smallwood and former American Vice-President, Richard Nixon, to visit our neighbour, former Premier Khrushchev, in April 1965. It was also Levy who was invited by the Soviets to attend a war crimes trial in Riga, Latvia, in October 1965 at which a Canadian resident, Haralds Puntulis of Toronto, was one of the defendants in absentia. Levy returned to Moscow very worked up at the evidence that had been presented on the murder of Latvian Jews and persuaded the CBC to run a programme on the case. Just three days before, we had sent a note to the Foreign Ministry refusing to extradite Puntulis and we were not happy at the prospect of a CBC airing of the charges against him. The Russians had calculated that Levy would react as he did.[45]

The third resident Canadian correspondent of my days in Moscow was Peter Worthington of the Toronto *Telegram* who had arrived in Moscow at the beginning of February 1965, just after I had left on a seven-week absence from Moscow on a course and holiday in the United Kingdom. I had met Worthington once before in 1961 in Pretoria, South Africa. Robert Ford gave a weekly briefing for Worthington and Best — and Levy when he deigned to come — principally on what we were doing in the area of Soviet-Canadian relations. Worthington was brash and out-spokenly anti-Soviet, qualities which did him little good when, after his wife left Moscow in September 1965, he began a conspiracy to help his female Russian translator to escape from the Soviet Union. His attitude towards the Embassy was disdainful: in 1984, he wrote in his aptly-named memoirs, *Looking for Trouble*, that, after he left Moscow, he learned that the Embassy "was (is?) considered thoroughly penetrated, top to bottom, by the KGB". He neither provided details nor revealed the source of this nonsensical charge in his memoirs.[46]

The foreign press corps included a few legendary newsmen. Although Edmund Stevens had lived in the Soviet Union for many years and had become more Russian than American, he always denied that he was a Soviet agent. The articles that he wrote for *The Times* and *The Sunday Times* simply reflected his concern that nuclear war be avoided between the West and his adopted country.

Eric de Maunay of the British Broadcasting Corporation was a famil-iar face at receptions and dinners and remained a familiar voice long after I left Moscow. Another British journalist, John Miller, achieved publicity for himself and his paper in a manner that spoke volumes for his initia-tive. He drove himself to receptions to places like the Praga Restaurant but, on leaving the party, made a practice of ordering the functionary standing at a loudspeaker to summon the limousines of the VIPs, to call for the car of the "Great London Newspaper, *The Daily Telegraph*". Then Miller slid away into the shadows to his car and drove himself off.

When I first met the correspondent of the *New Statesman and Nation*, Gloria Stuart, I described her in my diary as "improbable", a comment which had as much to do with her political views, so un-*Statesman*-like, as her striking beauty. A few months later, I learned from Sidney Weiland of Reuters that Stuart had acted as the intermediary for a deal between Gordon Lonsdale (Colonel Konon Molodoy) and *The People* of London for the Soviet master-spy's autobiography. This appears to have been her main work in Moscow for she was reported to have left when *The People* began to publish excerpts of the memoirs.

The correspondent of the *Evening News* of London was a Russian, Victor Louis, who liked to be considered the only "independent" Soviet journalist although he was known as a flyer of kites for various Soviet organs. His English-born wife, Jennifer, who had once been a clerk at the British Embassy, was the Moscow correspondent of *The Times Educational Supplement* and the compiler of the directory *Informatiom Moscow* which first appeared in January 1965. This was a most useful aid in a country where telephone books and lists of embassy staffs and other useful contacts were not published and previously had to be cobbled together by exchanging information with the foreign community. *Information Moscow* was a combined list of diplomatic missions, foreign correspondents, airline and business representatives, and Soviet agencies commonly contacted by foreign residents. The directory also provided the telephone numbers and addresses of museums, shops, cinemas, theatre, hotels, railway stations, airports and the like, as well as emergency numbers. In a nice touch in officially atheistic USSR, the book also listed religious services. It was probably the most useful source of information on Moscow to have appeared since the 1914 edition of Baedeker's *Russia*, an item that, in 1965, was still the best guide to the Soviet Union.[47]

The American press corps was the largest with correspondents from 20 media organizations, eight more than the British. Henry Tanner of *The New York Times* held the distinction of losing two cars in one day of political protest in Moscow. This happened on 28 November 1964, during the "spontaneous" demonstration by about 400 people, half of them African students, at the American, Belgian, British and Congolese Embassies against the rescue operation a few days earlier in Stanleyville (now Kisangani). Tanner parked his car near the American Embassy to observe the demonstration from that vantage point. The mob set fire to the vehicle and Tanner borrowed his wife's car to follow the story of the rampaging protesters at the Congolese and Belgian Embassies, ending up at the gates of the British Embassy. There the mob demolished the second Tanner vehicle.

The energetic and intelligent correspondent of the *Baltimore Sun*, Adam Clymer, was another who gained distinction in Moscow when he was declared *persona non grata* (PNG), the only newsman to be expelled during my assignment.[48]

For diplomats as well as foreign correspondents, reporting on the political, military and economic situation of the Soviet Union was an art rather than a science. To all intents and purposes, there was no raw material for the task in a country where anything resembling the truth was a state secret. The newspapers printed what they were ordered to print: untrustworthy statistics, a daily fare of attacks by the Kremlin on the West — especially the Americans over their war in Vietnam — florid banalities and distortions about state visits to the USSR, paeans of praise of the activities of the heroic workers and peasants and the glorious armed forces. We read what we could into this misinformation and sought to find the reality behind it, using methods that ranged from keeping our eyes and ears open, travelling where and as much as we were permitted to by the authorities, divining who ran the country by watching the body language of its leaders at state receptions and paying careful attention to such details as the relative positions of members of the Politburo in published photographs and atop Lenin's tomb in Red Square during the parades for May Day and the anniversary of the October Revolution. The gathering of intelligence was not the function of conventional diplomats although we were encouraged to use our powers of observation as we went about our daily business in Moscow or when we were permitted to travel in the countryside.

The search for information by diplomats in Moscow yielded little in comparison with the vast harvest of intelligence that was garnered through the satellite reconnaissance of Soviet territory and the electronic monitoring of the country's internal and external communications. Western military attachés in Moscow were professional observers, their status reluctantly accepted by the Soviets in return for the stationing in their own embassies of military intelligence officers. However, it was often the sharp-eyed diplomat who first detected the clue that triggered an informed guess on a crucial turn in Soviet politics or policy.

We were watched with unceasing suspicion by the Soviet counter-intelligence services because to them almost all information — political, social, economic or military — was closely held, even when it did not bear directly on the strength and intentions of the Soviet Union. The surveillance of the KGB (the *Komitet Gosudarstvennoy Bezopasnosti* or Committee for State Security) was intensive and extensive. Inside the mission, we had to be on guard against the listening devices that were employed against our offices. And in our contacts with the locally-engaged staff, we were mindful that they were selected to work for us by a Soviet agency and regularly debriefed by the KGB.

The senior locally-engaged employee was George Costakis, a legend at the Embassy for his renown as a collector and patron of art. From his first job with us as a chauffeur in the 1940s, Costakis had risen to be the administrative officer, responsible for dealing with the Soviet bureaucracy about our creature needs. Curiously, his brother occupied a similar function at the British Embassy.

Though born in Russia, George Costakis had held on to the Greek nationality of his father, a tobacco merchant who moved to Moscow before the fall of the Tsars. By virtue of his nationality, George was a privileged person in the Soviet society: he could travel abroad, maintain accounts in foreign banks and buy goods at the special hard currency shops in Moscow. Within the Embassy, his position was anomalous. While he had to be suspected like any other local employee because he was not immune from the attentions of the KGB, he seldom acted as anything but a faithful aide to the Canadian mission, giving help to a parade of Canadian diplomats for almost three decades.

Costakis was a first-class scrounger who seldom failed to satisfy the needs of the Embassy or the whims of an Ambassador's wife. If he could not find an item on the local market, he would search for it within the Canadian community whose imported supplies — from Stockmann in Helsinki, Ostermann-Petersen in Copenhagen, or T. Eaton's in Toronto — were cleared through customs by him, and remembered. It was a demanding role which Costakis did not enjoy but which he usually performed to the satisfaction of even the most insistent of his Canadian associates. It sometimes left him drained.

Christmas 1964 was such an occasion. The Ambassador's wife was preparing an evening's entertainment, a task to which she applied flair, hard work and expected the same from those who offered their assistance. Costakis was commanded to acquire the material needed for the party and went around the Embassy compound with a harried look as he sought to fill the list. He visited my wife to enquire if, by any chance, she had a spray can of artificial snow for the ambassadorial Christmas tree. Knowing that Costakis had read our import bills of lading carefully, she produced the can. Enormously relieved, the grateful George delivered it to Mrs. Ford and then returned with a gift, a watercolour depicting a dove, painted on cheap paper.

The reward for the can of artificial snow was our introduction to Anatoly Zverev and the art world of George Costakis. We learned that Zverev, an unofficial painter in a country where only official art was countenanced, had been subsidized by George for several years. For this support, George received hundreds of works dashed off by Zverev.

We were not the first owners of a Zverev thanks to Costakis: he had given or sold them to previous Canadian and other western diplomats for many years before. We eventually acquired three more Zverevs, two by purchase and the third as a farewell present from George. We learned to love the colour and the wildness of Zverev's imagination which was inspired, it was said, by the liquor that Costakis provided to the artist. Besides the dove, there was a portrait of a *babushka*, her gnarled hands held in prayer. A third depicted a fire, people running helter-skelter amidst a conflagration of colour. And there was an Orthodox church, a riot of oil and watercolour with the onion-bulb domes tilted at crazy angles.

Zverev was not the only painter helped by Costakis: he owned a large collection of art which he displayed in his double apartment on Vernadskova Prospekt. Wall-to-wall and floor-to-ceiling, the rooms were crammed with priceless icons of old Mother Russia and abstract paintings of the avant-garde artists of the years just before and just after the October Revolution, whose work had never been recognized by the Soviet state. His collection included a half dozen works by Marc Chagall and scores of pieces by artists less known in the West such as Eli Lissitzky, Wassily Kandinsky, Ivan Klyun, Kasimir Malevich, Liubov Popova, Alexander Rodchenko and Vladimir Tatlin. The collection that George Costakis had accumulated on his modest salary at the Canadian Embassy was a unique assembly of the art of the revolutionary period and the unofficial painting of the Soviet years. It was to be George's passport to freedom and fame a dozen years after I left Moscow.

In the spring of 1977, Costakis came to an arrangement with the Soviet Ministry of Culture under which he contributed some 300 paintings to the state in return for an exit permit for himself and about one-fifth of his collection. The works that the state selected were to be housed in a new wing of the Tretyakov Gallery in Moscow. And so the seal of Soviet approval was at last extended to artists long despised and suppressed and the name of George Costakis would be known in Moscow long after the fleeting memory of the Canadian diplomats for whom he worked had faded even in the archives of the KGB. With the paintings that he was allowed to take, George moved to the West to puff his pipe in quiet contentment and comfort. He had come a long way from his days as a driver and KGB informant.

Living in the *domik* in the compound gave Wynne and me insights into Embassy activities that were not seen regularly by the other Canadians. Across the courtyard from our side door was another small building that housed an automotive and appliance repair shop, the official cars and our personal Volga — and a store of lumber and other building material as well as packing material saved from shipments into Moscow and ready for use by the next to leave. We got to know well the Canadian soldier who was in charge of repairs and maintenance, helped by a couple of Russian *dvorniks* — as we called the locally-engaged yardsmen — whose language he did not speak. One of our more interesting times in the courtyard was when a grease pit was excavated in the garage, revealing evidence of Napoleon's occupation of the city and its burning by the defenders a century-and-a-half before. From our living room windows, we saw the arrival of food from Helsinki, Copenhagen and Amsterdam and liftvans of the personal effects of Canadian newcomers. One afternoon, Wynne watched in horror as a large crate of the possessions of Gary Harman — Godfrey Hearn's successor — was tipped off a flat-bed truck to smash open on the tarmac of the yard.

We were always reminded that we were a little island in a Soviet sea by the high brick wall that surrounded the compound and the guards at the gate at the end of the driveway out to Starokonyushenny Pereoluk. The militiamen were there not just to provide for our safety and to watch and report on our movements: it was also their mandate to prevent any Soviet citizen from having unauthorized contact with us. When we went outside the compound, on a walk or to a restaurant, theatre or other public place, we had to assume that any contact that we might have with a Russian was suspicious. Fortunately, there were encounters that were refreshing exceptions to this rule.

Tabs were kept on our movements in Moscow and when we travelled in the country. Stringent restrictions were placed on that travel. We were not permitted to go beyond a 40-kilometre radius from the centre of Moscow, and even within that zone entry was denied to several large areas, sometimes for understandable reasons of military sensitivity. For travel outside the circle, diplomats had to seek permission from the Foreign Ministry (from the Defence Ministry, known for short as OVS, in the case of military attachés) while arrangements were made with Upidika, the agency that existed to provide services to the diplomatic corps and controlled the purchase of air and rail tickets and the reservation of lodgings.[49] Travel by road was subject to the issuance of a pass by the Foreign (or Defence) Ministry. Large regions of the country were permanently closed to foreign representatives and frequently we were advised that others could not be visited for unexplained "temporary" reasons.

The preservation of the security of the Embassy was the responsibility of the Ambassador, when he was at the post; it was mine during his frequent absences. We were not under attack as intensively and ruthlessly as were the Americans, British and Germans, who were engaged in covert intelligence activities of their own. But the attention that the KGB paid to us was steady and involved efforts to compromise our Canadian staff and to place some of them in physical danger.

The Department of External Affairs in Ottawa gave us excellent backing on most problems of security and personal safety that were faced by members of the Embassy. Resources were generously provided to enable the Embassy to protect the staff as well as was possible from KGB harassment and other anxieties. We were helped by the fact that the

KGB was well aware that direct attacks on our personnel in Moscow could result in unpleasantness for Soviet Embassy officials in Ottawa. Moreover, there was a long history of reciprocity in the treatment of Soviet diplomats on those rare occasions when ours were declared *persona non grata* and required to leave the USSR.

However, there were instances when the Canadian Government turned down the requests of the Embassy and the recommendations of the Security and Intelligence authorities in Ottawa because bilateral negotiations were underway. The simple truth was that Canadian farmers and business people had more influence than the foreign service. Major wheat deals or questions such as Soviet participation in Expo'67 could and did lead to the refusal of the Canadian Government to agree to our recommendations that the same restrictions that we suffered under in Moscow be applied to the Soviet Embassy in Ottawa.[50] The result of this unwillingness of the Canadian Government to disturb a trade deal was that the Soviet Embassy in Ottawa seldom experienced more than a whiff of the surveillance, obstruction and harassment that was our daily fare in Moscow. This was a situation that prevailed despite the fact that the head of the Canadian Government was Lester B. Pearson, not many years before a member of the foreign service.

At the end of my first week in Moscow, Bill Warden took me to see the Novodevichy Convent, the beautifully restored convent of the maidens which had been created in 1524 by Tsar Vasily Ivanovitch to commemorate the reunion of Smolensk with the principality of Moscow. Beyond the main gate with its five-pinnacled tower was a striking five-domed cathedral, a handsome bell-tower and a large cemetery which was still in use. Ours was neither a cultural visit nor one concerned with modern Russian history despite the fact that the monastery cemetery contained numerous graves of the Soviet elite: Bill's objective was to demonstrate to me the high level of surveillance by the KGB that he had been subjected to in recent months. The KGB co-operated that morning: at least three cars of counter-intelligence agents followed us to Novodevichy and we identified four goons inside the convent grounds and cemetery. Some of the tails looked new to the game, nervously seeking cover by jumping behind trees or tombstones when we glanced in their direction.

It was Warden's belief that the KGB were especially interested in him and in Squadron Leader H.W. "Lefty" Madsen, the Assistant Air Attaché, because they spoke Russian better than other Canadians at the Embassy, apart from Robert Ford. Bill had also attended the Free University of Berlin, a fact known to the Soviet Foreign Ministry and to the KGB that made him suspect because they regarded the Free University as an American school for spies.

On our return from the convent, Warden suggested that we walk in the neighbourhood of the Embassy to gain an idea of the number of KGB cars waiting to shadow our personnel when they left the compound. As there were few private automobiles in the USSR in 1964, it was safe to assume that any in the vicinity of a western diplomatic mission were KGB vehicles. This assumption was even more reasonable when we saw that the motors of the cars were running and that they were occupied by two or three men listening intently to a radio dispatcher.

Back in the office, Bill filed a list of the licence numbers of the "goon" cars, commenting that the KGB seemed to employ the same teams in their surveillance of the Canadian mission for weeks on end. He also remarked that they had not learned to change the licence plates frequently in order to maintain their cover.

Just over a year later, the list of licence plates was to come into its own. Squadron Leader Madsen was on his way to his home in one of the apartment buildings in the Lenin Hills that were assigned to diplomats. He was driving across the bridge and the long embankment towards the university when, suddenly, he found that two cars were manoeuvring to force him off the road and down the side of the embankment. With remarkable coolness and presence of mind, Madsen memorized the licence numbers of the cars while evading them and escaping from the trap. We had the grim satisfaction of finding that the numbers matched some of those on the list of the KGB contingent parked in our neighbourhood.

Armed with this information, I called on Makharov, a desk officer of the Second European Division which looked after relations with Canada. My complaint to him was simple: I said that "hooligan elements" that parked their cars in the streets by the Embassy apparently had murderous intentions on our Air Attaché. I handed over the licence numbers, suggesting that the appropriate authorities might be interested in looking into the identity of the occupants of the cars. I could have sworn that Makharov mouthed the word *touché* before responding that the matter had been noted.

Harassment of diplomats in Moscow took many forms. It was the telephone ring in the middle of the night with no one responding to your "hello?", the shrill whistle of the militiaman on point duty commanding a diplomat to stop for a traffic violation that had not occurred, the deliberate delays in the supplying of services by Upidika. Harsher harassment was reserved for the military attachés and, especially, the technicians who were employed at western embassies to protect them from electronic eavesdropping. Milder torments were meted out to other embassy staff, often personified by enticing males or females who were domestic employees or apparently friendly and helpful people encountered in hotels or bars, especially on trips out of Moscow.

Inya, the curvaceous cook who was assigned to our house by Upidika, was a married woman and not at all flirtatious when my wife was around. She had been advertised to us as a *cordon bleu* cook and she certainly could make good *borscht*. Her knowledge of some English was also helpful to my wife. But we knew that her role in the house was not confined to cooking.

Like all employees who were supplied by Upidika, Inya had to report periodically to that agency to brief one of the KGB officers on its staff about our activities. From this officer, she received her instructions as to what to look for in our daily lives, and what to attempt. The KGB did not seem particularly intent on subverting the counsellor of the Canadian Embassy, probably because it assumed that back in Ottawa this might lead to reprisals in kind against my opposite number, the second in command of the Soviet Embassy. But if I were to succumb to inducements, the story would be different. Obviously the KGB had worked it out that Inya was my cup of tea and, in the autumn when my wife was away from Moscow, they put her to work.

It was lunchtime and I had returned to the house in the courtyard behind the Embassy to put my feet up and read the mail before the lunch table was ready. One of the items in my mail that day was the latest *Playboy* magazine, a gift from my daughter at school in England, featuring the pictures of the 12 best playgirls of the year: blondes, redheads, brunettes and various combinations of other attributes. When Inya announced that lunch was ready, I put the magazine on the *pouffe* in front of my easy chair, open at the 12 best. When I returned to the chair from the dining room, the magazine had disappeared. But it reappeared with the coffee tray, Inya setting it carefully in front of me. Fixing me with an appraising gaze, she asked: "*Gaspodin* Brown, which one do you like best?" I made a quick calculation: Inya had been instructed to determine what female type would best seduce a Canadian diplomat in his early forties. "All of them", I lied, and Inya left, rebuffed.

Inya — and the KGB — gave me up as a target for seduction, but Inya was put to work elsewhere. Occasionally, when another officer of the Embassy needed extra help for a party, I would ask Inya if she would like to earn a few more roubles.

Group Captain "Smokey" Drake, the Air Attaché, had been living the perilous life of a bachelor for some time after his wife had left the USSR in mid-November 1964 for health reasons, a casualty of the repressive atmosphere of Moscow. Drake wondered whether he should quit his post but agreed to stay when we told him that we would give him every support. By Christmas it was clear that Mrs. Drake would not return to Moscow and that Smokey might, after all, have to leave. But he was now determined to hold on and remained until May 1965, performing his duties effectively despite some KGB attempts to take advantage of his single state.

When Drake wanted to hold a dinner party at his apartment, he asked if Inya could be made available; Inya was willing and went, probably after a briefing by the KGB. When the dinner was over and before the last guests had gone, Smokey paid her off to let her catch the last bus to her home in the outskirts of the city. The guests left and Smokey settled down with a book to relax only to have his tranquility shattered by the reappearance of Inya holding Drake's cat in her arms. She explained dolefully that she had missed the last bus and added, stroking the cat, that she knew that the cat slept at the foot of Smokey's bed. Couldn't she, Inya purred, sleep like the pussy-cat that night.

Whereupon, Smokey assured me when he told me the story the next morning in the safe-speech room, he expelled her from the apartment, not caring how she got home.

Drake's posting to Moscow was abbreviated by his wife's illness. The Military Attaché, Colonel Curtis Greenleaf, and the Naval Attaché, Captain John Bovey, served out their two-year stints despite encounters with the KGB that made us wonder if Greenleaf would be declared *persona non grata* for spying and if Bovey might break under the pressure of an intense campaign to subvert him.

Soon after I arrived in Moscow, Greenleaf was harassed physically on a trip to Kishinev, the capital of Soviet Moldavia, in the company of two other Western service attachés. With the Ambassador's approval, I complained about this at the Foreign Ministry when I called on Madame Mironova, deputy head of the Second European Division. Mme. Mironova said, plausibly, that she knew nothing about the incident, but would make enquiries. My line was that we did not want to press the matter and would not publicize it. But we hoped the further "local" incidents of this kind would not recur. Mme. Mironova gracefully concluded our meeting by expressing regret that my first business call on her had to be on such a subject.

Although Greenleaf managed to stay out of harm's way on his travels in the Soviet Union for most of the time remaining in his assignment to Moscow, he was involved in an incident in mid-April 1965 which became highly-publicized a month later. In the company of three service attachés from the United States Embassy, Greenleaf went by train to Tambov, an industrial city about 260 km south-east of Moscow and checked in at the Hotel Tambov.[51] On returning to Moscow, he reported that he and his companions had been roughed up in the hotel restaurant during dinner by four men who said they were militiamen but were probably members of the KGB. During the altercation, a table was overturned and glasses and china broken but Greenleaf and the three American officers were adamant that the damage was caused by the Russians. We suggested to Greenleaf that he lie low for a while because we expected that a PNG might result.

Curiously, almost a month was to pass before we heard from the Soviet Foreign Ministry about the incident. We held our collective breath on 4 May when two members of the Soviet Embassy in Ottawa were declared *persona non grata* for industrial espionage, but there was no retaliation against us. Then, on 12 May, two events occurred that convinced us that the axe was about to fall. On the 11th, Robert Ford had been asked to see Roshchin, the head of the Second European Division of the Foreign Ministry. That appointment was cancelled an hour before it was due to take place but, shortly afterwards, a note came from Upidika billing Colonel Greenleaf 15 roubles and four kopecks (roughly Cdn.$ 17.00 at that time) for the damage caused at the Tambov restaurant.[52] We speculated that, at a senior level of the Foreign Ministry, a decision had been taken to defer action against Greenleaf. This, we surmised, had happened because, later that day, Ford was to be at the Ministry to exchange instruments of ratification of a protocol to the Soviet-Canadian trade agreement and, in the evening, he would entertain several Ministry officials at the Moscow première of the *Rideau Vert* theatre group of Montreal.

The drama unfolded quickly in the days that followed. The Ambassador was due to leave on Tuesday, 18 May, on a three-month absence. On Friday the 14th, he was asked to see Roshchin on Monday, an appointment about which he notified the Department. A nervous Ottawa then suggested that he put off his departure for a week. In another urgent telegram, the Department informed us of the observation of the Soviet Ambassador to Canada that the state of Soviet-Canadian relations was at such a low ebb that the USSR might decide not to take part in Expo 67.

Monday, 17 May, was a busy day. At 11:00 a.m., Robert Ford paid a courtesy call on President Mikoyan. The old survivor asked Ford to convey to the Canadian Government his warm expression of the great friendship of the Soviet Union towards Canada, despite, he added, his concern that we followed the United States too closely on some issues. At noon Ford saw Roshchin who read a note in which the Ministry addressed itself to us in the third person on the Tambov affair. Colonel Greenleaf's general conduct as a Military Attaché was described as "not correct, indeed unworthy". In a hurt tone, the note recalled that, at a reception, he had told a liaison officer of the Defence Ministry that he did not agree with Soviet policies. The note alleged that Greenleaf had been drunk at Tambov and had been restrained from attacking a Soviet citizen by the U.S. Assistant Air Attaché who was with him. Then came the surprise: we were asked to ensure that the Military Attaché behave himself better in future. No PNG was mentioned.

Ford decided that the unbelievably mild reaction of the Soviets justified his departure as originally planned. I saw him off the following morning and returned to the office to deal with an encounter with a Russian reported to me by a troubled staff member. A Kremlin reception for a Bulgarian visitor followed from which Wynne and I returned home to find the telephone ringing off the hook with calls from foreign correspondents who wanted my reaction to an article about Greenleaf which, they informed me, had just appeared in *Izvestiya*.

Headlined "The 'Machine-gunner' from Ottawa", the *Izvestiya* article began:

> A machine-gun rattle drowns out the strains of the waltz. Ra-ta-ta, ra-ta-ta. A grey-haired man pretending to be a machine-gunner "fires bursts" at neighbours at the next tables. The final burst stops abruptly and they hear the menacing cry: 'We'll destroy you' .

Describing the lead-up to this, the paper accused "his Nibs, the Colonel" of having been inebriated, displaying "brilliant erudition in obscenities", slandering communism and finally, having been asked to leave, rushing at one of the guardians of public order and crashing tableware to the floor. Other clients at the restaurant, the article noted primly, were disgusted beyond measure. *Izvestiya* concluded its 600-word report:

> It is usually the case for people like this to be arraigned in court for rowdyism in public places. However, Greenleaf enjoys diplomatic immunity. For that reason we hope the Canadian Embassy in Moscow will draw the appropriate conclusions and find ways and means of curbing its uniformed diplomat.

With Ottawa's approval, we rejected the *Izvestiya* account of the Tambov incident and decided to keep Greenleaf at the post until the end of his tour of duty in July. Knowing that he was badly shaken and in need of backing from his headquarters, I asked External Affairs to fill us in on the reaction to the affair in parliament and the press. The response was most supportive: Paul Martin, the Secretary of State for External Affairs, told the House of Commons on the 18th that the Government had full confidence in Greenleaf and, on the 19th, repudiated the allegations in the *Izvestiya* article, stating that they had no basis in fact. However, Ottawa suggested that Greenleaf confine his travels to the Moscow area and his contacts with the Defence Ministry and other Soviet officials to the bare minimum consistent with courtesy.

Concern for the security of the service attachés of the Embassy now shifted to the gentlemanly Naval Attaché, Captain John Bovey, who had been in Leningrad on a trip during the week of notoriety for Greenleaf. For some time, Bovey had been uncomfortable about the excessive show of friendship towards him by Colonel Prasnikov, a senior officer of OVS — the liaison staff of the Defence Ministry. Prasnikov was no simple liaison officer but a star intelligence agent.

While in Leningrad, Bovey telephoned me to say that he had heard, "in a most unusual manner", that he owed Greenleaf 25 kopecks. This, I learned from the other attachés, meant that Bovey had picked up information that Greenleaf would be declared PNG. Bovey continued on from Leningrad to Helsinki, his other post of accreditation as Naval Attaché, and sent a coded message explaining his phone call. Prasnikov had accompanied Bovey and other Western attachés on their visit to Leningrad and had told him that Greenleaf was going to be expelled because he was "rude and crude" while Bovey had been spared because he was "a nice chap". In his telegram, Bovey suggested that this was an approach intended to cultivate his co-operation with the OVS. If it was not that, it seemed to me at least a ploy to make John nervous.

Prasnikov's attentions continued and succeeded in making Bovey become more and more anxious as he neared the end of his Moscow assignment. Towards mid-July, Prasnikov informed Bovey that he had one of his "money belts" to return to him. As attachés used body pouches on trips to keep their notes secure, this was a clear hint that the OVS officer had found or fabricated a means of blackmailing Bovey. More pressure followed in the final fortnight of Bovey's posting. At a diplomatic reception on 23 July, both Bovey and Greenleaf were approached by Prasnikov and threatened with PNGs.

Melodrama was to be the backdrop to Bovey's last hours in the Soviet Union.

Bovey had decided to go from Moscow to Finland to pay the farewell visit there that protocol demanded. We now believed that prudence required that we send an escort with him to ensure that he left the country safely; the recently-arrived Assistant Air Attaché, Jim Kupkee, was chosen for this job. Late on 28 July, a number of us went to the *Leningradsky Vagzaal* to see the pair off. Sharing a compartment on the "Red Arrow" to Leningrad, they continued their trip in the same coach on the slow train to Helsinki. In the very next compartment was Colonel Prasnikov whose obvious intention to work on Bovey to the end was to be thwarted by Kupkee's presence.

From Helsinki the next afternoon, we learned that the journey had gone uneventfully. Though Kupkee remained awake all night guarding Bovey, Prasnikov did not appear until the train made its routine stop, just before the Soviet-Finnish border, to let off Soviet immigration and other officials. Prasnikov was among them that morning, his pursuit of Bovey ending as he walked a few hundred metres through the sparse birch woods at the border to a waiting limousine to drive back into the Soviet Union.

The period on the campaigns against Greenleaf and Bovey coincided with two important Canadian visits to the Soviet Union, those of Arthur Laing, the Minister of Northern Affairs, in May–June and the Parliamentary Delegation in July. Several days had seen my agenda alternate between hours of sharing Soviet friendship and hospitality with the Canadian VIPs and — unknown to them — seeing to the protection of the Embassy staff from Soviet machinations. The Embassy was undoubtedly saved from deeper trouble by the delegations because, for the Soviets, the political goal of improved Soviet-Canadian relations took precedence over whatever nastiness the KGB had in mind.

The presence of Mr. Laing in the USSR, however, did not prevent another attack on Canada for the expulsion of two junior Soviet diplomats, early in May, after they had been caught in the act of paying a number of Canadians employed in sensitive industries for information. We had been surprised that no publicity had been given in the Soviet Union to the episode which had been well-aired in the House of Commons in Ottawa on 10 and 11 May in exchanges between Prime Minister Pearson and the Leader of the Opposition, John Diefenbaker.

On 29 May, the newspaper *Sovietskaya Rossia* broke the silence in an article headlined "Dirty Work: Anti-Soviet Provocations in Canada". Branding the expulsion of the two Soviets as a "provocation", the newspaper said that a "slanderous anti-Soviet campaign had been launched in Canada and a veritable witch-hunt against Soviet Embassy officials." The expulsions of Bytchkov and Poluchkin had been based on "evidence fabricated by the [Canadian] intelligence authorities", the article continued, and the police maintained surveillance on Soviet citizens in Ottawa, searched their dwellings clandestinely, and set up listening devices in the Soviet Embassy. The expulsion of an *Izvestiya* correspondent in 1963 was cited as evidence of anti-Soviet activity as was an accident in which a car driven by a Soviet Embassy clerk went off the road killing a visiting Soviet scientist. *Sovietskaya Rossia* ended with this warning:

> These actions by the Canadian authorities cannot but harm the development of Soviet-Canadian relations which have been considerably extended and developed in recent years.

Appearing as it did in one of the lesser Soviet press organs, the article did not produce much concern for us although we were prepared to go public on the allegation that the death of the scientist was murder. It had been this incident in 1963 that finally produced Soviet agreement, after years of stalling, to the Canadian proposal for an exchange of notes granting immunity to Soviet non-diplomatic staff in Canada and Canadian staff in Moscow. When we had told the Soviet Foreign Ministry that we proposed to charge the clerk who had caused the accident with manslaughter, the Ministry caved in and, within 48 hours, the exchange of notes took place.

In two instances in 1965, junior members of the Embassy staff who seemed to be in danger of entrapment by the KGB were sent home. One case was of a female clerk who told me that on leaving a party at a diplomatic apartment in the early hours of the morning to walk back to her quarters alone, she had met a Russian man on the street and gone with him to his studio where she spent four hours in what she described as foolish conversation. Although the contact seemed innocent — and the thought crossed our minds that the woman had concocted the story so as to get away from the dreariness of the Moscow posting — the Department decided not to take any chances and she left for Canada a fortnight later, ostensibly for health reasons.

The second case was of a married clerk who was conducting an affair with a female on the staff of the British Embassy. The KGB were soon on to this and set the cat amongst the pigeons by phoning his wife to let her know of the trysts. Our clerk reported the matter to his superior in the Embassy but did not reveal all the details until we had a second interview with him. The probability that the KGB would follow up convinced us to send the clerk and his family home to Canada and the British to abbreviate their clerk's stay in Moscow.

One of the best examples of the way in which the KGB employed its resources in setting up a member of a foreign mission for blackmail concerned a Marine Corps guard at the United States Embassy who had been reprimanded by the Embassy's security officer, "Mr. X", for falling asleep on duty. A few days later, the Marine talked with a Russian switchboard operator who asked him why he looked upset. He replied that he was in trouble with "Mr. X". Two days after that conversation, when he went to a restaurant with his girlfriend from the British Embassy, a Russian in plain clothes — whom the Marines recognized as one of the Militiamen stationed outside the U.S. Embassy — came over to his table, ostensibly to introduce his wife. They left after a few minutes and the Marine and his companion went to get their coats. At the cloakroom, they were approached by two men who told the Marine that they knew about his problem with "Mr. X" and wanted to help. The Marine was later to claim that he told the two men that he was not interested in their help and left the restaurant. As he failed to report the incident until a week had passed, he was shipped back to the States.

It was a classical set-up which would have led to a far more serious predicament for the Marine had he tried to keep it from his superiors. The elements were familiar:
— the alertness of the Russian switchboard operator to the mood of an American staff member;
— the speed with which the KGB mounted an operation on the Marine after having been informed of his troubles by the switchboard operator, probably through her Upidika handler;
— the active role played by the Militiaman in fingering the Marine;
— the "sympathy" and offers of "assistance" made by the two KGB agents;
— the foolishness of the Marine in talking to a locally-engaged employee about his trouble and in not reporting the restaurant incident immediately.

A bizarre attack by the KGB took place one Sunday in the autumn of 1964. An electronic technician, who had been sent from Bonn to search for listening devices in the German Embassy, was visiting the *Troitskoya-Seroyevskaya Lavra*, a monastery at Zagorsk, about 75 km from Moscow on the Yaroslavl road.[53] By coincidence, 11 of us from the Canadian Embassy were there that day, seeing the monastery in the company of a pleasant Russian guide. While we marvelled at the fabulous icons in the Treasury and watched the services in the Trinity and Assumption Cathedrals, the German technician was being tailed by the KGB as he, in company with other German diplomats, made his way around the monastery.

A week later, the Germans broke the news that, inside one of the churches, an assailant had used a syringe to inject mustard gas into the technician. The efforts of the German Embassy to get him quickly out of the country were obstructed by Upidika which delayed issuing air tickets for him and an escorting diplomat, probably because the KGB wanted to force him into a local hospital and question him there. When the story was broken, the Germans briefed the NATO counsellors at a "tea party" and asked us to do what we could to let the Soviets know what we thought of their rough play.

It was only afterwards that it was learned from the Paris edition of *The New York Times* that the technician had been playing a rough game himself, using jolts of electricity to destroy intrusion equipment at the other end of the wire. It was a technique which could also give anyone working at the other end an unwelcome shock. The mustard gas attack assumed a different aspect and we wondered whether the KGB had not told their side of the story to the *Times*.

The activities of the KGB extended well beyond the service attachés and other diplomatic personnel of western countries. Neutrals and newsmen were not immune and resident and visiting foreigners also received the attention of the committee for state security. Exchange students from western countries studying at universities in the Soviet Union were especially vulnerable. It was in this period that Gerald Brooke, a former exchange student on a visit to the USSR, was arrested for allegedly passing to a Soviet citizen money, cyphers and other espionage material concealed in a photograph album. The British Embassy wondered if he had allowed himself to be used by an anti-Soviet emigré organization that had been infiltrated by KGB agents. The Brooke case was not the only one concerning the British Embassy, for an English exchange student was also the target of an attempt by the KGB to compromise him. At the Canadian Embassy, we had reason for concern for the welfare of the six Canadian exchange students in the Soviet Union and sought to keep in frequent touch with them.

During my first fortnight in Moscow, the dangers to guileless visitors were demonstrated by the experience of a young Canadian churchman who was in the Soviet Union seeking material for the religious publication of which he was an editor. On his arrival he had called at the Embassy and had been briefed by Bill Warden on the perils of travelling alone in the remote areas of the country. Duly cautioned, he had set out for Alma Ata where he met a friendly Russian "student" who took him on a picnic on a warm day with two attractive young women. Though not normally a drinker, he politely took part in numerous toasts to peace and friendship until the vodka made him drowsy and he found himself alone with one of the women whom he "tried to kiss". Three men suddenly detained him and took him to a police station in Alma Ata where they made him sign a statement about his "improper" conduct. Five days on, in Samarkand, the same policemen appeared and questioned him again about the purpose of his trip. He agreed not to write anything hostile to the Soviet Union and was warned not to tell the Canadian Embassy or anyone else of his experience.

Although thoroughly shaken and worried, the clergyman had the courage to come to the Embassy when he returned to Moscow a few days later. Bill Warden and I spent a morning with him in the safe-speech room explaining how blackmail might work in the months or years ahead and how it would be essential for him to protect himself by telling everyone close to him what had happened. We also got him to agree to take a flight that afternoon out of Russia. During the hour that Wynne looked after the traveller in our house while Bill and I made arrangements for his departure, he confided to her that he did not want to tell his wife. Accompanied by Warden, and with a parting word from me that I would be asking "friends" to meet him at Toronto the next day, he left to catch an Air France flight to Paris. This he succeeded in doing in spite of what Bill later described to me as "the most blatant harassment" of both of them at Sheremetyevo Airport. Word reached us soon after from the Department that he had arrived safely home.

For diplomats and foreign correspondents in Moscow, life was varied and exciting, every day's platter of activity challenging. Yet they knew that it was no place to be with a family and that, for wives, it was purgatory. Moscow meant drudgery to them because things did not work properly, basic foods were hard to come by, the care of small kids was a perpetual worry, and the absence of older children at schools abroad a chronic concern. To top all that off was the unpleasant knowledge that intimate relations with one's spouse were not private, thanks to the KGB bug in the apartment.

Insulated from the Russians by language, living in ghettos created by the suspicious Soviets, restricted in their travels within the country and unable even to leave it without an exit permit, Embassy personnel and their wives faced a difficult two-year posting in Moscow. Not surprisingly in these circumstances, the morale of the official Canadian community of about 50 was a constant preoccupation. Rank had little place in what was organized within the community and, unlike the situation at diplomatic missions in other countries, contacts among staff members included leisure time as well as working hours. A room in the basement of the chancery had been set aside a few years earlier as a "club" for all staff; it was the venue for occasional staff parties and, more regularly, for people to meet when they came to use the laundry facilities, to help in sorting out the frequent food shipments from the West or to pick up items from the storeroom — the *sklad* — where all of us had a section of shelving for our imported treasures. Canadians were welcomed at the clubs of the other Western embassies, the American Club being especially popular because movies and dances were regular features there. The British also showed films and held regular bazaars for the Save the Children Fund and other charities.

Summertime excursions were made fairly frequently by groups of staff members and their families to the diplomatic beach at Uspenskoye on the Moscow River, just within the 40-kilometre zone, and to the *dachas* (cottages) that were rented by Upidika to diplomats at Zavidovo, 125 km west on the Shosha River between Klin and Kalinin. Our people were often invited by friends to stay at the *dachas* that other Western missions maintained outside Moscow and to join in cruises on the Moscow River that were arranged by the larger embassies. Soon after we arrived in Moscow, Wynne arranged excursions for the Canadian community that saw groups of more than 20 visit the Kremlin on two occasions and a dozen go to the monastery at Zagorsk. In winter, hockey pitted the Canadian stars against the Americans to provide another forum for the community to get together.

The bathroom job at the *domik* not only gave us a taste of Thereza Ford's appetite for official funds but also the first personal encounter with the working habits of the Soviet worker. The need to arrange through Upidika for such matters as painting and plumbing repairs to the staff quarters inside the compound contributed to our education. A programme for the painting of Flat "A" had been approved earlier and work had begun on 3 August. By 31 August, I was able to record that the painters had completed the family and dining rooms and the front hall and its small toilet and had begun working in the large downstairs bathroom. When the matter of the new upstairs bathroom was resolved, a request was put through on 2 September to Upidika for that work to begin.

My weekly letters to my mother in Victoria chronicled the progress of the bathroom project. On 17 September, I reported that the work had begun but I doubted that it would be finished by October. A week later,

I said that the painting had begun and that, without the use of the existing downstairs bathroom, we were forced to use that of the administrative officer in the compound.

Over a month later, I told my mother that Wynne was celebrating her birthday by polishing the newly-laid linoleum in the downstairs bathroom. I added that the upstairs bathroom was coming along and should be done in a month "if we are lucky". We weren't. On 1 November — two months after Upidika had been asked to proceed — I wrote that, while the downstairs bathroom was completely finished and looked quite smart, no workmen had turned up in the previous week to continue the upstairs project. On 11 November, my message was:

> The workers are still on the job, spasmodically, in our new upstairs bathroom. One day they put tiles on a wall and a week later they take them off to make some adjustment to the pipes. Maybe by the end of the year ...

Almost four weeks later, I wrote that Wynne had been painting in the upstairs hall and that I had fixed rods in the new clothes closet. And a couple of days later, I was able to report:

> Wynne got the upstairs hall back in shape today, finishing up the painting herself. In the bathroom, all that remains to be done by UPDK is some tiling behind the towel rack.

That was done in mid-December, three months after the start of a project that might have taken a fortnight in the West.

It was not the only story of the inefficiency of Soviet labour during our time in Moscow. But it had illustrated, on a daily basis, the failings of the Soviet worker: not just drunkeness, absenteeism or long breaks for lunch, but inadequate tools, slipshod work, and the absence of skills accentuated by the total failure to schedule work in a logical order. It was, for us, an invaluable educational seminar on the competence of Soviet labour.

Another aspect of the ways of Soviet labour was illustrated the following summer when I decided that an old wall inside the courtyard should be demolished to give the staff access to a small lawn where they might relax in the rare sunshine. Not reckoning on the strength of century-old mortar, I thought that I could perform the demolition myself; a weekend of work with a sledge-hammer convinced me that I was mistaken. George Costakis was horrified that the Chargé d'Affaires of the Embassy should be engaged in menial labour and suggested that the services of Upidika be employed. My answer was that there were no funds for that, to which Costakis responded that all that would be necessary were a few bottles of vodka. I produced the vodka and, within a few days, armed with pneumatic drills, the hero-workers of Upidika finished the job.

Cynicism about things Soviet was tempered on occasion by incidents that revealed a humanity even in the Communist system. In a sense, this balanced what we knew of the Russian character: the odd mixture of coldness and warmth, of compassion and remorselessness.

My sister's husband died at a small hotel in Lubeck, Germany, in September 1965, when they were travelling from Sweden to France. When she sought my help by telephone from the hotel, the Soviet phone system performed without the usual delays then and in several hours of calls to the West that followed. No obstruction was placed in the way of my departure to Hamburg the following morning, an exit visa and airline ticket having been produced within hours. Clearly the officials of Upidika were touched by a human tragedy.

CHAPTER 6

A FROSTY RELATIONSHIP:
SOVIET-CANADIAN
CONTACTS

In the summer of 1964, the Secretary of State
for External Affairs of Canada, the Honourable Paul Martin pronounced
in the House of Commons that relations between the Soviet Union and
the West were showing "some real, though limited, improvement".
Acknowledging that it was impossible to say how deep the *détente* or "pause"
with the Soviets would go, he held that the intention of the West should
be to encourage it. The economic problems of the Communist countries,
he suggested, presented possibilities for trade and for the opening of channels of communication which might break down some of the barriers
between the Soviet world and the West and lead towards a *modus vivendi* —
an understanding — between the two blocs.

Three weeks after I arrived in Moscow, the United States contrived an
incident in the Gulf of Tonkin which cranked up the war in Indochina
and threatened to put an end to the hope that Paul Martin had seen only
a couple of months earlier. In spite of a mild appeal by Soviet Premier
Nikita Sergeyevich Khrushchev for the United States to show "compo-
sure and restraint" in order to reduce the mounting tension, the United
States Congress adopted the Gulf of Tonkin resolution "to promote the
maintenance of international peace and security in Southeast Asia". That
phrase was Orwellian for it set the stage for the bombing of North
Vietnam that followed. The Soviet Union was forced to throw its support
behind Hanoi, placing greater economic strains on the country and putting the leadership of Nikita Khrushchev at risk. The world entered
another long chapter of the Cold War.

My first contacts with the Soviet Foreign Ministry had been pleasant
enough. On 27 July, accompanied by Bill Warden the Second Secretary of
the Embassy, I made a courtesy call on officers of the Second European
Division which looked after relations with Canada. The head of division
was Alexei Roshchin, an even-handed professional in his early fifties. His

deputy, Madame Mironova, was a plump, matronly lady who always sought to be amiable and was disappointed when we would not be swayed by her good humour. The third member of the group that received us was Makharov, the officer in charge of the Canadian desk and therefore our normal contact on routine matters. A grey individual, Makharov was never to take a decision or provide an answer without consulting his superiors.

During the courtesy call, Roshchin had remarked that a forthcoming visit to the Soviet Union by a Canadian parliamentary delegation would mark a "major move" in the development of good relations between Canada and the USSR. A fortnight later, my ambassador, Robert Ford, had a substantive discussion of issues with the Foreign Minister, Andrei Gromyko, when he delivered a letter from Prime Minister Lester B. Pearson to Premier Khrushchev on the longstanding problem of the reunification of families. That issue involved our contention that close relatives of former Soviet residents in Canada should be allowed to leave the USSR; it was a question on which little progress was to be made until years later. The Ford-Gromyko conversation went on to current international concerns such as peacekeeping in Cyprus and the United States air attacks on North Vietnam.

Although the parliamentary delegation visit was postponed until 1965 because of the preoccupation of the minority Liberal Government of Mr. Pearson with the passage of the legislation on the new Canadian flag, exchanges of visits in other fields were to become increasingly frequent in spite of the worsening international situation. We were able to represent the visit of a large group from the Toronto Board of Trade as taking the place of the parliamentary delegation. Two technical visits took place in the summer: a group representing the iron ore industry of Canada and the Canadian Department of Mines toured some Soviet mines in August and, in September, four of the most senior executives of the Canadian asbestos industry spent over a week in Sverdlovsk and Asbest, east of the Urals, looking at the very large Soviet asbestos industry. The Soviets sent the Minister of Agriculture, P. Volovchenko, and five officials on a 21-day visit across the Canadian prairies to Vancouver, which yielded an immediate dividend for Ambassador and Mrs. Ford who, with Maldwyn Thomas, the newly-arrived Commercial Secretary, were allowed to go on a week's visit to the Soviet bread-basket, the "Virgin Lands" of Kazakhistan.

The visit of the Toronto Board of Trade covered four days in mid-September 1964. One hundred and twenty-six-strong, it was to be the largest Canadian delegation during my tour in Moscow. While arrangements were largely in the hands of the Soviet hosts, the Ambassador had the first words with the businessmen at a briefing on their first day. Fashioning his comments to his audience, Robert Ford was at his best in his outline of the changes that had taken place in the Soviet Union. He noted that the Russians were trying to form a new society which would be much closer to the western way of life than was "the semi-oriental and mysterious tyranny of Stalin". There was a growing realization within the Soviet leadership that western credits and technology were going to be necessary if the standard of living was to be improved and a modern society created. Ford contended that it was in the western interest to assist in the achievement of this goal and he pressed the view that Canadian business should be looking at the future possibilities of trading with the USSR.

Ford's message was well received: several of the visitors were to remark to me at the end of the visit that the briefing was the best they had heard on their European travels.[54] They were given a genuine welcome by their Soviet hosts and the visit was played up in the press as an indication of good bilateral relations.

Our calls on Soviet authorities were more frequent as a result of the visits; other matters contributed to these contacts. Among our concerns was the imminent arrival that fall of a half-dozen Canadian students who were coming to the USSR under an exchange programme between the University of Toronto and the University of Moscow. Five students were married and wanted to bring their wives. The Ministry of Higher Education, with whom we dealt on behalf of the students, had told us that married accommodation was out of the question. This, we responded, probably meant that the exchanges for the 1964–65 year would not take place; our comment did not seem to faze the Ministry. When we appealed to the Second European Division to intervene on our behalf, we were listened to sympathetically but told that the Foreign Ministry was powerless in putting its point of view across to the educational authorities.

In the event, all the students showed up, one without his wife, and were accommodated better than we had been led to expect. When my wife, Wynne, and I had them over for tea at the end of October, we found that they were well briefed on what the United States students were provided with by their embassy and wanted nothing less from us. We met some of their needs for imported food and Bill Warden and his wife kept in close touch with them and their spouses that winter.

Another question that took me to the Foreign Ministry was a request from Ottawa that we enquire about the Soviet plans for International Cooperation Year as 1965 had been designated. The acting head of the

International Organizations Division, whom I saw to make the enquiry, was a suspicious and dogmatic old-school Communist official. He dismissed the notion of limited national projects, telling me that the USSR wanted activities of truly international scope such as the elimination of colonialism and, I surmised, capitalism too, if that were possible.

For four weeks from 20 September 1964, I was Chargé d'Affaires during the absence on leave of Robert Ford. Although I had already had a taste of running the office during the Ambassador's trip to Kazakhistan, this period was to prove unusually interesting and rewarding because it coincided with the fall of Krushchev.

On 23 September 1964, I saw Khrushchev during the visit of the Egyptain premier, Ali Sabry, at St. George's Hall at the Kremlin and, the next day, at Vnukovo II Airport when the Egyptian left the Soviet Union. At St. George's Hall, the heads of diplomatic missions assembled in a square in the large vestibule at the foot of the stairs that led up to the magnificent reception area. Khrushchev and Ali Sabry walked inside the square, shaking hands with each of the diplomats who stood in an order determined by their precedence on the diplomatic list. Afterwards, we followed the pair up the broad, granite stairway and took our places, standing, at the far end of the section reserved for foreign VIPs. Both leaders made speeches and proposed toasts. Then, as the final rite of the ceremony, the diplomats approached them in turn, to clink glasses with Khrushchev and shake hands with the Egyptian.

Next morning the diplomats made their way to Vnukovo airport where a brass band, a 100-man army guard of honour and a rather small, "spontaneous" crowd of flower-bearing civilians were gathered to bid farewell to Ali Sabry. Once more, he and Khrushchev walked down the line of diplomats; within minutes, the visitor was waved aboard his aircraft and took off. We waited for Khrushchev to leave the tarmac in a long, black limousine and then we dispersed.

At the end of September, President Sukarno of Indonesia was greeted at Vnukovo by the Soviet head of state, Anastas Mikoyan. The next evening at the reception at St. George's Hall, Khrushchev was not present. Stuart Loory of the New York *Herald Tribune* wrote to his paper that reporters had been told by a foreign ministry press officer that the premier had begun a vacation earlier that day.

Two weeks later, on 13 October, I had a fleeting glimpse of Khrushchev when I was driving over the Kamenni Bridge across the Moscow River near the Kremlin. Coming towards me were three black limousines and I saw Khrushchev in the rear seat of the second, sitting between a pair of tall, uniformed KGB officers. I mentioned this to the western diplomats with whom I met that afternoon and we all assumed that the premier was simply back to work after his holiday.

President Dorticos of Cuba arrived in Moscow the next day to be greeted by Mikoyan and the diplomatic corps with the usual ceremonial. I noted that the affair was made different only by the lusty cheering, on college lines, of the hundreds of Cuban students on hand. Because Dorticos was a head of state, Khrushchev's presence was not required, and he was not there. At the airport, I exchanged tidbits with diplomatic colleagues and learned that they, too, had noticed that two militiamen were on duty outside diplomatic missions instead of the usual one and that gates into diplomatic compounds had been closed by the Soviet guards. We wondered why.

Thursday, the 15th of October, was a busy day at the office as we worked hard to fill the diplomatic bag with reports. Robert Ford was due back from his holiday, but a telegram notified us that he was postponing his return until Saturday. Still chargé d'affaires, I went to a reception at the Afghan Embassy whose ambassador, as dean of the diplomatic corps, fêted the Cuban president. A concert at the Kremlin followed which I left at the intermission to go to dinner at the Greek counsellor's apartment on Leninsky Prospekt.

What began as an ordinary dinner party took a dramatic change at about 10:30 o'clock. The Italian counsellor said that he had earlier picked up rumours of government changes; he phoned the Moscow correspondent of the *Corriere della Sera* who confirmed that changes were taking place which, though still unannounced, were thought to include the leadership. By midnight, when I left the dinner party for the office, it had been firmly established that Khrushchev was out: his portrait was disappearing from public buildings and those of Brezhnev and Kosygin were in, the former as the party secretary and the latter as premier.

Bert Spence, the security guard on duty at the Embassy, logged my unusually late arrival in the chancery with the line: "0010: Mr. Brown in re K out." I phoned Godfrey Hearn, the First Secretary, to ask him to come to the office and alerted Jeannine Charron, the communicator. By two in the morning we had put together a telegram analysing the *coup d'état*. Hearn and Charron delivered the cyphered message to the British Embassy to be transmitted by radio to Ottawa. We all had a drink at my house in the compound and I tried to ring the Department, succeeding at 3:00 o'clock in speaking to the Communications Centre and learning that they had tried to call us at 11:30 p.m., when the rumours were already on the news tickers abroad, but had been cut off. After the others left, I wound down by listening to the British general election returns, Harold Wilson's Labour Party holding a commanding lead in a different sort of *coup* from the one that had kept me up so late.

Four hours later, another full day began. A French diplomat visited us to get our views on the event; everyone at his embassy had slept through it all. We sent off two more telegrams replete with speculation on the significance of the overthrow of the plump, earthy Khrushchev who had made a lot of friends in the West and enemies in his own country.

Krushchev's decline had started long before I had arrived in the Soviet Union and was caused by his successes as much as by his failures. One of his greatest achievements had been to reveal many of the horrors of the Stalin era and free millions of political prisoners from the gulags. During his 10 years as leader, the Soviet economy leapt ahead but his efforts to translate increased production into social gains for the people were thwarted by his tendency to try quick fixes. His reforms were as often blocked by the structure of the Soviet state as by the inefficiency, corruption and conservatism of the bureaucracy. The party and the *apparatchniks* were nervous, not knowing how far Khrushchev would go in a renewed campaign of debunking Stalin or in meddling with the form of the establishment.

The afternoon of the 16th ended with a reception for President Dorticos at St. George's Hall. Anastas Mikoyan and Premier Kosygin were in attendance along with a large number of happy looking Russians, doubtless relieved to be survivors. Rumours abounded: it was said that Adzhubei, the son-in-law of Khrushchev, had been relieved of the editorship of *Izvestiya*, and that a wholesale purge of press and radio bosses was in progress. But it was to be a month before the rumours became reality in this bloodless change of government.

Apart from the disappearance of pictures of Khrushchev, Moscow was the same city that it had been a day earlier. However, there were almost tangible anxieties present as to what would happen to consumer goods and what the attitude of the new leaders would be towards the West. At the Embassy, we allowed ourselves a certain amount of satisfaction over the reporting that we had done when we received a copy of a telegram to Robert Ford in Paris from Marcel Cadieux, the Under-Secretary in Ottawa, which read:

> In view of yesterday's events, I expect that you are already hurrying back to Moscow. Wherever this may reach you, we look forward to your interpretation. Meanwhile we are grateful for Brown's tel 1001 Oct 16.

Ford got back on Sunday morning, the 18th. He commented ruefully to me as we drove from the airport that his batting average on Soviet leadership changes had been poor. He had been in hospital in Moscow in 1953 when Stalin died and had missed the 1955 changes, when he was in charge of European affairs in Ottawa, because he was on leave. In the office that Sunday afternoon, Ford discussed Khrushchev's departure with Hearn, Warden and me. Although he was somewhat surprised at the depth of our reporting of recent days, he was not deterred from cranking out his own commentaries in the days that followed.

He was not alone: in the next week, the downfall of the Soviet leader was flogged to death as a topic by various members of the Canadian foreign service who claimed status as Kremlinologists. Just after Ford returned, a 20-page analysis arrived from Ottawa which tied up our communications centre for almost a day. It had all the earmarks of having been prepared by Arnold Smith, Ford's predecessor in Moscow and now an assistant under-secretary in Ottawa, who was never known for brevity. In transmission, a priceless cypher corruption occurred to match the puffery of the analysis: a reference to Smith, in 1962, as "our *hon*[ourable] ambassador in Moscow".[55]

Khrushchev had disappeared without trace, or so it seemed for several weeks until Soviet contacts of foreign correspondents said that the former premier had become a pensioner and was living somewhere in Moscow. We did not attempt to guess where "somewhere" was and it came as a stunning surprise to learn in the course of time that he and his wife were living in an apartment block right next door to the Canadian Embassy.[56]

Though I do not recall any of us having clapped eyes on our renowned new neighbour, our proximity to Khrushchev led some visitors to Moscow to seek our services as intermediaries.

On a flight from London to Moscow in March 1965, Wynne and I met Shirley Temple — Mrs. Charles Black — and her husband when they joined our flight in Frankfurt. They were on their way to the Soviet Union to seek help for her brother's medical condition. Some days later, the Blacks came to the Embassy to tell me that they wanted to extend best wishes to Khrushchev with whom they had had a pleasant meeting in Hollywood in 1959 during his tour of the United States. They had already been next door but had been refused entry. They asked if we would translate into Russian a message expressing their greetings and I had a member of the local staff write their message on the back of Black's calling card. They went next door to deliver it but were again denied entry, this time by a pair of Russian women and a male "superintendent" who were stationed in the vestibule of the apartment building.

Just two days later, we received evidence that our neighbour's whereabouts were known abroad. A letter, postmarked Fort Nelson, British Columbia on 17 March, arrived at the office bearing the address: Nikita Khrushchev, Apartment next door to Canadian Embassy, Moscow, Russia. The censors had allowed the letter through, even stamping their own familiar imprint on the back of the envelope. And, we believed, they made a stab at a joke by delivering the letter to us.

Early in April, the proximity of Khrushchev to the Canadian compound provided a centrepiece to the visit to Moscow of the Premier of Newfoundland, the Honourable Joseph R ("Joey") Smallwood. We learned from the Canadian Ambassador in Helsinki that Smallwood would arrive in Moscow on Saturday, 10 April, accompanied by his legal adviser, none other than Richard M. Nixon, former Vice-President of the United States and a future president. One of my friends at the American Embassy also called to tell me about the visit, for which he was making arrangements at the request of the American Embassy in Helsinki. As Robert Ford was leaving in mid-morning that day for Uzbekistan, he asked me to meet Smallwood and provide him with any necessary help.

At the *Leningradsky Vagzaal* — the Moscow terminal for trains from Leningrad — on that cold Saturday morning, the American press corps turned out in force to interview Nixon, surrounding him with microphones and cameras. Smallwood, the nominal boss, had to settle for me and two Canadian newsmen, Jack Best of the Canadian Press and Peter Worthington of the Toronto *Telegram*. The Premier was peeved: Nixon, he told us, was just the lawyer for the company that Newfoundland had engaged for an economic development scheme. The two Canadian reporters and I chatted with the Premier for the 20 minutes that Nixon was detained on the station platform by the American newsmen. The visitors were then taken to their hotel by the American Embassy which looked after them during their one-day stay.

That evening, Wynne and I were invited by Foy Kohler, the American ambassador, to drinks at Spaso House for the Nixon-Smallwood party. We found Nixon very personable, projecting a far warmer image than he did on television. Premier Smallwood was pleased to learn that Spaso House had been occupied by the first Soviet foreign minister, Georgy Chicherin. The Premier displayed a thorough knowledge of the early Soviet communists whom he admired, describing them as a remarkable group of brilliant individuals. During the hour, Smallwood was called to the telephone twice to speak to his office in St. John's. At the time, we credited the KGB with being on the job knowing where Smallwood was, but I learned later that the operator had first tried the Canadian Embassy.

Wynne and I went on to a dinner party, returning to the Embassy compound after midnight. I checked into the office before going home. The security guard told me that Nixon, with Smallwood in tow and egged on by David Levy — the resident correspondent of the Canadian Broadcasting Corporation — had come to the Embassy at 11:15 o'clock, ostensibly to sign the visitor's book. Undeterred by the lateness of the hour, the trio had then gone next door to try to see Khrushchev. They had no more luck than Shirley Temple: the "caretakers" turned them away, probably with a lecture that retired citizen Khrushchev enjoyed the privilege of being protected from importuning foreigners.[57]

In the morning I left early for Sheremetyevo airport to see Nixon and Smallwood aboard a KLM Electra bound for Amsterdam. Though the two were treated with great respect by the immigration control officers, they were still required to produce all of their documents, including currency declarations. Nixon, who remarked to me on the relaxed manner of the immigration officers, compared his impressions of Moscow with those from his trip in 1959, when he had staged his famous argument with Khrushchev in the model kitchen of an American exhibition. The average Muscovite and the city itself, he said, still looked down at the heels.

In October 1964, all that was in the future. On the Monday after the Ambassador had returned from his holiday, he was obliged to perform his normal role as head of a diplomatic mission by going to Vnukovo Airport to stand in line in the greeting ceremony for Soviet cosmonauts. He skipped the parade for them at Red Square that afternoon so as to continue putting down his own thoughts on the fall of Khrushchev. I spent that day preparing for my departure the next morning for Moldavia on a five-day excursion organized by the Foreign Ministry.

At the Embassy, we were impressed in the month that followed the dismissal of Khrushchev by the care with which the new team of Brezhnev and Kosygin set their course. There had been concern among western countries that conservative hardliners would determine the direction of Soviet foreign policy. At the Kremlin reception on the evening of Revolution Day, an apoplectic speech by the Defence Minister, Marshal Malinovsky, about Soviet military might seemed to prove that peaceful co-existence was a thing of the past. Within minutes, however, Premier Kosygin approached the United States Ambassador to half-apologize by saying that it was a soldier's speech made on a festive occasion, and also went up to the British Ambassador, Humphrey Trevelyan, to speak to him in friendly terms. Kohler was told by Kosygin that it was up to the United States to take steps towards conciliation now that the presidential election was over and President Johnson firmly in power. The Premier said that the USSR had many difficult internal and external problems and the USA could help by proposing solutions to foreign policy issues; this theme was his toast to Kohler.

A few days later Kohler had an interview with Foreign Minister Gromyko during which the ambassador raised the establishment of a hot-line between Washington and Moscow. If President Johnson wanted to speak to the Soviet Government, Kohler asked, whom should he call. Gromyko responded strangely: it was, he acknowledged, "a very concrete question" which he would return to later for a government had to have "an authorized spokesman". The reply left the Americans wondering who was in charge in Moscow.

December brought a remarkably conciliatory statement by Premier Kosygin on foreign policy. While standing firmly in support of Cuba and North Vietnam and saying just enough unkind things about the recent American-Belgian rescue operation at Stanleyville in the Congo to retain the Soviet Union's appeal to the Africans, he offered negotiations on disarmament and a willingness to discuss all outstanding questions of international concern. The impression was given that the West would better know where it stood with the new regime than it had with Khrushchev and that Soviet policy would be conducted in a more businesslike manner. One highly interesting feature of the speech was that it contained not a single word about relations with China, this despite the fact that the Chinese foreign minister had visited Moscow just weeks previously. Kosygin's tone was far softer than we at the Canadian Embassy had expected because, a week before the speech, he had given Ford only five minutes when yet another letter from Prime Minister Pearson was delivered to the Soviet premier on the reunification of families. Ford had found him tense and preoccupied — a mood which may have reflected Soviet impatience with our badgering of them on that subject when other matters dominated their agenda.

In the late autumn of 1964, the question of the balance of Canadian press correspondents stationed in the Soviet Union and Soviet correspondents based in Canada was raised when the Russians wanted to send a new TASS newsman to Ottawa. I met this correspondent, Mikhailov, when I called on Yanchenko, the head of the foreign relations division of the agency, to enquire about subscribing to the TASS English-language wire service. Most diplomatic missions received the print out for a fraction of the price being demanded of us. Yanchenko slyly suggested that a lower price might be possible after they had become "better acquainted" with me and that circumstances would indeed improve if a visa were issued for Mikhailov. Ottawa approved the visa and a week later I closed the deal for the wire service with Yanchenko. Two days later we received our first "take", 77 pages long and, I recorded in my diary, obviously of great use.

The Soviets were entitled to send a new *Izvestiya* correspondent to Ottawa, not having yet replaced the one expelled from Canada in the spring of 1964 for spying. They recognized that this possibility existed and, so, when the Toronto *Telegram* applied through us for permission to set up a Moscow Bureau and send Peter Worthington as its correspondent, they raised no objection.

A month after gaining access to the TASS wire service, we pressed our request for the acquisition of a telex link, continuing a campaign for this facility that had begun in 1961 by Ambassador Arnold Smith. Up to this time in the history of the embassy, it had been necessary for us to deliver our telegrams to the Soviet telegraph office which despatched them. Our confidential traffic was taken, after being encyphered, to the British Embassy to be sent by their radio to the U.K. where the messages were passed to the communications centre of the Canadian High Commission at Canada House.

On the last day of the year, I was called to the Foreign Ministry by Mme Mironova to be told that we had been granted a telex line and that it would be available from 12 January 1965. I told her that this was a very nice New Year's gift. While our work pattern was changed sharply by the ease with which we could communicate henceforth with headquarters and they with us, the facility saved us a considerable amount of money and greatly improved our operational efficiency. Although it was always in the power of the Soviets to pull the plug on the line when they wished to, that did not happen in my remaining time in Moscow.

When the telex line was granted, we wondered if it resulted from a softening of the Soviet attitude towards Canada. A more cynical explanation seemed probable: the separation of our cryptograms from those going out over the British Embassy's radio would make it easier for the Soviet code-breakers to try their luck on our cyphers.

In the spring of 1965, the Department communicated a request to the Soviet Embassy in Ottawa that three ships of the Second Escort

Squadron of the Royal Canadian Navy be permitted to visit Petropavlovsk-Kamchatka. On a Pacific cruise from its base in Esquimalt, the squadron was due to visit Tokyo before the proposed call at the Soviet port. We became involved when we were asked to follow up on the matter with the Soviet Foreign Ministry. In the exchanges on the subject with Ottawa, we obtained their blessing for the idea that the Naval Attaché and I should go to the Pacific port to assist the RCN during the visit, should it take place.

At about the same time, the USSR's Baltic Shipping Line applied through its agents in Montreal, March Shipping Limited, for permission to send a merchantman up the St. Lawrence Seaway. On 7 April, I called on Mme Mironova to press for an early response on the proposed naval visit and to inform her that the proposed use of the Seaway by the Baltic Shipping Line required a decision by the Canadian Government. Inadvertently, I tied the two questions by remarking that both were urgent, one from our side and the other from the Soviet side.

Later in April, we were told by the Department that the Soviet Embassy in Ottawa had been informed of Canadian approval for two ships to make the passage of the Seaway. This approval was conditional on certain administrative conditions and, the Soviets were advised, future access would "depend in part upon an appropriate measure of reciprocity" on the part of the Soviet Government. That phrase was intended to cover the gamut of the bilateral relationship: it could mean the use of Soviet waterways by Canadian ships, freedom of movement for Canadian diplomats in Moscow, action on the reunification of families, or any other matter on which we sought change.

On 21 April, I gave a luncheon at home, with Godfrey Hearn and Bill Warden present, for Mme Mironova and two of her officials, Musin and Makharov of the Second European Division. Over dessert, we got down to business and I told the Russians of the conditional approval which had been granted for the use of the Seaway. Musin remarked that it was typical of Canadians to attempt to tie unrelated matters and I responded with the line that approval for the voyages of the ships was a gesture of Canadian goodwill which we hoped would prompt a Soviet response in some other fields. I suggested that "ships for ships" might be a reasonable starter: the approval of the RCN visit to Petropavlovsk. Musin acknowledged that a Soviet denial of the naval visit might jeopardize the use of Canadian ports by Soviet naval and fishing craft and added that the difficulty was not over a visit but the choice of Petropavlovsk. I took this as a hint that an alternative port might be offered.

The negotiations now moved ahead quickly. The next morning, Mme Mironova telephoned Ambassador Ford to tell him that Petropavlovsk could not be visited "for technical reasons" and to offer Severo-Kurilsk, on the most northerly of the formerly-Japanese Kurile Islands, as a substitute. At noon at the Foreign Ministry, Mme Mironova gave this offer to me in writing when I called on her for a prearranged meeting to take up five other matters besides the naval visit. On returning to the Embassy I fired off telegrams recommending that the change be accepted and the visit still take place. We added that as there was no civil air connection between Moscow and Severo-Kurilsk, Captain Bovey and I could go to Tokyo and board the RCN ships there. Ottawa approved the change in ports on condition that the Soviets provided marine charts, made available oil and water during the visit and gave transportation to Severo-Kurilsk to Bovey and me. Perhaps because the port of Severo-Kurilsk was thought to be little better than a fishing harbour, the RCN was not enthusiastic and we were instructed to cancel the visit if all conditions were not met.

We communicated Ottawa's conditions to the Foreign Ministry. When no response had been received three days later, we sent a note regretting that we would have to cancel the visit if an affirmative response to all of our requirements were not forthcoming that day, 27 April. In mid-afternoon, I was called in by Safronchuk of the Second European Division to be given a *note verbale* stating, firstly, that the necessary charts would be passed to the Canadian ships on the high seas; secondly, that water and oil would be made available; and, thirdly, that travel by Bovey and me was impossible to arrange because there was no regular air or sea link to Severo-Kurilsk. Safronchuk added to the note by saying that some of the problems had been of a "very complicated nature", which I took as an allusion to an intra-ministerial battle between the Foreign Ministry, possibly supported by the Navy, and the KGB. He chided us for not having made known our requirements earlier.

Safronchuk was shocked when I told him that on the basis of the Soviet failure to meet all of our requirements, the visit could be regarded as cancelled. As for the delay in making our needs known, I said that these had been of Soviet making because they had refused the proposal to visit Petropavlovsk and offered us at the last minute an obscure fishing village. On returning to the Embassy, I told Ottawa of the outcome. Four hours later, the Second Escort Squadron set sail from Tokyo for the Aleutians. They were probably happy to have avoided the Kuriles.

The failed naval visit was a useful exercise in demonstrating the tensions that existed amongst Soviet agencies and the domination of the issue of state security — the domain of the KGB — over all other considerations. There was probably little intelligence to be garnered by the RCN in or around Severo-Kurilsk and the Soviets were comfortable about that port. Hence, it was of much interest to us that the point on which the visit foundered was the request that Bovey and I be given transportation to the port that could have been provided easily by the Soviets. Plainly, therefore, the KGB was nervous that we would see too much on our way to the remote port, especially if we had been routed by way of the closed facilities of Petropavlovsk.

Six months later, on the eve of my departure from Moscow, I had another encounter with Safronchuk on the subject of naval visits. The Soviets had asked us to permit two naval hydographic ships to visit Vancouver. I took along an *aide-memoire* asking in return for an assurance of favourable consideration to future RCN visits to the Soviet Pacific ports of Vladivostock and Petropavlovsk. Safronchuk stated that the proposed visit to Vancouver was off, but claimed that by giving us any one of 10 "open" ports (Nakhodka and nine on Sakhalin Island) reciprocity was being offered for Vancouver. Perhaps appropriately, this stand-off marked my last call on the Soviet Foreign Ministry.

On 18 May 1965, Robert and Thereza Ford left Moscow for leave and duty in Ottawa. Their absence was to last for just over three months which meant that I was in charge of the Embassy during the two principal Canadian visits to the Soviet Union of my posting there, the first that of the Minister of Northern Affairs and National Resources, Arthur Laing, and the second the much-postponed parliamentary delegation. These were the most important visits to the USSR by Canadian political figures since that of Lester B. Pearson as Minister of External Affairs nine years earlier.

The purpose of the Laing visit was to gain knowledge on how the Soviet Union dealt with permafrost in its vast northern regions, a problem that we also grappled with in our North. The visit had been long in the making and followed a tour of the Canadian northland in 1964 which was arranged by the Northern Affairs department for a group of ambassadors accredited to Canada. Before coming to the Soviet Union, Mr. Laing and his party had visited the Scott Polar Institute in Britain and gone on to Denmark, Norway, Sweden and Finland to discuss and view development programmes involving the subarctic. The Minister was accompanied by his parliamentary secretary John Turner, the deputy minister of the department Ernest Coté, the Minister's special assistant Jacob Austin, and two officials, Graham Rowley and Harry Rosenburg.

On 25 May, with Bill Warden who was to accompany the party on their travels in the Soviet Union, I went to Sheremetyevo Airport for the arrival of the Minister. He was greeted by Georgy A. Karavayev, Minister and First Deputy Chairman of the State Committee for Construction, better known by the acronym *Gosstroy*. In the usual Soviet fashion, it was necessary to negotiate the details of the visit the next day. No objection was raised to the request to go to Irkutsk and Bratsk after an agreed visit to the Arctic Institute in Leningrad, but the northern centre of Tiksi, on the shores of the Arctic Ocean at 72° N. Latitude and 128° E. Longtitude, was refused. Next morning, before a lunch at my home for the Laing party and the Soviet hosts, I called on Safronchuk at the Foreign Ministry, having warned him that I would be pressing the case for the Tiksi visit. Safronchuk had already been in touch with *Gosstroy* and made a counter-offer of the addition of a mine near Yakutsk.

That evening, the Laing party with Bill Warden and Jack Best of the Canadian Press took the night train to Leningrad. Two days later, they flew 4500 km east to Irkutsk, where they were shown the hydro-electric station and an aluminum smelter, and then to Bratsk to see a massive hydro-electric project, under construction in the seasonal deep freeze of this area north of the Mongolian Republic, and a forestry complex, where Canadian sawmill equipment was eventually to be installed.

While the party was in Yakutsk, I put more pressure on the hosts to allow the visit to Tiksi, writing to Karavayev on 4 June and copying my letter to him to the Foreign Ministry. Tiksi was again denied but Norilsk — the world's most northerly industrial city and built on a deep bed of permafrost — was offered. This was a unique concession for it was the first time that the Soviet Union had permitted a group from the West to see this community of 100,000 inhabitants. The party was informed in Yakutsk of the addition of Norilsk to their itinerary but instead of arranging for them to fly there by way of the regular Aeroflot service from Novosibirsk, the *Gosstroy* guides required them to return 4000 km to Moscow before setting out on the 2800 km trip to Norilsk. On the evening of the 7th, I met the Minister and his party at Domededevo, the new airport south of Moscow, and brought them back to bed them down in the Embassy compound for a few hours' rest.[58] At midnight they were off to Vnukovo Airport only to find that the flight to Norilsk was cancelled because of heavy snow in the Arctic city. The delegation was put up at the Ukraine Hotel and I got to bed at 3:45 a.m., in broad daylight.

A few hours later, the group left once again for Vnukovo and took off for Norilsk only to have to break the journey for 20 hours at Syktivkar because their destination was now fogged in. Eventually they made it to Norilsk on the morning of the 9th. What they were shown made up for the fatiguing trip: the vast smelter complex, eight-storey buildings and other facilities built on the solid foundation of the permafrost, water and sewer services distributed through insulated tunnels below the frost level more than 30 metres underground.

On 10 June, the party returned to Moscow and the following day had a final session with Karavayev at which the details were discussed of a return visit by *Gosstroy* officials to Canada in August. Mr. Laing suggested exchanges of permafrost scientists but Karavayev insisted that the proposal be studied only after the August trip. Writing shortly after he arrived back in Canada, Mr. Laing described it as "one of the rare and privileged experiences of a lifetime to be able to see contemporary Soviet society at work in so many parts of the country". He made a special point of thanking Bill Warden for his work in accompanying the delegation and my wife for the hospitality that she had produced on short notice.

The visit of a Canadian Parliamentary Delegation — the first ever to the Soviet Union — was put on track again in June 1965 when we notified the Foreign Ministry that the delegation would like to come to the Soviet Union from 17–30 July. This proposal was quickly approved by the Soviets but the event was almost upon us before Ottawa informed us of the last-minute wishes of some delegates and the head of the foreign relations section of the Supreme Soviet gave us an outline of the programme.

Led by the Speaker of the House of Commons, Alan Macnaughton, and the senior Senator, David Croll, the delegation of 14 parliamentarians and three officials, including Alan McLaine of External Affairs, arrived at Sheremetyevo on the afternoon of Monday, 19 July. I went on to the aircraft to greet the party and introduced them to Chairman Jan V. Peyve of the Council of Nationalities who took them to the terminal for a half-hour televised ceremony of welcome which the next morning's *Pravda* described as warm. Then the group moved to the Sovietskaya Hotel in 10 limousines, Soviet-built Chaikas and Volgas, which were assigned to them for their stay.

That evening, Wynne put on a dinner for the visitors who included, besides Macnaughton and Croll, some other distinguished past and future politicians such as the Hon. Michael Starr, Senator John Hnatyshyn, T.C. Douglas, the leader of the New Democratic Party, and Donald S. Macdonald, then 33 years of age and Parliamentary Secretary for Justice, who was to impress me as being the most level-headed of all the group. Inevitably, there were a few duds; an MP representing part of my home-town was to prove a real menace.

On the second day, the delegation was received by Peyve at the Supreme Soviet and we heard the details of the programme for the first time. The requests of Senator Croll to visit his birthplace in a Byelorussian village and Michael Starr to go to his ancestral home in the Western Ukraine were agreed to by the hosts. Peyve announced that Chairman Anastas Mikoyan — the old Armenian survivor of governments from Lenin's to Brezhnev's, now serving as nominal head of state — would receive the delegation in the afternoon. That event was preceded by a tour of the Kremlin and Lenin's Tomb and lunch in the Palace of Congresses at which Senator Croll provided light relief by speaking of the thrill at having seen the Kremlin, Red Square and the tomb of *Stalin* all on one day. (The nimble interpreter turned this smartly into "Lenin's Mausoleum".)

Mikoyan gave the delegation a half-hour display of his renowned sly and acerbic humour. He told the Canadians that they were free to see everything in the Soviet Union adding: "Everything except our rocket bases because you are in NATO". When Tommy Douglas distanced his party from Canadian policy on Vietnam and opined that a Commonwealth Peace Mission held promise, Mikoyan called it "illusory", saying that the only way to stop the war was to speak to the United States. Later, Mikoyan balanced the earlier gaffe by Senator Croll with one of his own when he recalled that, a few years earlier, during an unexpected stopover in Nova Scotia when he was on the way from Moscow to New York, Prime Minister Diefenbaker had sent his foreign minister, *Paul Martin*, to call on him.

The Canadian parliamentarians spent their second full day in the Soviet Union sight-seeing in Moscow. I accompanied them on their visit to the Metro, on which I had not yet travelled. (When I mentioned this to Alan McLaine, he told me that it was also a first for him because he had not made a trip on the underground system during his posting in Moscow from 1960 to 1962.) The comments of some of the members of the delegation that day made me wonder if they were trying to win votes among the Russians who conducted them around the city. The Canadians spoke to me about the trip as a "unique experience, different and exhilarating", described the Soviet Union as a "big, vigorous and vital" country where "there is something to see and appreciate and things are happening". To a Soviet guide, one member remarked in my hearing that the Soviet people were "struggling to improve themselves, and succeeding"; they were "a people who are awakening", a "lovely and wonderful people".

Accompanied by L.I. Lubennikov, a member of the Supreme Soviet, the parliamentary delegation left Moscow on the 22nd for Tbilisi, Sochi, Kiev and Leningrad. Six days later, I met them at the *Leningradsky Vagzaal* on their arrival on the overnight "Red Arrow" train from Leningrad, and went with them to the Kremlin for a lengthy meeting with Chairman Peyve and other personalities of the Supreme Soviet and officials of various ministries. Alan Macnaughton extended an invitation to the Supreme Soviet to send a delegation to Canada, expressed satisfaction at the Soviet decision to take part on a large scale in the world exposition at Montreal in 1967, and put forward a request that the Soviet Union participate in the opening gala of the National Arts Centre in Ottawa, due to be completed in 1968. Senator Croll followed with an impassioned appeal on the reunification of families which, I noted in my diary, may have done more than anything else to convince the Russians of the positive value of taking action on this issue. T.C. Douglas made some useful suggestions on exchanges in various fields.

In the evening, Wynne and I held a reception for the delegation and their Soviet hosts in the outer office area of the Embassy. TASS later reported that, from the Soviet side, there were present "the Vice-President of the Presidium of the Supreme Soviet of the USSR Georgi Dzotsenidze, Chairman of the Soviet of Nationalities Jan Peyve, deputies of the Supreme Soviet, Deputy Foreign Minister Mikail Zamyanin, and members of the public". They seemed pleased with the event; Alan McLaine was to report to us that Speaker Macnaughton had expressed his gratitude — and that the Canadian parliamentarians were appalled at the poor accommodation of the chancery.

The Supreme Soviet gave its reception for the visitors on the afternoon of the 29th at the House of Receptions. It was the usual stilted ceremony: Peyve gave a prepared speech and made the usual toasts and the Canadian leaders, obviously tired, made impromptu replies. From there, the delegation was taken to the Kremlin for a meeting with Premier Kosygin. He listened through short speeches by Macnaughton, Croll and Starr and then, without notes, made a very coherent statement of the Soviet desire for the development of closer ties with Canada, following this with an exposition of Soviet policy on Vietnam and a denunciation of the American escalation of the war there. Kosygin made a great impact on the Canadians.

That morning, the Soviets had given us a draft communique on the visit which we re-worked to ensure that it reflected our position on what had happened. After the meeting with Kosygin, Godfrey Hearn and I returned to the Sovietskaya Hotel with the delegation to sit down with Musin and Makharov of the Foreign Ministry and reach agreement on the text. The two accepted all of our changes except our attempt to include a reference to the reunification of families, an issue which had never been accepted as a problem by the Soviets. We cleared the draft with our respective masters, Macnaughton of the Delegation and Lubennikov of the Supreme Soviet. The next morning at the departure ceremony at Sheremetyevo Airport, the communique was signed, more speeches made, toasts and embraces exchanged, and flowers presented by small girls while TV cameras recorded the historic scene.

As we walked with the delegation to the Czech Airlines Tupolev-124 which would take the Canadians to Prague for their next visit, Senator Croll provided the last of his many vacuous remarks. Seeing the Czech logo on the aircraft, the senator said to Chairman Peyve: "I see it is a Czech plane. I would feel safer in one of the Russian planes we have flown in during the past week." Peyve demurred: "It *is* a Russian plane." "Ah", Croll responded, "then I feel safe. Your planes are the best in the world."

The delegation left and I returned to the office to look after a caller of a different sort — Percival Price, once the Dominion Carilloneur in Ottawa — and tend to more customary matters like the final day in Moscow of the Military Attaché who, under intense pressure from the KGB for months, had probably been saved from being declared *persona non grata* by the visit of the parliamentarians. Not only he, but the Naval Attaché had received menacing attention from the Soviet counter-intelligence that week and, towards midnight two days earlier, after our reception for the parliamentary delegation, I had gone to the *Leningradsky Vagzaal* to see him off for Helsinki, escorted out of the USSR by another of our officers. The care that we had to take to protect the two Canadian attachés in their final days and hours in the country perhaps explains the moments of cynicism, even nausea, that we had experienced when listening to the platitudes that had laced the exchanges of the Canadian parliamentarians and their Soviet hosts.

Another event had occurred early in the visit which was of personal importance. A telegram arrived on 21 July from the Under-Secretary of State for External Affairs, Marcel Cadieux, asking if I would agree to my name being submitted to Paul Martin for appointment as ambassador to the Democratic Republic of the Congo. By coincidence, the communicator delivered the message to me after dinner just as I was leaving for Vnukovo Airport to attend the arrival of Prime Minister Milton Obote of one of the Congo's neighbours, Uganda. I asked Godfrey Hearn, who had served in Ghana, to drop over for a drink and we chewed over the job offer until midnight. Godfrey urged me to take it. Wynne and the girls were delighted at the prospect of getting away from Moscow. Next morning, before going once more to Vnukovo to see the parliamentary delegation off to Tbilisi, I sent a wire to Marcel saying simply "Agreeable. Brown".

I had three more weeks in charge of the Embassy before the return of Robert Ford on 21 August from his long absence. The visits of the King of Afghanistan, the Prime Minister of Turkey and the President of the Republic of the Congo — the other one which I now easily spoke of as "Congo (Brazza)" — added to the impressive total of my visits to the Kremlin and to the number of times that I had shaken the hands of Brezhnev and Kosygin.

The good state of Canadian-Soviet relations was demonstrated on 10 August by the announcement in Ottawa of the signing of a massive wheat deal which would be worth over $400 million to Canada. It came as a surprise to the experts in the western diplomatic missions who had forecast that the 1965 Soviet harvest would be only slightly below that of 1964. When I mentioned the deal to my NATO colleagues at a tea party that day, Brimelow of the British Embassy said that he had been told by Zamyanin, the Deputy Foreign Minister, that the crops in Kazakhstan had been gravely damaged by drought. Brimelow also said that a British farmers' union delegation, which had visited the Volgagrad Oblast on the lower Volga River, had described the harvest there as "miserable".

We judged that the deal meant a lot to us and that it would help to keep the Russians less adventurous for another year at least. It was not until later that we learned that a price had been paid by Canada to clinch the wheat agreement and also to ensure Soviet participation in Expo 67. For some time, the Canadian counter-intelligence services had wanted to restrict Soviet and other East Bloc diplomats in Ottawa to a 25-mile (40-kilometre) zone around the capital, to match what we were confined to in Moscow and down from the 50 miles (80 km) that the Communists enjoyed in Canada. Robert Ford told me that the proposed, more stringent, restriction was vetoed by Prime Minister Pearson himself on the urging of the Department of Trade and Commerce.

Ambassador Ford had returned from Ottawa with a letter from the Prime Minister to Premier Kosygin which commented on the improvement in bilateral relations and appealed for Soviet support on disarmament and the end of the chronic crisis in the finances of the United Nations. Cordial and relaxed, Kosygin received Ford on 27 August and responded to the delivery of the letter by issuing an unexpected invitation to Mr. Pearson to visit the Soviet Union. Such a visit, Kosygin said, could mark a turning point in Soviet-Canadian relations.

A month later, as he neared the end of his first year in office, Premier Kosygin took firm control of Soviet economic policy with a lengthy *doklad*, a lecture, to a plenum of the Central Committee of the Communist Party, on the reorganization of the economy and the introduction of a version of the profit motive into industry at large. These and other revolutionary proposals kept us busy assessing their importance. They also gave rise to a comment by a Soviet professor in the English-language *Moscow News* to the effect that the proposals had been made because "we are no longer satisfied with our existing successes". He was obviously on a different wavelength from Premier Kosygin who was plainly concerned with dealing with existing failures.

While it was heartening that the Premier sought to improve the country's economic performance, Soviet utterances on foreign policy continued to remind us that the East-West confrontation was largely responsbile for the sad state of the Soviet economy. In a decade when the United States was confident that it could have guns and butter, military demands were already crippling the Soviet Union. At a diplomatic reception for the visiting Danish Prime Minister in early October, Kosygin revealed how deeply the Soviet Union was alarmed by western strength when he delivered a stinging attack on NATO, German "revanchism" and the escalation of the Vietnamese conflict by the Americans. While his tirade seemed threatening to his Western guests, it was also a reminder that the Soviet Union, like Tsarist Russia before, was a nation that considered itself threatened by its neighbours.

The final weeks of my relatively short Moscow posting were dominated by the imminent assignment to Leopoldville, for which I left the Soviet Union on 29 October. But there was time for reflection on what my experience with the Soviet authorities had meant to Canadian-Soviet bilateral relations. Under the regime of Brezhnev and Kosygin, by then one year old, were those relations better or worse than they had been under Khrushchev? Or was there no change?

Looking back to what had seemed the balmy days of Nikita Sergeyevitch, I recalled progress in areas such as the accreditation of resident Canadian newsmen, the development of the first student exchanges, the visit to the Soviet Union of the Toronto Board of Trade, the delegations from the Canadian iron ore and asbestos industries, the visit to Canada of the Soviet Minister of Agriculture, the first tour of a Canadian theatrical group, our proposal for a Canadian naval visit and the Soviet agreement to receive a Canadian parliamentary delegation. Most of these developments had resulted from Canadian initiatives and were efforts to flesh out the policy enunciated by Paul Martin on the promotion of *détente*. The visit of the parliamentarians was proposed during Khrushchev's days and went ahead smoothly and in an atmosphere of some warmth nine months after his fall. That of Arthur Laing and his northern affairs experts — organized under the new regime — was extensive and reward-ing despite some difficulties. The naval visit did not happen because of obstacles placed in its way by the nervous Soviet intelligence agencies but its failure did not mar relations with the regime.

Some other developments had been the result of Soviet initiatives: the use of the St.Lawrence Seaway by Soviet merchantmen, the inauguration of a Leningrad-Montreal passenger-ship service, and a USSR-Canada air link. By and large, they represented a Soviet calculation of economic ben-efit. Still other developments were more closely related to a Soviet desire to promote bilateral relations but had less to do with *détente* than with hard-headed assessments of the advantages to the Soviet Union. A slight yielding by them on the reunification of families was in this category.

Taken together, the points on which we rubbed shoulders added sub-stance to the Canadian-Soviet relationship and, to the extent that private as well as official contacts were involved, seemed to assist in conditioning the Soviets to accept a more normal place in the international community. Yet the historical barriers remained: suspicion as well as ignorance of the outside world stood in the way of co-existence, and the KGB was well-staffed and well-equipped to protect these dams against what the Russians had always regarded as attempts to breach them. Thus, what we tended to perceive as improvement resulting from contacts often led to the opposite effect on the relationship: what we hoped for was not what we got. And, when we reacted to Soviet attacks on embassy staff, or took measures over the improper activities of Soviet diplomats and visitors in Canada, we had to stand up to the overt and covert hostility of the KGB. However, these were not attacks based on policy questions, a fact borne out by the repeated assurances of officials of the Foreign Ministry that "little things" should not be permitted to interfere with the general pattern of relations.

On other, more fundamental questions of foreign policy, the Canadian and Soviet positions were totally opposed. Whatever the state of the bilateral climate, the Soviet Union always criticized us for being too close to the United States on the big international issues, and reserved its applause for those occasions when we took issue with the Americans, such as on aspects of the Indo-China war. Though we had taken the initiative in convening an international conference on peacekeeping, the Soviets saw the American hand behind it. We were not seen as important players on the world scene and the Soviet Union cultivated us only to the extent that good relations with us suited their larger aims. If they did not, any hope of agreement was illusory.

Because relations between the Soviet Union and the United States were bad in the autumn of 1965, the Soviet hard line was applied towards the West in general. The Soviets took advantage of every opening that Canada made in the bilateral relationship to press for concessions in fields that mattered to them. The wheat deal of 1965 paid off for them in the lifting of restrictions on Soviet diplomats in Canada, but left the Canadians in Moscow boxed in. Soviet hints of uncertainty over their participation in the Montreal exposition of 1967 provided them with leverage to play on Canadian vulnerabilities. Only when we made it known that they could not blackmail us — that we could deal with them on the basis of long-established principle and that we recognized the weaknesses in their bargaining position — would it be possible to maintain bilateral relations on an even keel. Although these truths had not invariably guided the Canadian Government authorities in Ottawa, we had tried to adhere to them in the embassy in Moscow and had used them to stand up to repeated challenges in 1964 and 1965.

CHAPTER 7

TRAVELS IN THE
SOVIET UNION

The sixteen months that I served in Moscow gave little scope for trips inside the Soviet Union. One reason was that I made three journeys to the West which added up to an absence of almost 10 weeks. Then there were over four months when I was in charge of the Embassy and had to stay close to Moscow. A six-month slot in the middle of the posting, from October 1964 to April 1965, proved to be the only time when I could get out into the country. During that period, I managed to go on four trips.

Each trip took me to a republic of the Soviet empire where, for good historical and cultural reasons, the rule of Moscow was not entirely accepted. The first visit was to Moldavia, a Rumanian province that had been annexed soon after the start of the Second World War. On the next two, I travelled to Estonia and Lithuania, sovereign states until their fate was sealed by the infamous deal between Hitler and Stalin on the eve of that war. My final trip was to Georgia, an ancient land which had enjoyed a brief renewal of freedom between the collapse of Tsarist Russia and the consolidation of the Leninist revolution. The Moldavian visit was organized by the Soviet Foreign Ministry and made in company with a number of other diplomats. I went to Lithuania with an officer of the German Embassy and a Canadian colleague. The Estonian and Georgian trips were made with my wife.

The visit to Moldavia took place from Tuesday the 20th to Friday the 23rd in October 1964. Coming on the heels of the removal of Premier Nikita Khrushchev from power, it was seen by some of my diplomatic colleagues as a neat way of getting inquisitive foreigners out of the way while the new regime took over. In my own case, the trip began less than two days after the return of Ambassador Robert Ford to Moscow from a month's absence. I had written all the analyses of the fall of Khrushchev that I wanted to and was happy to get away from the office while Ford added his thoughts to the volume of comment pouring into and from Ottawa as all the Department's sovietologists had their say.

About 40 members of the diplomatic corps and a half-dozen Foreign Ministry escorts and translators arrived in the Moldavian capital of Kishinev soon after noon on the 20th. After we had taken up our rooms at the Hotel Kishinev on Negruzzi Boulevard, we were officially welcomed to Moldavia by A.D. Dyorditsa, the Chairman of the Council of Ministers of the Soviet Socialist Republic, in the large government building on the main street of the nondescript city. Dyorditsa was nothing if not thorough in detailing for us the achievements of the collective farms and other agro-based industries located on the fertile plains of the Republic in the basin of the Dniester River. We learned that the population of the republic was two-and-a-half million made up of Moldavians (the word Rumanian was not uttered), who accounted for two-thirds of the total, Ukrainians (14 percent) and Russians (10 percent), the remaining 10 percent being divided equally among an exotic tribe, Bulgars and Jews. Fifty years earlier, one-half of the 125,000 people of Kishinev had been Jewish. There were now few in the city of close to 300,000.

As part of our education we were taken to the library of the University of Moldavia. Claiming to have two million volumes, the library had already reduced the number of books on its shelves by removing those about Khrushchev. The foreign languages reading room was pathetic: the works of Lenin and a few other books in English and, in the magazine section, the famous British periodical *Shoe and Leather*, the trade journal of the footwear industry. We were shown three documentary films. One was intended to contrast the good life of Soviet Kishinev with the bad old days when it was part of Rumania but left the assembled diplomats believing just the opposite, partly because all the street and shop signs of yore were in the Latin alphabet, now totally replaced by Cyrillic.

At an evening of lively Moldavian culture, we were entertained with folk dancing by an energetic and noisy Cossack group. One dancer played the clown brilliantly and, even in the *de rigueur* anti-religious skit, got us all laughing. The folk singing was gypsy, some of the music close to *flamenco*. The concert was not only the best entertainment of the trip: it was the only real insight into Moldavian culture during our stay. There was to be no opportunity to wander around Kishinev on our own and we never rubbed shoulders with non-official citizens. Thus we missed visiting the Russian Orthodox Cathedral of the Nativity in the heart of the capital; built in the 1830s, it was considered the outstanding building of Kishinev and so it seemed to be in this city that had suffered badly during the Second World War.

The second day of the visit had taken us along the narrow paved road that paralleled Kishinev's river, the Byk, to its confluence with the Dniester River at Bendery. The countryside often seemed neglected and still showed the scars of war. We stopped at a silk factory where 2800 workers in three shifts spun silk from cocoons and wove natural and artificial fibres together in textiles of extravagant design; the experts among us noted that the machinery was all of Soviet manufacture and not modern. Sprawled along the west bank of the Dniester, the city of Bendery had been the headquarters of Charles XII of Sweden from 1709 to 1712 in the war against the Ottoman Turks. We crossed the river, once the Soviet-Rumanian boundary and climbed up the eastern bank on a circuitous road that had been designed to slow down rather than facilitate transborder-movements. As we drove over the bridge, our attention was diverted by our guide to a Bulgar settlement on the down-stream side. We lunched in Tiraspol and toured a winery where we were conducted by a cork-shaped plant engineer to a session of wine-tasting and toasts.

On the return crossing of the bridge we had a good view of the fine Turkish fort that once guarded this north-easterly corner of European Turkey against the Russian Empire and was now garrisoned by the Soviet Army. I remarked to the Intourist guide that it was a pity that we could not stop for a closer look at the fort. He agreed, adding that there was no particular reason why we should not have seen it because it was "not a vital link in Soviet defences". He was a Ukrainian and I asked him what he thought of the departure of Khrushchev and whether it would make any difference. He replied that one "K" had gone and been replaced by another "K" — Kosygin — and that it was a good thing to replace leaders every four or five years.

The visit to the winery at Tiraspol was only one of a succession of sumptuous feasts that were the main activity of the trip to Moldavia. At these Bacchanalia we sampled fruit and wine between toasts to peace, friendship and other virtues. The first had come early on the first day at a state farm, near Kishinev, which also served as a technical training school. We drove through large fields of grape-vines and then were treat-ed to a great variety of wine of excellent quality. Outside Kishinev on the third day, we were shown a research institute of gardening, grape-growing and wine-making where we were asked to work at our sampling by judg-ing the wines. At a collective farm at Kojooshna, the manager described the glorious achievements of this socialist enterprise and then invited us to sample the wine produced by the happy peasants. Carried away by his own enthusiasm for proposing "bottoms-up" toasts, the manager loudly proclaimed the visit a superb success as we took our leave.

On the eve of our return to Moscow, a dinner at the residence of Chairman Dyorditsa rounded off the hospitality of the Moldavians. When we were seated at tables in the colonnaded dining room, a television set was wheeled in and we were shown a news story of our stay in the republic. Seven courses followed, countless toasts were drunk and a string of speeches made by the hosts and the diplomats.

The next morning, we flew back to Moscow in the aircraft that had brought us to Kishinev; a VIP-version of the Ilyushin-16, it had remained on the tarmac waiting for us. I sat with one of the interpreters on the trip, Oleg Krokholev from the Bureau of Translations of the Foreign Ministry, and chatted about Alan Moorehead's *Blue Nile* that I was reading. Later, when I finished the book, I sent it to him in Moscow.

Four weeks later, on 21 November, Wynne and I left on our visit to Tallinn on the bay of that name on the Gulf of Finland. The "Town of the Danes", known in the past in the West as Reval, had a population of about 300,000 in 1964. As we travelled by air to and from Leningrad and by rail the rest of the way, we had the bonus of almost two days in that great city, St. Petersburg, the former capital of Russia. At Sheremetyevo Airport, we waited with the other passengers, all Russians and keenly interested in our Canadian winter coats, hats and boots. Boarding for the one-hour flight to Leningrad, we carried our baggage to the TU-104 where it was checked in on the tarmac alongside the plane on this snowy cold day. At Leningrad, we were received royally by an Intourist agent at the foot of the steps and taken to the terminal as the only passengers of a bus. From there a ZIM limousine swept us to the Astoria Hotel where we were given a suite for our brief stay.

The best hotel of pre-revolutionary St. Petersburg, the Astoria retained that standing in 1964 and was indeed considered the best in the entire Soviet Union, its Victorian trappings dowdier but still resplendent. Our suite was located on the second floor above the corner of the street nearest to St. Isaac's Cathedral. The suite was full of baroque furniture and there was an adjoining study with old leather chairs and a high bench. Still, it was warm and the bathroom was monumentally equipped.

We ate that evening in the cold dining-room, an orchestra playing American hits of the 1940s and 1950s. An Intourist car took us afterwards to the railway station where we boarded the night train to Tallinn, a milk-run that left at 11:22 p.m. and took eight-and-a-half hours and many stops on the 360 km to the Estonian capital. There we were again met and driven to the Intourist Hotel, a small modern building situated below the old city walls.

After breakfast, we set out on a walk about the old town, skirting the moat along Sustern Street to enter the lower town where we were drawn to the Church of the Holy Ghost by the sound of an organ and the singing of a hymn. We entered this 14th-century Lutheran church to join the large congregation in their Sunday morning service and to admire a wooden clock carved by Christian Ackerman in 1684.

Pikh Jag — Long Street — took us to the Town Hall, a magnificent Gothic structure built from 1371 to 1404 on the Market Square, for centuries the heart of life in the lower town and long the only medieval city hall extant in the Baltic States. A beautiful spire crowned the building: the vane at its top depicted an ancient warrior of the town and was known as "Old Thomas". From the Square, we walked up the steep *Pikh Jalg* or Long Leg, the old lane that, until the 17th century, was the only one connecting the lower to the upper town called *Toompea* or Dome Hill. A service was in progress in the onion-domed Orthodox Cathedral of Alexander Nevsky but the 13th-century Lutheran Cathedral, the Gothic *Toomkirk* or *Domkirk*, was not "working" that day.

We walked past the pink-stuccoed government building, once the Palace of Russian Governors, to an observation point off a courtyard at No. 12 Kohtu Lane. From here we had a superb view of more than 30 hectares of high-gabled, red-tiled houses of medieval Tallinn, towers and steeples rising above them, the *Pikh Jalg* leading down below us to the Town Hall and beyond to the Old Market, the *Vanaturg*, and to the sea. I took several photographs of the town and nearby port, without inhibition for we were in the company of a group of visiting foreign Communists who were also rapt by the panorama and busy with their cameras.

We descended to Victory Square to visit the *Oleviste* or St. Olaf's Church, one of the oldest and largest churches in the Baltic republics with a tower almost 150 metres high that provided a landmark anywhere in the town. A congregation of many hundreds was at worship. We returned to the hotel for lunch, passing the *Strandpforte* — the Coast Gate — with its massive medieval tower called *Dicke Margarete* or Thick Margaret, and another working church where a funeral service was in progress. We had now seen enough of this wonderfully preserved medieval city of the Hanseatic League to whet our appetite, and regret that we had given it only a day.

In the afternoon, we walked back to Victory Square and took a taxi to Pirita, a couple of kilometres east of the city, to visit the ruins of the

Cloister of the St. Bridget's Nunnery, built from 1407 to 1436 and destroyed by the Russians in 1571 during the Livonian War. A Russian girl posed for her boyfriend in the graveyard, arms outstretched in crucfix form in front of the cross of a tombstone. On the way back to Tallinn, we stopped at Kadriorg Park on the Pirata Beach to visit the enormous concrete open air bowl. Created for the Tallinn Song Festival four years earlier, it seated an audience of more than 100,000 before a stage on which 30,000 singers could perform. Nearby we saw the *Rusalka* (Mermaid) Monument — a memorial surmounted by a bronze angel to a Russian man-of-war that had foundered in 1893 off the coast in the Gulf of Finland — and the small seaside château built by Peter the Great in 1713 for his wife Catherine.

The sun set early that afternoon and we rested before going to dinner at the Kevad Restaurant, a very large place with a dance-floor and orchestra, located on Lomonosov Street in the modern downtown area. The manager recognized us as foreigners and tried to seat us in a corner near the entrance door, but I pointed out to him that there was a nice table near the orchestra and, with reluctance, he led us there. When we told the waitress that we did not speak Russian, she brought a young man from the next table to translate. A Lithuanian, he stayed and talked, informing us that he had a brother in Detroit and relatives in Kitchener, Ontario. Things were not all that good in Tallinn, he remarked, and he wished he could go back to Lithuania.

An older man joined us. Estonian and a tailor, he had apprenticed in his trade in Paris from 1929 to 1931. He fingered the material of my inexpensive sports jacket and pronounced it far better than the cloth available in the Soviet Union. He danced with Wynne as did the Lithuanian. Two young couples at a nearby table sent us a bottle of champagne and told us how happy they were to chat with Canadians. A couple of vodkas on, the older man expressed his dissatisfaction with the Russians, who accounted for almost half the population of Tallinn, saying that Estonia could do without them. He became worried that he had said too much and I could see that the manager and some others in the place were becoming interested in us in a less than friendly way. But the Estonians near us had proved their spirit of independence to us. They told us that their nationalism was helped not only by memories of Russian domination, but by the fact that their language, a branch of the Finno-Ugric family, was close enough to Finnish to enable them to listen to Western news from Helsinki, only 90 km across the Gulf.

We left at 10:30 o'clock to return to the hotel and rest; giddy from the champagne, Wynne remarked, "What I do for Queen and Country!" At midnight, we were on the train to return to Leningrad and, this time, I did not count the stations during the eight-hour journey.

It was cold when we arrived back in Leningrad and ice was forming over the Neva River. At the Astoria, we resumed our occupancy of the corner suite, the one that most diplomats were given on their stays at the hotel because, so we all believed, it was the best-bugged accommodation there. We were well-tailed when we walked over to St. Isaac's Cathedral — in 1964, a museum rather than a "working church" — to admire the malachite and lapis lazuli columns in the iconostasis. After lunch, we went to the Hermitage for a conducted tour of the Gold Room by a female student who, pleasingly, kept propaganda out of her descriptions of the fabulous archaeological treasures found in the burial mounds of the Scythians. Snow fell that evening when we went to the Kavkazsky Restaurant on Nevsky Prospekt for Georgian food and music. And, next morning, we returned to Nevsky Prospekt to walk past drab shops and older monuments like the Stroganov Palace and the Cathedral of Our Lady of Kazan, built at the beginning of the 19th century and approached by a semi-circular colonnade of 136 Corinthian columns, modelled on that of St. Peter's in the Vatican.

Our baggage had already been brought down to the reception area when we returned to the Astoria to prepare for the trip back to Moscow. Intourist took us to the airport where we were met and seated in an empty wing of the restaurant, away from the Soviet travellers and with no view of the tarmac, until we boarded our TU-104 flight and took off for the flight to Moscow. Winter had arrived there during our brief absence. On Saturday, the Moscow Canal was flowing; on Monday it was frozen solid and the fishermen had already drilled holes through the ice and placed their heated huts over the holes.

A two-day visit to Vilnius in Lithuania followed in mid-December. Travelling with me were Rudolf von Wistinghausen, a First Secretary at the Embassy of the German Federal Republic, and Maldwyn Thomas, the recently-arrived Commercial Secretary of the Canadian Embassy. We went to Vilnius by rail, a journey of 800 km by way of Smolensk and Minsk. The train was bound for Kaliningrad, on the coast 280 km farther on in the former East Prussia, of great strategic importance since 1945 as the most southerly region of the USSR on the Baltic Sea.

We left in the early evening of the 14th from the Bielorussian Railway Station in Moscow, settling into our compartment for the overnight journey. A Soviet railway official bound for Smolensk occupied the fourth berth of the compartment. Though he spent most of the evening in the corridor, he talked to us before he left the train after midnight. He had lived most of his life in Siberia and had none of the Moscovites inhibitions about talking to foreigners. One of his experiences on the Siberian railway had concerned the 1942 removal of Chinese from Khabarovsk, Irkutsk and other cities east of Lake Baikal to places in Kazakhistan to the west. This had been necessary, he said, because the Russians could not trust their troops to tell Soviet Orientals from Japanese invaders if a hot war had developed on the Pacific coast. When our railwayman friend left at Smolensk, his place was occupied by a Soviet Air Force officer who promptly took to bed, an action that persuaded us also that the night was no longer young.

The train pulled in to Vilnius at 8:14 a.m. We were met by an Intourist guide who took us the Intourist Hotel, once the George (*Georgiyevski*), on the prospekt of that name that led to Gedimnas Square which was the heart of the ancient city. We breakfasted and, in mid-morning, set out on a walking tour of the old town with our guide. A Lithuanian, he was proud of his city's heritage and not at all reluctant to show us working churches. I could not help recalling that on the official Foreign Ministry tour of Moldavia, no opportunity had been given to the foreign diplomats to see any church, let alone a working church.

Our first stop was at Gedimnas Square, named — like the castle above it — after the legendary founder of the city, the prince of Lithuania who ruled in the early 14th century. There we visited St. Stanislaus, the erstwhile Roman Catholic Cathedral built in the form of a Greek temple which was now employed by the Soviet regime as a picture gallery. The Cathedral had been founded in 1387 on the site of a sanctuary of Perkunas, a pagan god of light, whose name, our guide told us, is often invoked by modern Lithuanians. We descended to the vault which holds the bones of Polish kings and queens.

The tall, pointed belfry in the cathedral grounds, a free-standing structure, was built from the stone of the lower castle which was once situated on the other side of the nearby town hall square. Not far from the belfry, we visited St. Peter and St. Paul. A 17th century Catholic Church with an impressive baroque interior of white stone and the tomb of St. Casimir, it was designed by Italian architects who were responsible for much of the architecture of Vilnius.

Beyond Pushkin Park, we entered Gorky Street, once Great Castle Street, near a striking high-eaved house. We turned off down a narrow lane; the walls of its old buildings covered with Stars of David and swastikas proving that Vilnius had not forgotten the past when its population was Lithuanian, Polish and Jewish living uneasily together in approximately equal proportions. The lane brought us to the complex of old buildings and beautiful squares of the university which, founded in 1579, was the oldest in the Soviet Union. At this institution of 11,000 students, we were told, all instruction was in Lithuanian. We continued along Gorky Street to the most renowned place in the city, the *Medininkai* or Austos Gate, over the arch of which is located a famous shrine to the Black Madonna of Vilnius, the chapel known in Lithuanian as the *Ostruiya Vorota* and in Polish, the *Ostro Brama*. Many women were praying at the shrine and men removed their hats as they passed by in the lane.

Lenin Prospekt took us back down to Gedimas Square and our hotel; once called the *Bolshaya*, the street paralleled the River Neris. There was much evidence in the walls of buildings of post-revolutionary name changes, while bullet and cannon holes in the masonry reminded us that medieval Vilnius had not totally escaped the ravages of the Second World War. That was only the latest of the centuries of conflict that had swirled through the city. Napoleon had been here in 1812 on his way to Moscow and had said of St. Anne's — a 16th-century brick Gothic church still in use — that he would like to take it back to Paris. He had occupied the old palace of the Catholic Archbishop of Vilnius in Kutuzov Square, so-named afterwards for the Russian general who retook the city when the French retreated later in the campaign.

On our last morning, our guide showed us something of modern Vilnius. The numerous apartment blocks along Antakalnio Street seemed much more attractive than their Moscow counterparts because of the better use of exterior colour and landscaping; it helped, too, that they were set against a pine-covered hillside. On our way to another area of apartments in the western part of the city, we passed an industrial zone with a large machine tool plant and building materials factories. This brought us to the outdoor "song theatre", a twin of that in Tallinn.

We had gone out on our only evening in Vilnius to a modern dinner-and-dance restaurant but our KGB tails ensured that we had little contact with the locals. Maldwyn Thomas made a couple of friends by dancing with some young unescorted women. He had to forsake them after the goons took one of the girls aside and talked threateningly to her. We were joined at our table by a man in his twenties, very civilized in appearance, who described himself as a student of economics. He insisted on paying our dinner bill with a 50-rouble note; because a note of that denomination was then seldom seen in the hands of ordinary Soviet citizens, we suspected that our benefactor was a practitioner, rather than a student, of economics — if he was not a KGB agent.

Our most pleasant contact in Vilnius was with the 77-year-old manager of the restaurant at the Intourist Hotel who sat with us at our table during both of the lunches we had there. A remarkable man of distinguished appearance despite his threadbare formal clothes, he spoke excellent English and six other languages. An officer in the Imperial Army in the First World War, he had been captured by the Germans in 1917 and placed in a prisoner-of-war camp with other Allied officers, including a Canadian who had taught him English. At lunch on our second day, he produced a photograph of a group of officers in the POW camp and pointed out the Canadian, whose name was Andrews, and himself. His conversation was mostly of the past when his life had been "different", but he did not hide his disapproval of what was going on in modern Russia.

We travelled back to Moscow by air. Bad weather had prevented the scheduled TU-104 from landing and we had to travel in an Antonov-14, a turbo-prop that was the uncomfortable short-haul workhorse of Aeroflot. We bounced around for over two hours that evening on the way to Sheremetyevo Airport and home.

In April 1965, Wynne and I decided to visit Georgia and Armenia in the Caucasus for the Easter weekend; our daughter Jane, who had come back to Moscow with us from England a month earlier, accompanied us. Tbilisi, the Georgian capital, was the first objective and we intended to fly on from there to Yerevan in Armenia. Weather prevented us from carrying out the second part of this plan.

Early in the afternoon of Thursday, 15 April, we left Moscow's Vnukovo I Airport on a three-and-a-quarter-hour, 1800-kilometre flight in what I now knew as the long-distance mainstay of Aeroflot, a TU-104. The security authorities had taken no chances with us for we were seated in Row 4 of the aircraft, the row without a window, and saw nothing of the Russian countryside all the way to Georgia. Our fellow passengers included many dark-skinned Georgians and the luggage racks were crowded with newspaper-wrapped parcels and bags of oranges which, we deduced, could not be bought in Tbilisi.

The plane let down at Tbilisi through heavy cloud. Disembarkation was delayed for 10 minutes because steps were not available. We were met by Intourist and were soon at the Tbilisi Hotel, once named the Palace, at 13 Rustaveli (formerly *Golovinski*) Prospekt. On checking into a three-bedded room with bath, we realized that prices could have barely changed since the hotel was built in the grand manner in 1912: the charge for the three of us for three days was only 12 roubles, less than $15. However, standards had declined since the Revolution. The bathroom was a comedy of communist inefficiency: towels torn; the tub installed the wrong way around; an ornate gilt lamp over the sink concealing half of the mirror; a smart new Czech-made sink supported by a makeshift bracket contrived from metal water pipes; two "hot" and no "cold" taps — and no plug in the sink.

We went out to eat in the Daryal Restaurant which was located below street level on Rustaveli Prospekt. The meal was disappointing though there was plenty of *shaslik* and mountains of unleavened Georgian bread as well as cheap good wine to wash it down. Informality was the mark of the grubby-looking, unshaved waiters. One used Wynne's dinner knife to open the wine and sampled the *shaslik* served to three young Georgians seated next to us. When we returned to the hotel, the streets were swarming with younger men, dark mustached types who gave Wynne and Jane the eye. We agreed that the place had atmosphere.

In 1964 a city of 800,000, Tbilisi stretched a dozen kilometres along the banks of the swift-flowing Kura River and in the hills on either side. The houses of the old town were most attractive, particularly those with iron-grilled balconies perched high up on the cliffs above the Kura River gorge and the Metekh Bridge. On our first morning we walked along sycamore-lined Rustaveli Prospekt — a boulevard reminiscent of Paris — to Lenin Square and then to the sixth-century Sioni (Zion) Cathedral where a Lenten service was in progress. On the other side of the Kura, narrowed to a gorge barely 30 metres at this point, soldiers were rehearsing for the May Day parade. .A bystander pointed to my camera, said something in Georgian and clapped his hands. As he did not follow us, I assumed that he was warning me of the presence of troops. Sure enough, around the corner were six armoured personnel carriers.

We took a taxi up the winding road to the top of *Mtatsminda* (David's Mountain) to admire the spectacular views of the wild countryside around Tbilisi. To the south-east towards the Kura was the ancient Persian fortress called Narykala, dominating the area where the bazaars once stood and the old bridges to the Metekhi quarter across the river. I took a number of photographs from the funicular station near the ruins of St. David's Convent, and we then returned to Lenin Square to lunch on apple-filled doughnuts in a *gastronom*, the Soviet answer to New York's automats.

In the afternoon, we visited the State Historical Museum which had most interesting exhibits of the stone and bronze ages in Georgia, a presentation representing the Georgian renaissance of the 11th century and a room of revolutionary souvenirs that included photographs of kilted Scots of the British force that occupied Georgia in 1919.

We hired an Intourist car with a guide who introduced himself as Tonika Kvirikvshvili and mercifully allowed us to call him "Tony". In the newer areas of the city, we saw numerous institutes, parks and sports stadia, all of which evinced expressions of nationalism from our guide. Tony was especially pleased to tell us how proud Georgians were that their football team had beaten the Moscow team and that their basketballers were the European champions. We noticed that verandahs had been added to the standard Soviet apartment buildings, an ornamentation that was at once a concession to local custom and a great improvement to their appearance. Sadly, however, the quality of workmanship was as shoddy as in Moscow. A striking difference from the Soviet capital was to see men, not women, at work sweeping the streets; this suggested that the male-female ratio was more normal in Georgia — or that full employment did not exist.

At dinner in the pillared dining room of the Tbilisi Hotel, we were joined by two Embassy wives, Anne Madsen and Barbara Brockly, who had flown down from Moscow for the weekend. The room was crowded but most of the diners were Georgian men who were obviously curious why I had four women with me. Two officers of the Netherlands Embassy were at a nearby table to add a cosmopolitan touch to the clientele. We had Chicken *Tabaka* (for tabasco sauce) and a veal stew called *Soljanka* and washed it down with an excellent Georgian red wine named Tsollikaori Number Seven. The orchestra played all evening but only one song at a time, resting between each number. The music was a mixture: oriental, waltz, foxtrot and "beat". We enjoyed the evening and thanked the staff with ceremony for their efforts. The pleasure of the headwaiter on being given a tip was distinctly un-Socialist.

On Saturday the 17th, we left with Tony the guide in an Intourist car for a memorable 130-kilometre drive up the Georgian Military Road, a spectacular mountain highway built by the Russians during the first half of the 19th century to consolidate their hold on the Caucasus against the Ottoman Empire. The highway connected Tbilisi with Ordzhonikidze — the capital of the North Ossetian Autonomous Region of the Russian Republic — about 210 km north along the winding, spiralling road, by steep gorges, rushing rivers and wooded foothills to a pass at 2500 metres through the Caucasus Mountains. Baedeker had called the road one of the most beautiful mountain roads in the world; but we could not tell whether his description was apt because low clouds covered the tops of the foothills that Saturday and heavy rain kept us in the car more than we would have liked. Yet, despite the weather and though we travelled only as far as Ananouri, 68 km from Tbilisi, and spent less than five hours on the road, we looked on an astounding panorama of more than two thousand years of Georgian history.

Just 13 km from Tbilisi, where the valley of the Kura River closes in, we came to the sixth-century monastery of Dzhvari with a remarkably well-preserved church on the top of a high hill commanding the town of Mtskheta, eight kilometres farther north. The church had been damaged only once in its history: in the 10th century when it was set on fire by Arab invaders. Arriving at Mtskheta, near the confluence of the Kura and Aragvi, there was a view of the bridge of Pompey which dated back to 55 B.C.

Though little more than a village today, Mtskheta is one of the oldest continuously-occupied towns in the world. The ancient capital of Iberia, as Georgia was once called, it was the centre of a highly developed culture from the third century B.C. whose inhabitants had trade and military connections with Greece, Persia, Parthia and Rome. Christianity was brought to Mtskheta, according to legend, by Nina of Capadocia, the daughter of a Roman general stationed in Jerusalem, who came to Georgia in 314 A.D. in search of Christ's robe, converted King Mirian and performed miracles which led to her canonization. King Mirian built a church, the first of many that were to stand on the spot where a miraculous cedar tree associated with the robe had grown, and where the present-day *Sveti Tskhoveli* (Twelve Apostles) Cathedral was erected in the 15th century. Still "working", the Cathedral was the burial place of Georgian kings and the princely family of Bagrationi, one of whom had fought with the Russian Army against Napoleon at Borodino in 1812. There was an icon to the famous Queen Tamara of Georgia and a holy water shrine where by tradition the miraculous tree had stood. Carved on the facade of the Cathedral were reliefs, some in red stone: mythical birds, lions, bunches of grapes, two pigeons drinking from a cup. Over an arch, the right hand of the architect was depicted holding a set square; his name, Arsudkidze, was inscribed there.

From the Cathedral, we went to the Samtovro Convent where there were now only 10 nuns, replacements having been denied by the Soviet state. King Mirian and St. Nina were buried there. Built in early Georgian style in the 11th century, the church of the convent was named after St. Nina. Elsewhere in the grounds was a very old chapel said to have been built on the site of the hut where the saint had lived when she first came to Mtskheta. High above the town were the ruins of a Persian fortress.

We continued on towards Ananouri passing the spectacular battlement-like cliffs, their sides pocked with ancient caves, between Tzulkani and Dushet. Then we came to the Aragvi Valley and stopped where the broad gravel-bottomed river ran through fields of violets, primroses and cowslips. Tony, our guide, picked a bouquet for my wife. Shepherds watched flocks of sheep on the hillsides above the fields and pigs wandered unattended. In Ananouri, we visited the 16th-century fortress with its three churches and then, after these hours of immersion in the fascinating past of Georgia and splendid scenery of the Military Road, we returned to Tbilisi.

That evening, we went to the Paliashvili Opera House on Rustaveli Prospekt for a performance of a new Georgian opera by Sh. Mshvelidzye with, appropriately, a theme relating to the day's drive to Mkstheta. Entitled "The Arm of the Great Master", it told the story of the architect of the Sveti-Tskhoveli Cathedral using the allegory of the miraculous cedar. The architect loses his arm in a rebellion against the king but later, when the city is destroyed by an earthquake, only the church is left standing. Like the plot, the music and staging was deeply religious and the performance of the cast of 70 was impressive.

There were other manifestations of religion that weekend, Easter Sunday for us but Palm Sunday for the Russian and Armenian Orthodox Churches. On Saturday afternoon, we had stopped at the Kvashvetskaya Church in Rustaveli Prospekt to watch the service. Many of the congregation were young people and when they left, they carried laurel branches into the streets, an affirmation which would have led to retaliation from the goons in Moscow. Next morning, we visited three other churches where Palm Sunday services were in progress. At the Sioni Cathedral, the Metropolitan conducting the Armenian service looked like a bearded Mikoyan, the Soviet president who was also Armenian. The symbolism of the crossed candles and the Metropolitan's conductor-like gestures with his hands were beyond my understanding, but we were impressed by the singing and the devotion of the congregation. I noted that all three churches were full and the congregations represented a full range of ages and sexes.

Because very heavy rain discouraged us from sightseeing and our plane for Yerevan was several hours late, we decided to forego that leg of the Caucasian trip and return to Moscow. We left Tbilisi in the late afternoon and were rewarded by being given seats with a view on the TU-104. And, away from the rain clouds, what views we had: the peaks of the Caucasus

Range sparkling from new snow, the Russian steppes with the straight strips of houses along the edges of collective farms, the semi-circular patterns of the streets of a new town and, as we neared Moscow's Vnukovo Airport, a surface-to-air missile site. Our descent was a rare, long glide and the landing was the smoothest I had ever experienced in a Soviet aircraft. The taxi ride home was somewhat less comforting because the driver was drunk, but we were glad to be back in the sunshine of Moscow.

The final two months of my Moscow posting were dominated by the imminent assignment to Leopoldville and educational and other arrangements for Jane and Tricia. Wynne and I were due to take a train from Moscow to Vienna at the beginning of September where we would have a holiday after enrolling Jane at the American International School in Vienna and seeing Tricia off to England, where she was to begin her second year at Ellerslie School in Malvern. On 31 August, the day before we were to leave, my sister Win phoned from Lubeck in West Germany to tell me that her husband, Gordon MacKenzie, had died there an hour earlier; they had been on their way to Paris for a year at the Sorbonne, Gordon on sabbatical leave from the Royal Roads Military College in Victoria. She wanted me to come to help her. I told her to phone the Canadian Consulate General in Hamburg and shortly afterwards, when I called Consul General Roy Blake, I learned that he and his office were already doing everything that had to be done.

I left for Germany at noon on the 1st of September and Wynne and the girls entrained that evening for Vienna where I joined them on the 4th after seeing my sister off to Vancouver. Jane entered her boarding *Heim* near the school that day while Wynne and I went to Semmering for a few days with Tricia before she flew to England on the 17th. The next day, we said farewell to Jane and began the return journey to Moscow by train.

Wynne and the girls had experienced the journey already on their way to Vienna but for me this was a first. The train left Vienna at 10 in the evening and we were ensconced in a narrow two-bunked compartment in which we had to let down a third, upper bunk to accommodate our luggage. Except for us, all in the coach were Russians. After an hour, we reached Hohenau on the Austro-Czech border where we waited for 15 minutes, eventually moving across the border with the doors of the coaches locked. The exterior of the train was searched meticulously by armed Czech soldiers and we looked back to the frontier delineated by the double fence of barbed wire that marked the start of the Iron Curtain.

Shortly after midnight, we trundled into Breclav — *Breslau* in other times — and were visited by two two-man teams of immigration and customs officers, the second of which did not bother with the Russians on board but only with us. At one in the morning, we were on our way again, having travelled about 50 km in three hours. Another three and a half hours on, we had crossed Czechoslovakia. At the Czech-Polish border, we were checked out by two teams of Czechs and checked into Poland by two teams of Poles. It was impossible to avoid the conclusion that suspicion within the Curtain was as great as it was deep inside the Soviet Empire.

Yet, when we arrived at the small international station at Warsaw, at 11:15 in the morning, and were permitted to descend to the platform, we were astonished to see that *The New York Times* was on sale and a tag-day was in full swing. We wondered why charities were allowed in a workers' paradise. As we pulled away from Warsaw, we had a glimpse of the rebuilt old city, and gained some impression of the awesome destruction of the Second World War.

Five hours later, we were across the Polish-Soviet border at Brest-Litovsk where a procession of Soviet officials vetted us. Ninety minutes were spent at this historic border crossing while the carriages were lifted from their narrow-gauge bogies on to wheels for the wide Russian tracks. We mingled with the Russians on the platform, who looked unhappy at their return to the Soviet Union. The onward journey to Moscow was made comfortable by the broad track and we awoke only shortly before arriving, just after 10 in the morning, at the Bielorussia Station in the grey and cold capital. I wrote that evening in my diary: "Moscow is so dull and depressing after Vienna". The journey had been one of the most impressionable of our travels in eastern Europe.

Wynne left Moscow on 22 October on an Austrian Airlines flight. In my last week in Moscow, I met the new British Ambassador, Sir Geoffrey Harrison (who was to distinguish himself by having an affair with a Russian upstairs maid at his residence), dealt with a minor security matter at our own embassy, completed the packing for the Congo — and gave a party on the eve of my departure that emptied my wine cellar and liquor cabinet. Early on the morning of Friday, 29 October 1965, my Moscow days ended as I flew in an Austrian Airlines Caravelle to Vienna to visit Jane, proceeding to London the next morning to rejoin Wynne and Tricia and spend 10 days in England preparing for the journey south to Africa and the posting to the Congo.

CHAPTER 8

LEOPOLDVILLE:
THE FIRST SIX WEEKS

The Democratic Republic of the Congo, later to be known as Zaire, had never occurred to me as a possible posting in the foreign service. My mind was soon made up. Although we had been in Moscow for just over a year, its allure had already dissipated and there was a definite attraction in having my own post. Canada had maintained a trade commissioner in Leopoldville for a dozen years before the Congo's independence, but the chaos that ensued soon forced the closing of the office.[59] Our involvement in the UN peacekeeping operation that followed led to the establishment of a diplomatic post in 1962 headed by a chargé d'affaires. I took pride in the knowledge that I would be the post's first Canadian ambassador and only the second in a sub-Saharan francophone country. My Ambassador in Moscow, Robert Ford, who was in Ottawa for the summer, wrote:

> As you can imagine, I was in a dilemma over the question of your posting. I was not particularly keen on the idea of your moving after such a short time in Moscow but I did not want to stand in the way of your getting a more important job. You were considered for Saigon but in the end this was dropped, and I think the Congo assignment will be considerably less trying on the nerves and on the health than the Vietnamese post.

He added that the target date was mid-October.[60]

My wife and I were soon busy with preparations for the move: brushing up on our French, ordering food and other supplies, and making plans for Jane, our elder daughter, to attend the American International School in Vienna. (Early on we had decided that the younger, Tricia, should continue to attend Ellerslie School in Malvern, England.) Cabinet approval for the Congo appointment came at the end of August and the agreement of the Congolese was requested in Leopoldville a few days later. Douglas Hamlin, the Third Secretary — indeed the only foreign service officer in Leopoldville — supplied us with many helpful hints on living and working conditions. We read everything about the place in our files and at friendly embassies, but that left much unanswered and unknown.

The third largest country in Africa, the Democratic Republic of the Congo had been established only five years earlier, on 30 June 1960, when Belgium gave up control of its major and richest overseas possession to an indigenous population that was almost totally unprepared for self-government, let alone for independence. Since that time, the Congo had been a synonym for bloodshed, instability, assassinations, civil war and secession.

Almost delineated by the basin of the Congo River, the country occupied the heart of Africa, bordering on Angola, Congo (Brazzaville), Central African Republic, Sudan, Uganda, Tanzania, Rwanda, Burundi and Zambia. The eastern fringes of the modern Congo had been known over a millennium ago to the ancient peoples of Khami in the south-east and to the Arabs of Sofala on the Indian Ocean coast of the continent. European awareness of the region came in the 1500s when the Portuguese explored the Atlantic coast, established themselves on the banks of the vast Congo River and tried to penetrate into the interior. For three centuries more, however, the Congo Basin remained unknown to the West. It was still the heart of darkness when the Welsh adventurer-turned-American-journalist and explorer, Henry Morton Stanley, thrust his way ruthlessly across Africa from east to west in the years 1874 to 1877, following the Congo River from Lake Tanganyika to the Atlantic. A year later, he entered into the service of Leopold II of Belgium to administer, in the same remorseless spirit in which he explored, what was to become the Congo Free State. In 1884, he drew its boundaries and Leopold obtained the approval of other European powers for his African acquisition, 80 times larger than his European kingdom.

The Free State became the Belgian Congo in 1908. By that time, the infrastructure of colonial government was in place, a network of railways and riverboat transportion had been established and the mineral wealth of the Katanga and the diamonds of the Kasai were being developed. A third of a century later, the Congo was so rich that it was able to launch Belgium swiftly from occupation during the Second World War to recovery well ahead of other European countries. On the eve of independence, the enormous wealth of the mineral deposits together with the agricultural possibilities of the land and the energy potential of the rivers constituted an immense dowry for the new African republic. But there was no heritage of political experience among the Congolese. No educated class existed to take the place of the white administrators and technicians. In the police and military, no black commissioned officers were available to take charge of the country's security. Industry was totally dependent on white leadership.

The political awakening of the Congo was late. Only in 1959 was there a serious campaign for independence and it was confused and incoherent. Neither Patrice Lumumba, the leader of the leftist Congolese National Movement (MNC), nor the more moderate Joseph Kasavubu, head of the Bakonga Alliance (ABAKO), spoke to each other about tactics though both wanted independence. It was only the collapse of Belgian will to hold its only colony in the face of United Nations denunciation and the tide of anti-colonialism that led to the abdication of power, on 30 July 1960, when the totally unprepared Congo became a sovereign state.

The first team of Kasavubu as President and Lumumba as Prime Minister enjoyed a fragile stability for barely a half dozen days until it was shattered by mutiny within the army — the *Armée Nationale du Congo* (ANC) — which threw out its European officers and was at a stroke completely Africanized. Most of the Belgian administrators, military officers and technicians rushed to get out of the country, abandoning their cars at the airports and often selling their houses for a fraction of their cost to Lebanese and Cypriot businessmen whose money-sense steadied their nerves. A few days later, the immensely rich Katanga seceded under the leadership of Moise Tshombé and with the support of Belgium. Separatist regimes also cropped up in the Orientale province and in Sud-Kasai.

For the ill-trained hands that had assumed power, the country proved to be a huge ungovernable shell. With the economy in tatters, even the central authority came apart. The United Nations intervened with its largest peacekeeping force ever up to that time — ONUC — with 20,000 troops at its peak but with a mandate that lacked teeth. Canada contributed from the outset with a sizeable communications unit whose bilingual capability facilitated contact between the UN Force, which worked mainly in English, and the Congolese government and army, which employed French. What the United Nations was able to achieve in its first year was to save the country from total disaster by restoring some semblance of social and political machinery and combating famine and disease.

The Congo was now an arena of conflict that was multi-sided and confused. The big game of international politics was played alongside the battle of contending multinational economic corporations. The West sought to counter the East. The Belgians tried to fend off the Americans.

The French schemed against the rest and the British waited for opportunities to come their way when the others fought themselves to a standstill. Throughout, Congolese vied against Congolese and played the foreign interests against each other.

In September 1960, Prime Minister Lumumba, who had thrown away whatever sympathy he had had at home and abroad,[61] was dismissed by President Kasavubu and in turn dismissed Kasavubu. Colonel Joseph Mobutu — the ANC Chief of Staff and probably already the chosen instrument of the U.S. Central Intelligence Agency to bring stability to the country and a regime favourable to the United States — took over the government in October, imprisoning Lumumba and expelling the Soviet and other Communist-bloc embassies. Lumumba attempted to escape, was recaptured and died in February 1961 in circumstances that were seen later to implicate Mobutu. That same month, Lumumba's former deputy Prime Minister, Antoine Gizenga proclaimed himself the head of the legitimate government and set up his administration in Stanleyville. Frustrated, Mobutu ended his dictatorship and handed power back to Kasavubu. Through the efforts of the UN, the Congolese parliament was recalled in September 1961 and a government of national unity created under Cyrille Adoula who had been a co-founder of the MNC.

The Adoula government was to endure for three years during which reconciliation was effected with the Kalonjists and the Gizenga group and growing pressure was applied on the breakaway Katanga. ONUC made little headway against Tshombé's mercenary-led army until authorized to engage in outright war; it was the first and last time until the end of the century that a UN peacekeeping force was allowed to fight. The UN Secretary-General devised a plan for the reintegration of Katanga, and Tshombé and the central government at last reached agreement in January 1963 to end the province's secession.

ONUC remained in the Congo until 30 June 1964; it left in the midst of another military threat to the Congo, pulling out because it had bankrupted the world organization. The new threat was a revival of the old Gizengist regime which had fled from Stanleyville in 1963 and gone to Brazzaville in the neighbouring Congo whose president, Massamba-Débat, connived at East Bloc training and arming of the exiles. In Brazzaville, a National Liberation Council was set up to direct the rebellion which, by mid-1964, extended over much of the eastern and northern region of the Congo. This clear danger to the existence of the central government, coinciding with the withdrawal of ONUC, led the United States to intervene vigorously through its diplomats in Leopoldville.[62]

Mobutu, now commander-in-chief of the ANC, was persuaded to accept Tshombé, the erstwhile Katanga secessionist, as Prime Minister and to hire Colonel Mike Hoare, Tshombé's legendary mercenary commander, to assemble a force of 1000 soldiers of fortune to fight the rebels. But Tshombé's accession to power was not to be the end of the drama.

Stronger measures became necessary when the rebels occupied Stanleyville on 5 August and fanned out from there to control two-fifths of the country by the end of that month. In early September, Christophe Gbenye, the head of the CNL in Brazzaville, arrived in Stanleyville and proclaimed himself president of "The People's Republic of the Congo". The mercenary columns of Mike Hoare began to roll back the rebels in the east and on 24 November, Belgian troops parachuted from United States Air Force planes into Stanleyville and liberated it from the rebels.

The liberation of Stanleyville and the rescue operation that followed did not solve the country's problems. The task of mopping up rebel-held pockets was to occupy the ANC and the mercenary columns for 20 months until the middle of 1966. Equally serious was the fact that extensive damage had been done to the large agricultural plantations on the eastern Congo. Moreover, the civil servants and technicians who had administered the infrastructure of the region had been eliminated by the rebels: almost half of the country was in chaos and beyond the control of the Tshombé government. The restoration of the bureaucracy and the resurrection of the economy was to take much longer than the elimination of the rebels.

Prime Minister Tshombé was in difficulty for other reasons. The legality of his government was questionable and his political opponents clamoured for the resumption of the parliamentary process which President Kasavubu had suspended in September 1963. Tshombé obliged by calling for elections in early 1965. While his party won convincingly, Tshombé was unable to hold together its disparate elements or to prevent the opposition parties from turning the country's political life into renewed confusion. Kasavubu began to worry that Tshombé might take the presidency from him in the election due in February 1966.[63]

On 13 October 1965, Kasavubu dismissed Tshombé and replaced him with Evariste Kimba who had been Tshombé's Foreign Minister in the Katangan regime. The change of government was not without benefit to me for, on 22 October, the Congolese gave their informal agreement to my appointment, seven weeks after it had been requested. Patience, I had been told, was the cardinal quality required of the diplomat in the Congo: the wait for the Congolese agreement gave me my first lesson in the virtue.

I had been counselled, too, never to be surprised by the unexpected: surprises galore in the first weeks brought home this truth to me.

The announcement of my new job was not made in Ottawa until two days after the Canadian general election of 8 November. Four days later, Wynne and I flew from Brussels by Sabena and arrived in Leopoldville shortly after dawn on 13 November, a Saturday.

We were met by Douglas Hamlin, the Second Secretary, and his wife Daphne and the other members of the small Canadian Embassy. With them were Kalamazi, the tall, courteous and, I was soon to learn, always helpful Chief of Protocol, and Ngambani, his assistant. Ngambani was familiar for he had been in Moscow with me where he was in charge of the Congolese Embassy when it was sacked by the Soviet-authorized mob protesting the Stanleyville rescue operation. Doug Hamlin had experienced some trouble in getting the two Congolese to the airport that morning to pay the appropriate respects to the new Canadian representative. He had given a lift to one of them after waiting for him to dress and shave. The VIP treatment cost us time: it was 40 minutes before we set out from the airport to the residence where we were then required to exchange pleasantries with the protocol officials over champagne. It was hard to say who was more tired when that was done — the Congolese or Wynne and me.

We had a rest after we had met the servants and inspected the house which had been rented some years before for the Canadian Trade Commissioners who had enjoyed the easy life of the colonial Congo. The residence was set amidst the palms, acacias, casuarinas and eucalyptus of Parc Selemba, an enclave of imposing villas in the Leo suburb of Kalina.

With memories of four years in southern Africa still fresh in our minds, there was much in our surroundings that seemed familiar. Verdant Africa and its smiling people, busy at the simple tasks of the daily routine; women walking elegantly erect, babies on their backs, balancing head-loads of firewood or water with swaying hips. The air was warmer and more humid than we had known on the worst of Ottawa summer days. It was also richer in human odours. Leopoldville, like most major African capitals, was a modern western city existing side by side with a black slum: the black inhabitants merged with the landscape while the whites stood out against the stone and stucco of their architecture. The city business district and some parts of the formerly all-white suburbs had lost their shine in the five years since independence. Grass had been worn away where it had once carpeted lawns and boulevards: it grew, instead, through cracks in the pavement and along the edges of buildings.

Congolese politics did not wait for me to settle in. Prime Minister Kimba failed to obtain a vote of confidence on 14 November because the supporters of Moise Tshombé still dominated the parliament. Kimba was reappointed the next day by President Kasavubu but observers saw no hope of political stability until the presidential elections had taken place. Speculation was intense as to what might happen in the interval. Tshombé, who was manoeuvering to obtain places for his supporters in the new Kimba cabinet, threatened Kasavubu with a real rebellion if he did not agree. The President found it expedient that week to promote Mobutu to the rank of Lieutenant-General and Mobutu demonstrated his power and popularity in the Army Day celebration on 17 November. That event gave me my first taste of the country's predilection for interminably long ceremonies.

Doug Hamlin filled me in on the mood of uncertainty and instability that prevailed and I encouraged him to prepare a report to External Affairs assessing the various outcomes that were possible and giving Ottawa a prediction as to what was most likely to happen. This he did and, in a telegram of 23 November — the first major analysis of the situation since my arrival — we forecast a take-over by General Mobutu.

That day I had my first meeting with President Kasavubu. It was completely unexpected. I was under the shower at 7:30 in the morning when the telephone rang and my wife came to tell me that someone who sounded like an important Congolese wanted to speak to me. I replied tersely that she could see that I was in no state to answer the phone and asked her to tell the caller to ring back. Wynne persuaded me, however, that if I was going to be a diplomat in the Congo, I should conform to what appeared to be a custom of the country. I splashed across the bedroom to the telephone, grunted "Brown", and heard a high-pitched male voice stating that he wished to speak to the Canadian Ambassador. I told him that it was the Ambassador speaking. "Non, he insisted, "je veux parler avec l'Ambassadeur *lui-meme*." "C'est l'Ambassadeur lui-meme qui parle," I replied. "Non," he reiterated, "c'est Son Excellence l'Ambassadeur avec lequel je veux parler." I gave up, replaced the phone on its cradle and dried myself. A few minutes later the phone rang again and the same voice, this time in a chastened tone, immediately recognized me as the Ambassador and identified himself as Kasavubu. For a moment I did not get his name and asked, "Kasa qui?" "Kasavubu," he replied, a little hurt, "Président de la République Democratique du Congo." I thought it prudent to sound more friendly in asking him what I could do for him. He said that he would like me to come to the Presidency as he had "un petit service" to request.

He wanted me immediately and we agreed that I would be there at eight o'clock. Fortunately my driver arrived on time and, full of anticipation of some portentous news, we raced up to the presidential palace on Mount Stanley, were waved through the gates by two completely uninterested soldiers and stopped under the portico. There was no doorkeeper and I walked into the entrance hall expecting to face a guard. A servant who was waxing the floor scuttled away and, a moment later, I was greeted by the President himself, in shirt-sleeves, and invited into his office.

Kasavubu told me that his son, Adolphe, who was on a Canadian External Aid scholarship at the University of Ottawa, had written that he was short of money. Could I, Kasavubu asked, send some by diplomatic bag. I readily agreed. Kasavubu opened the door of his desk and took out four $100 United States bills. I asked if he would like a receipt and, when he agreed that he would, scribbled one on a scratchpad. I told the President that I would send a telex to a friend of mine in Ottawa who would ensure that Adolphe received the money quickly.

Before leaving the President, I reminded him that I hoped to present my credentials to him soon. All would be arranged, he replied. At my office, I spent an amusing half-hour drafting a telegram to the Department asking them to look after Adolphe and adding that the job of Ambassador to the Congo seemed more varied than I had believed it would be.

A more formal meeting with President Kasavubu had been arranged for Thursday, 25 November, when I was to introduce myself to him in the traditional diplomatic way. A few hours after the currency transaction, however, the credentials ceremony was advanced to Wednesday, the 24th at 2:30. That afternoon, the Chief of Protocol came to the residence in the presidential Buick convertible with an escort of 16 motor cyclists of the presidential guard, dressed in baby-blue uniforms. Sirens sounding, we roared along the street to the Presidency only to wait in the car for 15 minutes while a blown fuse was replaced and lighting restored inside the palace. Entering the salon, I approached the waiting Congolese, bowed to Kasavubu who on this occasion was resplendent in a blue uniform matching that of his guard, a wide red sash supporting his sword. I read my speech in which I reviewed the development of Canadian-Congolese relations, recalled the participation of Canadian troops in the United Nations Force, referred to our common linguistic heritage and concluded with this extravagant flourish:

Permettez-moi, Votre Excellence, de vous dire combien je me sens honoré de présenter mes Lettres de Créance comme Ambassadeur du Canada a Léopoldville a Celui qui est entré dans l'Histoire Congolaise comme le Père de la Nation, et qui est resté son guide supreme dans la marche vers un avenir brillant.

Kasavubu replied in equally smarmy terms emphasizing that Canada was one of the few countries to have aided the Congo in a disinterested manner. During a brief conversation after I had handed over my letters, the anti-Belgian impact of this remark became clear when Kasavubu lectured me on the sins of the Belgians who, he insisted, wanted to regain control of the Congo. Photographs were taken in the garden, Kasavubu saw me to the door and the presidential guard played a fanfare. Thus installed as Canadian Ambassador, I was delivered in the Buick back to the residence where the Chief of Protocol drank champagne with Wynne, the staff and me and the 16-man motor cycle escort put a dent in my stock of beer.

It was the first anniversary of the Stanleyville rescue operation and, two hours after returning from the credentials ceremony, I went to *Notre Dame du Congo* for a requiem high mass to mark the occasion. Kasavubu, Kimba, Mobutu and all of the official Congolese world prayed together and then went their own ways to the intonations of *Dominus Vobiscum*. Mobutu and his friends left to plan the last details of their *coup d'état*.

At five o'clock the next morning, Kasavubu was awakened by a group of army officers and informed that he was no longer President. Our cook, Antoine, passed the news to me at breakfast, saying in whispered confidence that Mobutu had taken over. My thoughts went back over the previous two days: I wondered if General Mobutu had found my receipt for $400 in Kasavubu's desk; I was struck by the irony of my hyperbolic reference to poor Joseph as the supreme guide, leading the Congo to a bright future; I recalled the piety of the previous evening at the cathedral.

I also proudly remembered having signed Doug Hamlin's telegram predicting Mobutu's takeover. When we wired an account of the *coup* to Ottawa that morning, we allowed ourselves the preface "As we predicted ...". A puzzled External Affairs replied wondering when and how we had made the forecast: Doug and I were floored when we learned that the last part of the telegram, in which the guess was advanced, had been lost in the communications jungle on its way to the Department. It was an object lesson in the importance of putting the conclusion of a message at the beginning as well as at the end.

The bloodless *coup d'état* of the early morning of 25 November 1965 was not unpopular. Mobutu vowed to respect the constitution and named the well-liked Colonel Leonard Mulamba, the only senior officer in the ANC whose courage was proven and respected, as Prime Minister.

Tshombé declared himself pleased and recalled that once before Mobutu had taken over from the politicians only to return power to them after a brief rule. Even if Mobutu were to be the victor in the promised February elections, he might not want the job and Tshombé could again take over.

Mobutu summoned the resident diplomats the next day in two groups, Africans at three o'clock and the rest at five, to his army residence in the para-commando camp on Mount Stanley. Speaking simply and with what seemed to be great sincerity, he promised to end the corruption and anarchy which, he said, had impelled his seizure of power. He would, he went on, instill in the population the same discipline that he had imposed on the ANC. But, he argued, his takeover had not been a military *coup d'état* despite the martial music on Leo Radio which, he admitted wryly, may have convinced listeners otherwise. He read a letter from Kasavubu accepting his dismissal and thanking Mobutu for the consideration shown to him and his family. Mobutu introduced us to the new Prime Minister and we left after 75 minutes persuaded that the crisis of recent weeks had passed.

For the diplomatic corps, the *coup d'état* raised questions of accreditation and recognition. Was I, less than 24 hours after presenting my credentials, still Canadian Ambassador to the Congo? Would I have to go through it all over again when Ottawa decided to recognize the new regime? The Congolese Foreign Ministry, indeed, asked all of us for new credentials. A few days later, however, the new Foreign Minister, Justin Bomboko, told me to disregard the request. This, our first meeting, was appropriately at a reception launching a new beer in the Congo. I made an early recommendation that Canada should recognize the new government but Ottawa took the line that African changes should first be sanctified by Africans and it was not until 20 December that I was able to inform Bomboko of our wish to carry on normal relations.

Early in December, it seemed time to set a course for my two- or three-year assignment in Leopoldville. There were plenty of problems to tackle. The office, satisfactory years earlier for the Trade Commissioner and a few assistants, bulged at the seams: a new workplace was obviously needed. Staff housing had to be sought. Among the other administrative questions that demanded attention were those created by the steady decline of the Congolese franc from its official rate of exchange of 150 to the U.S. dollar to the current rate of 350, a figure which rose steadily as the months passed. Staff security was a continuing concern: to the ordinary Congolese, Canadians stood out like other foreigners not only because of their appearance but also because they were wealthy. At the residence, my wife and I viewed the return of the jungle in the garden and began a major assault on encroaching bushes and trees to clear the lawn for a badminton court and to reduce the hiding places for snakes and other intruders.

Substance had to be put on our bilateral relations with the Congo. Until its independence, Canada had enjoyed a modest but worthwhile trade with the country, enough to encourage the government to station a trade commissioner in Leopoldville at the end of the Second World War. Leo was, indeed, the first Canadian government office of any kind to be established in Francophone Africa. With the disasters that followed independence, this trade had almost disappeared and the state of the Congolese market in 1965 afforded little promise of improvement. Yet Canadian sales were still at the annual level of a million dollars, about the highest of those to any French-speaking country in sub-Saharan Africa. We looked to the day when things would change and the vast potential of the Congolese market could be tapped.

Politically, there existed some goodwill for Canada in the Congolese administration. As President Kasavubu had said to me, the non-combatant role of the Canadian troops in the UN Force — most of whom were signallers — was remembered with gratitude by the Congolese. This was unusual for the Congolese had little good to say about the other national contingents, least of all the Indians who had pillaged what they had not destroyed in the campaign against Katanga. Under most circumstances, Congolese support of Canadian viewpoints in the United Nations and other international organizations could be counted upon. It was the Embassy's function to ensure that this support continued and that the Congolese were made aware of what we wanted in international forums. That was not always easy: the lower levels of authority could not be relied upon to follow up on their undertakings and even the higher-placed Congolese had to be continually reminded of their promises and of our hope that they had communicated them to their spokesmen abroad.

Given the unhappy economic state of the country and the glaring need for development in every sphere except, miraculously, the copper industry, it was clear that the Canadian-Congolese relationship would for some time to come be that of a donor and a recipient of aid. We had already committed ourselves to giving $500,000 annually to the United Nations Development Programme (UNDP) in the country. Monitoring how that aid was spent was a preoccupation. Earlier in 1965, the Embassy had done the spadework on the gift of a large quantity of Canadian paper for the production of school textbooks by the Roman Catholic educational printing press in Leo. This gift was to come to fruition in 1967. A few scholarships had been made available for Congolese students at Canadian institutions. We contemplated what further forms of assistance might be offered but it seemed premature to enquire into new aid projects before we had recognized the Mobutu regime and before its lasting power had been assessed. Continued threats to the safety of foreigners did not make it easy to recommend programmes involving the presence of technical experts from Canada, although there were several in the country under UNDP auspices. Certainly we wanted no part of young volunteers of the Canadian University Service Overseas (CUSO) who were going to other parts of Africa. Then there was the question of providing donations of capital: in spite of promises by Mobutu to clean out the stables, we doubted that this was the time to entertain proposals of this kind.

Through the efforts of a variety of Canadian churches, there already existed a substantial Canadian aid programme in the educational field. About 200 Canadian missionaries were scattered about the Congo, most of them engaged in education at all levels. Several husband and wife teams were at work in remote areas, teaching and providing basic social and health services to villagers. Our contact with those in the interior was limited and their safety during periods of trouble was a considerable concern. One Canadian missionary, Hector McMillan, had been murdered by the Stanleyville rebels in November 1964. We were conscious that it could happen again.

The daily routine of the first weeks left me little time to explore long-term objectives. My agenda was set by a plague of Congolese ceremonies and calls on members of the government, the bureaucracy, other diplomats and the officials of the UNDP. I enjoyed meeting my diplomatic colleagues, the dean of whom was the saintly and sympathetic Monseigneur Maury, the Papal Nuncio.

On an earthier plane was G. McMurtrie Godley, "Mac" for short, the energetic, tough, likeable and well-informed United States Ambassador. Godley had served in Leo in 1961 as U.S. Chargé d'Affaires during a six-month interval between the departure of one ambassador and the arrival of another. His bold interventions then into the Congolese political situation worried the State Department and brought rebukes. But when Godley's gambles paid off, State's admonitions were replaced by praise and Godley was recognized as a winner. In June 1964, he returned to the Congo as ambassador and established a close relationship with Tshombé when he took over as Prime Minister. Godley's key role in the Stanleyville rescue operation followed and, by the time I arrived 16 months later, he was in a class by himself in the diplomatic corps for his influence and knowledge.

The Belgian Ambassador, Charles de Kerkhove, was nearing the end of his tour. For a man who had been in the front line of a very troubled bilateral relationship, he was superbly detached in his observations. He was also appealingly cynical. When I called on him for the first time, he remarked that the Congolese never expressed gratitude for Belgian assistance, never stopped asking for it, and always gave the Belgians hell when things did not seem to be going right. Albert Osakwe, the Nigerian

Ambassador and an Ibo, had a calm, intellectual approach to the problems of the Congo that made his counsel valuable. It saddened us all later that he was caught up in the civil war in Nigeria, on the Biafran side, when he left the Congo on posting to the Hague and happened to be in Biafra as the civil war began.[64] The Tanzanian Ambassador, Andrew Timbandebage, found little African brotherhood in Leo. He became a close friend and I was to meet him again years later in Dar-es-Salaam when he was foreign affairs adviser to President Nyerere. Obeid, the Sudanese, had waited six months to present his credentials to Kasavubu. He viewed the Congolese with a distaste close to contempt.

Willem Zeylstra, the Netherlands Ambassador, was a steady source of rumours, some of which proved well-founded. John Cotton, the United Kingdom Ambassador who arrived just after me, had served in Leo in better times and found the contemporary Congo distinctly odd. Jacques Kosciusko-Morizet, the French Ambassador, had established a French presence in depth which, to others, did not always appear to be any more in the interests of the Congo than it was of those of France's western allies. This style of diplomacy was to take him on to be France's representative to the United Nations and to NATO.

The diplomatic corps consisted in all of 40 missions to which was appended the very large office of the United Nations Development Programme. The Resident Representative of the Secretary-General for this programme was Dr. Bibiano Osorio-Tafall. A Mexican by adoption, he had been a general in the Spanish Republican Army at the age of 30 and a minister of the republican government in its last days. He was a botanist whose hobby was orchids. Osorio-Tafall directed the activities of almost 700 experts from a well-guarded headquarters in *Le Royal*, one of the last apartment buildings constructed before independence. His dealings with the Congolese were daily, for the funds and technical services at his command were of crucial importance to the country at this stage.

A requiem mass for Queen Elisabeth of Belgium and a *Te Deum* for the new government; the final parade of the departing Nigerian police who had provided reassurance to the residents of the capital throughout the troubled years;[65] a ceremony on the occasion of the London Missionary Society's "Bible House" — such events set the tone of my stay in the Congo in those early weeks of my posting.

There seemed to be enough to do and enough to plan. As Christmas 1965 approached and we arranged for our first large party for the Canadian residents of Leopoldville, the job looked interesting enough. We had little inkling of how occupied we would be, before Christmas arrived, in events beyond the borders of the Congo.

CHAPTER 9

OPERATION "NIMBLE": THE OIL AIRLIFT TO ZAMBIA

En route from Moscow to the Congo, I was on the steps of Canada House in London on the morning of 10 November 1965 when Dorothy Burwash of the High Commission rushed by, saying that it looked as if Southern Rhodesia would declare itself independent that day. My part of Africa, she added, would be even more interesting as a result. The significance of Dorothy's remarks did not sink in until six weeks later: the unilateral declaration of independence (UDI) of Southern Rhodesia on 11 November was submerged for me by the journey to Leopoldville to take up my new post and by the unfolding of dramatic events in the Congo. Eventually, in December, I recorded in my diary a conversation with the Nigerian Ambassador, Albert Osakwe, which centred on the ultimatum of the Organization of African Unity (OAU) to Britain to "crush" the illegal Rhodesian regime.

At Addis Ababa on 3 December, the OAU foreign ministers had given Britain until the middle of the month to "restore law and order" in Rhodesia, failing which the member states of the Organization would sever diplomatic relations with the United Kingdom. Osakwe said that his country was divided over Rhodesia and unhappy about the rift between Britain and the black Commonwealth, but would have to do what other Africans agreed upon. He accepted my observation that by threatening to leave the Commonwealth over the issue, Nyerere of Tanzania was perpetuating the myth that Britain headed the Commonwealth. This, I said, was a common misconception amongst African countries, one that Canada could not accept. At dinner the next day, I met the Tanzanian Chargé d'Affaires who seemed elated by the prospect that Tanzania, on the expiry of the OAU's ultimatum, would break off relations with Britain, and perhaps leave the Commonwealth.

It was only later that I learned that the remarks of the Nigerian and Tanzanian diplomats accurately reflected their countries' respective attitudes. On 13 December, the Nigerian Prime Minister, Sir Abubakar Tafawa Balewa, flew to London to propose to Prime Minister Wilson that a meeting of Commonwealth Heads of Government be held in Lagos with Rhodesia as the sole item on the agenda. It was Sir Abubakar's hope that a Commonwealth initiative would render the OAU action unnecessary. Mr. Wilson reluctantly agreed to the proposal and the other Commonwealth leaders were canvassed on it. The Tanzanians were not dissuaded from breaking relations with Britain, a step which they took on 15 December; only Ghana among the other Commonwealth African countries followed suit. The idea of a Commonwealth meeting was generally approved and it was agreed that it should be held in Lagos beginning on 10 January 1966.

While Wynne and I were looking forward to our first Christmas in Leopoldville, events were taking place in London, Washington and Ottawa that were to determine how we would spend the holiday season. In anticipation of Rhodesian UDI and the imposition of sanctions on that country, contingency planning had begun in October. It was accepted that, in retaliation to the sanctions, Rhodesia might institute its own blockade of Zambia. That land-locked country was dependent on rail lines through Rhodesia for its imports from South Africa and for most of its supplies from overseas, which came through the port of Lourenço Marques on the Indian Ocean coast of Portuguese East Africa (Mozambique). If these rail links were blocked, only the Benguela Railway to the Atlantic port of Lobito in Portuguese West Africa (Angola) would be available to Zambia. As the Benguela line was used almost to capacity by the copper industry of neighbouring Katanga in the Congo, it could carry no more than a small portion of Zambia's imports and exports.

It was recognized that total economic sanctions against Rhodesia would be ineffective because neither the Commonwealth nor the United Nations could expect co-operation from the Portuguese or the South Africans. Oil was the only commodity which offered hope of applying pressure on Rhodesia because there were no oilfields in southern Africa and the SASOL coal-to-oil plant in South Africa met only a small proportion of that country's needs.

In 1965, oil for Rhodesia and Zambia was imported by pipeline from the port of Beira in Mozambique to a refinery at Ferukwe, near Umtali, in eastern Rhodesia. Refined products were shipped from there by rail and road tankers throughout Rhodesia and Zambia. To keep Zambia going after the imposition of an oil embargo on Rhodesia, the British contingency planners foresaw the necessity of an airlift to handle Zambia's essential imports and to maintain the economy — above all, the copper mines — on a care and maintenance basis. The British reckoned that 21,000 tons of goods a month would have to be airlifted, a task which would have demanded more than 30 flights a day by the largest transport aircraft then in production (and on order by the Royal Air Force but not yet delivered), the Lockheed C-130 "Hercules".[66]

In mid-December, Prime Minister Wilson and U.S. President Lyndon Johnson decided at a meeting in Washington to impose oil sanctions on Rhodesia and agreed on the need for an oil airlift to supply Zambia. The oil embargo was imposed on 17 December and, as expected, the Rhodesians retaliated at once by forbidding the transhipment across their territory of petrol, oil and lubricants (POL) to Zambia.

The Canadian Government had been informed of the Anglo-American decision. After it was put into effect, Ottawa received a request on 19 December from President Kenneth Kaunda of Zambia that Canada participate in the airlift. That Sunday afternoon, Prime Minister Pearson discussed the matter with Prime Minister Wilson during the latter's brief stop-over in Ottawa on his way home from Washington. More or less on the spot, Mr. Pearson promised that Canada would help. On the 20th, Cabinet confirmed his offer by deciding that Canada would take part in the emergency operation with four Hercules aircraft of the RCAF for an initial period of one month. The same day Prime Minister Wilson announced the airlift in the House of Commons in London.

My first intimation of Canadian involvement came on 21 December in a telegram from External Affairs, addressed to a number of posts, stating that the RCAF would operate an airlift to Zambia and would probably use Leopoldville as its base. Knowing by now that the Americans were in it with the British, I went to the U.S. Embassy to discuss the project with Ambassador Godley. Although the Ottawa telegram had contained no instructions concerning the use of Leo as a base, Mac opined — and I agreed — that I should speak to the Congolese about our intentions. Never one to hesitate, Mac picked up the phone. He got the Secretary-General of the Foreign Ministry on the line, identified himself as "the Canadian Embassy" and arranged for me to see the Congolese official.

Late in the afternoon, I called on the Secretary-General and told him of the Canadian plan and of the possibility that we would be asking for the use of Leo as our base. When I returned to my office, our primitive communications were closed for the night and I used the Americans again to send a telegram to Ottawa saying that I had warned the Congolese of a possible request.

My message crossed one from Ottawa that reached us the next morning. I was told to make a high-level approach to the Congolese Government to obtain approval for the operation of Canadian aircraft from Leopoldville to Elisabethville in the southeastern Congo and, on occasion, to Lusaka in Zambia. Another telegram informed me that a Yukon aircraft of the RCAF would leave Canada on 22 December to conduct a survey of facilities in the Congo and Zambia for the operation which was given the code name "Nimble".

Douglas Hamlin used all his ingenuity to get an appointment for me with Foreign Minister Justin Bomboko. In the afternoon I presented a note to Bomboko containing the requests that Ottawa wanted me to make — the use of Leo as the base, permanent landing rights during the operation and immunities for the RCAF personnel — to which I added a fourth suggested by Godley: that the Congolese waive airport landing fees. Bomboko was obviously pleased with my pitch that the airlift would be a joint Canadian-Congolese collaboration in aid of Zambia and agreed to all of our requests with that succinct Belgo-Congolese Gallicism "OK".

That morning I had attended the first of what became daily meetings on the airlift at the United States Embassy. The participants were the American, British and Canadian Ambassadors and their officers, together with the local representatives of the oil companies (Mobil Oil, Petrocongo, Shell and Texaco) who had to arrange for tanker deliveries to the port of Matadi of oil that would be flown to Zambia by the Canadians from Leo and by private U.S. contractors operating from Elisabethville. It was obvious from the outset that decisions on the operation of the airlift would be made at these meetings and that we would, in effect, control the situation. Back at the office, I sent messages to Ottawa asking for the assignment to Leo of an additional French-speaking FSO and another stenographer to assist Hamlin and my hard-pressed secretary, Verna Dollimore. Answering a telegram in which I was told that the British had volunteered the assistance of their Embassy to me, I responded that we could stand on our own feet, adding that if we needed help, we would get it from Mac Godley and his staff who were much closer to the Congolese than the British and their newly-arrived Ambassador.

Thursday, 23 December, was a hectic day as we arranged for the arrival of the advance party in the RCAF Yukon aircraft. After the morning meeting of the airlift group at the U.S. Embassy at which I reported on developments on the Canadian side, I returned to the office to arrange ground transportation and accommodation for the aircraft crew and survey team. They numbered 23 officers and men plus Yolande Dibattista, a foreign service stenographer from headquarters who had gone to work as usual the morning before only to find herself on the long trip to the Congo at the end of the day. I sent a telegram to Ottawa proposing that I go to Zambia on the survey flight and that I invite representatives of the Congolese Government, the other embassies concerned and the oil companies to accompany me. Noting that the first flight was of some political significance, I also proposed that we take in a symbolic drum of oil and bring out a symbolic bar of copper. Throughout the day, I tried to get an appointment with President Mobutu but had no luck. With some annoyance over the difficulty of doing business in the Congo, I later told a Foreign Ministry official that I expected a "high Congolese personality" at the airport for the Yukon's arrival.

Wynne and I had scheduled a Christmas cocktail party at the residence for all Canadians in Leopoldville for that evening. Wynne saw it through while Doug Hamlin and I, with a number of the Embassy staff and two Canadian members of the International Civil Aviation Organization (ICAO) mission in Leopoldville, left for Ndjili Airport at 7:00 p.m. for the expected arrival of the Yukon at 7:50. It was an hour late in landing. Disembarkation delayed things further as it had to be done by forklift because there were no steps at Ndjili tall enough for the aircraft. I greeted and introduced the team leader, Wing Commander Gordon Webb, to the two Foreign Ministry officials whom we had corralled for the occasion and the members of the diplomatic corps who were present. After transportation and other problems had been sorted out, Doug and I returned to the residence with Webb and the other officers to enjoy the rest of the party. They would be lodged with us for the week.

Friday morning, Christmas Eve, I took the officers of the advance party to the morning meeting of the airlift group at the U.S. Embassy. We outlined our plan to send the Yukon on its survey flight on Monday the 27th and invited representatives of the Congolese Government, the British, United States and Zambian Embassies, the oil companies and the press to come along on the flight. From the meeting, the RCAF officers and I went to Ndjili Airport to look at facilities for parking, loading and maintenance. They were pleased with what they saw. They were especially happy with the co-operation proffered by the American-financed WIGMO, which provided logistic support to the Congolese Air Force and had a large hangar and European staff at the airport.[67] The survey team was less than pleased about the only accomodation that seemed available to accommodate the proposed 120-member main party. The survey party indignantly rejected a suggestion that they repair and use a derelict Congolese Army barracks at Ndjili, reminding me that the modern serviceman expected first-class hotel lodgings. As there were none available in Leopoldville after five years of chaos, the airmen would have to settle for something less than they were accustomed to.

Telegrams flew to and from Ottawa that Christmas Eve., I notified the Department that the survey flight would take place on the 27th and that, in the absence of their comments, it would be a public relations operation. A flash message came back that Ottawa did not like the idea of a Congolese Minister being invited but acknowledged that, as I had made arrangements for one, I would obviously have to go through with the plan. The wire reluctantly agreed with the delivery of a symbolic barrel of oil but added "please — no copper bar" be brought back. Some problems had been encountered with the United Nations Development Plan (UNDP) mission in Leo which was reluctant to release items from its stores that the RCAF needed. I asked the Department to put pressure on the United Nations in New York to ensure the co-operation of the UNDP and, within 24 hours, the Resident Representative had received instructions to give us whatever help we needed. Doug Hamlin and I agreed that our day had really been made when we received a note from the Foreign Ministry acceding to all the requests that I had made to Bomboko two days earlier. It was less surprising that Bomboko had kept his word than that a written confirmation had been prepared in such short order by his usually inept Ministry.

Christmas 1965 was the first on which Wynne and I had been without the company of our two daughters, in schools in Vienna, Austria, and Malvern, England. Instead we had three wing commanders with us at breakfast that morning. They went with me to the United States Embassy for the daily meeting after which we stopped at the chancery to read telegrams and draft a couple of replies. Back at home, we had Christmas dinner with our Canadian guests, returning to work in the evening when we had a meeting at the residence with a Royal Air Force officer who had flown from Lusaka where he was responsible for airlift planning.

Boxing Day was also spent, largely, at work. After the meeting that day at the American Embassy, I found the communicator, John Beranger, knee-deep in ticker-tape at the office. The day saw the accommodation problem largely resolved when we obtained 56 rooms from the American Embassy hostel to add to those already booked at a hotel. On the strength of this, the advance party asked the Air Transport Command in Trenton, Ontario, to send the second and third C-130s on 28 December, the first having already been called. I wrote to Bomboko expressing thanks for the co-operation which had been extended to the RCAF and I also sought an interview with President Mobutu, again without avail. The Congolese moved, however, on the invitation to them to send a representative of the Government on the survey flight. Kalamazi, the Chief of Protocol, came to the residence after lunch to ask what it was all about. He soon grasped the idea, went straight to Mobutu and in a half hour was back to tell me that the Congo would be represented by the junior minister for Foreign Affairs, Joseph Kalumba. All was now in place for the journey to inaugurate the airlift.

At nine in the morning of the 27th, we took off for the three-hour flight to Lusaka. The welcome there was larger than I had expected but, with our impressive Yukon aircraft, six drums of oil and a speech in my pocket, we were prepared for the ceremony that proceeded. Two Zambian cabinet ministers — Hyden Banda of Communications and Nalumino Mundia of Labour — were on hand to greet us as were British High Commissioner Sir Leslie Monson, United States Ambassador Robert Good, and the Commander of the British Forces in Zambia, Air Commodore Ian MacDougall.

I had a moment of difficulty in persuading the Zambians that this was a Canadian show after I had introduced the Congolese Minister, Kalumba, to them but a programme for the ceremony was soon organized. With two of the oil drums mounted on a forklift as a backdrop, the two Zambian Ministers on one side and Wing Commander Webb on the other, I made a short speech while the news cameras recorded the event. I referred to the request for help of President Kaunda to which we were responding, the support extended by the Congo and the presence on the flight of representatives of all who were involved in the oil airlift. Concluding, I said:

> This trip has two purposes. It is intended to survey the problems which the RCAF will face in the airlift operation. For this purpose, Wing Commander Gordon Webb has come today with a group of officers who will discuss the hows and wheres and whats of the Canadian oil lift. The second purpose is to deliver a token shipment of oil. It is a symbol of the resolve of the Canadian Government to assist the Government of Zambia in this operation which the RCAF will be joining on an important scale in a few days' time.

I gave Banda a Canadian flag and he conveyed his Government's gratitude to Canada. At this point, Kalumba insisted on delivering a long speech in French which none of the Zambians understood. It was just as well that they did not for the speech was full of hollow promises of Congolese assistance that were far beyond their capacity to perform.

We had a few words with the press and were then taken off to State House for tea with President Kaunda. Wynne and I made sure that we were seated flanking the President so as to underline again the Canadian character of the occasion. He expressed very cordial appreciation for Canada's offer of help and spoke in glowing terms of Prime Minister Pearson. Kaunda was deeply worried about the oil and coal shortages and concerned that the Zambian copper mines, on which the economy was almost totally dependent, would have to stop production within days. The impact of the isolation of the country on its political future, just 14 months after independence, obviously troubled Kaunda. I sensed that he was disturbed that only white, western countries could and would give effective aid to Zambia.

I was greatly impressed by President Kaunda at this first meeting. A handsome, soft-spoken, dignified man, he was to be friendly and hospitable in all of my later calls at State House.

Two hours after arriving at Lusaka, the Yukon took off north to Ndola for a look at the airport facilities there. While the RCAF team was busy at this task, Wynne organized a reverse airlift, buying a case of fresh milk unobtainable in Leopoldville to take back on the return journey. The shortage of fuel was as striking at Ndola as it had been in Lusaka. Few cars were on the roads and, at the airport, the maintenance vehicles were propelled by manpower instead of gasoline. One wag called that "Black Power".

The Yukon survey flight was followed the next day by the arrival of the first Hercules and within a few days Operation Nimble was underway. We started to relax at the office. I had time on 29 December to drop a line to Jim Nutt, the head of the Defence Liaison Division in Ottawa who, with Tom Carter, the head of the African and Middle East Division, had been as busy with the airlift at headquarters as we were in Leopoldville. I wrote:

> Just a note to thank you very much for all the support you have given us in the last few days on the airlift. You know better than I do there were some matters that I had to take by the horns myself. I hope you feel that I didn't get Canada gored too badly. I have just heard that the Americans are going to be bringing copper out. I thought I should confess to you that I did bring copper back from Ndola on Monday when the Yukon flew there. The piece that I brought out is attached as evidence.[68] The lift starts tomorrow

and I think most of our immediate problems have been solved... Derek Arnould arrived today ..."[69]

There was no need to be apologetic about the inaugural flight and the delivery of the first oil drums. The event attracted attention worldwide: a wire-photo of the scene as I read my speech in front of the forklift was on the front pages of many newspapers during the next days, including the Paris edition of *The New York Times* of 30 December and more exotic publications like the *Jerusalem Post* and the *Tehran Journal*. Although the British and Americans were to play a larger role in supplying Zambia with oil, the publicity that the Canadian airlift received from the ceremony attending the survey flight of the Yukon was to create the impression abroad that Canada was first with the most.

The initial Canadian delivery of fuel to Zambia was made on 30 December in Hercules 10312 carrying 62 drums or 2728 gallons of motor gasoline. Two more C-130s arrived on 31 December when 10312 carried 100 drums to Lusaka. New Year's Day 1966 was the first occasion on which two aircraft made the trip. The full complement of four planes was reached on 5 January and Operation Nimble began to gain momentum. By the end of January, the RCAF had delivered 1673 tons of POL, or over 400,000 gallons. In mid-January, the Canadian Government decided to extend the operation for an additional month and, a fortnight later, to continue it until the end of April, reducing the number of aircraft from four to two on 1 March. Although mechanical trouble and "crew time" prevented the flying of all four aircraft on any one day throughout the airlift, the cumulative tonnage increased steadily to about 3000 by the end of February. In March, 712 tons were added and in April, 938 — to make the total carried over 4750 tons. In terms of volume, 1,163,884 gallons of oil, motor gasoline, aviation gasoline and some lubricants had been flown by the Canadian planes to Ndola or Lusaka by the time the operation terminated on 30 April. Another million gallons of aviation fuel had been burned up by the engines of the C-130s.

While the Canadians were flying from Leopoldville to Zambia, the Americans were employing two Boeing 707s of PanAm and TWA on carries to Elisabethville, the closest airport to Zambia on which large jets could land. Their deliveries were then railed across the border to the Copperbelt. The British airlift was based on Nairobi after the RAF had been ordered out of Tanzania; the British used Britannias and other smaller aircraft which carried much less than the C-130s. However, as they were employed longer and made more flights on the shorter haul from Nairobi, they delivered much more than the Canadians. Together, the three airlifts freighted over 40,000 tons of fuel to the Zambians in the first four months of 1966. This achievement undoubtedly saved Zambia by enabling life to go on in that country, albeit at a slower pace, and giving time for the development of alternative surface routes for imports of POL and other goods, and for the export of copper.

The Canadian airlift was unique because the C-130 was better suited for the job than the planes used by the Americans and British. The short take-off and landing capability of the Hercules allowed it to use with ease the relatively short airfields at Lusaka and Ndola, both located close to the city centres. But more important was the fact that, because the electrical systems of the Hercules were installed overhead through the cargo bay, volatile fuels could be safely transported. This advantage was demonstrated at the beginning of February when an urgent appeal was made to us by the Zambian authorities to meet a shortage of aviation gas. For several days, the RCAF flew this dangerous cargo and forestalled the grounding of commercial aircraft in Zambia as well as the light planes of the Zambian Air Force. President Kaunda acknowledged this particular service in a letter of 7 March to Prime Minister Pearson in which he said that "the whole situation was saved by the RCAF and its Hercules aircraft".

As good as their aircraft were, the RCAF team still faced hazards on their daily trips to and from Zambia. During the first weeks, the route took them through storms of such intensity that it became known as "thunderstorm alley". Several lightning strikes were taken by the gasoline-heavy planes. Exposed to the tropical humidity, the radar of the C-130 frequently failed. More serious was the uncertain state of navigational aids at the Leopoldville end of the run. Communications, too, were a problem until the RAF established a radio station at Ndjili Airport in Leo. Nearing the end of one return flight from Lusaka on 25 February, my wife and I experienced a hair-raising combination of these hazards when a heavy thunderstorm knocked out the aircraft's radar and the airport's beacons. A fortuitous glimpse through a break in the clouds of Stanley Pool — the broad waters of the Congo River just above Leopoldville — showed us where we were and, 28 minutes late, the Hercules set down at Ndjili with little fuel left. Wing Commander Chris Cooling,[70] who was waiting for us at the airport, confided that he had spent that time mentally drafting messages to the Air Transport Command reporting that he had written off one C-130 and crew and one ambassador and wife.

Throughout Operation Nimble, demands were made on the Embassy and the RCAF for services above and beyond the carriage of POL. As no direct commercial air link existed between Leopoldville and Lusaka, those who had to make the journey were attracted to the four-hour, daily flight in a C-130. Though most were deterred when they learned that they would have to pass the time in company with 20 tons of gasoline, some persisted and we found it necessary to lay down stringent rules to restrict passengers essentially to those on airlift business. Yet there were exceptions almost from the outset, one of the first passengers being President Kaunda who flew from Lusaka to Leo on a Hercules on his way to the Commonwealth meeting in Nigeria.

There were a few other more unusual exemptions from our restrictions on carrying passengers. A notable case concerned a young Canadian couple who had begun a Cape-to-Cairo safari driving a Volkswagen "Combi" from South Africa through Zambia and into the eastern Congo from where they put their van on a riverboat to Leopoldville. When they arrived, the vehicle was in bad shape and their route to the north was blocked because the ferry across Stanley Pool to Brazzaville was not working. More serious was the fact that their visas to the Congo had already expired. When threatened with arrest, they came to the Embassy, a fortunate move because, a few months earlier, two Canadians had been severely beaten by the Congolese police in similar circumstances. We convinced the couple that they should take the opportunity which was provided by the airlift to go back to Zambia where, as Canadian citizens, they needed no visas. They agreed and we smuggled them aboard a departing Hercules early one morning. The "Combi" was disposed of by being towed to a dark street where, little by little, parts and pieces were stolen by the Congolese until it disappeared.

Another occasion when the presence of the planes helped to resolve a serious problem involved a Belgian Jesuit suffering from polio. We were asked by the head of the hospital of Lovanium University in Leopoldville if the priest could be flown to Europe on a C-130 which was returning to Canada for major servicing. The priest had to be treated in an iron lung: none was available in Leo and international air transport regulations forbade the carriage of a polio patient on a normal commercial flight. The request required ministerial approval in Ottawa. This was given within hours of the request along with permission to fly to the airfield nearest the hospital of Louvain University in Belgium. It was a generous response that led to much publicity for Canada in the Belgian press and messages of gratitude from the Belgian Government.

The freight-carrying capability of the C-130 also attracted requests and some tons of equipment urgently required by the Zambian economy were carried by the RCAF. The Save the Children Fund was also helped by the transport of a shipment of special dried milk from England, badly needed for the Fund's mission in the Congo. One instance of unofficial cargo-carrying caused amusement. When a Hercules was grounded in Lusaka over a weekend, the members of the crew were offered the use of a car on the understanding that they would replace the gasoline. This they tried to do on the next trip. They purchased some jerrycans of gasoline in Leo and took them to Lusaka along with the usual official cargo. After delivering the cans to the owner of the car, however, they were apprehended by detectives of the Zambian Criminal Investigation Branch for breaching the rationing regulations by illegally importing motor fuel. That brought an end to their private oil lift.

For several weeks from late February, the presence of the Canadian aircraft had an important consular application. In the tiny central African state of Rwanda, the perennial trouble between the governing Hutu tribe and the Tutsi minority had flared up again. The safety of foreigners in the country, who included some hundreds of Canadians, seemed endangered. An evacuation plan was worked out between the Canadian residents in Rwanda — whose unofficial leader was the rector of the University at Butare, Father Levesque — and the United States Embassy in the Rwandan capital, Kigali. Under this plan, we would send a Hercules to Kigali on their recommendation to fly Canadians and Americans to safety in nearby Nairobi, Kenya. All Operation Nimble crews were briefed on the action to be taken and we ensured that the contingency plans dealt with what was to be done should orders be sent to a plane that was in the air on its way to or returning from Zambia. In the event the call never came, but the availability of the C-130s was of comfort to the Canadians in Rwanda during that period of unrest.

I was a frequent passenger on the Leo-Lusaka run because of my responsibility to Ottawa to monitor the Zambian situation. I had been asked at the beginning of January to take on consular tasks in Zambia. To these were added duties in the field of aid administration and, eventually, diplomatic representation. Before I flew to Zambia in a C-130, I had gone to Lagos in one, in early January, to attend a regional conference of Canadian heads of post which was held in conjunction with the Commonwealth Heads of Government meeting at which Prime Minister Pearson was present. It was a happy gathering and Mr. Pearson was in a relaxed mood. He joked about the airlift but I knew that he was pleased with its progress and that he was finding it a useful tool in the difficult discussions on Rhodesia with the other Commonwealth leaders. Ralph Collins of the Ottawa team asked me if I had realized that the departmental bureaucracy was prepared to ditch me if the inaugural flight of the airlift on 27 December had gone wrong. I was quite prepared to believe that but pointed out to Ralph that our planning had been careful and we had pulled off a coup. Ralph retorted that, while I was taking symbolic drums of oil to Lusaka, some of my friends were preparing a symbolic Brown to drop from the top of the Peace Tower. I rejoined that it was nice in the age of theoretically instant communications for an ambassador in the field to prove that not all initiatives had to originate at headquarters.

I recalled Ralph's words with some amusement towards the end of the airlift when instructions came that "an appropriate ceremony" in Lusaka should mark the last flight on 30 April. Within days, the Department countermanded this order but the Zambians had decided that they would celebrate the event. There had already been days of ceremony for the men of the airlift, especially on 24 February when a "working crew" was invited to tea with President Kaunda at State House. The day of the last flight was made memorable by Air Vice Marshal E. ("Jimmy") James, then the Commander of the British Forces in Zambia, who sent up two RAF Javelin fighters to meet our lumbering Hercules and escort it on a low-level pass over the Lusaka airport. My daughter, Tricia, on Easter holidays from school in England, accompanied me on the trip and snapped a number of photos of the two Javelin pilots in the air.

On landing, I found that I faced a welcoming party led by Mwiinga, the Minister of State for Commonwealth Affairs, who asked me to make a speech. I was followed by the American Ambassador, Robert Good. Then Mwiinga spoke, concluding his thanks for the American and Canadian airlifts by presenting us with Zambian flags, copper tankards inscribed "POL Airlift Zambia 1966"[71] and scrolls that proved to be blank. Kenneth Knaggs, the Zambian civil servant who had masterminded the contingency planning of which the airlifts were part, had the crew and Bob Good and me to lunch at his house. And then we winged our way back to Leopoldville in the C-130, full of satisfaction at the results of the 130 days of Operation Nimble.

There is no doubt of the value of the Canadian contribution to the survival of the Zambian economy in 1966. (Sanctions against Rhodesia, which had created the need for the airlift, unhappily did not have the desired effect of returning the Smith regime to legality which British

Prime Minister Wilson, at the Lagos conference, had promised would happen "in a matter of months".) Operation Nimble produced political dividends for Canada. It demonstrated our support for the independent black states bordering white-ruled southern Africa. It enabled us to assert the value of the Commonwealth connection and to silence those African countries — notably Tanzania — whose rhetoric about the wickedness of the western world in the Rhodesian affair was not accompanied by practical brotherly assistance to Zambia. It established a strong bond with President Kaunda and other Zambian leaders which was to last for many years.[72]

Operation Nimble gave me a rare chance to work closely with the Canadian and British military. I enjoyed my collaboration with the members of the RCAF contingent and their frequent visitors from head-quarters. The airlift took my mind off the difficulties of life in the Congo and the frustrations of dealing with the Congolese. Above all, it was the beginning of a long, often satisfying association with Zambia.

CHAPTER 10

THE CONGO: PLANS, PLOTS AND MUTINY

During the first four months of 1966 in Leopoldville, my main interest was the Zambian Airlift and the situation in central Africa. That and administrative problems in Leopoldville took most of my time in the office and I was not able to devote a great deal of attention to events in the Congo. May 1966, the first month after the oil lift ended and the RCAF detachment returned to Canada, gave me the opportunity at last to concentrate on the Congolese scene and, above all, to assess the performance of General Joseph-Désiré Mobutu as President.

Mobutu had set a monumental task for himself and had already taken a wide range of initiatives to restore the country to health. What were his objectives and how was he going about achieving them? Looking back on his first half year since seizing power, it was plain that he was seeking to assert his government's control over the entire vast country and to bring an end to chaos by stamping out rebellion, reducing the divisive influence of tribalism, eliminating political squabbling and instilling a sense of national purpose. A major preoccupation in those early months was the effectiveness of the *Armée Nationale Congolaise* (ANC) and Mobutu looked to ways in which to widen the authority of its elite nucleus, his power base, which was stationed in Leopoldville. In the administration, he aimed at putting a stop to the bribery and corruption of others and at creating a civil service worthy of the name. In this he had to build anew, for the bureaucracy was so hopelessly inefficient that, as a rule, Congolese ministers produced results only through the Belgian and other foreign experts who were provided under technical assistance programmes.

Mobutu's economic goals were equally daunting. There was an urgent need to slow down the rate of inflation, to restore the value of the currency and to attract large-scale foreign investment and development assistance. Mobutu sought to satisfy the urge of nationalism by gaining control of the major sources of industrial wealth while continuing to attract

European managerial and marketing skills. Like his goals, his methods were often mutually contradictory: they were also naive and simplistic when viewed against the complicated and chaotic economic situation. At the beginning of the year, for example, he attempted to resolve the currency crisis by ordaining an end to the black market in Congolese francs. Foreign currency transactions were henceforth to take place at the official exchange rate of 150 francs to the United States dollar. Foreign Minister Justin Bomboko called in the heads of diplomatic missions to give advance notice of decrees which were aimed at this objective and to seek co-operation. He declared that rents for housing and office accommodation under lease to diplomats must in future be paid in the Congo and not, as was usually the case, to the foreign bank accounts of their owners. A few days later, it was learned that all travellers entering the Congo must exchange the equivalent of US $20 into Congolese money for each day of their proposed stay. Accounting for expenditures was to be demanded on departure and, in theory, the traveller would be allowed to reconvert excess francs into hard currency.

The scepticism with which these edicts were received was absolute. Their immediate effect was to drive the free rate of the franc down, within a fortnight, from 450 to 600 to the dollar. Later, a 30 percent increase in the minimum wage was granted to offset rising food prices and a new sales tax was imposed on goods and services. These measures were followed by a price freeze designed to prevent mark-ups reflecting higher wages and taxes. The freeze soon ended when it was realized that the impact of the economic measures was hardest on those businesses which had been the most honest in conducting their affairs on the basis of the official rate of exchange. Mobutu had not yet come to accept the fact that only through a comprehensive economic plan could success be achieved.

In foreign affairs, Mobutu had undertaken to stabilize the Congo's relations with neighbouring states in order to cut off support to the rebels in the eastern Congo. As an enterprise in the longer term, he bid for a place in African affairs consistent with the Congo's size and potential strength. His first incursion into the international field had taken place at the end of March when he attended a summit meeting of east and central African countries in Nairobi. It was a fruitful trip, for he persuaded President Julius Nyerere of Tanzania and President Milton Obote of Uganda to prevent arms and supplies from flowing across their borders to rebels in the Congo. Mobutu also used the occasion to show himself as a militant African nationalist and thus dispel the suspicion that he was a Belgian or American stooge. As proof of his African authenticity, a few weeks later he decreed that all provincial capitals with Belgian names should receive Congolese names on 1 July 1966. Among them, Leopoldville would be known as Kinshasa, Elisabethville as Lubumbashi and Stanleyville as Kisangani.

Yet Mobutu also had endeavoured to maintain close relations with western countries, above all with Belgium and the United States. His actions, however, often seemed to be ill-considered and, in some instances, placed great strain on the fundamental goodwill of the Belgians and Americans, whose presence was so important to the Congo and to Mobutu's regime.

On seizing power, Mobutu had not tampered with the constitution except to declare that he would rule for five years as head of state. The cabinet, which was headed by General Leonard Mulamba but otherwise consisted of civilians, was presented to and confirmed unanimously by Parliament three days after the coup. Mobutu permitted Parliament to remain in session long enough to approve his decrees and to pass his constitutional amendments, but then sent it into recess. When he called a new session of Parliament on 7 March 1966, he made his contempt of its members clear. With other diplomats, I attended the formal opening of the session which lasted but 20 minutes. A roll call, revealing many absences, was followed by a stern speech by Mobutu, who was angered that the parliamentarians had spread rumours against him during the recess and were threatening to annul some of the measures that he had decreed since he took power. In Cromwellian terms, Mobutu told Parliament to do what he directed or be sent home. That day he issued an ordinance under which, a fortnight later, he assumed legislative powers and dismissed the senators and deputies without formally dissolving Parliament.

In his first six months, Mobutu had not brought stability and prosperity to the country and his performance had to be judged as spotty. We were encouraged, however, by the appearance that he was in control. May had seemed a quiet month except for the continuing duel between the Congolese and the Belgians over economic matters and a new anti-Portuguese twist in foreign policy, which had resulted in the termination of air service between Leopoldville and Luanda in neighbouring Angola. Older hands counselled me that June — the eve of the annual exodus of expatriates to Europe on vacation — was always a nervous month in which disasters were feared and often happened. But in looking back over the hectic time that I had already had in the post, I was tempted to describe the situation as quiet.

The apparent calm broke on 30 May. Antoine the cook was the bearer of news at breakfast, as he had been six months earlier. He told me about rumours sweeping the African *cité* that Kasavubu, Kimba and other important politicians had been rounded up. The population, Antoine declared, was in a hostile mood towards the military regime.

It was a holiday and we went ahead with an outing on the river. All was quiet when we drove to the marina to board the launch of the Shell Oil Company skippered by the resident manager, George de Freitas. When we got to the sand-bar in the middle of the Stanley Pool, we tuned in on Leopoldville Radio and heard the announcement that a *coup d'état* had been thwarted and its four leaders arrested. It was alleged that they had planned to murder General Mobutu, throw his body to the crocodiles in the Congo River and seize power for themselves. The four were identified as former Prime Minister Kimba and three former ministers in the Adoula Government, Jerome Anany, Alexandre Mahamba and Emmanuel Bamba, the latter also a leading member of the Kimbanguist religious sect.[73] A rumour that former President Kasavubu had also been arrested proved false. Later, still on the sand-bar, we heard the Minister of Information, Jean-Jacques Kande, speak at a broadcast press conference. He stated that the plot had begun in March and had become known to the Government when an army officer in Matadi was approached by the plotters. He had reported the matter to Colonel Bangala, later the Governor of Leopoldville, who had passed the information to Mobutu. According to Kande, the President had ordered the officer to play along with the conspirators; we wondered whether his role had been that of monitor or agent-provocateur. Now that the facts were fully known, Kande pronounced, the four politicians would be tried and hanged publicly.

Tried they were, the next day, before a military court held outdoors. No lawyers were present. The accused were permitted to make only brief statements which were barely audible because of the catcalls from the audience. The judges withdrew to reach their decision and returned five minutes later with a long typewritten judgment sentencing the prisoners to death. The "trial" had lasted two hours.

Just before the trial, Foreign Minister Bomboko convened a meeting of heads of diplomatic missions to whom he repeated the official version of the plot. Bomboko declared that the embassies of four western countries — Belgium, France, Germany and the United States — had been approached by the plotters. A Belgian First Secretary, Alain Rins, had "listened sympathetically" to them; for this he was declared *persona non grata* and expelled from the Congo. At the other three embassies,

Bomboko asserted, the plotters had been turned away. Bomboko was received coldly by the diplomats and looked very embarrassed. This was not the only impression that he left with us for he also seemed thankful that he had not been in the dock with the others.

Like many of my colleagues, I found the official explanation of the alleged coup highly dubious. However, when I expressed this view to a CIA agent at the United States Embassy, he bridled. The Americans, he said, had been informed of developments from the beginning and considered that Mobutu had handled matters well, up to and including the time of Kande's revelation of the plot. But the subsequent kangaroo court and the sentences had horrified the Americans just as they had cast a pall over the entire city.

On the first of June, the executions were set for the following morning in a public square. Messages poured into Mobutu's office. Those from the Congolese were fawning and bloodthirsty while those from the outside world expressed disgust at the mock trial, dismay at the sentences of death and horror at the decision to carry them out in public. The Pope and the Secretary-General of the United Nations counselled clemency. Efforts were made to persuade Kenyatta and other African leaders to follow suit. At a sombre National Day reception at the Tunisian Embassy that evening, Bomboko was approached by most of the African ambassadors and asked to pass on their misgivings to Mobutu; the western diplomats refrained from intervening, considering that African opinion would carry more weight. Later, however, we learned that the United States Chargé d'Affaires had called on Mobutu three times that day to deliver messages from Washington arguing in favour of clemency. A joint meeting of the Congolese cabinet and the army high command had discussed the issue for three hours. Prime Minister Mulamba, it was said, sought a stay of execution but General Bobozo, the commander of the ANC, insisted that he would quit if the hangings did not take place. Mobutu agreed and ordered the army to carry out the sentences.

The Kenyatta message came at 8:35 o'clock the next morning, too late to sway Mobutu. Two hundred thousand people had already gathered in the *Grand Place* of the African *cité* to watch the spectacle for which a national holiday had been declared. According to the handful of western journalists present, there was some excitement when Kimba was executed just after nine o'clock but, as Anany, Bamba and Mahamba followed on the gallows, the crowd became subdued and dispersed quietly and sadly.

Coinciding with the Congolese Execution Holiday was the Italian National Day. The reception that evening at the Italian Embassy was a gloomy affair. No Congolese ministers or officials attended and little but the hangings was discussed. The next evening, Bomboko gave a cocktail party at *La Devinière* Restaurant in the suburb of Binza for a visiting Zambian delegation led by Justin Chimba, the Minister of Commerce and Industry, and Hyden Banda, Minister of Communications. I attended because I was accredited to Zambia but few other diplomats were present. One of them asked me to introduce him to the two Zambian ministers, which I did. A little later, he accused me of making a bad joke when I had given their names during the introductions. He thought that I had said Kimba and Bamba — two of the four who had been hanged — instead of Chimba and Banda. As I left with the other diplomats after a brief half-hour stay, Bomboko asked me if there was another reception on. I lied that there was but I doubted if he believed me.

We learned the next day that it was not only foreigners who were depressed by the week's events. The *Courier d'Afrique*, Leopoldville's principal daily newspaper, bravely reported the appeals that had been made for clemency and a statement by United States President Lyndon Johnson deploring the executions. The newspaper quoted the *Manchester Guardian*:

> President Mobutu has just demonstrated the extent to which the Congo has still to learn respect for the law and human decency.

and *The Sun* of London:

> The hangings were a revolting spectacle which a westerner has difficulty in understanding... It is true that one African leader after another has been overthrown by violence. This can explain but still does not excuse ferocious counter-measures.

The *Courier's* own comment was even more pointed:

> Une page noire de l'histoire congolaise a été tournée. Page noire, truffée d'intrigues politiques, voire de 'complots'; page macabre: la pendaison de quatre personalités qui furent toutes bien connues à la population et qui... avaient partagé parfois les memes idéaux et participé a des plans communs avec les autorités du régime actuel.

Into this situation, Prime Minister Eshkol of Israel arrived on an official visit. Whether or not to come as scheduled was a difficult decision for Eshkol but the right one for Israeli-Congolese relations and for the atmosphere in Leopoldville. Accompanying Eshkol was Herzog of the Israeli Foreign Ministry — a former Ambassador to Canada — with whom I spoke when the visit was ending. He offered the view, without much basis, that it had pierced the gloom of the previous week. The Congolese, he said, had tried to justify the hangings as necessary to restore discipline. Mobutu was seriously concerned over the morale of the ANC and tense and resentful about what he saw as the antipathetic Belgian attitude towards him. Despite his claim about the usefulness of the Israeli visit, Herzog predicted serious trouble, even an explosion, in the near future.

There had already been three unexplained plastic bomb explosions in Leopoldville, on the eve of the Israeli visit, to remind Mobutu that dissent persisted. Road blocks became part of the scenery again and elaborate, if inefficient, security precautions were put into force. We became involved in these through three incidents in early June.

The first occurred on Saturday, 11 June. At breakfast, I had a call from a British colleague telling me that our office building was surrounded by ANC troops. Doug Hamlin and the communications clerk arrived at the residence a few minutes later to report that they had been refused entry to the building by soldiers. We worked out our tactics. Hamlin went to the Foreign Ministry to make oral representations to anyone he could find there about the breach of diplomatic usage involved in the denial of entry to a diplomatic chancery. I took off with my driver, flag flying, for the building which was located directly across the principal boulevard of Leo from the PTT, the main post office which was also the telegraph office.

Samuel drove on to the lawn in front of the building. When I got out of the car, a soldier blocked my way with his bayonet-tipped rifle, to the satisfaction of a nasty group of Congolese onlookers. I explained who I was and what I wanted, but it was soon evident that the soldier understood little if any French. He was equally uncomprehending when I asked where his officer was, but, when I substituted sergeant for officer, he got the message and produced this personality. Again I put my wishes and received the answer that there was "no way" (*pas moyen*, a favourite Congolese expression) of letting me into the building. To that I responded that there was *pas moyen* that he could tell me *pas moyen*. The sergeant thought this over and then, curtly, told me to go ahead.

I asked for an escort and was given the soldier who had first stopped me. We went up to the second floor of the building on the elevator and walked along the outside corridor on the back of the building to the entrance to the chancery. I determined that the grill and locks had not been tampered with and returned to the elevator. As we descended and walked out of the building, my escort — who had seemed willing to skewer me a few minutes earlier — asked me if I would give him 30 francs for a beer. I ignored him. Mike Codel, the resident United Press

International correspondent, complained to me later that when, from the PTT office, he saw me emerge safely from the building and get back in my car to drive off, he knew that he had lost a good story.

Hamlin, in the meantime, had located the Chief of Protocol and taken him in tow to the chancery. When they arrived there, the drama was over and the soldiers had left, having seized — they claimed — six truckloads of automatic weapons and ammunition. Weapons had, indeed, been found in the Belgian-occupied apartments of the nine-storey building because most whites in Leopoldville considered it prudent to have firearms. But the quantity seized that morning bore little relationship to the official report which General Bobozo probably exaggerated to convince Mobutu of the existence of a Belgian plot against the regime. General Bobozo himself had led the operation as he was later to direct other farcical forays.

The second and third incidents of mid-June 1966 were related to the overnight stops of an RCAF C-130 Hercules of the Royal Canadian Air Force en route to and returning from Dar-es-Salaam. At the Embassy, we had no inkling of anything amiss during the first stop-over until, some hours after the aircraft had left Leo, the Belgian manageress of the American Guest House, where the crew had spent the night, informed us that a Canadian airman had been arrested by the ANC. The airman had been picked up in a bar by the military police during the small hours of the morning and held in a cell at the para-commando camp at Mont Stanley. When questioned, he had eventually persuaded his captors to accompany him to his lodgings to get his passport. By this time the others of the crew had left; his visit in the custody of the ANC had alerted the manageress who then brought us into the picture. We made enquiries to the Foreign Ministry which had their effect because the airman was released to us two hours later.

That evening, the C-130 returned from Dar-es-Salaam with 25 Tanzanian Air Force ground crew aboard, making the first stop en route to Canada for six months of training. Late the next afternoon, the Congolese Army intervened once more.

I had just returned from the office when a Belgian civilian drove up to the house to tell me that a bus taking the crew and the Tanzanian passengers to Ndjili Airport had been stopped by soldiers in the Limete area of the city. A few minutes later, another Belgian arrived with the same information. I hurried out to Limete, located the bus and learned that the Tanzanian Ambassador, who was on his way to the airport to see his compatriots off, had already intervened. It seemed that some members of the crew had taken photographs of the military prison as they passed it in the bus. The prison guards had pursued them and were in the process of arresting Canadians and Tanzanians alike when the Tanzanian Ambassador came on the scene. With three of the crew, including one who had failed to conceal his camera, the Ambassador went to the prison where the matter was settled by the surrender of a roll of film. When they came back to the bus and all were re-boarded, my Tanzanian colleague and I placed our cars at the front and rear of the bus and convoyed it to the airport where we waited until the aircraft took off. On the drive home, I drafted a message to Ottawa asking that no more flights be staged through Leopoldville until the atmosphere became more relaxed.

While the Congolese Army was, thus, remaining vigilant against foreign and domestic dangers, General Mobutu had been persuaded that less tension might be good for the country. He withdrew an earlier threat against the foreign press corps that they would all be expelled if their reporting did not become flattering to the Congo. Suddenly, the radio ceased its attacks on Belgium and the Belgians and began to broadcast appeals for calm. At a cabinet meeting on 14 June, Mobutu declared that the national day celebrations at the end of the month would be conducted in a climate of tranquillity and serenity. In this mood, the sentencing of Cléophas Kamitatu, a radical nationalist and the Foreign Minister in the Kimba Government — who was present at my credentials ceremony on 24 November 1965 — to five years imprisonment by a military court caused surprisingly little stir.

For the sixth anniversary of the independence of the Congo, Mobutu could not give the people bread. But he could offer them a circus. The celebrations lasted two days, Wednesday, 29 June and Thursday, 30 June. They began, as was appropriate in the Congo, with a *Te Deum* at *Notre Dame du Congo*. At one o'clock that Wednesday afternoon, Mobutu gave a reception at the Mont Stanley Presidency at which the chiefs of mission were presented in order of precedence, determined by the dates on which they had presented their letters of credence. We were introduced to General Lundula in his capacity as head of a new honours system called the Order of the Leopard. Lundula modelled the new ANC uniform which was touted as being distinctive but still looked Belgian. As a gesture of reconciliation to the white community, almost one-quarter of the 208 recipients of the new Order were whites, among them a Canadian, Dr. Melvin Loewen, Rector of the Free University of the Congo.[74]

Mobutu proudly showed us his new thatch-roofed office to the north of the Presidency and drew attention to the new *livre d'or* which, at this beginning of the seventh year in the history of the independent Congo, had just replaced the one whose cover was inscribed "Congo Belge".

Mobutu scored a considerable diplomatic success on this national day with the presence for the occasion of President Nyerere of Tanzania, President Kaunda of Zambia and Vice-President Bahiiha of Uganda. When they arrived at Ndjili Airport, Mobutu said in his welcoming remarks that their visits would not have been possible seven months earlier. On an impulse, Mobutu invited the entire diplomatic corps — on hand at the airport for the arrival of the eastern African leaders — for a drink with the visitors. A mad drive from the airport followed, limousines alternately careening along at high speeds and screaming to sudden stops as the uncontrolled procession went towards Mont Stanley. The corps assembled outside the Presidency awaiting the President's call only to learn after some minutes that he and the visitors were at the "new" residence, the house that Mobutu had built before he seized power. We drove over to this place only to find that its doors were closed to us, Mobutu having forgotten his offer of hospitality. Had he proved that he could make the diplomatic corps do anything for a drink?

The 30th of June, 1966, was exhausting. By 8:30 a.m., the diplomatic corps together with cabinet ministers, judges and other Congolese luminaries were assembled in the stands of the Place Braconnier on the Boulevard du 30 Juin. Mobutu, Nyerere and Kaunda arrived in jeeps three-quarters of an hour later and the installation of the companions and officers of the Order of the Leopard proceeded for an hour.

The parade was next: the Israeli-trained, female parachutists of the ANC led the armoured cars, ambulances and marching troops of the military portion. Then came boy scouts, girl guides, civil servants, church groups, school children, floats advertising the barely functioning commercial life of Leo, trade unionists and, finally, 8000 members of Mobutu's newly-organized political party, the *Corps des Volontaires pour la République* (CVR). The parade lasted for five hours and brought our time in the stands to seven, with no time off to move from our places. There were no refreshments of any kind, fortunately, perhaps, because neither were there any toilets. In these circumstances, we voted the float of a local brewery, its deck crowded with happy workers drinking beer, as the worst of the parade. What the visiting East Africans thought of the ordeal was best expressed by Hyden Banda of Zambia when he described it to a newsman as "diabolical".

The impression of "tranquility and serenity" achieved by Mobutu at the beginning of the ceremony was destroyed by the parade of the CVR.

Their leaders, dressed in collarless tunics, broke away from the column as it arrived at the reviewing stand and took up places in front of Mobutu. The marchers carried well-produced cartoons bearing anti-Tshombé, anti-white, anti-capitalist slogans along with some faintly pro-Mobutu placards. One of the least edifying depicted Tshombé on the gallows, a rope around his neck, this only four weeks after the executions that had done so much to confirm the Congo's image of darkness. The parade left us with the conviction that Mobutu could be destroyed by the CVR — his own political creation — if he did not watch out.

From the stands, dignitaries and spectators moved to the traffic circle in front of the Foreign Ministry, near the *Parc Selemba* where the Canadian Residence was located, for the laying of the cornerstone of the new monument to independence. A vast crowd was present, attracted by beer and soft drinks on sale at half price. Mobutu made a half-hour speech promising economic independence and announcing the rehabilitation of Patrice Lumumba as a national hero. The party at the roundabout continued long after the principals had left for a ball in the garden of the Presidency. A fantastic traffic jam was created there by the 8000 guests and it was some time before the ball began. My recollection of that party is of a cacophony of amplified sound and an orgasm of black movement on and towards the bars and the dance floor; and of President Kaunda, the quiet, moral man, dancing with gusto with a shapely, undulating young woman, put at his disposal for the night by his Congolese host.

Through that night at the Residence, sleep was interrupted by the noise from the direction of the Foreign Ministry as people helped themselves to the unguarded cache of refreshments. Drunks staggered along the streets with cases of beer and soft drinks and thousands of broken bottles littered the area for days afterwards. It was said that one brewery alone lost 170,000 bottles; we worried that, without bottles, there would be a beer drought in the city.

As June ended and July began, Leopoldville became Kinshasa, a city exhausted after the national day celebrations. The apparent calm did not last long. On 6 July, the government and embassies received copies of an anti-Mobutu broadsheet entitled *Le Léopard Libre* by mail from Luxembourg. It was cleverly done and clearly written by people who knew what was going on in the Congo. One article in it purported to be a detailed record of Mobutu's currency transfers to banks in Switzerland. Another was a pro-Kimbanguist article which noted that Bamba, one of the four hanged in June, was a member of the sect. There was a take-off on Mobutu's appeal for honesty and an item on the discontent of Prime

Minister Mulamba. Most observers agreed that the broadsheet was the work of Tshombé. Barbed by its charges, so close to the mark, Mobutu was furious.

During July, Mobutu pressed forward his plans to control the major sectors of the economy. The nationalization was announced of *Kilo-Moto*, which operated the major gold mines, *Forminière*, the diamond enterprise in the Kasai Province, and *Ossam*, the Belgian-established properties firm in which social security funds were invested. The quarrel with the Belgian national airline, Sabena, over the future of Air Congo — up to that time totally dependent on the Belgian line — also came to the fore. Mobutu had already taken on the *Union Minière du Haut-Katanga* (UMHK), the enormous copper mining company under the control of the *Société Générale* of Belgium. But that was to be a longer dispute even though the company had already announced its willingness to move its headquarters from Brussels to Kinshasa.

Mobutu explained his difficulties with the economy at a dinner which he gave on 21 July to the diplomats representing the countries whom he evidently regarded as sources of investment. Apart from the Communists and the Portuguese and Spanish representatives, all of the white heads of mission were invited. In a well-organized, extemporaneous monologue lasting 90 minutes, Mobutu sought to justify the take-over of the Belgian companies. Though he talked about Belgian "treachery", his language was not particularly violent. The Belgian press, whose attacks never failed to sting him, had called him a *spoliateur*. But, he declared, it was the Belgians and not he who were the real plunderers. Mulamba and Bomboko were the only other Congolese present at this curious justification of policy by a head of state. True to form, Bomboko chipped in from time to time with sycophantic echoes of Mobutu's comments. The next day, Mobutu gave a press conference in which he repeated his rationale for the expropriation of the companies.

It began to look as if Mobutu was working up to a renewed anti-Belgian campaign of the kind that had made the first weeks of June so tense. It was true that he had much to worry about, as the *Léopard Libre* pamphlet had demonstrated. New rumours had circulated in the middle of the month that Tshombé was organizing another Katangan secession and credence was lent to them by reports of clashes between men of the former Katangan gendarmerie and the ANC in Bukavu.

On 23 July, the trouble erupted. At Kisangani, the Katanga gendarmes chased away one or two of the new, supposedly elite, battalions of the ANC which had paraded so proudly on 30 June in Kinshasa. It was at first reported that the Katangans had the support of elements of the Sixth Commando — the French-speaking unit of white mercenaries — but this explanation of the ANC rout was soon proven false. Mobutu was at wit's end and had to be consoled by his chief Belgian military adviser, General Delperdange. Eventually he agreed to engage in a parley with the mutineers whose complaints were basic: their pay had been embezzled by Mobutu's provincial governor. General Bobozo wanted to go to Kisangani but was dissuaded when the Katangans said they did not want to talk to him. But Prime Minister Mulamba was acceptable to them and he flew the next morning to begin the talks.

That weekend, the Americans flew a C-130 to Kisangani to evacuate their nationals. They also gave a ride to a Canadian missionary named Harms who had experienced two previous abrupt departures from his mission in the eastern Congo resulting from earlier insurrections. We reported to Ottawa that he was safe and added our hope that we would be kept out of Harms' way in future.

Prime Minister Mulamba settled down bravely in Kisangani to a typical African palaver with the Katangan mutineers. The word that filtered back to Kinshasa was not at all pleasing to Mobutu: the mutineers asked for nothing less than the dismissal of General Bobozo and seemed also to want Mobutu to step down and be replaced by Mulamba. General Bangala, the governor of Kinshasa who had played a leading role in the entrapments that led to the June hangings, expressed his paranoia at events when he told a diplomatic colleague that he believed that the Belgians were about to reoccupy their old military bases of Kitona and Kamina. Mobutu acted with similar fecklessness when he declaimed to the Belgian Ambassador that the Congo could do without the 1200 Belgian teachers who were provided under technical assistance. Tension, never far from the surface, rose again and roadblocks in Kinshasa testified to the regime's nervousness. Fearful of an invasion, Mobutu even forbade the use of private pleasure boats on the Congo River at Kinshasa.

Life was not all serious that week as my diary entry for 30 July, a Saturday when I was at home, suggests:

> At 4 p.m. someone purporting to be Kalumba, the Sec'y of State for Foreign Affairs, phoned to ask for money. I could barely understand him & asked for his phone number so as to call him back. That number didn't answer so I gave up. An hour later he phoned again to tell me that his wife was ill, had to go to Europe & needed some hard currency. He asked for $600. I told him that I didn't have that much but did have $50 at the office. He asked me to get it & send it to him. I said that I would be glad to do so

on Monday but would not be able to today, whereupon he hung up. At the Portuguese [reception, that evening]... I learned that he had also tried to touch Mac Godley (for $2000!), Osorio-Tafall and the Swiss Chargé. Mac spoke to Bomboko who described it as the work of an agent provocateur! C'est le Congo.

Bomboko was wrong, as I learned when the Japanese Ambassador — my neighbour in *Parc Selemba* — told me that he had been touched by Kalumba for $200 and had a receipt from him to prove it.

My wife had left for London at the beginning of July to have an operation and we had planned to link up there later in the month before starting home leave in Canada to use up the credit that 16 months in Moscow and eight in the Congo entitled me to. I was in Zambia on business from 8 July for just over a week and the threats that I heard while there about Zambia pulling out of the Commonwealth added to my workload when I got back to Kinshasa. As the Congo also seemed to be descending into gloom, I began to wonder whether I would have to cancel my leave.

Evidence of the recurrence of chaos in the country mounted as Prime Minister Mulamba remained in Kisangani negotiating with the mutineers. On 4 August, he returned to Kinshasa and the *Agence Congolaise de Presse* gave circulation to wild rumours of the landing of foreign troops near Jadotville in Katanga and of Belgian troops and materiel at Lobito in Angola. But all was not desperate. Though the mutineers remained in control at Kisangani, President (later Emperor) Bokassa of the Central African Republic was due to arrive for a seven-day state visit. It was time to get away. On the sixth, I flew out of Ndjili Airport on Alitalia's weekly flight to Rome, just as the flower of the ANC paraded on to the tarmac to greet Bokassa.

CHAPTER 11

THE CONGO'S DRIFT
TOWARDS STABILITY

When I returned to the Congo from home leave in early October 1966, I was assured that the situation was still as confused as ever. Disillusionment with President Mobutu was almost total among members of the diplomatic corps although it was grudgingly accepted that he was in charge. The mutiny of the Katangan Gendarmerie, begun three months earlier, had ended on 24 September in a short, sharp action undertaken by 100 white mercenaries led by Lt. Col. Bob Dénard of the Sixth Commando. In Kinshasa the next day, a mob of members of the CVR, the activist wing of Mobutu's new political party — attacked, looted and burned the Portuguese Embassy in the Avenue des Aviateurs, next to the United States Embassy. Relations with Portugal were broken off, restrictions placed on travel by diplomats, and consulates closed. The state-controlled radio had inspired the mob's assault and the breach in relations with Portugal by reviving old rumours that Tshombé-recruited mercenaries were being allowed to cross Angola on their way to Katanga.

Mike Codel of UPI came to see me soon after I returned. One of only two western correspondents left in the Congo, he was thoroughly fed up with the Mobutu regime which he considered to be in a state of complete disarray. Yet, he added ruefully, the other western correspondent, Max Coiffait of Agence France-Presse (AFP), was reporting the nicest things about Mobutu, so flattering that he had to be in the pay of the Congolese. Watch the French game in the Congo, Mike concluded.

In mid-October Mac Godley, told his friends that he was leaving the Congo for good, his relations with General Mobutu having become strained to the point of rupture. The falling out of the Congolese President and the United States Ambassador was not a sudden development. Mobutu was suspicious of Godley's close friendship with Tshombé, now the General's number one enemy. Moreover, the forceful, sometimes insensitive, manner in which the Ambassador pressed American interests and wishes on the regime grated on the proud young President who had resolved to assert his African identity and his independence from western influence. At the beginning of 1966, Godley had angered Mobutu by urging him to revoke his order to diplomatic missions to make all their financial transactions, including the payment of rents, through the Congolese banking system and not, as was often the case, through banks abroad.

When Godley returned from a long vacation in June 1966, he found that he no longer had easy access to Mobutu. The rift between the two men soon widened. When the CVR attacked the Portuguese Embassy, the American Ambassador went impulsively into the street to point out the looters to the police and demand their arrest. Neither the CVR nor its patron, the President, could have appreciated this. In early October, Godley was accused of intervening in the internal affairs of the Congo when he told Mobutu what he thought of the President's action in ordering the closing of the Belgian and Portuguese consulates. By this time, the relations between the two men were ruptured and Godley put into effect the plan for his quiet departure from the Congo which he and the State Department had agreed upon as early as July. Ostensibly, he left for consultations in Washington, but this was merely a cover for him to get out before he was declared *persona non grata* and thrown out.

On 15 October, we said a fond farewell to Mac Godley at the U.S. residence just before he left on the weekly Alitalia flight. Emotional about his departure, he had nothing good to say for Mobutu, declaring baldly that he had done more than any other Congolese to ruin his country. Bob Blake, whose tour of duty in Kinshasa had been extended in July when the trouble had begun, was to be the U.S. Chargé d'Affaires until the arrival of a new ambassador, not expected before March 1967. The Americans had not lost all their influence over the President, however, as two key players remained. The CIA station chief Larry Devlin and Mobutu's personal physician and confidant Dr. William T. Close remained as channels for getting Washington's views to the President.[75] The Congolese were as keen as the Americans to avoid a public airing of the circumstances of Godley's departure and, on 18 October, expressed the hope to Blake that there be no publicity about it. When an officer of the Canadian Embassy in Washington asked the Congo desk officer at the State Department about the affair, he was given the line that Godley had returned for consultations.

From the 21st to the 29th of October, I made a visit to Lusaka to look into the possibility that there would be a request for a renewal of the oil airlift to Zambia. When I had called on Basil Robinson[76] in Ottawa on 14 September, he had surprised me by saying that the question of a resumed airlift had been raised by the British during the Commonwealth Heads of Government meeting which was then taking place in London. This was so serious a possibility that Basil had alerted the Chief of the Defence Staff. But the Zambians had not been informed that renewed help might be given because of an outburst during the conference by Simon Kapwepwe, the Zambian Foreign Minister, accusing Prime Minister, Harold Wilson, of being a racist and charging him with preparing a sell-out to the Rhodesians.

On my return to the Congo a month later, the question was still alive. The U.S. Embassy had prepared a study of the technical aspects of a renewed airlift and I used some of its material in a telegram to Ottawa on 14 October, discussing as well the political and security considerations that would affect a role by the RCAF. I concluded that the operation would be much more difficult from Kinshasa than it had been in the days of Operation Nimble mainly because of the prevailing xenophobia.

In Zambia, I found that the consensus among the experts was that the fuel situation in the country was parlous. Basil Napper of the Roan Selection Trust (RST) predicted that one-third of the copper smelters would have to close down within a month, this despite the fact that RST was now operating C-130s, flying copper to Mombassa and bringing oil back. The Shell Oil representative estimated that current stocks of gasoline would last only nine days and of diesel a mere six days. Yet, he added, this was an improvement over recent weeks though he worried that the road to Dar-es-Salaam would fail to hold up during the coming wet season. The United States Ambassador in Lusaka shared his pessimism but the former head of the Zambian contingency planning organization thought that stocks were sufficient for three weeks. A new twist was added to the supply problem, two days after I got back to Kinshasa, when 400,000 gallons of oil went up in smoke in the Copperbelt town of Kitwe and Africans attacked whites, suspecting them of sabotaging some of Zambia's meagre reserves. While the situation seemed grim, the months to come were to see a steady increase in deliveries of oil by road from East Africa and the resumption of the airlift was never again raised.

My trip to Zambia had been made memorable by a Congolese event. Prime Minister Mulamba had also travelled to Lusaka to represent the Congo at the ceremonies in celebration of the second anniversary of Zambia's independence; no sooner had he arrived than rumours spread that he had been dismissed from his office. As the other visitor from

Kinshasa, I found myself being asked by Zambian officials and the press whether I knew anything about the matter. Mulamba carried on as if nothing was amiss. On the night of the Zambian National Day, 24 October, Marcel Lengama, Mobutu's roving ambassador, flew into Lusaka with a personal message from Mobutu to President Kaunda telling him that Mulamba had been fired. The next morning, when I called on Valentine Musakanya, the Secretary to the Zambian Cabinet, he expressed his irritation that the Congolese would demonstrate their instability in this manner and insult Zambia to boot by sending a representative to their celebrations — Mulamba — who was a non-person.

Mulamba left that morning to face the music in Kinshasa. At Lusaka airport, he was in full control of himself during the departure ceremony and at an informal press conference that followed. He remarked that Mobutu had denied the reports of his dismissal and said that he had not been in touch with Kinshasa, a statement that I found entirely plausible given the abysmal communications facilities between the two capitals. Bravely, and in words that seemed aimed at Mobutu, he went on to say that the Congolese people were their own worst enemies: no individual should stand in the way of peace and harmony and he or any other man should step down if this were the will of the people. He added that he wanted to remind the Congolese people that he was a man who had done much for them. It was a fighting performance by Mulamba and typical of his well-known directness and courage.

I returned to Kinshasa a few days later to find that the post of Prime Minister had been abolished and that none of my colleagues knew whether Mulamba was alive or dead. But he reappeared on 13 November at the baptism of the Mobutu's latest child, a daughter called Claudine, at the chapel of Lovanium University. Mulamba sat near Mobutu and looked cheerful. His presence started the rumour that, on the first anniversary of the coup d'état, there would be a general amnesty for all those currently in disfavour. At the end of the month, Mulamba was named president of the state company SONAS, which was created to be responsible for all insurance in the country. Even in this capacity, Mulamba must have worried Mobutu, for the President appointed him as Ambassador to India in October 1967, a post at which he was to remain in unhappy exile for several years.

Mobutu's purpose in dismissing Mulamba was seen as the elimination of a possible alternative head of state. By doing away with the office of Prime Minister, Mobutu avoided having to elevate another potential rival. The Kisangani mutineers had made it clear that they preferred Mulamba to Mobutu and Mulamba's role in the negotiations to end the mutiny had demonstrated, once again, his superior leadership qualities.

Even more than Mobutu, Mulamba disliked politicians. Privately, he often expressed his disagreement with Mobutu's decision to have only civilians, most of them politicians of past regimes, in the cabinet. Mobutu's increasing militancy and his courting of the "progressive" African states that had supported the Simba rebellion, did not please Mulamba who was stoutly pro-western. As professional soldiers, Mulamba and the new cadre of properly-trained officers did not hold Mobutu, the ex-journalist, in esteem as a military man. They regarded General Bobozo, whom Mobutu had installed as commander-in-chief of the ANC, with utter disdain; they were contemptuous that Mobutu had elevated Bobozo to the position because he was Mobutu's tribal superior. It was evident that, if Mobutu was to retain control of the ANC and even hold on to the presidency, the Army's most popular general had to go.

As he approached the first anniversary of his regime, President Mobutu unveiled a number of measures designed to put a radical stamp on his government and assert its African authenticity. At the beginning of November, he appointed the first woman to membership in a Congolese cabinet. The choice of Madame Sophie Lihau was less a recognition of female emancipation, however, than a gesture to militants at home and in exile because Mme. Lihau's brother was the noted Stanleyville rebel, Thomas Kanza.

The first non-clerical Congolese to have attended university in Belgium, Kanza had been a member of the cabinet of Patrice Lumumba while serving as the Congo's permanent delegate to the United Nations in 1960. After the fall of Lumumba, Kanza sided with Gizenga's break-away regime in Stanleyville in 1961 and, when it was reconciled with the government in Leopoldville, was appointed Congolese Ambassador in London. 1964 saw him once more in disagreement with the central government as a member of the *Conseil National de Libération*. He became Minister of Foreign Affairs in the rebel Gbenye regime in Stanleyville in August 1964 and, when it fell, took refuge in Cairo. In 1966, he returned to London as a student, working on advanced degrees at London and Oxford universities. Among younger intellectuals, he was a hero in the class of Lumumba and it suited Mobutu's policy of appeasing them to recognize Kanza through the Lihau appointment.

Mobuto now turned to action against former Prime Minister Tshombé for his role in the secession of Katanga and also the death of Lumumba, ironically a deed in which Mobuto himself had been the instrument. Both the Belgians and the Americans abandoned their former protégé when proceedings were begun in a military court in September and a charge of high treason laid in October, the first steps towards the imposition of the death penalty the following March. Mobutu gave further satisfaction to the radicals by dismissing Godefroi Munongo, the former Governor of South Katanga, who had been a close associate of Tshombé. The appointment of a Lumumbist, Bernardin Mungul-Diaka, as ambassador to Brussels seemed a studied insult to the former colonial power and was also welcomed as such by those whom Mobutu was now cultivating.

Action against political opponents had been the name of the game in the Pentecostal hangings and the founding of the CVR was also a part of the elimination of the opposition. Parliament had by now been reduced to a cypher and political parties had ceased to exist, except for the CVR. The political dictatorship of Mobutu was now firmly in place. Security was also much improved: for the first time since the independence of the Congo, there were no armies in the country other than the ANC, cadred though it was by white mercenaries and propped up by a CIA-furnished Air Force and Israeli training.

Mobutu's earlier economic policies had generally been half-baked. But, in the second half of 1966, he took sound advice from Congolese, notably the head of the National Bank, Albert Ndele, on how to stabilize and gain control of the economy. For his battle against Belgian control of the copper industry, Mobutu hired the American Theodore Sorenson, once the legal adviser to President Kennedy, to put together the case against the *Union Minière du Haut-Katanga* (UMHK).

Mobutu had been active in mending the Congo's relations with other African countries during the second half of 1966 and had shifted the emphasis in these relations from the members of OCAM (the conservative association of former French colonies) to the more progressive states of East Africa which were dominant in the Organization of African Unity (OAU). Marcel Lengama was the point man in this campaign. During the OAU meeting that November, Michel Gauvin, my colleague in Ethiopia, reported that Lengama had appeared at a reception in what Gauvin said to him seemed to be Tanzanian dress. Lengama had responded that it was East African, not Tanzanian, and that he wore it because Congolese were also East Africans.

All these activities raised Mobutu's stature at home and abroad and were accompanied by steps to surround the presidency with pomp and circumstance and splendour of a kind never before seen in the country. On 13 November, after the baptism of Claudine, the diplomatic corps was invited to Mont Stanley for a reception. I wrote in my diary that the Presidency was much improved since my last visit five months earlier:

> Not only has Mobutu his outdoor office, but next door to it is a very large cage for a leopard (now the national animal) and a grand gateway or arch is being built. The electrified fence has... been completed and a new guard house, inside the fence, is being built.

It was but a hint of what was to come in the next year as Mobutu added to the trappings of his office.

The first anniversary of the regime was observed on 24 November as if to confirm that it was on that day in 1965, following the requiem mass at *Notre Dame du Congo* for the first anniversary of the Stanleyville operation, that the coup d'état had been launched. Perhaps Mobutu wished to erase the association of that date with the rescue operation to placate his new radical African friends. The coup had, in fact, not been announced until 25 November 1965.

Once again the dignitaries of the Congo took their places in the stands on the *Boulevard du 30 juin* in the *Place Braconnier* at 8:30 a.m., well before the announced time of the President's arrival. To the noise of a 101-gun salute, Mobutu appeared an hour late with President Massamba-Débat of the Republic of the Congo (Brazzaville), King Ntare of Burundi and other African guests. During the hour-long wait, we had been treated to music through loudspeakers set up along the street. At one point, they broke into "God Save the Queen" and the diplomatic corps broke into titters. The anthem stopped, only to be played in full a few minutes later. This time, led by the Papal Nuncio who was the Dean of the Corps, the ambassadors stood up and were joined by others in the stands, much to the pride of the British Ambassador and the amused delight of the foreigners present.

As usual, the parade was interminable. Although the army march-past lasted only an hour, it was succeeded by three hours of firemen, police, boy scouts, church groups and school children and, for an equal time, by the CVR and its new youth wing, the *Jeunesse Pionniere Nationale* (JPN). Having learned my lesson on 30 June, I had brought my camera on this occasion to while away the time, and a binocular case filled with sandwiches and lemonade to fortify myself.

The slogans of the posters carried by the CVR that day were more subdued than they had been for the independence day parade but their militancy was unmistakable. The on-lookers were exhorted to hang Tshombé, and Mobutu's name was linked with Lumumba's. Massamba-Débat and Sékou Touré of Guinea, Africa's two most radical leaders, were saluted. A dilettantish touch of foreign affairs trivia was provided by one poster praising UNESCO for having acknowledged the greatness of the Congo; not many Congolese could have known that, at the last general conference of the organization, the Congo had been elected to a vice-presidency, a distinction that came to every member state in rotation.

During the seven-hour ordeal, I resolved to try to persuade my diplomatic colleagues that we should attend only the official section of such parades and leave when it ended, as the diplomats did in such places as Moscow where hordes of happy workers marched for hours after the armed forces had goose-stepped out of Red Square. I found few supporters for this suggestion. Happily, duty and holidays called me away from Kinshasa when the two annual parades were held in 1967.

The celebration of the first anniversary of the coup d'etat continued the next day with a five-and-one-half-hour rally under the broiling sun at the Tata Raphael Stadium. Ernest Hébert, who had arrived in Kinshasa in September to augment our strength of foreign service officers, took in this event for the Embassy. Mobutu spoke for 90 minutes, summing up his accomplishments in his first year of power and setting goals for the second year. He declared that economic independence had been achieved and would be crowned by the nationalization of the insurance companies. In 1967, the emphasis would be on food production, housing and public health; work would begin on a steel industry. The President said that the number of provinces would be reduced from 12 to nine. When the crowd responded by chanting "Six", ironically the pre-independence number, Mobutu said it would be six if that was the people's will. He made much of the end of the Congo's isolation in Africa. His speech was peppered with references to imperialism and colonialism and he announced that a memorial would be built to Patrice Lumumba. On foreign affairs, he called for a round table conference to deal with Vietnam and he condemned Britain for its handling of the Rhodesian crisis. When he said that he hoped to resume diplomatic relations with the Soviet Union, which had been broken off in 1964, the crowd took it as an announcement of the resumption of relations and cheered before he had completed the sentence. In what seemed to some of us as an allusion to his quarrel with Mac Godley, he stated that donor countries should not base their policies towards the Congo on the assumption that the Congo would always require aid. The tenor of Mobutu's speech clearly identified the Government with the CVR, which suggested to many foreign observers that leftists were in command of Mobutu's policy.

A third day of celebrations followed for the edification of the foreign guests. But eighteen-year-old King Ntare enjoyed his visit too much, staying on longer than he should have. On 27 November, the news came of a coup d'état in Burundi. Ntare was no longer King and a group of army officers led by Captain Michel Micombero proclaimed a republic. It was difficult to feel sorry for Ntare for, only in July, he had deposed his father and provided him with a pension to live in Geneva. We wondered whether Ntare would now join his father in Switzerland and whether both would receive retirement allowances from the military junta. Mobutu, however, permitted himself to be quoted to the effect that the coup, occurring when Ntare was a guest, was an embarrassment to the Congo. Perhaps the President had not been told how the Zambians felt a month earlier when Mulamba was their guest.

For the small Canadian Embassy, Mobutu's first year had been extraordinarily hectic: the airlift to Zambia had been the main preoccupation for five months out of 12 and the Zambian accreditation had taken much of my time when concerns for the security of Canadians in the Congo did not dominate. Problems of self-administration plagued the office and housekeeping was a constant bother in a country whose shop shelves were usually empty. Normal bilateral relations between the Congo and Canada hardly existed and the Embassy spent little of its time on matters of substance of the kind that filled the working days of Canadian diplomats in less dangerous and more prosperous parts of the world. Now that there seemed to be a glimmer of hope that the dictatorship of Joseph-Désiré Mobutu might bring stability to the Congo, we hoped to flesh out the relationship.

For some time, three questions concerning Canada's presence in the Congo had been in abeyance: only at the top could decisions be taken by the Congolese and the top Congolese had had other preoccupations such as the June hangings and the preservation of their own skins. The three questions were the Congo's participation in Expo 67 at Montreal, a major gift of paper for the printing of school textbooks, and scholarships and our offer to provide 10 professors to Lovanium University.

Oscar Mulelenu, the Minister of Foreign Trade, had told the Expo authorities in Montreal in January 1966 that the Congo would be a major participant in the international exposition with a pavilion of its own. Prior to Mulelenu's visit to Canada, the Congo had placed a deposit of $15,000 on a stand in the *Place d'Afrique*, a building which had been designed to cater to African states with low budgets. Mr. K.L. Marshall, an official of Expo, visited us in March to establish the Congo's real intentions. I accompanied him on a call on Mulelenu who was extremely uncomfortable when he tried to explain that his problem was not one of telling us what the scale of the Congolese exhibit might be, but that of informing us that the Congo would not take part at all. This, he said, was the decision of Foreign Minister Bomboko. Mulelenu as much as appealed to me to see Mobutu with a view to having the Government change its mind.

It was not until June that we obtained anything definite on the Congo's intentions and then only in the form of an article in the Kinshasa daily *Le Progrès* describing a grandiose national pavilion. My next contact with the subject was when I was on leave in Ottawa in September and called on a bank manager who told me that the Congolese Chargé d'Affaires had been refused a loan of $300,000 from the bank but had raised the money from a source in the United States. Three months later, notwithstanding the story of the loan, the Congolese were far behind with the advance payments for their space in the *Place d'Afrique* and I was asked to intervene in Kinshasa. I decided that I should see Mobutu himself about the problem but had to begin by following the channel of the Foreign Minister.

Getting to see even Foreign Minister Bomboko was no easy matter but Ernest Hébert succeeded in setting up an interview by spending the morning of 7 December at the Ministry. He cornered Bomboko himself in the corridor shortly before noon and obtained a promise of a five o'clock rendezvous for me. Miraculously Ernest and I were ushered into Bomboko's office at 5:05 p.m. and I had 15 minutes with him to raise the Expo problem and a number of other current concerns in the aid and administrative fields. By now, the question was not simply whether the Congo would participate in Expo but whether Mobutu would accept an invitation to visit Canada during the celebration of the centennial of Confederation, on a date to correspond to the day set aside at the fair as the Congo's "national" day. Bomboko promised to look into everything and to call me within a few days, preliminary to my meeting with Mobutu.

Despite daily enquiries by Hébert, two weeks were to pass before I heard from the Foreign Ministry again. I recorded what ensued in my diary:

> Ernest and I had a wild goose chase this morning after Protocol had told us that Alphonse Zamundu, the Acting Min. of Foreign Affairs (& Min. of Agric.) would see me at 11 a.m. Just before we left the office, the MFA [Foreign Ministry] phoned to say that Zamunda would see me at his residence in Rue Banning. We got there and were told by a houseboy that Zamundu was at his office on the corner of 8e Armée and Blvd 30 Juin.

There we learned that he had 'just' been called away to Mont Stanley to see the President. We gave up.[77]

Finally, I got to see the President on Christmas Eve for an audience which was my first full business meeting with him. Ministers were gathering for a cabinet meeting when I arrived and Mobutu was talking with a small group at the entrance to his garden office. He led us straight in and we got down to business. I told him that I appreciated that it was a busy day for him and asked how much time he could give me. He replied that we had 15 or 20 minutes to which I responded that I would not cover all the ground but only the important questions. On Expo, I raised the matter of the invitation and the financial problem. Mobutu told me that he had instructed the Foreign Ministry to accept on his behalf and to let us know that he planned to go to Canada in April or May. I responded that we wanted him there at the end of August; he found this timing quite agreeable. On the money owed to Expo, Mobutu declared that the Congo would honour its undertakings and that an order would be given immediately to pay what was due. His words were reassuring but they were not the end of the tale.

Of the two aid questions, that of the gift of paper was the happiest although it had a vexing beginning. Under the project, which had evolved from a request by the *Bureau d'Enseignement Catholique* to my predecessor, 300 tons of paper were to be supplied each year for three years for the printing of some 1.2 million textbooks. Through this scheme, I met and came to know *Père* Martin Ekwa, a pleasant and intelligent Congolese Jesuit who was in charge of the Bureau and whose co-operation was never lacking. It was a different story with the Government whose formal acceptance of the gift had to be sought. There was one catch: the Congo had to pay $17,000 each year to cover the cost of ocean freight. I assumed, charitably, that my difficulty in obtaining acceptance was caused by this condition, one that recipients of Canadian aid had long resented and only later, in 1970, succeeded in having removed. In mid-February 1966, I was instructed to notify the Congolese that the gift was to be made. As it was the most important single aid project to the Congo up to that time, I decided that it was newsworthy of Mobutu's ears and spoke to Bomboko to ask for an audience with the President. I was to wait a long time for it.

In anticipation of the audience, I had a formal note prepared which I proposed to hand to Mobutu; for many days, I carried it around in my pocket in case of a sudden summons. Three weeks later, I was called in by the Ministry of Foreign Affairs to see Bomboko's deputy, Kalumba, who told me that as Mobutu was busy and Bomboko ill, he had been directed to see me about the gift of paper. I handed the now dog-eared note to Kalumba, asking him to pass it up the chain of command. Written acceptance came within a reasonable time but the Congolese were predictably slow in paying for the freight. Only when I saw Mobutu on 24 December was I able to tell him in person about the gift.[78]

The arrival of the first shipment of paper in January 1967 was the occasion of a happy ceremony arranged by *Père* Ekwa. The Minister of National Education, *Abbé* (defrocked) Athanase Ndjadi, took delivery of the paper from me and passed it to Ekwa. Some days afterwards, the Catholic School journal, *L'Antilope*, carried a long article about the gift and summed up its significance to the children in this paragraph:

> Qu'est ce que vous pouvez faire, de votre coté, pour montrer votre gratitude vis-à-vis des donateurs? En premier lieu, vous devez apprécier ce geste; en deuxième lieu, vous devez détruire dans votre coeur l'énorme distance qui existe entre l'Afrique et le Canada, en vous sentant proches de ce peuple ami; en troisième lieu, vous prierez le Bon Dieu, afin qu'il protège toujours cette Nation. A Montréal, au Canada, se déroulera cette année l'Exposition Mondiale: vous souhaiterez, dans votre coeur, que cette Exposition soit couronnée par une joyeuse réussite.

A year late, *Père* Ekwa gave me copies of the textbooks that had been produced with the first 300 tons of paper. In each was a red maple leaf and an inscription stating that the book had been printed on paper given by the people of Canada. Of all the aid projects with which I was involved during my time in the Congo, none gave me more satisfaction, none seemed so useful, and none provided so much publicity for Canada.

The third area in our bilateral relations on which we sought to make progress in 1966 also concerned aid. We had in mind the extension of our modest scholarship programme and the provision of staff to Lovanium University; other projects came to our attention from time to time. Ottawa was anxious to increase Canadian aid to the Congo as part of the new policy of increasing development assistance generally in Francophone Africa.

Sensing our wish to be generous, some Congolese seemed to spend their time devising schemes which would profit them at our expense. One such was the son of a "High Customary Chief" of the Lake Leopold II district who came to my office in June 1966 on an appointment requested by the Foreign Ministry. The visit, I was assured, had the blessing of Mobutu. The visitor provided me with a murky exposition of a remarkably vague plan for fisheries and timber development so incomprehensible that I took refuge behind a request that he provide details in writing. He agreed to do so and then calmly asked me for a gift in order that he might eat over the weekend before returning home. Sensing that his request was probably genuine, I gave him a thousand francs out of my pocket but hoped to myself that that would be the full extent of Canadian aid to the Lake Leopold II district.

There were obstacles in the way of being generous even in the fields of technical assistance and scholarships. As an Embassy, we favoured the presence of more Canadian teachers in the Congo but the Kisangani mutiny and tension elsewhere convinced us that all should be assigned to Kinshasa or the immediate area. A detailed request had been made by Lovanium University for the services of a large number of professors and, in November, Ottawa agreed to furnish 10. The University of Montreal wanted to send a medical team to Lovanium because it was branching into tropical medicine and the local mission of the World Health Organization supported the idea as an extension to the team of 11 medical technicians at Lovanium hospital who were already there under the Canadian aid programme.

An increase in the number, then miniscule, of scholarships in Canada for Congolese students was more of a problem. The students had to be nominated by the Ministry of National Education through the Foreign Ministry; selection had to show some semblance of merit and had to be undertaken with some regard to the calendar of the university year in Canada. Ernest Hébert applied himself diligently to this problem throughout his days in Kinshasa: often he did the paperwork required by the two ministries for their own purposes as well as that needed from us by the External Aid authorities in Ottawa. But the number of students put forward for the Canadian scholarships was disappointingly low. During my Christmas Eve call on Mobutu, I observed that the Congo had frequently lost places in Canadian universities because of the lack of co-ordination between the two Congolese ministries. Mobutu said that he realized that co-ordination was poor and promised that he would soon be turning his attention to the objective of having ministries work more closely together. Unfortunately, the results of this promised attention were not apparent during the remainder of my stay in the Congo.

Mobutu had bigger fish to fry at the end of 1966. He made his first major cabinet shuffle which saw eight of the 18 ministers sent to oblivion and 10 re-confirmed. Among those retained were Bomboko and Nendaka. They had been founding members with Mobutu of the Binza Group, so named after the Kinshasa suburb where these like-minded,

young politicians had met in the months before Congolese independence.[79] Many of the new ministers seemed to represent the fire-eating
nationalists now dominant on the President's staff. However, they were a
more intelligent lot than their predecessors and welcome for that.

The event of paramount importance at the end of 1966 was the
denouement of the struggle between the UMHK and the Congolese
Government. It was Mobutu's position that the UMHK owed the Congo
4000 million Belgian francs. He wanted the company to take up Congolese
domicile and threatened that, if it did not, he would nationalize it. Foreign
Minister Bomboko spent some time in Brussels in December negotiating
with the UMHK and returned on 22 December apparently empty-
handed for, the same day, the company announced that it would not
comply with the order of the Congolese Government to move its headquarters to Kinshasa. Mobutu countered by telling Parliament on
Christmas Eve that an administrative council would look after the affairs
of UMHK from 1 January 1967 and that, if the company had not paid
up the money owing to the Congo by 15 January, assets in the Congo of
the parent *Societé Générale* to that value would be seized.

At very short notice, Bomboko called in the heads of diplomatic missions in Kinshasa on Boxing Day to brief us on the background to the
dispute. At the very end of his statement, he made it clear that the
Government was by no means sure of its grounds when he said that, if
the UMHK would agree by 1 January to set up its headquarters in
Kinshasa, the Government would lift all of the measures that it had
threatened to take against the company.

The UMHK did not respond and, on the stroke of midnight of the
new year, the company was expropriated and Gécomin (the acronym for
the *Société Générale Congolaise des Minerais*) was created. Although the UMHK
announced that it would sue anyone who bought Katangan copper from
the Congolese Government, the UMHK agreed to arrangements for its
technicians in the mines and smelters of Katanga to remain on the job.
The energies of friendly countries were concentrated on the marketing
problem. The Americans, in particular, were concerned at the consequences that might arise given the existing world shortage of copper and
the heavy demands for it in the war in Vietnam. Ted Sorenson worked
day and night on the problem as the Government's counsel. (When
I met him, I remarked that he would find life interesting as
there was a crisis in the Congo every 10 days. "Every 10 hours", he
responded, "since I've been here.") The Congolese were equally anxious
for a settlement. When the CVR celebrated its first anniversary with a

demonstration against the Belgian Embassy that featured a coffin marked "UMHK", the army was much in evidence and the protest passed peacefully. A settlement was also very much in the interests of the Belgians whose large refineries were dependent on Congolese copper and rarer ores.

To the relief of all parties, the first of a series of agreements between Gécomin and the Belgian refining company Sogémin (*Société Générale des Minérais*) was signed on 17 February 1967. Mobutu presented the agreement as a victory in the struggle for independence, but this rhetoric mattered little against the fact that copper would continue to be produced and exported and that there would be hard currency in the hands of the Congolese for the first time in 1967.

The Canadian Embassy had not been involved in the big copper game except to follow it closely because of its impact on the stability of the Congo. When the dispute ended, it was succeeded almost immediately by a short-lived crisis at Lovanium University which concerned us more because it threatened the safety of the Canadian experts and their families who lived on the campus. The crisis had been caused by a disturbance brought about by a confrontation between the student body, on the one hand, and the university authorities and the Government, on the other hand. It was but the first of a series of clashes which were to continue long after my time in Kinshasa.

Located atop a hill about a dozen miles south-west of Kinshasa, Lovanium University had been founded in 1954 by the Roman Catholic Church. It was a serious institution with the distinction of having the first atomic reactor on the African continent and a good medical faculty and hospital. Two other universities existed, in Kisangani and Lubumbashi, but both had suffered gravely from the chaos in the country since 1960. The rector of Lovanium in 1967 was an extremely able and energetic Belgian priest, Monsignor Luc Gillon, who was later replaced by a thoughtful Congolese, Monsignor Bakole.

The trouble at Lovanium in February 1967 was touched off when the wife of a student was allegedly denied treatment at the university hospital clinic. The left-leaning students' council vented its nationalism and anti-clericalism in a strike to which the university authorities responded by closing the university for a week and demanding the re-registration of students with a view to weeding out undesirables. When the students refused either to leave their quarters or to re-register, a battalion of paratroopers was called in to maintain order. Entrances to the campus were sealed off and the paratroopers put the lid on the situation. The students refused to negotiate with anyone but Mobutu, who gave them the face-saving formula of collective rather than individual re-registration while declaring his support for the university authorities in most respects. The mini-crisis was over in five days. During that tense period, the Embassy kept in close touch with the Canadian aid personnel who, like the students, had been all but prisoners of the army surrounding the campus.

For Mobutu, the most important event of 1967 was to be the meeting of the heads of state of the OAU in Kinshasa in September. Mobutu was resolved to show other leaders that he was a progressive, solidly in command, and that his country was a real leader in Africa. Despite extravagant preparations for the conference, which were underway by early spring, the atmosphere of Kinshasa continued to be charged and Mobutu was to experience serious tribulations before September. For us at the Embassy, the Congolese situation took second place to events at home, where the unfolding of the centennial celebrations was paralleled by the emergence of Quebec on the world scene. We were put to work to counter the strong support which France was giving to the province especially through *La Francophonie*, the new instrument of the international influence and prestige of France under its President, General Charles de Gaulle. Like the Congo, Canada was in for rude shocks in the months ahead.

CHAPTER 12

CANADA'S TROUBLED
BIRTHDAY PARTY

In 1967 Canada became a centenarian and the
country, like people at that age, seemed to be losing its grip. National
unity had been put in question early in the sixties by the growth of
Quebec nationalism. The assertion by the province of the right of its
French-speaking community to be the master of its own destiny had, early
on, manifested itself in the field of external relations where Quebec began
to insist on its right not only to control the international extension of
matters falling within provincial jurisdiction but to do so on a quasi-
diplomatic level, treating with foreign countries without the intermediary
of the federal government.

The Quebec thrust to place its French identity on firm social, cultural
and economic grounds had grown out of the quiet revolution in which a
new generation cast aside old beliefs that had been the bases of Quebec
life and questioned the soundness of every pillar and post of the old
structure of institutions and relationships. Accompanying the assertion
of nationalism were acts of violent protest, but these were not as damaging to the fabric of Canada as the deliberate and incremental expansion
of provincial power within the boundaries of Quebec and abroad. Almost
more damaging to the Canadian fabric was that Quebec nationalism
struck a responsive chord in France which became the patron of the
province and a sponsor of its foreign ambitions.

Faced with threats to the integrity of Confederation from within and
without, the Canadian Government sought to respond with a variety of
strategies. At home, the creation of distinctive symbols of Canadianism
such as the maple leaf flag and the Order of Canada was intended to raise
the level of national pride.[80] Hand-in-hand were measures to enhance and
protect the bicultural character of Canada. At the federal level, it became
obligatory to use both French and English on official stationery, in publications and for all signs on federal property. Food packaging became

bilingual. Federal services became available across the country to unilingual Canadians in both languages.

The Department of External Affairs was put to work to deal with the Ottawa-Quebec dispute in the international theatre. Posts abroad were given the task of ensuring that foreign leaders understood the constitutional realities of Canada and were sympathetic to the federal position. To ensure that sympathy, the Canadian aid programme became an instrument in the third world. Nowhere was this more the case than in those countries where French was an official language or one used widely because many of them had already been targeted by Quebec or by France on Quebec's behalf.

The celebration of the hundredth anniversary of Canadian Confederation would have taken place in 1967 even if there had been no disagreement between Ottawa and Quebec. However, because foreigners were to be involved, the birthday party proved to be a perfect backdrop for the unfolding of the dispute beyond Canada's shores. By the start of the year, the battlelines were already being drawn in the heart of Africa where, Ottawa had decided, the Embassy in Kinshasa would also carry the campaign to Rwanda and Congo-Brazzaville.

Our first indication of how serious the tension between Ottawa and Quebec had become was an immediate telegram that came on 6 March 1967 setting forth the Government's views on *La Francophonie*. A "solidarity association" for the new grouping of French-speaking states had been established in Paris which Ottawa feared would be dominated by France unless it was converted into a true international non-governmental body composed of representatives of national French-language associations from around the Francophone world. We were instructed to make the Canadian view known urgently to the Congolese.

When Foreign Minister Bomboko came to the Embassy two days later to sign the book of condolences that we had opened for the death of Governor-General Georges Vanier, I had a brief conversation with him on *La Francophonie* and arranged to call on him the next morning.[81] At that meeting, Bomboko said that he was in entire agreement with us because any French-led organization would smack of neo-colonialism. While this might be all right for the African countries that had been French colonies, he went on, it was not good enough for the Congo, nor, he assumed, for Canada. Clearly, Bomboko was on our side, for the moment at least.

A week earlier, Quebec had incurred Ottawa's wrath — expressed in a stern statement from Prime Minister Pearson — by setting up a Ministry for Intergovernmental Affairs with all the trappings of a foreign ministry.

This action and the creation of the "solidarity association" by the French led, later in March, to a speech by Paul Martin in which the claim of Canada as a whole to play a full part in any international Francophone organization was restated and Ottawa's responsibility for the conduct of foreign affairs re-emphasized. A full head of steam was thus building up on the eve of the centennial celebrations.

The centrepiece of the Canadian centennial year was the world-class exhibition in Montreal, Expo 67, into the planning of which went great imagination and countless tax dollars. While participation by countries of the developed world was on a prestigious scale, an effort was made to stamp the exposition with universality by ensuring broad participation from the third world. Among the inducements used on them was the provision of venues at Expo such as the *Place d'Afrique*, in which 22 African countries were eventually persuaded to take up small spaces in which to represent themselves modestly and relatively cheaply. As early as 1965, the Congo had placed a deposit on a stand in the building; by late 1966, they were far behind in the installment payments due on their space.

A further inducement to participating countries was the promise that their heads of state would be invited to Canada on state visits during the centennial year and to be present in Montreal on a "national day" at which their country would be honoured. President Mobutu had been invited by the Governor-General in September 1966 and I had reminded him on Christmas Eve that an answer would be appreciated. Arrangements for the state visits and the three-score "national days" were well advanced, for most countries, in early 1967. At the Embassy in Kinshasa, we were fortunate that of the five countries in our territory, only the Congo and Rwanda had signed up for Expo. While Rwanda seemed to know what it had signed up for, the Congo was dilatory about, if not oblivious to, the obligation that it had assumed. With other countries also vacillating on their participation, the Expo management was becoming nervous as the Canadian spring approached.

The problems over the participation of the Congo were multifaceted. One concerned the invitation to Mobutu to pay the state visit, which Ottawa had scheduled, arbitrarily, for the end of August. The second concerned the Congolese pavilion in the *Place d'Afrique* and the third involved payments due to Expo 67.

Mobutu had assured me at Christmas 1966 that an August date for his visit would present no problem and that there would soon be a formal reply to the Governor-General's invitation. When no response had been received by mid-February, we made enquiries through Commandant Jean

Powys, Mobutu's Belgian aide, who took the matter up with the President. Powys warned us, however, that it was unlikely that Mobutu would travel much in 1967, especially because the summit meeting of the Organization of African Unity (OAU) was due to be held in Kinshasa in September. A fortnight later, Powys reported that the President had ruled out late August but would accept a July date.

July was turned down by Expo, because it was crammed with dignitaries ranging from President de Gaulle of France to my own President Kayibanda of Rwanda. The Expo visits organization suggested reverting to 30 August, with a "high personality" representing the President, or a date in October, if Mobutu really wanted to go. When I delivered this message to Foreign Minister Bomboko, I inverted the suggestions. Eventually, Jacques Bongoma, the economic adviser in the President's office, told me that 20 October would suit the President who hoped to make the visit himself. Bongoma had been to Canada in April in connection with problems at the Congolese Embassy and had paid a visit to Montreal to ascertain whether the Congolese exhibit would be worthy of the presence of Mobutu.

The affair that had given rise to Bongoma's trip to Ottawa had everything to do with Expo. On 11 April, the Kinshasa daily *L'Étoile* ran an article reporting trouble between the Chargé d'Affaires, Pierre Mbale, who was also his country's Commissioner-General for Expo, and Likita-Bemba, the Assistant Commissioner-General, who was the anchor man in Kinshasa. Commandant Powys told us that Bongoma would investigate a shortage of $150,000 in the Embassy's accounts. A week later, Expo authorities told us that Bongoma's visit had greatly agitated the Embassy, which wanted them to keep him off the site of the fair. Mbale, it was reported, was seriously ill in hospital in Montreal.

Expo opened its doors for six months on 27 April but it was to be almost eight weeks before the Congolese stand — Expo's 64th and last — was ready for business. When Bongoma returned to Kinshasa, we learned that Mbale had been relieved of his Embassy duties for alleged misappropriations amounting to a million dollars and that Likita-Bemba was also heavily involved and would be going to jail. A new Chargé d'Affaires, Charles Sumba, was appointed but for several weeks his position remained nebulous because the Foreign Minister failed to send a message of appointment to his Canadian counterpart. In the situation, Expo refused to deal with Sumba. On 3 June, I wrote in my diary that we had received a telegram from Marcel Cadieux, the Acting Under-Secretary of External Affairs in Ottawa, bringing us up to date.

My diary entry was not sympathetic towards the Expo authorities:

> The MFA here has obviously not yet regularized Sumba's position as Chargé and no new Commissioner-General has been appointed. Meanwhile the Congolese still owe the final rental payment on their stand in the Place d'Afrique and some of their officials who are living at the Mount Royal Hotel haven't paid their bills since they arrived. Ottawa wants money or else they will close the unopened Congolese show — an action which would do wonders to our relations! I think that my line will be that as we accepted the Congolese at Expo — indeed put pressure on them to participate — we must pay the shot...

The next problem that vexed Ottawa was Mbale's diplomatic status. Bomboko's office was surprised to learn from us that Mbale was refusing to comply with its direct order to return home. We asked the Ministry if it would waive his diplomatic immunity so that we could deport him. Mbale was still in hospital recovering from surgery when the Congolese stand was opened on 19 June. But he was well enough to give an interview to the Toronto *Star* after he was told that the Congolese Cabinet Minister, Jean-Marie Kititwa, who was present for the official opening, had charged in a press conference that the delay in opening was the fault of Mbale. Kititwa, said the *Star*, had "blandly" accused Mbale of "shooting the bundle in two years of high living" as the Congo's man in Ottawa. Mbale denied the accusations in the interview, describing them as "political demagoguery" and asserting that not a single dollar was unaccounted for.[82]

My attention had now turned to Rwanda which I had to visit in order to present my credentials as Ambassador so as to be able to accompany President Kayibanda on his state visit to Canada in August. Before flying to the Rwandan capital, Kigali, at the end of June, my wife and I gave a reception at the residence in Kinshasa for the centennial of Canadian Confederation. The Congolese invitees stayed away in droves and the party could not be described as a great success. What made the centennial memorable to some Congolese, however, was that we at the Embassy had created a special Canadian "Order", the medallion for which was the bronze commemorative coin minted in Canada for distribution to school children. We obtained enough of these coins to send some to Madrid where clasps were attached through which the red and white ribbon of Canada could be threaded. They arrived on the 29th and we paraded the Congolese office and domestic employees; I bestowed them with the "Order", pinning the ribbons to their tunics and kissing them in good Gallic fashion on both cheeks. Four years later, when I was in the residence in Kinshasa as a member of the visiting party with External Affairs Minister Mitchell Sharp, the domestic servants still proudly wore the "Order" on their white uniforms as they served dinner.

On 30 June, I left for Rwanda before the celebrations of the seventh anniversary of Congolese independence began, happy to avoid broiling in the sun on the bleachers watching another interminable parade. While the trip gave me the opportunity of seeing much of this small, alpine land and of visiting the Canadians who ran the national university at Butare, the main purpose was to present my credentials. The date for that ceremony had not been firmly fixed when I arrived in Kigali and was set — for Saturday 8 July — only on the 5th, the day that the mercenary mutiny in the Congo led to the closing of all borders and the cancellation of flights into and out of the Congo. There was an opportunity to get back to my post on the Friday on an American military aircraft but the Rwandans refused to advance the date and so forced me to make a long, time-consuming detour to return to Kinshasa to responsibilities that were far heavier than those involving Rwanda.

The episode did not make me look forward with much pleasure to Kayibanda's state visit to Canada. Before it began, General Charles de Gaulle, with his cry of *"Vive le Québec libre"*, was to ensure that my journey was to have all the attraction of walking through a political minefield. This was especially so because the Federal Government had set up the state visits to give the distinguished guests a taste of Canada beyond Ottawa, where the visits would normally begin, and Montreal, where the focus was on the visiting country's participation in Expo. In the case of the visits of leaders of French-speaking countries, their appearance in Quebec was considered *de rigueur*. The Rwanda visit was the first from the Francophone world since that of de Gaulle's France. The provincial government was the host and in charge of the agenda. Each of these occasions was to provide the Quebec Government with an opportunity to add facets to the image of *La Belle Province* as an entity separate from the sway of Ottawa and sovereign in many aspects of international relations.

There was an upside to the experience. The state visits of 1967 demonstrated that there was pageantry in the Canadian psyche and a recognition, now that we were a hundred years old, that it was good to have a celebration and to entertain our friends in the world in a cosmopolitan style, a style forbidden until so recently by the dour puritans who had ruled us.

The Rwandans arrived in Montreal on Monday, 8 August, for their visit which would last six days. They were welcomed to Canada by the

Hon. Lionel Chevrier, who had returned from the post of High Commissioner in London to serve during the centennial year as the Commissioner-General for State Visits, the Government's official greeter. My work began when I conducted the visitors on the short flight to Ottawa on a Cosmopolitan aircraft of the RCAF and, then, from the airport in Ottawa to Parliament Hill where there was a ceremony of welcome complete with red-coated Canadian Guards who dwarfed the tiny Kayibanda. I saw the party to Government House and returned there in the evening for the dinner given in Kayibanda's honour by the Governor-General and Mrs. Michener.

There were 48 seated at the glittering table and the Micheners made their guests at ease by the friendliness and warmth of their hospitality. Afterwards, we went into the garden which was illuminated in the red and white of the national colours that had become Canada's only 30 months before. Mr. Pearson, whom I had last seen at the Commonwealth meeting in Lagos in January 1966, asked me about Kayibanda and was impressed when I mentioned that his salary was a mere $400 a month and that he was reputed to be the most honest leader in Africa.

The second day of the visit took the Rwandans on a tour of Ottawa. The first call was on the mayor of Ottawa at City Hall from where the party went to Parliament Hill to be received by Jean Marchand, then Minister of Manpower and Immigration and Senator Maurice Lamontagne. The third stop was at the cattle-sheds of the Central Experimental Farm of the Department of Agriculture where the size of the cows startled these visitors from a land where the animals, like the people, suffered from malnutrition and both animals and people were stunted and scrawny. Paul Martin, the Secretary of State for External Affairs, was the host at a lunch at the Country Club, across the river in Aylmer, from which we were whisked to the spanking new railway station in Alta Vista to depart for Montreal.

For the next two days in Montreal, protocol demanded that I stay close to Kayibanda while he was feted at Expo and by the City of Montreal. On the Rwandan "National Day" — Thursday, 10 August — he was greeted by the Commissioner-General for Expo 67, Pierre Dupuy. After a lifetime in the foreign service, Dupuy had come out of retirement at 71 to provide a distinguished front to the large staff of managers and hucksters assigned to the exposition. He was the host at a lunch at the attractive restaurant of the *Pavillon d'Honneur* which was set on the small island called *Hélène de Champlain*.

In the afternoon, the Rwandans entertained the official parties and the spectators at Expo that day with a programme of dancing and music that was divided into four parts repeated at 30 minute intervals: Watutsi dancing by *Intore*, traditionally the sons of chiefs, who performed a choreography that was as spectacular as their costume of leopard skin skirts, fringes of white *colobus* monkey fur around their heads, brandishing bows and lances decorated with long tails of raffia fibre; a "Kayibanda-Rwanda" chorus, a sort of "Hail to the Chief" called *Ama Sunzu* sung by a dozen nubile girls with butterfly hair styles; and gourd-horn and drum concertos, interspersed with the monotony of bass drums. From all this, after two-and-a-half hours, we were mercifully released by a sudden rainstorm. We returned to the *Pavillon d'Honneur* for a reception given by the Rwandans where I met sundry Commissioners-General of whom there was one for each national pavilion.

The next day marked the divide between the Federal part of the state visit and the Quebec City section for which the Quebec Government would be responsible. In the morning, we toured some of Montreal and returned to the Expo site to pay rapid visits to the pavilions of Canada, Quebec, the United Nations, Czechoslovakia (one of the most beautiful of the Fair), the Soviet Union and the United States. From Expo, we drove straight to St. Hubert to board the RCAF Cosmopolitan for the trip to Quebec City. On the flight I was uncomfortably aware that, as on the first Cosmopolitan that had taken the Rwandans from Montreal to Ottawa, none of the flight attendants spoke French and the luncheon menu was in English only. From our arrival in Quebec City until our return to Montreal, I as "Head Fed" walked on unfriendly ground.

On landing at the Ancienne Lorette Airport that afternoon, the Rwandan President was met by the Lieutenant-Governor of Quebec, the Honourable Hugues Lapointe, and three cabinet ministers of whom Marcel Masse, the Assistant Minister of Education, was to be the provincial presence over the next two days. After a tour of the city and of Laval University, the visitors were installed at the Chateau Frontenac where we of the small federal group — an RCMP Inspector, a conducting officer from the State Visits organization and myself — were separated by 11 floors from the Rwandans. We smelt a rat.

In the evening, Hugues Lapointe held a friendly reception at the Citadel which was followed by dinner at the *Café du Parlement* with Premier Daniel Johnson as host. Premier Johnson greeted me in the receiving line with "*Monsieur* Brown or *Mister* Brown?", probably a jocular reference to his own surname. Before dinner, Marcel Masse outlined his background to me in a chat that seemed to be going in a friendly enough fashion and then astounded me by drawing himself up to his full stature and exclaiming: "Have a good look at me: I am the new Quebec man!" I sat at the table next to the Minister of Justice, Armand Maltais, who made no effort to respond to my attempts at conversation. Across the table and equally uncommunicative was Jean-Noel Tremblay, the Minister of Cultural Affairs. When Johnson spoke that evening of *l'État du Québec*, and the word "Canada" was not even mentioned in any of the speeches, I felt that Quebec's separation was no longer merely a possibility. I wrote in my diary:

> I have been treated correctly but very much as the representative of a foreign power.

A couple of days later, I was to write about the "studied rudeness" of the Quebeckers.

After the dinner, those of us of the federal party, accompanied by Father Levesque of the University of Rwanda, walked the Dufferin Terrace by the Chateau Frontenac. Inside the hotel, Premier Johnson paid an unscheduled call on President Kayibanda.[83] Inspector Theriault had earlier learned that an aid agreement between Rwanda and Quebec was in the works, the very thing that I had warned the Rwandans against. When I woke up the next morning, the radio was reporting that a three-year agreement had been signed. The Rwandans told me that there had not been an *entente* but merely a *déclaration*. As the day wore on, this intelligence was replaced by word through Father Levesque that there had been an exchange of letters with the Rwandans asking Quebec for whatever aid it could afford and Quebec doubling the $25,000 that it already gave.

Marcel Masse was in charge of the Quebec handling of the Rwandans on the final two days as the visitors were shown Quebec City, taken to Kent House — once the home of Governor Haldiman — for lunch, shown more cattle at a farm on the Ile d'Orléans and entertained at drinks at the summer home of the Mayor of Sillery. At Kent House, I had joined Masse and two priests in a discussion they were having about the visit of General de Gaulle, whom Masse was defending. Masse pretended to ignore me but then turned to put me in my place — and, through me, Prime Minister Pearson whose criticism of the French President had been raised in the discussion. "I am sorry, Mr. Ambassador", Masse said, "I forgot you are a representative of the Federal Government and I must observe that statements decrying the General, his great success in Quebec and the close relationship between Quebec and de Gaulle are themselves unacceptable." The young minister could not have made his position on the future of Canada clearer.

On the last day, a Sunday, the Rwandans went to the cathedral and we then left Quebec City for Montreal by the Trans Canada Highway in a Quebec Government motorcade escorted by a detachment of the Quebec Provincial Police. For the first hour, a fairly rational speed was maintained but the lead police car then stepped up the pace to 90 miles an hour. When a rear tire disintegrated on the Cadillac in which Kayibanda and Masse were riding, we held our breath as the drivers of the other cars pulled up without piling into each other. There was no back-up vehicle in the convoy and neither the QPP escort nor Masse suggested that the Rwandan President be placed in another car so that the motorcade might continue. We stood in the median of the busy highway for a half-hour while the wheel was changed. In security terms, it was an instance of utter incompetence for which the provincial hosts were solely responsible. Inspector Thériault and I refrained from intervening though Thériault directed a few blunt words on the situation to the head of the QPP escort.

Farther along the road to Montreal, we lunched at an inn at St. Marc. While we waited to dine, Kayibanda and Masse signed the *déclaration*. In it Quebec acknowledged the Rwandan request for aid — thus asserting that *l'État* had been approached directly by a sovereign state — and responded by doubling its existing aid of $25,000 to $50,000 for each of the next three years. What had led up to this ceremony had been done clandestinely. Now, Masse arranged the signing in the open, so that everyone present was aware of what was happening, so as to prove that the Feds had been had.

After the luncheon at St. Marc, the motorcade sped on to Montreal and through the city to Dorval Airport where Lionel Chevrier was waiting to bid the Rwandans farewell. They were soon off on an Eastern Airlines flight to New York and I returned with my federal companions to Ottawa. We were enormously relieved to have the visit behind us. And profoundly depressed about the future of Canada.

Next morning I put my impressions of the visit in a memorandum that described the events leading to the "declaration", the behaviour of the Quebec Government hosts towards the federal party and the motorcade incident. But, dramatic events were taking place in Kinshasa that day, highlighted by anti-white demonstrations and the sacking of the Belgian Embassy. These quickly took my mind off the Rwandan visit and led to the scrapping of my arrangements for a holiday in England, where my wife and daughters had been for almost four weeks. Within a few days, I was back in Kinshasa.

Much had been happening in the Congo, as the summer days passed in Montreal, to prevent the Mobutu Government from thinking about state visits and Expo. Major developments dominated the domestic scene. The currency had been reformed in June, the mercenary mutiny began in July and, in spite of both, lavish and expensive preparations were going ahead for the OAU Summit that would be held in Kinshasa in September. It was, indeed, only after the OAU meeting had ended that we heard again about the President's travel plans; on 22 September, Powys phoned to tell me that, on instructions, he had booked the President and Madame Mobutu and their personal entourage on the *Ile de France* sailing on 13 October to New York; there, Mobutu would speak to the United Nations and, after visiting Washington, go on to Ottawa. A few days later, when I had a brief chat with the President, he told me that he still hoped to find the time for the trip to Canada but "everything depended on the situation in the east" — the settlement of the mercenary uprising.

There had not yet been a formal response to the Canadian invitation from the Foreign Ministry. With little time remaining for the Visits' Panel in Ottawa to make arrangements, I decided to set a deadline of 5 October and warned the Congolese that, on that date, the invitation would be withdrawn. To back up my case, I enlisted the help of Charles Sumba, who was visiting Kinshasa from Ottawa, and was even more anxious than I to know if the President would go to Canada. I gave him copies of all of our correspondence to the Foreign Ministry concerning the visit, including a draft of a note declaring the invitation null and void, and this Sumba passed to Bomboko.

On 3 October, Robert McBride, the U.S. Ambassador, told me of two indications that Mobutu would not be going to Canada. The first was that Nyerere of Tanzania had called a meeting of neighbouring states for 18 October and Mobutu wanted to attend. The second was the President's alarm at hearing that a bomb had been found at Expo during the visit of the Secretary-General of the United Nations. I noted that it had begun to look as if Kititwa, the Minister of Foreign Trade would be "the high Congolese personality".

Results came on 4 October. The morning papers said that Madame Mobutu accompanied by five women would visit Expo. A note arrived from Kititwa, saying that he had been named to represent the President. This was followed by a note from the Foreign Minister stating that the President regretted that he could not accept the Governor-General's invitation, and naming Kititwa. Sumba, who delivered the note, told us that he had drafted it and obtained Bomboko's signature; his effort, he said modestly, had been "*une véritable tour de force*".

We were not yet out of the woods. The next day, Mobutu shuffled the

Cabinet. Kititwa was dropped and, when we asked to Foreign Ministry if that meant he would still be going to Canada, we were told that Bomboko would take on the assignment and we would be formally so notified on the morrow. Then we were told that in place of Bomboko, the representative would be Jean-Théodore Umba di Lutete, the new Vice-Minister of Foreign Affairs. Sumbu came to the Embassy to say goodbye before flying back to Canada; the poor man left not knowing who would be in the official party or whether Madame Mobutu still intended to cause him incredible protocol problems.

It was not until the 9th that the Congolese formally notified us of the appointment of Umba di Lutete who, we were told, would be accompanied by his newly acquired bride, Foreign Minister Bomboko's daughter, Marie-Jeanne. There was no further mention of Madame Mobutu. Umba di Lutete would leave the next day for his introduction to international diplomacy at the United Nations General Assembly. Given the level of Congolese representation, I wondered if I could beg off going to Canada for the visit. What stopped me from asking was the knowledge that, as for the Rwandan visit, I would be the senior Canadian representative with Umba di Lutete when he was in Quebec City, and responsible for being on guard against ploys by the Quebec Government. And so, I flew to Ottawa on 16 October to prepare for the arrival of the Congolese party on Friday the 18th.

If getting the Congolese to Ottawa and Expo had been infinitely more difficult than it had been to involve the Rwandans, the reverse was true of the visit itself. Umba di Lutete was anxious to please everyone on his first excursion into diplomacy and his junior status reduced the length of guest lists. The Canadian hosts were relaxed, happy that the long summer of repetitive and tedious ceremony was ending with the Congolese visit. And the illness of Premier Johnson of Quebec had led to the cancellation of the visit to Quebec City, thus abbreviating the schedule and making this one of the briefest as well as least confrontational state visits of the year by the representative of a French-speaking country.

In Montreal, the mood among the Expo authorities was as relaxed as it had been in Ottawa. The official dinner offered by Mayor Jean Drapeau in the superb *Hotel de Ville* and the Expo luncheon were light-hearted affairs. The weather, barely above freezing, curtailed the rhetoric of the speeches at the Congolese "National Day" ceremony and reduced the enthusiasm of the Congolese dancers when they performed in the open-air theatre. That evening, the Congolese gave their own party at the new Bonaventure Hotel. Advertised as a reception and dinner, it was attended by 600 guests and gate-crashers, of whom 500 stayed for dinner. Umba di Lutete delivered a speech in which he gave all sorts of advice which most of the crowd did not want to hear: there were groans from the separatists present when he opined that the continued use of English and French was as good for Canada as it was for Africa. When he proposed — quite properly in terms of protocol — a toast to the Queen, a fifth of the guests remained seated, uttering their disapproval with cries such as "Don't you know you are in Quebec!"

The next morning, the Congolese asked me if I would arrange for them to leave Canada that day, a day early, so that they might spend more time in Paris on their way home; they went shopping while we attended to this travel change. I spent the afternoon in the Laurentians with friends, getting back to Dorval Airport in Montreal in time to see the Congolese safely on their way. An hour later, I boarded an Air Canada flight for London to begin my own journey back to the Congo.

When I returned to Kinshasa and the Embassy, the continuing search for a resolution of the mercenary crisis was to take my mind off the problems of Canadian national unity for some months. Well before the mercenaries had been removed from the scene, however, there were renewed skirmishes between Ottawa and Quebec and, as 1968 rolled in, *La Francophonie* and the future of Canada were to be at the centre of the Embassy's activity.

CHAPTER 13

THE OTTAWA-QUEBEC
CONFLICT WIDENS

In February 1968, in Libreville, capital of the small west African country of Gabon, the Quebec Government flexed its newly-developed international muscle and pulled off a coup in foreign affairs that limned the background against which much of my last 10 months as Canadian Ambassador in Kinshasa was set. With the active sponsorship of the France of General Charles de Gaulle, Quebec was invited to send a delegation to the semi-annual meeting of education ministers of the members of *La Francophonie*.

The subject matter of the meeting interested Quebec only marginally: what mattered was the opportunity that it afforded to take part in an international gathering on an equal footing with representatives of sovereign states. Just as Canada itself had done earlier in the century, so Quebec had determined to obtain recognition as an international personality incrementally, step-by-step and brick-on-brick. Its authority in education and certain other fields under the federal constitution seemed to point the way in which this could be done. What made the Libreville conference especially significant for Quebec was that it was invited and Canada was not.

As invitations were formally the responsibility of the host country, the Canadian Government took the position that Gabon's action was tantamount to interference in the domestic affairs of Canada. This charge was becoming a familiar one: it had been made twice by Prime Minister Pearson against President de Gaulle in the aftermath of his cry of *"Vive le Québec libre"* in July 1967. Canada suspended its minimal diplomatic relations with Gabon, provoking the Gabonese to respond in a spirited and scathing statement. This reply referred throughout to the Canadian Government as the Government of *Ottawa* and to Prime Minister Pearson as *Mr.* Pearson whose action against Gabon was described as a "tantrum". Sneering reference was made to the low level of Canadian aid (two

Canadian advisers in Gabon and two Gabonese students on scholarships in Canada). The statement concluded by parroting the French and Quebec line that, as culture and education were exclusive provincial powers, Ottawa had no cause for complaint at not having been invited to the Libreville conference.

But while Ottawa could act against Gabon, it seemed incapable of controlling Quebec and unable to do much with France, the prime opponent and the mastermind behind Gabon's insult, except to make an oral protest to the Quai d'Orsay.

Libreville had the effect, however, of stiffening the resolve of the Canadian Government to launch a counter-offensive before the second meeting in 1968 of the education ministers, which was to be held from 22 to 26 April in Paris. There had been earlier attempts to ensure that Ottawa's version of the workings of the Canadian constitution were understood abroad. One that was still fresh in our minds was an instruction from the Prime Minister, near the end of 1967, to Kinshasa and some other posts to re-educate the locals on the powers of the central government in Canada. An opportunity to carry out this request came at the new year's levee when I found President Mobutu and Foreign Minister Bomboko together. Mobutu expressed understanding of the problem and agreed to use the Congo's influence to ensure that only Canada, and not Quebec, be invited to intergovernmental meetings such as those about to take place in Libreville and Paris. I told the President that we would regard an invitation to Quebec in the same light as one to Katanga. I followed up on this brief exchange by giving a piece of paper outlining the Canadian position to Jacques Bongoma of the President's office. The conversation with the President was to prove of immense value to me in the months ahead.

On 3 April, we received a telegram from the Department of External Affairs, signed by the Under-Secretary, Marcel Cadieux, instructing us to take up the cudgel to ensure that Canada was represented at Paris, and Quebec excluded as a separate delegation. I saw the Congolese Education Minister, Bernadin Mungul-Diaka, at his residence and asked for the Congo's understanding and respect for the Canadian view on invitations to the Francophone education conferences. In expressing full sympathy with our position, Mungul-Diaka referred to the Congo's own unhappy experience with secession in Katanga. But he claimed that he could not raise the question at the Paris meeting. Quebec would be at Paris, he said, because it had been at Libreville; it needed no further invitation. He added, however, that the Congo would be the host of the next meeting in

January 1969 and he could promise that Canada would be invited. Meanwhile, he observed wisely, the problem lay between Canada and France.

On 18 April, I took a similar message to Brazzaville where I called on Levy Makany, the Minister of National Education of that Congo. He, too, promised sympathy and understanding at the Paris meeting for which he was leaving later that day. He also made the interesting remark that there were no invitations to the Paris conference, only reminders: hence, Quebec, having been to Libreville, would be at Paris. As I left Makany's office, I noticed the French Ambassador arriving. My *démarche* was certain not to remain private for long.

At the Paris meeting, events went much as Mungul-Diaka and Makany had implied they would. Quebec attended as a full participant and Canada was excluded. But a hopeful decision was the acceptance of the Congolese offer to be the host of the 1969 conference. At the Embassy, we knew that a testing time lay ahead and we thirsted for information on the subject. I wrote a personal letter with this thought to Arthur Blanchette, then head of the division dealing with Federal-Provincial affairs in the Department, and sent a telegram enquiring about the state of play. One of my officers who returned from home leave a few days later had an explanation for the lack of news. Officers at headquarters, he said, ran for cover whenever *La Francophonie* was mentioned.

Not everyone was in hiding in Ottawa for, in mid-May, a telegram was received at the Embassy asking for an expression of views on the possible Congolese course of action on invitations to the January conference. Would they formally invite Quebec as well as Canada or would there be some alternative, such as including Quebec by way of a "reminder"? In Kinshasa, this question could not be answered with precision except for the confident and gloomy assertion that any pressure by France on the Congolese would be of great importance, given the role of France as an aid donor and a supplier of military equipment. Without such pressure, there would be no problem because the Congolese would invite only Canada. But pressure was likely and the result would be that invitations would be extended to both Canada and Quebec.

In the Embassy, we were concerned that the low level of Canadian aid to the Congo gave us little leverage in our relations with the Congolese. There had been only 11 Canadian technical assistance experts in the country when I arrived in November 1965. Chronic political instability had taken its toll and only two were left in June 1968. I noted in my diary:

> If we don't have more when the meeting of the Francophone education
> ministers takes place in Kinshasa next January — a meeting which Quebec

will probably attend — the Canadian programme of aid will invite ridicule.

Two days later, I sent a telegram to Ottawa urging this line and proposing that CUSO (Canadian University Service Overseas) volunteers also be assigned to the Congo. On 14 June, my campaign was reinforced when Mungul-Diaka called the Belgian Chargé d'Affaires and me to his office to make a pitch for the assistance of friendly governments in a programme by the Congo to recruit teachers for senior educational institutions. I explained to the Minister that I was trying to get CUSO to come to the Congo and also promised to recommend in favour of his general request. It seemed to me at the time that we could have a direct confrontation with Quebec over teachers which was not possible over such matters as aid through the United Nations Development Plan (UNDP) or paper for school textbooks which we had been giving for the past couple of years. If we could get one or two dozen teachers to the Congo before January under External Aid or CUSO auspices, I thought that we might be able to make the Congolese realize that the aid programme of Ottawa also covered education.

Early in May, I was asked to accept the assignment of High Commissioner to Cyprus with a probable departure date from the Congo of just after the middle of the year. The reluctance of the Secretary of State for External Affairs, Mitchell Sharp, to put new ambassadorial appointments to the Prime Minister before the 25 June federal general election, delayed the process. Further delay was caused by the ill-health of the colleague in Nicosia whom I was to replace. Repeatedly, I expressed concern that my successor should arrive as early as possible in order to become well-established before the January conference.

A major, new element in the evolution of the Canadian aid programme to the Congo was that of assistance to Air Congo, the country's sole airline. In addition to a domestic service of sorts, Air Congo also flew to some African points and to Europe. Victor Nendaka, the Minister of Transport, had summoned me to his office, on 29 April, on what I was told was an urgent matter. I arranged to get there at noon and that hour passed as I sat in his waiting room. A half hour later, I told his *chef de cabinet* that I had another appointment and regrettably would have to leave. I was quickly presented to Nendaka. He told me that he wanted Canada to provide personnel for a thorough study of Air Congo's operations and to recommend courses of action. He indicated that there would be sales possibilities. I agreed to let Ottawa know and to sound them out on the idea. Uppermost in my mind was the conviction that, despite the appalling state of Air Congo and the hazards of doing business with the

Congolese, there could be an advantage to the Canadian aircraft industry and Canadian airlines if we played the game hard.

Ottawa was slow in responding fully but we were given to understand that the request was being considered favourably and that Air Canada was involved. We learned later that the Americans had suggested to the Congolese that they turn to Canada for this assistance and, on 19 June, Charles Mann, the director of the office of the U.S. Agency for International Development (AID) in the Congo, came to see me to enquire about progress on the request. He confirmed that the Embassy had favoured Canadian participation in this field because it would help to diversify the sources of aid on which the Congo depended. With diversification, there would be a political bonus for the west because, with more countries than Belgium involved, the Congolese would be less able to afford the luxury of anti-foreign — meaning anti-western — outbursts. Diversification would also make Mobutu less vulnerable to the often-heard charge that he was handing control of operational areas of the economy over to the Belgians.

Mann was less than subtle when he continued his analysis of the advantages of a positive Canadian response to the Congolese. He said that he knew why Canada wanted to obtain the favour of the Congolese Government. He had had a conversation with Mungul-Diaka in which they touched on the forthcoming meeting of Francophone ministers of education in January in Kinshasa. Mungul-Diaka, Mann told me, had said that there would be only one invitation to Canada and it would go to the federal government and not to a province. Mann's foxy addendum was an interesting confirmation of the promise that the Minister had made to me in April.

External Affairs advised me on 22 June that two experts of Air Canada would be sent to the Congo to undertake a study in depth of Air Congo's operations: their eventual report and recommendations would be given "sympathetic consideration", but no commitments would be made in advance. I felt that this was promising as did the Congolese when I passed the information to them. A few days later at a reception on the presidential riverboat, I spoke to Nendaka who asked that we hurry up the arrival of the two experts. Bomboko was also aware of the favourable Canadian reply as a result of a note that we had sent to the Foreign Ministry and he asked me to thank Ottawa.

About this time, it became clear that we were not alone in the Air Congo act and that the Congolese had invited others in the West to look into their air transport problems. A British firm had been employed to do an audit of Air Congo. The Dutch had been negotiating with Air Congo for the sale of 10 Fokker Friendships. So, quite naturally, the Dutch Ambassador wanted to know if Air Canada would be supplying technicians, this well before our experts had arrived. A few weeks later the Dutchman expressed his disillusion to me because of the failure of the Congolese to produce any money for the Friendship contract. I was not sympathetic: in my view, the deal should not have been pursued at that time. However, a financial agreement for the aircraft was eventually signed in September, long before the Air Canada team would have the opportunity to make recommendations on a multitude of things, including the aircraft types that Air Congo should have in its future fleet.

It would have been extraordinary if the Americans had not also been in the Air Congo act. In June, a team from the Federal Aviation Authority (FAA) and the Civil Aviation Board (CAB) arrived to study airfield construction and maintenance, navigational aids and electronic and equipment requirements, notably of aircraft. As their terms of reference overlapped those of the Canadian survey, liaison was clearly necessary. After discussions with the leaders of the U.S. team, I decided to ask Ottawa to send the Air Canada group to Kinshasa a fortnight before the Americans left so as to benefit from what they had learned of the Congolese requirements. Later in July Robert McBride told me that the State Department hoped for great things from the Canadian survey and deemed it conceivable that Air Canada might operate the international service of Air Congo. McBride went on to say that the Import-Export Bank would approve the sale of Lockheed C-130s to the Congo if the Air Canada team recommended these aircraft for internal freight runs. He did not need to add that C-130s would also be useful for military trooping in emergencies, thus satisfying American strategic objectives in the Congo without having to continue committing the U.S. Air Force.

Towards the end of July 1968, we learned that the Air Canada team was to arrive within a week. Instead of two members, there were four. We noted, however, that only one of the four names was French and asked ourselves what proficiency in that language the other three possessed. We were dismayed to find, when they arrived, that it was nil. It was a bad beginning. I sent a blistering wire in French to the External Aid Office in Ottawa telling them that they knew very well that this was a Francophone country and that it was folly to send a team three-quarters of which was unilingual English. Ironically, the specialty of the one French-speaker of the group — flying — was the only one in which knowledge of French did not matter because most of the air crew of Air Congo were from

English-speaking countries. The External Aid Office replied surlily that it was holiday time in Canada and that, in any case, the team was not performing technical assistance but merely making a survey; I did not get the relevance of that distinction. A few days later, I was advised that three Francophones were on their way to Kinshasa.

The Air Canada group made preliminary contact with the American teams and with the Belgian who was the linchpin of the Air Congo operation. Jim Bonthron, the Second Secretary at the Embassy, took the team to the Ministry of Transport where they were unexpectedly received by Nendaka. He made it clear that he was after Air Canada's management of Air Congo for a five-year period and, though he used the term "technical assistance", he said that there was plenty of money available for the airline. We wondered, afterwards, if we should not offer a management contract sweetened by Canadian training of technicians, sales staff and administrators.

Within days the Air Canada team had come to preliminary conclusions. A basic one was that Air Congo was in such bad shape that it would have to be rebuilt from the ground up. Experienced as they were in the air transport business, the members of the team were finding flying hazardous in the Congo: they had to make a domestic flight with Air Congo in the course of their survey and it had worried them. They were impressed by the frank admission of shortcomings by the senior Congolese of Air Congo and by their relative efficiency in spite of all the muddle. The judgment of the team was less kind about the attitude of the Belgians who were employed by Air Congo: the Canadians thought that many of the Belgian advisers and technicians were deliberately obstructing the advancement of Congolese in the airline.

The team left after two weeks. When they departed, there was yet another change in Mobutu's cabinet, Nendaka going to the Finance portfolio and handing over Transport to Faustin Nzeza. Nendaka told me that he would retain his interest in the future of Air Congo and might visit Canada later in the year to keep in touch with the outcome of the Air Canada survey. A few days later, Nzeza called me in to go over the Air Canada visit. He said the Congolese Government wanted Air Canada to appoint a senior French-speaking officer as director-general of Air Congo with full powers to carry out reforms; if we could not send someone immediately for a four-year term, they would take an interim appointee for six months, but they wanted our help and early action. While reminding Nzeza that our only commitment was to produce a report, I promised to transmit his request.

The report of the Air Canada survey team arrived in October. Predictably, it was in English only. I delivered it to Nzeza with an abbreviated list in French of its recommendations. He was upset that we were delaying implementation until CIDA (the Canadian International Development Agency, the new name of the External Aid Office) had discussed them with Air Canada. He did not want a government-to-government relationship but one between companies.

On 15 October, CIDA advised me by telegram that Air Canada would welcome a direct approach by Air Congo for a Canadian management comprising a director-general, a technical director and other experts. Air Congo was to foot the bill, although it was possible that CIDA would later provide an aid umbrella. The telegram added that Air Canada would insist on certain strong conditions such as no interference from other advisers, control of military flights and the improvement of air traffic control to international standards. I passed all this to the Minister of Transport by letter and learned that his personal assistant, Oscar Muyayi, and the President of Air Congo, Louis Lumumba, were to leave shortly for discussions in Montreal with Air Canada. A tentative agreement between the two airlines was reached at the beginning of November. The first members of the management team, headed by Hervé Lesage who was to be the new director-general, arrived on 15 November, just before I left Kinshasa for good.

The Air Congo enterprise was the largest and most exciting of the various aid schemes that developed in 1968. More than the other projects, it was also more visible to the members of the Congolese Government whom we hoped to influence in time for the January meeting of education ministers. Our efforts in the teaching field, however, bore a more direct relationship to that meeting and so we worked hard to ensure a visible Canadian presence in Congolese schools. The External Aid Office had agreed at the end of June that something could be done to meeting Mungul-Diaka's request for senior teachers for the coming school year; however, university lecturers were more difficult, the Office added. We were asked to obtain more details. Our excellent working relations with the Ministry of National Education faltered before we could do this. On 6 July, the morning newspapers carried the announcement that Mungul-Diaka had been dismissed from the cabinet and from Mobutu's party for *manquements* — omissions, failures and shortcomings — prejudicial to the aims of the revolution. We felt that we had lost an ally in the battle of the January conference.

A few days later, the former Minister of Labour, Alphonse-Roger

Kithima, was given the portfolio of National Education. Once more we began to pick up the pieces. After we had settled with the Congolese on a figure of a dozen high school teachers, we eventually received six. CUSO came through in September with five volunteer teachers. Alain DesGroseillers, the CUSO co-ordinator for our part of Africa, had visited Kisangani in August and had been appalled at the sight of large colleges and schools, not to mention the University of Kisangani itself, standing empty and abandoned because of lack of staff. Requests for over a hundred volunteers had been put to him. Even with the arrival of the modest total of five, I was pleased that we had succeeded in interesting CUSO in the Congo. Their presence, like that of the CIDA teachers, would help us to build up the case for the Congo's support at the January meeting.

Earlier in the year, I had proposed that, as an additional sweetener to the Congolese Government, we should participate in the Kinshasa Trade Fair of 1969. This was to be the first international fair held in the Congo since independence in 1960 and large resources were being poured into the project. At the end of July, the Department responded that they were interested in the fair and would send an exhibit. Two weeks later, we were instructed to ask for 1600 square feet of space. Clearly, my successor would have his hands full in 1969.

Although quite a substantial package of Canadian involvement in the Congo was being put together, I felt that more was needed. In a telegram in early September, I reviewed Canada's relations with the Congo in order to encourage Ottawa to provide us with guidance on tactics in the event of a confrontation with Quebec at Kinshasa. I noted that our aid in education and civil aviation and our announced exhibit in the 1969 trade fair all helped to make the Congolese authorities sympathetic towards Canada. But, I went on, some more concrete arguments, in the form of aid, were needed to bolster the constitutional position that we held and, to that end, I asked that a senior official of CIDA come to Kinshasa in November with authority to approve projects on the spot.

Pre-conference tactics also concerned me. While Mobutu and his ministers and top bureaucrats were well-disposed to Canada, they were capable of blunder and the French had proved that they could create mischief. I put to the Department a number of reasons why we were better placed in relation to the Kinshasa meeting than we had been to Libreville. Notably, we had a diplomatic mission in Kinshasa and were thus able to follow closely the intentions of the host government, to bring persuasion to bear on it and to employ a wide range of diplomatic techniques. I proposed that we make use of some of our friends by asking them to make clear, in their dealings with the Congolese, their support of our position on invitations to the meeting. I also suggested that we should include in the Canadian Delegation to the conference someone versed in the Canadian political realities of the problem as well as its international implications. But I added to my confident assessment this warning:

> ... it is foolhardy in the Congo to take fidelity for granted and the French, who have covert as well as overt means of exerting pressure here, might easily make cuckolds of us at the last minute.

A few days later this fear was revived when the Belgian Embassy passed on the information that the Congolese hoped to be able to invite both Quebec and Canada. According to the Belgians, the Congolese felt that an invitation to Quebec would be hard to avoid because it was France's wish that Quebec be invited and France was "the patron of *La Francophonie*". This prompted me to recommend that our views be conveyed to the Congolese at the highest level and I suggested this be done by means of a personal letter from Prime Minister Trudeau to President Mobutu.

My sundry suggestions were acknowledged privately by Arthur Blanchette. He wrote flatteringly that he appreciated Kinshasa's telegrams, "timely, foresighted, perceptive and elegantly and wittily written". A good deal of contingency planning, he assured me, had been done in Ottawa. An aid mission was being sent to the Congo at the end of October or early in November. CIDA planned to post one or two officers to Kinshasa in 1969 and the Trade Commissioner Service was sending a senior officer to study the question of restoring the presence that it had had at the post until independence. Blanchette thought that these and initiatives already underway would put us in a fair bargaining position with the Congolese. Discussing the other elements of the situation, he referred to imminent federal-provincial constitutional talks whose outcome was anybody's guess. But, he noted, the Quebec economy was under pressure and that might "cause Mr. Johnson to pause a bit". By coincidence, the letter arrived on the day of Premier Johnson's death.

When Joseph Ndanu, my Congolese counterpart in Ottawa, came to see me on 27 September, our conversation centred on *La Francophonie*. Ndanu told me that he had been approached in Montreal by a Quebec official who had expatiated upon the well known argument that the competence of Quebec in education extended into the international field. To this, Ndanu said he had responded that, as far as he was concerned, there would be only one invitation to the January meeting which would be delivered to Ottawa; if the Canadian Government wished to ask Quebec to participate, that was a Canadian affair. I emphasized to Ndanu that it was of the greatest importance to the development of bilateral relations between Canada and the Congo that there should be no repetition of the Libreville situation in January. I recalled that, after Libreville, Canada had suspended diplomatic relations with Gabon. If this were to happen after the Kinshasa conference, we, as the resident diplomats in each other's country, would have to leave our respective posts. Ndanu, a non-career ambassador, took the point and reassured me that he would be pressing the Canadian view on the Congolese authorities during his visit. Then, as an afterthought, he remarked that what worried him was that the Congo was simply the host-country for the meeting; invitations were the responsibility of the organizing committee which, he presumed, was in Paris. It was a clairvoyant observation.

I had hoped that my successor would be in place when the CIDA mission arrived. Ottawa was still having trouble, however, in finding someone to replace me at the post which did not rank as a plum in the foreign service. At the end of September, I was assured that my own departure, already once postponed, would probably be possible at the end of October. Details of the aid mission were received on 7 October. In a telegram signed by Mitchell Sharp, we were instructed to tell the Congolese that to demonstrate Canada's capacity and willingness to increase its aid, we envisaged a technical assistance programme of one million dollars annually and would consider requests for two or three capital assistance projects of a million dollars each. The Congolese were invited to provide us with a list of projects for study by the CIDA mission.

I transmitted the outline of the aid offers to the Vice-Minister of Foreign Affairs on 10 October. At the same time, I informed him of the nomination of Marc Baudouin, a 38-year-old foreign service officer, as the next Canadian Ambassador and requested the agreement of the Congolese Government to have him. This seemed to clear the way for my departure but my hopes to leave before the visit of the CIDA team were dashed when I was instructed to stay for their arrival and to go to Rwanda to pay my farewell calls there. On 23 October, a long, apologetic telegram came from Ottawa asking me to remain in Kinshasa throughout the visit of the aid mission from the 7th to 17th of November. This was the fourth change in my departure plans. I decided that it must be the last and arranged to leave on 17 November on the same flight that the CIDA group would take.

On 30 October, I paid my farewell call on President Mobutu. He received me at the Presidential Palace, in an upstairs drawing room elegantly furnished in the heaviest of Belgian styles. Our conversation began with diplomatic exchanges of mutual admiration and an expression of appreciation on his part for Canadian aid, the details of which I outlined to refresh his memory. Mobutu said that he was impressed by the growth of this aid and by our intention to send a special mission to examine new areas of assistance. We then moved on to the January meeting of education ministers. I wrote afterwards in my diary:

> He was well briefed on the education ministers' meeting and without prompting from me said 'Oh, yes, the conference before [the] OCAM [conference]'. 'The Congo is not Gabon,' he went on, 'We don't take orders from France in the manner of some of their former colonies.' He went on that he had his own troubles with the French. If any foreign state tried to deal direct with a Congolese province or a provincial governor, he wouldn't tolerate it. What, he asked, would de Gaulle say if a foreign state meddled in Alsace Lorraine or Brittany or the Pays des Basques? He expressed full understanding of Canada's position and assured me that only Ottawa would be invited to the meeting.

It was sweet music to my ears. I was also pleased at my good fortune in having been given a farewell audience, a courtesy that had been denied to every departing ambassador since Jacques Kosciusko-Morizet of France had left in February. (Ironically, *he* was at this point a director of the Secretariat of State for Co-operation in Paris, masterminding the French strategy for the Kinshasa meeting and the presence of Quebec.)

The CIDA mission arrived on 7 November just after I returned from my farewell trip to Rwanda. The mission consisted of Henri Gaudefroy and Adelard Gascon of CIDA and George Rejhon of External Affairs. Our discussions covered the gamut of aid philosophy and projects and there was no difficulty between the visitors and the Embassy over these matters. The first contact with the Congolese was less auspicious. A call had been arranged on Umba di Lutete for noon on 9 November. I met the members of the mission at the Foreign Ministry where we were told by a junior protocol officer that the Vice-Minister could not see us because he was indisposed. When Kalamazi, the Chief of Protocol, passed by, I told him what had happened and asked that Umba di Lutete be informed that this was the mission's first contact with the Congolese Government. Kalamazi disappeared and returned to tell me that the Vice-Minister was actually with Foreign Minister Bomboko and too busy to receive the visitors. We arranged a new appointment for another day. As we left the Ministry, I spotted Umba di Lutete sneaking out of the back door of the building.

In spite of minor obstacles such as this, and other difficulties of doing business in the Congo, the CIDA mission spent 10 useful days in the country. On 15 November, with the mission members present, Umba di Lutete and I signed an entente which, as we were to say in a press release, "marked in a tangible manner the wish for closer and closer co-operation between Canada and the Congo". Amongst other things, the agreement governed the privileges and terms of service of Canadian technical assistance personnel in the Congo. At that ceremony, I gave the Vice-Minister a letter addressed to President Mobutu informing him that the Honourable Paul Martin, now Leader of the Government in the Senate, would visit Kinshasa on 10 December. The letter went on to say that Mr. Martin would deliver a personal letter from Prime Minister Trudeau explaining — in line with my suggestion to Ottawa in September — the Canadian Government's position towards the conference of education ministers; the Trudeau letter would also invite Mobutu to visit Canada.

My last full day in Kinshasa, 16 November, was spent almost entirely on aid matters. The CIDA mission briefed me on the proposals which had been made to them by the Congolese. The list began with the proposal, conceived by the mission and readily agreed to by Nzeza, that Canada take over effective control of the civil aviation function of the Ministry of Transport, to complement the work of Air Canada with Air Congo. The Congolese asked us to undertake a scientific study of Lake Tanganyika to determine how to stabilize the level of the lake. They wanted us to establish an agricultural college, a school for aviation mechanics and a school for commercial secretaries and administrators. There was more: we were requested to furnish personnel and equipment for a technical school and the Lake Moero navigation and fishing institute. Additional paper was needed for the printing of school textbooks. And, finally, the Congolese wanted us to do a study of forest resources in the Mayumbe and Lake Leopold II areas. It was an impressive shopping list.

At the end of the day, the CIDA team and the Embassy prepared a press release on the mission's visit to Kinshasa. In the evening, we held a meeting with the four members of the advance party of the Air Canada management team, who had left for the Congo as soon as Air Canada had been asked officially by the Minister of External Affairs to undertake an operation in support of Air Congo. Although a formal agreement had not yet been concluded between the two airlines, the management team and I agreed that the team should act as if it possessed full authority. I suggested that a first test of their authority might be to request the Congolese Government not purchase new aircraft for the time being.

When I left the Congo the next morning, I felt that the ground had been well laid for my successor. Though I did not envy him the role that he would have to perform in the weeks leading up to the January meeting, things were to go better for Canada at that conference than I thought possible. Senator Martin's visit in December was most successful in obtaining further assurances from the Congolese Government that Canada would be invited to the meeting and Martin came away impressed by Mobutu's knowledge of the Canadian constitutional situation and by his firm intention to invite only Canada. A week later, the Congo delivered a letter to the Embassy inviting Ottawa to take part in the January meeting. All seemed to be going well.

In Paris, Kosciusko-Morizet was pulling strings to achieve a different result. One week before the meeting, these new French efforts led to the despatch (via the Senegalese official of the secretariat of *La Francophonie* in charge of the administrative arrangements) of an invitation to the Quebec Minister of Education to participate in the conference. Supported by the French Embassy in Kinshasa, the official claimed that the Congolese Government was agreeable to this course of action. Marc Baudouin rapidly obtained proof from the Congolese that this was not the case and, faced with this, the Senegalese official sent a new message to the Quebec authorities explaining that his earlier telegram was to be considered as an invitation to Quebec to join the Canadian Delegation. This did not put an end to the designs of the Quebec Government to be represented on its own.

In Ottawa, intense activity in the Department of External Affairs had led to the conclusion that a Canadian delegation representing the three main French-speaking provinces should be fielded. Thus, Ontario and New Brunswick were also in the plan. Negotiations on the issue had been underway for some weeks between Ottawa and Quebec but, on 10 January 1969, three days before the conference was to begin, the matter was still not resolved. Prime Minister Trudeau, then in London, found it necessary to send a long message to Premier Bertrand of Quebec. This telegram, which was made public in Ottawa, declared bluntly that only one Canadian delegation could be present at conferences such as that at Kinshasa, and reiterated the hope that Quebec, duly identified, would be at that meeting as part of the Canadian Delegation. The telegram concluded by informing Bertrand that the Delegation would be led by Premier Robichaud of New Brunswick.

Before the day was out, Quebec had come to terms. The chairmanship of the Delegation was to be shared by Premier Robichaud and the Quebec Minister of Education, Jean-Marie Morin. If the choice of Robichaud indicated the grim seriousness of Ottawa's approach to the conference, so did the inclusion of Marc Lalonde, the Prime Minister's powerful private secretary, as an adviser.

Yet, it was a complicated compromise and a shaky one. Incidents were bound to happen and did. From a friend, I learned of the transit through Brussels of the "Canadian" delegation on 11 January. The group led by Premier Robichaud had arrived first and waited in the VIP lounge at the airport for the Sabena night flight to Kinshasa. Meanwhile the Quebec component arrived from Paris in a French government aircraft with the French Delegation and went straight to the waiting room at the departure gate. Two officers of the Canadian Embassy located the Quebeckers and invited them to join the Canadians in the VIP lounge. Only a couple of junior officials accepted and paid a brief visit. Morin, their leader, refused when he was encountered whiling away the time by walking the long corridor of the departures wing. By sheer coincidence, Mrs. Marc Baudouin and her four young children were on the same flight to Kinshasa. That night, Sabena had to extend the front section of the Boeing 707 to accommodate more than 30 first-class passengers.

On the opening day in Kinshasa, only the flags of Canada, Ontario and New Brunswick flew in front of the conference building, the Quebec flag having failed to arrive. But one was quickly made available by the French Delegation. For some technical reason, the Canadian flag had to be lowered first to raise the *fleur-de-lys*, an event which was duly recorded by a *Radio Canada* film crew. The next evening, viewers of the French-language service of the Canadian Broadcasting Corporation were informed that the incident represented not a mechanical hitch but the replacement of the Canadian by the Quebec flag on the orders of a French official.

There may have been a grain of truth in the Radio Canada interpretation because, throughout the conference, the delegation of France persisted in its attempts to cause trouble for Canada and managed to create embarrassment on several occasions. However, the French failed to disrupt the compromise between Ottawa and Quebec and, when the meeting was over, it was clear that the complicated arrangements for the curious Canadian Delegation had been successful. The compromise and the contact between the Federal Government representatives and those of Quebec were to provide the basis of a stronger Canadian presence at the next meeting of Francophone ministers of education in Paris in May 1969. In retrospect, indeed, the Kinshasa conference was a pivotal occasion: if it was not a turning point in the strained relations between Ottawa and the Province of Quebec, it was at least the first sign that the Quebeckers had become reserved in their eagerness to accept a French embrace that looked to others like neo-colonialism.

The Ottawa success at Kinshasa was even more satisfying to look back on a year later when the growing contacts within the French-speaking world led to the establishment, at a meeting in Niamey, Niger, of the Agency for Cultural and Technical Co-operation. The Agency was set up to provide a focus for all international French-language organizations and to foster co-operation in educational, scientific and technical matters among countries that were partly or entirely French-speaking. With the Canadian role in *La Francophonie* by then accepted, Canada was a founding member of the Agency and, with France, a senior partner in meeting its expenses.

CHAPTER 14

CYPRUS 1969:
THE SETTING

My assignment to Cyprus began on 10 December 1968. A year and three weeks later, I closed the doors of the High Commission in Nicosia to business and left the island on 18 January 1970. It was too brief a stay in this place of high interest.

We lived and worked in the Greek sector of Nicosia. As Greek Cypriots accounted for 78 percent of the population of the island,[84] it was inevitable that we depended for administrative support on Greek bankers, travel agents and air service, communications, grocers, insurance agents and other businessmen. Although we attempted to keep up an appropriate level of contact with the smaller Turkish Cypriot community (18 percent of the population), the less developed character of their community limited the possibility of extensive commercial and social ties. Despite these circumstances, it was not difficult to maintain an impartiality which was probably right on target when we seemed pro-Turkish to the Greeks and pro-Greek to the Turks.

The Canadian High Commission had been in Nicosia since the arrival of the first Canadian contingent of the United Nations Force in Cyprus (UNFICYP) in March 1964. The first resident High Commissioner was Arthur Andrew who was Ambassador to Israel but soon found that his responsibilities in Cyprus necessitated his presence there rather than in Tel Aviv. Andrew set up the office in Nicosia; in August 1965, after enduring the worst of the Cyprus crises, he handed the post over to Tom Wainman-Wood, a High Commissioner responsible solely for the island. From Wainman-Wood, I took over a mission with over four years of experience behind it and procedures well in place for the role of backing up the Canadian contribution to UNFICYP and peacekeeping.

The staff was tiny. Most important of all was the Canadian Forces Adviser, Lieutenant-Colonel William D. (Bill) Little who had been in

Cyprus since August 1966 and was well acquainted with the situation on the island and well known to the key players of UNFICYP and the Greek and Turkish sides. There was only one political officer, the Third Secretary, Kenneth D. Harley. On his first posting, he was to be replaced in mid-1969 by the more experienced Ray E. Caldwell, a Second Secretary with a posting in Prague under his belt.

A foreign service secretary and a communicator, both from External Affairs, and my chauffeur, a Canadian army sergeant-driver, rounded out the staff. We were guarded by four corporals of the Canadian Provost Corps who slept on the chancery premises. We employed a Cypriot receptionist-telephonist and a driver-messenger and there was one servant at the residence on the government payroll. In addition to the staff in Nicosia, four officers of the Canadian Embassy in Tel Aviv were accredited to the High Commision, two from the Trade Commissioner Service and two from Immigration.

The troubled island had a long and complicated history which had seen it flourish in ancient times when it was dominated successively by Egyptian, Greek, Roman and Byzantine dynasties and empires and the Crusaders and Venetians, only to fall to the Ottoman Turks in 1571. In 1878, Britain took over the administration of the island which it annexed in 1914. Independence came in 1960 after a guerrilla war conducted against the British by the Greek Cypriots who were backed by Greece and led by a Greek Army officer, Colonel George Grivas. By international agreements reached through immensely intricate negotiations at Zurich and London in 1960, Cyprus obtained its independence under a delicately-balanced mechanism which required the best of goodwill to work.[85]

Basically, the agreements recognized the historic separateness of the two communities and perpetuated it within the institutional framework of the new Republic. The president was to be a Greek Cypriot and the vice-president Turkish Cypriot, each being elected by his own community. Of the cabinet of 10 ministers, seven were to be Greek and three Turkish. This ratio was used also in the membership of the House of Representatives and the public service, police and gendarmerie. For the army, the ratio was set at 60/40. Separate communal chambers were established to exercise legislative power on religious, educational and cultural matters and on personal status, and taxation powers were accorded to the chambers to provide funds for these purposes. Separate Greek and Turkish municipalities were created in the five largest towns.

Independence was attained on 16 August 1960 and, in the following three years, a number of serious constitutional problems were encountered.

Some provisions of the constitution were never implemented. When the Turkish ministers vetoed the budget in August 1963 because they believed that they were not receiving their constitutional rights, President Makarios sought a way out of the financial impasse. He proposed constitutional amendments involving 13 measures to facilitate the smooth functioning of the State and remove causes of intercommunal friction, but these were rejected by the Turkish side. On 21 December 1963, the first shot was fired in the intercommunal war; it put an end to constructive discussions on the constitution for the next four and a half years, but the constitution remained legally in force in spite of the troubles that followed.

The constitution was only one of a series of basic documents signed when Cyprus became independent. Safeguards were spelled out in great detail to guarantee the rights of Greece, Turkey and the United Kingdom. Under the Treaty of Alliance, Greece and Turkey were given the right of intervention and the right to station contingents in Cyprus. Under the Treaty of Establishment, the United Kingdom retained sovereignty over two areas totalling 99 square miles (256 sq. km) known as the Sovereign Base Areas (SBAs).

These external interests remained in play when I came to Cyprus at the end of 1968. Although the Agreements had ruled out *Enosis* (union with Greece) and the partition of the island into separate Greek and Turkish states, some elements of the Greek Cypriot community had never given up on *Enosis* and some in the Turkish Cypriot community still thought in terms of partitioning the island. Pan-Hellenism dictated to Greece its support for the Greek Cypriots while strategic considerations and the right to protect the Turkish Cypriot minority determined Turkey's attitude. When the fighting had broken out in 1963, both countries supported their respective communities with arms and men and, as it had been during the fifties and earlier, Cyprus was once more a flash-point in relations betwen Greece and Turkey.

Shortly after the outbreak of fighting, Britain acted quickly at the request of the Government of Cyprus to separate the two sides and so forestall the threat of an invasion of the island by Turkey. Ceasefire lines, the "Green Lines" of several communities, were established in a little over a week and, in January 1964, the British called a conference in London to be attended by delegates from Britain, Greece and Turkey and the leaders of the two Cypriot communities. This conference failed but meanwhile the United Nations sent an observer to the island. A proposal for a NATO peacekeepng force was amended to include United Nations participation.

When this scheme was turned down by the Cyprus Government, it was superseded by a Security Council resolution of 4 March 1964 creating a United Nations peacekeeping force. On 13 March, Canada agreed to take part in the Force and the first Canadian troops wearing the UN blue beret arrived in Cyprus three days later as part of a small UN army that soon numbered over 6300.

UNFICYP had an eventful beginning but after two months it had gained the respect of the Cypriots and some control over the situation. Between that time and my days in Cyprus, there had been two very critical periods: in August 1964 and November and December 1967, intense local battles occurred and invasion by Turkey was imminent. The fighting in 1967 marked a watershed because Turkey, having made it plain that it held Greece responsible, demanded and achieved the removal from the island of Colonel Grivas of *EOKA* fame in the 1950s, along with several thousand Greek Army troops who had been introduced illegally.[86] There was also a mutual realization by Greece and Turkey that they had come very close to war over Cyprus. When, on 7 March 1968, the Cyprus Government lifted its economic blockade of the Turkish Cypriot enclaves, the stage was set for the Secretary-General of the United Nations to appoint a Special Representative whose task was to persuade the two communities to stop shooting and start talking.

Though Cyprus was quiet in December 1968 when I took over the High Commission, the island presented a warlike face. It was not necessary to travel far to see evidence of past conflict or the makings of future strife. In the heart of old Nicosia, on either side of the line separating Greek from Turk, there was no street without a barricade of rusting, rock-filled oil drums, no path unwatched by a Turkish fighter or Greek National Guardsman. Along that twisting line through the old city, bisecting the circular area enclosed by the walls of the Venetian fortifications, blue-helmeted soldiers of UNFICYP patrolled. In the countryside, barbed wire ran along the ridges and circled the peaks of the mountains between the capital and the once-idyllic port of Kyrenia. Below the fairy-tale Crusader castle of St. Hilarion and near the groves of Lawrence Durrell's *Bitter Lemons* at Bellapais, gun positions pocked the hillsides. Greek and Turkish flags were everywhere, the blue emblem of the Greek cross competing with the red standard of the Turkish crescent across the usually narrow no man's land where UNFICYP outposts were identified by the blue-and-white United Nations flag.

It was apparent that armed confrontation had existed so long that it was part of the Cypriot way of life. To a large extent the economy depended on it, especially in the Turkish-held area north of Nicosia. The Greek and Turkish contingents, respectively 950 and 650 strong, that the two countries were entitled to station in Cyprus were still there in 1968. There were more from each country, thousands more, on the island illegally, providing the officers and specialists for the Greek Cypriot National Guard and the Turkish Cypriot Fighters. In the two Sovereign Base Areas of Akrotiri and Dhekelia, there were around 6000 British servicemen and many more dependents who employed large numbers of Cypriots and relied on others for services and supplies. Some Americans were on the island, in civilian clothes, operating two radio stations. And largely because the others were there, so was UNFICYP whose well-paid 3700 soldiers and policemen poured millions of dollars into the economy. In 1968, these Canadians, Swedes, Finns, British, Irish, Austrians, Danes and Australians were Cyprus's tourists: the mass influx of European vacationers came later.

These circumstances ensured that my work would centre on the practice of diplomacy in its purest form, barely hampered by the usual concerns of trade, aid and consular problems. The job was also one of those rare ones in which the military and civilian elements of government worked hand-in-hand in what was for Canada, if not for Cyprus, a peacetime situation. In addition to the professional attractions, there was the fascination of Cyprus itself: a history stretching back into antiquity, each period amply attested to by the stones around us; the natural beauty and variety of the island with carpets of anemones in the spring, golden beaches and the deep blue of the sea in summer, the dry hillsides and parched Mesaorian Plain in autumn, snow on the Troodos Mountains and the green transformation of the countryside when the winter rains began.

Getting acquainted with a divided country is at least twice as difficult as getting to know a unified state. I was accredited to the President of the Republic of Cyprus, Archbishop Makarios, in his constitutional capacity as head of the government of the whole island. That he governed all of Cyprus only in some matters and was accepted as leader only by the Greek Cypriot community was not part of the legal basis of my presence as Canadian High Commissioner. Nor did it prevent me from going to his Palace to present my credentials while knowing that there would be only Greeks present at the ceremony. This ambiguity, however, was the reason for my visit, immediately after seeing the Archbishop, to the titular Vice-President, Dr. Fazil Kuchuk. To compound the confusion, I did not see Kuchuk because he was head of the Turkish Cypriot community, though only Turks were there when I called on him, but rather because he was Vice-President of the Republic of Cyprus. We carefully disregarded the complication that, in 1964, he had resigned from this position and pronounced both the Republic and its constitution dead.

The President and Vice-President and the *de facto* governments that each headed lived on opposite sides of the Green Line in Nicosia. That physical barrier placed difficulties in my path when I wanted to discuss matters affecting both communities and all of the island such as questions of Canadian trade or the visit of parliamentarians or other things not related to our military presence. Meeting the lesser lights was relatively easy on the Greek side because the ministers and bureaucrats were surrounded by familiar trappings of government and occupied the buildings of the erstwhile unified Republic. It was not as easy to keep up contact with the Turkish authorities because their bureaucracy was neither as extensive nor as sophisticated as that of the Greeks. Nor were the Turks as open, probably because many of their senior officials were imports from Turkey who did not want to reveal their identity. Another barrier to close dealings with the Turkish side was that telephone calls were listened to by the Greek security service.

Access to the leaders of the two communities was easy and frequent. I saw more of Archbishop Makarios than of Dr. Kuchuk. Makarios was the head of state and head of government of the Republic of Cyprus while Dr. Kuchuk's authority was proscribed by the exclusion of the Turkish community from the running of the country as a whole and by Turkey's exercise of control over the community.

To say that I saw President Makarios often is not to say that I came to know him well; no one that I met in Cyprus ever made that claim. Born Michael Mouskos on 13 August 1913, he was the son of a shepherd in the district of Paphos. At 13, he entered Kykko Monastery as a novice and, nine years later, resumed his education in Nicosia and went on to the University of Athens to study theology, becoming a priest in 1946. He then studied law at Athens and in 1948 went to Boston University on a scholarship from the World Council of Churches for post-graduate studies in theology. While there, he was elected Bishop of Kytium and within two years, in 1950, was elected Archbishop and Ethnarch of the Autocephalous Orthodox Church of Cyprus.

As the leader of the church and the Greek Cypriot community, Makarios was immediately immersed in the politics of the island which, for the Greek Cypriots, meant freedom from British colonial rule and *Enosis* with Greece. As these objectives seemed attainable only by revolution, it was accepted that armed struggle must be planned. With the connivance of the Greek Government, Colonel Grivas went to Cyprus in 1951 to establish contact with the Archbishop and lay the foundations for the campaign of guerrilla warfare and sabotage that Makarios would eventually finance from church funds.

The Archbishop's overt contribution to the goal of independence was to travel abroad, especially to the United States and Britain, to create sympathy for the Greek Cypriot cause and mobilize international pressure that might eventually force Britain to yield. In 1954, he went to the United Nations General Assembly to watch from the wings as Greece tried to have the "Cyprus Question" debated, only to be out-manoeuvred by the British. As a junior adviser on the Canadian Delegation with Cyprus as one of my reponsibilities, I saw the Archbishop then for the first time.

When Makarios returned to Cyprus in January 1955, Grivas had already begun organizing military operations on the island; the Archbishop gave him the green light to begin the sabotage campaign at the end of March. A year later, the British exiled Makarios to the Seychelles where he remained for a year. Released in March 1957 on the condition that he would not go back to Cyprus, he lived in Athens until the signing of the Zurich agreements. On 1 March 1959, he returned to the island and, after elections, he became the first president of Cyprus when it came into being on 16 August 1960.

My first meeting with President Makarios was on 20 December 1968 when I presented my letters as High Commissioner. I thought that he looked older than his 55 years: "his beard and hair graying and his skin a bit blotchy", I wrote in my diary afterwards. He was serious and expressionless when he replied to my speech but warmed up when he talked about the Canadian role and when we chatted informally at the end of the ceremony. My impressions were mixed: he was undoubtedly a charmer and a person of some magnetism but I was disturbed by his smile, which conveyed sweet priestly humility rather than warmth, and I could not read his hooded eyes.

Within the Greek Cypriot community, the great majority held Makarios in reverence as a St. George-like prelate of extraordinary political skill. Those among the Greeks who differed from this view were few in number in 1968 but their dislike bordered on hatred because he appeared to have abandoned *Enosis* as a practical goal. This minority began its own campaign of sabotage in 1969 and, shortly after I left the island in 1970, attempted to assassinate the Archbishop.[87] Among Turkish Cypriots, there was no confidence whatever in the Archbishop's word.

They regarded him as an unscrupulous devil whose black robes concealed the most venal designs against their land and lives. Some members of the British civilian and military establishment were almost equally antipathetic towards Makarios. Remembering darkly the murders of Ledra Street in the 1950s and convinced that he remained a dishonest finagler, albeit astute, they could not speak of "Black Mak" without disdain.

In my encounters with the President, I seldom sensed the deviousness which was considered one of his characteristics but I was aware that the care that he took in phrasing replies to questions meant that his intentions and methods would usually be a matter of mystery to me. During calls at the Palace with visiting Canadians, I noticed that well-framed questions received well-crafted replies while fuzzy questions resulted in obfuscation or ambiguity. Sometimes he would play games with an importuning or impertinent visitor. When a Canadian clergyman tried to draw agreement that a Canadian diplomatic mission to the Vatican would be wrong, the Archbishop responded with sly humour by saying that, in the case of Cyprus, an ambassador to the Holy See was unnecessary because he himself had a direct line to the Pope. It was one of those occasions when Makarios beamed with pleasure at what he had said or done.

Whenever I talked to the Archbishop about the intercommunal problems of the island, I felt that his comments made sense, especially when he expressed caution or spoke of the need to avoid optimism. I could detect steel in the man in his replies to questions concerning the extremists within the Greek community. Once when I remarked that the Greek language press appeared to be counselling restraint, he said there was an exception: *Makhi*, the organ of the *EOKA* hit man, Nicos Sampson, still called for war.

My relations with the dour Vice-President were less challenging or meaningful. Born in 1906, Dr. Kuchuk had studied and practised medicine until 1941 when he became a newspaper publisher in Nicosia. In 1945, he founded the Cyprus Turkish National Union Party which, in 1955, became the "Cyprus is Turkish" Party. He represented the Turkish community in the Zurich-London talks and signed the final agreement on their behalf. Under the constitution of the new country, he was elected as Vice-President in the elections of December 1959 and, in 1969, we still considered him as the incumbent of that position even though he had withdrawn from it after the intercommunal war erupted.

Although Dr. Kuchuk spoke better French than English, he managed to upstage me frequently by speaking French when I was ready with English and English when I expected French; I consoled myself with the knowledge that all of his remarks were prepared by someone else. In the early years of the Republic, Makarios and the Greek Cypriots had been tactless in their treatment of Dr. Kuchuk. By the time that I met him, he was old beyond his years and a mere figure-head of the Turkish community.

Below the President and Vice-President, two very similar men were the principal forces in their respective communities, on the Greek side, Glafcos Clerides, and on the Turkish, Rauf Denktash. They were the two principals in the intercommunal talks which had begun in June 1968 and which were to continue throughout my time in Cyprus and beyond. They held similar positions in their communities, Clerides as President of the House of Representatives where the 35 Greek Cypriot legislators sat, and Denktash as the President of the Turkish rump of 15 members who had left the House to establish their own Turkish Communal Chamber.

Denktash was relatively more powerful within his group than Clerides was within his. Denktash had to check his positions only with the Government of Turkey, more often than not through the Turkish Embassy in Nicosia; he could usually disregard Dr. Kuchuk. Clerides was not as fortunate: he had to seek direction from a community that lacked cohesiveness and from a leader who often hesitated to come down on one side or the other. Moreover, he could never be certain whether the regime of the colonels in Athens would blow hot or cold on his ideas or attempt to impose their own. Clerides made frequent trips to Greece to sound them out.

Physically alike, Clerides and Denktash were moderate, intelligent and realistic. Both were English-trained lawyers. During the rebellion, Denktash had been a Crown counsel and Acting Solicitor-General prosecuting *EOKA* terrorists while Clerides defended them. Of Clerides, a British reporter of those days was to write:

> Klerides, a key man in *EOKA*, had managed to retain the confidence of British officials throughout... the rebellion. His ability, his influential position in the community, his usefulness as a go-between, his moderation and courtesy when dealing with the British may well explain his escape from arrest and detention, long after the security forces suspected his activities.[88]

By 1958, Denktash had left the colonial service to work for the Turkish community. In 1959, Denktash joined with Clerides and Michael Triantafyllides (another Greek lawyer with close links to *EOKA*) in representing Cyprus on the Joint Constitutional Commission which prepared the framework for the independent republic Until the intercommunal conflict of 1963, Clerides and Denktash worked politically for their communities on the unified island. From then until the inter-communal talks began, their paths split as Clerides remained as presiding officer of the House of Representatives while Denktash went to Turkey, returning only in April 1968 to represent the Turkish Cypriot community in the talks.

I saw much of the two men, though seldom when they were together, and was pleased to be taken into their confidence. Of the two men, Clerides was the calmer and more sophisticated and flexible in his think-ing and actions. Five years younger,[89] Denktash was more emotional, more open and more direct. They were personal friends who spoke with real regret of the circumstance that led to their sons knowing each other only as enemy uniforms in the sights of their rifles.

My first priority on coming to Cyprus had been to establish a rapport with the Canadian troops in UNFICYP whose headquarters was located at Camp Maple Leaf, a former British Army cluster of Nissen huts near the Nicosia Airport. When I arrived, the 3rd Battalion of the Royal 22nd Regiment, the renowned Vandoos, was on the island under the command of Lieutenant-Colonel Jean B. Riffou. In the rotation at the end of March 1969, a sister battalion, the 2nd R22eR, commanded by Lieutenant-Colonel Charles Belzile, took over. Six months later it was the turn of the 2nd Battalion of the Royal Highlanders of Canada, the Black Watch, whose commanding officer was Lieut.-Col. Bentley ("Bill") Macleod. Other Canadian soldiers were attached to the headquarters of UNFICYP. In overall command of the Canadians was Brigadier-General E.M.D. ("Ted") Leslie who also served as Chief of Staff of UNFICYP. In that capacity, he was also the most senior member of the peacekeeping force after its commander, Lieutenant-General Armas Martola of Finland.[90] Ted Leslie had come to Cyprus six months before me and was thoroughly conversant with the work of UNFICYP and with the politico-military situation of the island by the time I arrived.

Numbering 574 officers and men, the Canadian contingent, known to the military as "Cancon", had two tasks: it was responsible for the Kyrenia district north of Nicosia and also for providing a reserve company for UNFICYP. The Kyrenia district component was centred in Tjiklos, a hill camp high above Kyrenia on the road to Nicosia. From Tjiklos, the contingent manned a dozen outposts which were situated in between points where the Greeks and Turks confronted each other at close range. Each commanded usually by a corporal with a section of eight or nine men, the outposts were scattered through the district along the western and northern limits of the main Turkish enclave. At these lonely places, the Canadians pitted their wits against the belligerent schemes and ruses of the soldiers of the two opposing sides and used a skilful mix of firmness and good humour to keep the guns quiet.

I saw the outposts for the first time on Christmas Eve of 1968, two weeks after my arrival in Cyprus. The day started with a briefing at Camp Maple Leaf on the general situation, the location of the outposts (all named years before, when the Canadians took over the area, for soldiers or memories of Canada or, more prosaically, for geographical features) and the efforts of the contingent to assist in the restoration of normal economic life in their district. Then Bill Little and I left on a tour of the outposts in a Wessex helicopter of the British contingent. Our first call was at "Hanley's Hill", a slight elevation located in the most inhospitable and isolated part of the arid Mesaoria to the west of the salient of the Turkish enclave that thrust south towards Nicosia. A quick briefing from the corporal on his role and on the positions of the Greek and Turkish bunkers and we were off in the helicopter for similar briefings by the section leaders at "Martin's Mound", "Oneisha Farm", "Hill Top" (the most spectacular of all the posts, atop a ridge and close to the falcons soaring above), "Stampede Corral", "Saddle", and "Paquin's Hill". The rest of the outposts were accessible by jeep or car: at Temblos, an isolated Turkish village on the Kyrenia Plain surrounded by Greek farms, "Sami House", the headquarters of the contingent's reconnaisance platoon which was equipped with jeeps carrying heavy machine guns or anti-tank guns, "Thompson's Farm", and "Borehole" on the road from Bellapais to the top of the pass between Kyrenia and Nicosia. It was a day memorable not just for magnificent scenery but for observing the cool efficiency and quiet discipline of the Canadian troops.

In the weeks that followed, I visited most of the outposts of the other national contingents of UNFICYP. Long distances were not involved: Nicosia is located roughly in the middle of the island. Cyprus has only 9251 sq. km: it is just half again as large as Prince Edward Island or half the size of Wales. The island is but 224 km east to west and 96 km from north to south. There is no corner that cannot be visited in a one-day excursion from the capital, especially by helicopter.

The visit to the Danish contingent ("Dancon"), a force of 461 men, involved almost no travelling at all for the Danes guarded the line through Nicosia which was demarcated, at the end of the fighting in 1964, by a green chinagraph pencil and hence known as the "Green Line". We walked along the line where some 420 Turks faced half that number of Greeks, each side manning about 25 positions. Some were underground and others on roof-tops. Every street running off the Green Line was blocked with piles of sandbags or rubble-filled barrels or wrecked car bodies. Houses along the line had been derelict for five years and those built of sun-baked brick had collapsed. Cypriot honesty was illustrated by the 12 UNFICYP outposts, unmanned because the size of the Force had been reduced, each equipped with a blue helmet and a field telephone that worked. These articles had never been stolen or interfered with by Greek or Turk.

Half-way through our walk, we stopped for refreshments in a wine shop, barely on the Greek side, which was totally medieval in character except for the metal taps on the kegs. (The prices seemed medieval, too, with brandy at a dollar a gallon.) Our walk ended at the headquarters of Dancon in the Ledra Palace Hotel, the most luxurious of all UNFICYP accommodation. The hotel was close to the Ledra Gate of the city wall which had been the scene of fierce fighting in 1963 as it was to be again in 1974 when the Canadians guarded the Nicosia District.

The 422 Irish soldiers were stationed west of Nicosia where they lived in marked contrast to the Danes, under canvas and in the worst conditions of all contingents. Irish coffee and Irish Mist were the principal, indeed essential, ingredients of the winter's day when I visited the Irish at their headquarters at Xeros, amidst the copper mines that gave Cyprus its name.

"Ircon" had a company in the Lefka area close to Xeros. Nearby, the Turkish villagers of Ambelikou lived surrounded by their enemies and protected by the Irish in a hilltop outpost near an abandoned lime kiln, 300 metres above the valley floor. Across the February almond blossoms of the valley nestled the Greek village of Galini, looking pastoral and innocent but, like all Cypriot villages, full of guns. Another Ircon company was located at Kokkino, between Morphou Bay and the more westerly Khrysokhou Bay, where a miserable Turkish enclave stretched along the coast, hemmed in by the Greeks who dominated the mountains above and separated on the seaward side by the Greek-held town of Mansoura. The poverty at Kokkino was stark: we watched as villagers queued at a spring inside a cave and carried water away in old jerrycans and older clay pots back to the crumbling hovels that were their homes.

From ancient Salamis and medieval Famagusta to the equally hoary city of Larnaca, 412 Swedish troops maintained a difficult truce, employing Volvo personnel carriers that looked like great bathtubs on wheels to make up with mobility what the contingent lacked in numbers. The headquarters of "Swedcon" was at Carl Gustav Camp just north of Famagusta in the coastal plain where Jewish refugees trying to get to Palestine before Israel was created were detained by the British. Camp Goldfish, so named for the goldfish in a large reservoir nearby, was the location of the Swedish company responsible for the walled city of Famagusta and its Turkish community.

Before the conquest of Cyprus by the Ottoman Turks in 1571, it was said, there was a church within the walls of Famagusta for every day of the year. Few remained intact though the Gothic cathedral of St. Nicholas still functioned as the Lala Mustafa Mosque and the Church of St. Peter and St. Paul was a Turkish community centre. The sole UNFICYP outpost was in the Venetian citadel known as Othello's Tower, overlooking the modern, Greek-occupied port of Famagusta. A handful of Swedes lived there with the mission of ensuring that the Greeks did not place observation posts on the roofs of two tall buildings in the port and so dominate the walled city. At Larnaca, Swedcon manned posts along a local "green line" between narrowly-separated Greeks and Turks and patrolled Artemis Road where the evidence of past and present confrontation was everywhere.

The British furnished logistic support to all of UNFICYP through the administrative and medical facilities at the Sovereign Base Areas at Akrotiri and Dhekelia and provided helicopters and a reconnaissance squadron of armoured cars in support of all contingents. Numbering 1078 men, Britcon was the largest in UNFICYP. It also served British interests by its location which screened the SBAs and controlled most of the connecting roads between them. There was little doubt in anyone's mind that the British would use their contingent forcefully to control the Cypriot territory that lay near the SBAs if these were threatened in any way.

The headquarters of the British contingent was at Polemidhia Camp, six kilometres north of Limassol, the principal port of Cyprus and the heart of its vineyards. Turkish enclaves existed in all of the main towns as well as in the scattered villages of the Limassol, Paphos and Morphou Districts for which Britcon was responsible. Limassol was often troublesome but the British were able to keep control in the city without separating the Turks from the Greeks with a Green Line; it was the only city on the island without one. It sufficed to threaten to take the business of the nearby SBA at Akrotiri elsewhere and employ labour from farther afield if the two communities were overly fractious.

On my visit, we went by helicopter to Ktima, near Paphos, the ruins of the former testifying to the destructive fighting of 1963 as the ruins of the latter attested to the ancient glories of Greece and Rome. Some

32 kilometres north, at Polis, we visited a detached platoon which, with help from a dozen UN policemen, kept the area reasonably quiet. From Polis, the helicopter took us to an outpost in the hills at Anadhou where a Turkish *mukhtar* (headman) drove up ostensibly to say hello but more likely to find out for the Fighters on his side who we were. At Kophinou, on the main road from Limassol to Nicosia, the Britcon company commander took us to an observation post on a high point overlooking the battlefield of November 1967 when both sides had fought each other to a bitter standstill.

With 478 personnel in Nicosia East, Finland had the smallest district, but it was an area full of hot spots. Fincon's headquarters was at Kykko Camp on the outskirts of Nicosia and their district was largely to the north-west of the capital. The Finns had a reputation for toughness which was enhanced by their wearing of camouflaged uniforms. With responsibility for the scene of one of the most brutal massacres of the fighting of December 1963 and with numerous points of current Turk-Greek confrontation in their zone, they had to be tough.

On an early drive to get acquainted with the countryside and the official car, I had felt something of the tension of the Nicosia East District. In the foothills of the Kyrenia Range below Mount Pentadactylos with its five stubby peaks, I passed the Greek-held, once mixed village of Bey Keuy, where the mosque now served as a stable. I visited the Byzantine Monastery of St. Chrysostomos and then drove west along what had been a cobbled road but was now little more than a dirt track. Between a scruffy Greek village and an even poorer Turkish hamlet, I passed in turn a National Guard bunker, an UNFICYP post manned by Fincon, a Turkish Fighter checkpoint — where I had to insist that the Canadian flag on the car gave me right of passage — and then a Turkish military camp. A few miles along on my way home, I came to the Nicosia suburb of Ormophita and passed back into Greek-held territory.

With the Finnish contingent commander, I was later to walk along one of the most dangerous streets in Cyprus, Naousis Street in Ormophita, which had become well-known to me in February 1969 because of several incidents. The walk revealed how much devastation had occurred six years earlier when the Greek Cypriot irregulars drove the Turks from their homes, killing hundreds. We were watched closely by sentries on each side of the line. The Fincon commander pointed out two Turkish Fighter officers to me, telling me that they were both Finnish-speakers and probably intelligence officers of the regular army of Turkey. Their linguistic ability was emulated by the "bar-girls" and shopkeepers of Nicosia East.

The smallest military contingent was the Austrian with 55, all members of the UNFICYP field hospital.

Although the United Nations Civilian Police Force (UNCIVPOL) numbered only 175, the concept of unarmed policemen working to effect liaison between the police forces of the Greek and Turkish Cypriots was considered most useful by the UNFICYP commander and the national contingents. In a future smaller UN presence, it was foreseen that a proportionately larger police presence would be deployed throughout the island in what were called rural constabulary posts. Contributing to UNCIVPOL were Australia, Austria, Denmark and Sweden. The Australians worked with Britcon in the Limassol District and the Austrians in Nicosia and Kyrenia with the Canadians and Finns. The Danish police were located in the Irish district and with Dancon; the Swedes, similarly operated in their national contingent's area.

The contingents provided teeth to UNFICYP which had its headquarters at yet another former British base at Nicosia Airport. There the Force Commander worked in tandem with the Special Representative of the Secretary-General of the United Nations, Dr. Bibiano Osorio-Tafall, "Bibi" to his friends.[91] I had been fortunate to have known Bibi in the Congo where he headed the Mission of the UN Development Programme. Since taking up the job of Special Representative, he had applied his tremendous intellectual ability and negotiating skills to the intricate Cyprus situation and had laid the foundations for the intercommunal talks that were quietly and delicately in progress when I arrived in Cyprus. Assisting him as political and legal adviser was a Swiss lawyer, Dr. Rémy Gorgé, who combined reverence for the law with tact and great political acumen.

Working with the United Nations team to find a solution to the Cyprus problem were the representatives of some of the score or so countries that maintained resident diplomatic missions in Nicosia. Four of these — Greece, Turkey, Britain and Canada — had troops in Cyprus.

The Greek Ambassador and the Turkish Chargé d'Affaires were the most important diplomats on the island because of the presence of the treaty-permitted national contingents and the more numerous troops which formed the backbone of the two contending sides. Of these two envoys, the Turk was in the stronger position of authority because Turkey was all important to the Turkish Cypriot community as a defender and provider; the Greek Ambassador could not give orders to President Makarios as easily as the Turk could tell Vice-President Kuchuk what to do. Moreover, with the removal from Cyprus of major elements of the

Greek military after the events of November 1967, the Greek representative in Nicosia did not hold as many high cards as before in his dealings with the Government of Cyprus. But the Cyprus Government was dependent on the Greeks for diplomatic communications and Greek diplomatic missions looked after Cypriot interests in much of the world.[92]

With contingents from their countries in UNFICYP, the British and Canadian diplomatic missions merited and received special standing in the peacekeeping *cum* peacemaking drama that was played in Cyprus. The British High Commissioner was not responsible for the Sovereign Base Areas. When he drove to an SBA, he stopped at the border to remove the Union fanion that flew on his car to denote his status as British representative in Cyprus. The fact that there were British arms in the Bases as well as with Britcon entitled him to an edge over the Canadian. However, the British carried baggage from the past history of the island that diminished their credentials as *interlocateurs valables*, as credible go-betweens in the peacemaking process. The Canadian High Commissioner could intervene in the process because his country was seen by the disputing sides as impartial.

Listing 18 diplomatic officers, the United States Embassy was the largest in Nicosia and probably the busiest. For the Americans, the existing stand-off in Cyprus was the next best thing to a settlement because it reduced the tensions that had brought two NATO partners close to war. The United States was therefore a strong supporter of UNFICYP, the most important single contributor to its costs and a major backer of Osorio-Tafall's efforts to keep the intercommunal talks going. There were other reasons for the active American interest, not the least the location near Kyrenia of the large U.S. communications listening post, its antennae ranged on the Middle East and the southern flank of the Soviet Union.

Although the Soviet Embassy was slightly smaller than the American, the Soviet Union together with those of its Warsaw Pact allies who were represented in Nicosia (Bulgaria, Czechoslovakia, Hungary and Poland) had a combined strength of 36 diplomatic officers, sufficient to pose a significant intelligence threat to western interests on the island. The British installations in the SBAs were the main target of the KGB and its associates who were also active in other areas and may have attempted to subvert members of UNFICYP. It was of lesser importance that the Cyprus Communist Party, *Akel*, benefited from the strong east bloc presence; but *Akel* was a potentially useful instrument to use if it suited the Soviet purpose to stir up intercommunal trouble.

France had a moderately-staffed embassy in Nicosia which maintained a low profile on matters affecting UNFICYP to which France had made no contribution, in manpower or money. On one occasion, the French Ambassador toured the Canadian Contingent outposts in a visit that his office had arranged directly with the Cancon commander in breach of UNFICYP etiquette. When I learned about the tour after it had taken place, I remarked to the Ambassador that I hoped that he had reported to Paris how favourably impressed he was by what he had seen and had suggested that France should become financially involved. To my surprise, he replied that he had, indeed, made such a recommendation.

Franco-Cypriot diplomatic relations were relatively new, having been given priority by the Cypriot Foreign Minister, Spyros Kyprianou, who found an ally in the French Under-Secretary of State for Foreign Affairs, Count Jean de Lipkowski. To reward Lipkowski, Kyprianou arranged for unusual honours to be accorded to him when he visited Cyprus in October 1969. Lipkowski made the most of the opportunity, going so far as to raise the question of Quebec during his call on the Archbishop.[93] We would have been much more concerned over this had not Lipkowski begun his call by kissing His Beatitude's ring, an act of homage that amused even the Archbishop.

It would have been easy to come to an early conclusion that the situation in Cyprus was intractable and that there would not be a solution to the intercommunal problem in this century, if ever. One of my colleagues, the Lebanese Ambassador, counselled me not to be too serious about the situation and to enjoy the *dolce vita* that the island offered. It was tempting advice, but the troubles that punctuated the talks between Clerides and Denktash in the year ahead were to remind me frequently that my involvement was far greater than that of my Lebanese friend.

CHAPTER 15

CYPRUS: TENSION
AND TALKS

In the absence of open warfare, the tension between Greek and Turkish Cypriots in 1968–69 manifested itself in the extraordinary importance that attached to minor incidents. Like hundreds of clashes, some small, some large, that had taken place in the previous four years, these troubles reminded us that we were living in a volatile atmosphere.

Though there were not many incidents during my time at the Canadian High Commission in Cyprus, each had the ingredients for an explosion. Each involved most of the major players; each was marked by their reassertion of what they considered to be their legitimate roles in the drama; each imperilled peacekeeping and impeded peacemaking. The United Nations Force in Cyprus (UNFICYP) and the UN civilian advisers dealt with these flare-ups in a professional manner. Supported by the resident diplomatic missions of western countries and the moderate politicians of the Greek Cypriot and Turkish Cypriot communities, UNFICYP had prevented the recurrence of hostilities on the scale of those of December 1963. To that extent, the peacekeeping process had worked. The job of the interested diplomats was to back the UN Secretary-General's special representative in his efforts to ensure that the atmosphere remained right for negotiations, for peacemaking. That process, involving ongoing talks between the two communities and the normalization of life on the island through intercommunal contacts, had begun in the middle of 1968, six months before I arrived in Cyprus.

But we continued to be diverted by confrontations.

The first incident in which I was indirectly involved took place on 15 January 1969. In the village of Meladhia in the western part of the island, 15 miles from Ktima, a Turkish Cypriot went berserk and shot a woman and two men, all Turkish Cypriot. The Cyprus (Greek Cypriot) Police, known as Cypol, asked the commander of the local detachment of

UNFICYP to provide an escort to go with them to investigate the incident and a patrol led by a corporal was assigned from the British Contingent. At the request of the police, the corporal disarmed and detained the alleged murderer. For an account of what followed, the United Nations version is best:

> At this point, an argument developed between the Cyprus Police and Turkish Cypriot villagers as to who should have custody of the suspect. Despite UNFICYP's efforts, the dispute became heated and weapons were displayed on both sides. It became apparent to the UNFICYP ... on the spot that all restraint would probably be lost with the onset of darkness and that quick action had to be taken should a serious incident be avoided. With the agreement of the local Cyprus Police commander and the local Turkish Cypriot leaders, the suspect was removed from the village in an UNCIVPOL vehicle and kept overnight in UNFICYP protective custody.
>
> During the night, the Government authorities insisted that the suspect be handed over to them; for their part, the Turkish Cypriot leadership requested that he be delivered to them, either in the main enclave of Nicosia or in the Turkish sector of Ktima (Paphos). In the light of the prevailing situation, UNFICYP felt that the suspect ought to be returned to the village and handed over to the headman of the village (mukhtar). This was done the following day. The Government ... took exception to UNFICYP's action as being an infringement of the Government's authority and responsibility for the maintenance of law and order.[94]

Absent from Cyprus when the Meladhia incident occurred, I returned two days later to find that it was the principal subject on my desk. I learned that it had been the decision of the UNFICYP Chief of Staff, General Leslie, to remove the murder suspect from Meladhia to protective custody at the UNFICYP camp at Limassol; Leslie had arrived on this scene by helicopter an hour after the British corporal had made his brave intervention.

On Monday, 20 January, Osorio-Tafall came to my house at the end of a busy day to speak to me about the "irregularities" that had been committed by the corporal and the "mistake" made by General Leslie. Osorio-Tafall said that he had reminded Leslie earlier in the day of the necessity of consulting the political side of the UN presence in future. This rebuke must have shaken Leslie for Bibi asked me to reassure him that everyone retained full confidence in him.

Next day, Leslie told me his side of the story. When he arrived at Meladhia village, he realized that he had only a few minutes to decide what to do: his assessment was that if he released the suspect and the

Cyprus Police arrested him, the shooting would begin. After arranging for the removal of the arrested man to Limassol, Leslie had returned to Nicosia and consulted Dr. Rémy Gorgé who had advised him that it would be exceeding the UNFICYP mandate to continue holding the suspect. I told Leslie about Osorio-Tafall's expression of confidence in him and added my own view that he had done the right thing in the circumstances.

I heard of Meladhia again when, the following day, I paid a courtesy call on the Greek Ambassador. He called the return of the murderer a "serious mistake" because it aligned the UN with the Turkish Cypriot side by acknowledging the existence of a separate Turkish authority in the person of the *mukhtar* of the village. Alexandrakis did not criticize the military decision taken on the spot by General Leslie, but only the action of Osorio-Tafall the next morning in ordering the return of the man to Meladhia where he was handed back to the *mukhtar*. I disagreed with Alexandrakis, knowing that I could discount his interpretation because, in a conversation the previous evening with Foreign Minister Spyros Kyprianou, I had learned that the Cyprus Government did not intend to pursue the matter with the United Nations.

Omorphita was the scene of the second incident in which I was involved as a bit player. This north-eastern suburb of Nicosia had been occupied by Turkish Cypriots before the civil war broke out in December 1963. In the fighting that ensued, the villagers suffered heavily at the hands of the Greek Cypriots who, in April 1966, arbitrarily incorporated Omorphita into their sector of Nicosia. Most houses had been heavily damaged during the earlier troubles and the abandonment of the area contributed to its dilapidation. However, when the Cyprus Government lifted the barriers to the freedom of movement of the Turks, some former residents repaired their houses and moved back to Omorphita. By the end of 1968 this movement was of such a size as to alarm the Greeks and make them fear that the Turks were about to incorporate Omorphita into their sector.

The middle of Naousis Street in Omorphita was the boundary between the two communal sectors known locally as the "Red Line". On 10 February 1969, a patrol of the Cyprus Police moving along the street was stopped by a Turkish Cypriot fighter. That incident passed peacefully but, when Cypol patrolled on the following two days, the fighters had built up their strength and were spoiling to take on the Greek Cypriots. On the 12th, a house that was owned by a Turkish Cypriot but located on the Greek side of the Red Line was set on fire and destroyed. It had only recently been rebuilt and refurnished and the owner was about to reoccupy it. The fire added a new dimension to the dispute on Naousis Street. When the Turkish Cypriot leadership protested to UNFICYP about the patrols, the Government maintained that it had patrolled the street regularly and had the right to do so. While UNFICYP records supported this contention, they also showed that the patrols of the past were neither as frequent as they had become nor as extensive. Many recalled anxiously that the savage fighting of November 1967 had been provoked by aggressive Cypol patrolling at Ayios Theodoros.

While Omorphita was brewing up, I was looking after a visit of the National Defence College of Canada. On the round of calls that we had arranged for them, the new problem was raised repeatedly and, at the reception at my residence for the College, spice was added by the incident. The telephone was busy during the party. Archbishop Makarios called to speak to one guest, Christodoulou, the Public Information Officer of the Cyprus Government. Ted Leslie was frequently on the phone to consult the headquarters of UNFICYP. and held a conference in the hall with his officers including the commander of the Finnish Contingent whose troops had been interposed in Omorphita. The next morning, during the courtesy call by the visitors on the Turkish Cypriot authorities, Rauf Denktash, the Turkish representative in the intercommunal talks, described Omorphita as the most serious incident for some time. Its occurrence, he said, had made him less optimistic about the departure of UN peacekeepers in the foreseeable future.

A few days later, Leslie told me that he had become concerned that the grave state of the Omorphita problem could result in the cancellation of a scheduled meeting between Denktash and his opposite number, Glafcos Clerides, the Greek Cypriot negotiator. Leslie also feared that if the Greek Cypriots pursued their intention of sending a patrol along Naousis Street later in the week, shooting would result. This was of special concern to Leslie and to me because Canadian troops formed the UNFICYP reserve in the Nicosia area and would be deployed in Omorphita if needed. The next day, I saw Osorio-Tafall who was especially gloomy about the political effects of the situation though less pessimistic about the possibility of a military clash. He remarked, however, that Omorphita had put an end to the general plan to return Turkish Cypriot refugees, who lived in squalid conditions in the Turkish enclaves, to their homes throughout the island. He had reached this conclusion because Omorphita had convinced him that the real intention of the Turkish Cypriot leadership in encouraging refugees to go back to their old homes was to prepare the way for the seizure of territory.

On 18 February, I made a routine courtesy call on the Chargé d'Affaires of the Turkish Embassy, Ercument Yavuzalp. A person of ambassadorial rank and probably the most influential player on the Turkish side, Yavuzalp was a good listener to my concern about the current situation. Afterwards I wrote in my diary:

> Yavuzalp has a wonderful map on his wall, designed to acquaint or re-acquaint his visitors with the geopolitical situation of Cyprus. There is a little island, 40 miles [64 km] off the Turkish coast and 400 miles [640 km] from Greece! I reminded him that Leslie intended to position Canadian troops on the red line in Omorphita if there were trouble and remarked that if I had to explain the death of a Canadian soldier, I hoped that I would not have to say that he had died because of a deliberate decision of either the Turk Cypriot or the Greek Cypriot leaderships to unleash the dogs of war.

Much of the tension went out of the Omorphita situation after the Americans suggested to Greece that it intervene with the Cyprus Government in the interest of moderation. The Greeks obliged. The Turks, too, cautioned the Turkish Cypriot community to let the situation cool down. It was just as well that tempers were cooled in this way. The situation had shown that the political leaders of both communities had less control over the "hawks" in their military and police forces than was patently desirable. Clerides had felt obliged to tender his resignation as the Greek Cypriot negotiator in the intercommunal talks as a way of forcing Archbishop Makarios to rebuke the bellicose elements. The rebuke had little lasting effect for, although things briefly became calmer, the Cyprus Police let it be known that they would insist on patrolling Naousis Street "when necessary". When patrols were sent out on three successive days late in February, the Turkish Cypriots gave out the word that if UNFICYP did not stop Cypol, they would.

That the Omorphita mini-crisis was having effects everywhere had become clear throughout the second half of February. The strain on the members of the Danish Contingent, in whose district Omorphita was located, became evident during March. Ted Leslie came to see me on 14 March about a new incident in which a Danish soldier had tried to stop an unannounced Cypol patrol along the Red Line only to have the police threaten him with their guns. Leslie's protest to Cypol had drawn the response that they did not take orders from the top, the "top" having promised UNFICYP earlier that no patrols would be sent into the area without 24 hours notice. The commander of the Danish Contingent issued orders to his troops to shoot if the police drew guns again. As Chief of Staff, Ted Leslie quickly overruled the Danish commander, leaving him and his troops smouldering with discontent. The Cyprus Police concluded from this that the Danes were fair game and increased their harassment along the Red Line. When a Danish soldier was knocked down by a Cypol patrol car, UNFICYP at last blew the whistle: Osorio-Tafall, accompanied by the Force Commander, visited Epaminondas Komodromos, the Minister of the Interior, to complain. Komodromos pleaded ignorance and promised to investigate. At a subsequent meeting on the issue, it was the Director-General of the Ministry, Komodromos's deputy, who did all the talking, making it clear who ran the ministry.

A ceasefire violation with an amusing *dénouement* occurred on Naousis Street on 19 June when a Turkish Fighter fired a sub-machine gun at a National Guard post 20 metres away. The bullets damaged the sandbags but nothing else and the Greek Cypriots refrained from responding. While the incident ended there, it caused nervousness and a state of alert on both sides in Nicosia itself. During the following week, a flap on the Green Line one evening convinced the prostitutes of nearby Regina Street that an attack was about to take place. They closed their houses and moved out of the area for the night. General Leslie remarked that his intelligence section would have to take the temperature of the red light district more often.

Other, even more minor, incidents took place during the first half of 1969 and others were to occur in the second half of the year to disturb the superficial tranquillity. The intercommunal talks played no small part in maintaining the relative calm. On the day that I had arrived in Cyprus, the United Nations Security Council had renewed the mandate of UNFICYP for six months. It was the seventeenth time that the Council had reaffirmed its resolution 186 of 4 March 1964 by which the Force had been created. It was the first time, however, that this action — which had become almost routine — was taken in the knowledge that the authorities of the two communities were talking to each other. It was a hopeful moment. Even my friend the Lebanese Ambassador, who considered the Cyprus problem insoluble and predicted that the talks would come to naught, admitted their usefulness in keeping tempers down while other influences worked towards a modus vivendi.

Begun in June 1968, the intercommunal talks were already a monument to the determined diplomacy of the Secretary-General's Special Representative. The talks were meant to provide a bridge from peacekeeping to peacemaking. The initial contacts between Denktash and

Clerides had established that there existed a sufficient identity of views to proceed to a second phase in which written proposals were exchanged on the major constitutional issues. When I arrived in Cyprus, difficulties had already been identified that stood in the way of the search for new arrangements under which the two communities might co-exist.

At the beginning of the third round of the intercommunal talks, the principal point of contention was the degree of autonomy to be given to the Turkish Cypriot community under a new constitution. The Greek Cypriots held to their preference for a "unitary" state which would guarantee representation to the minority group in the executive, legislative and judicial branches of government. At the local level, the Greeks were prepared to accept communal autonomy in education and some other fields but they insisted that control and supervision of other matters by the central authorities must go right down to the local government level. The Turkish Cypriots disagreed. They demanded autonomy for their community not only at the local and district levels but through to the central bodies of government. This, in turn, was rejected by the Greek Cypriot side. As Clerides put it in a speech later in the year:

> Such a system would mean the existence of three governments in Cyprus exercising jurisdiction, each in its respective sphere, on all the territory of the Republic, the two central local government authorities, Greek and Turkish, having respectively exclusive jurisdiction on local government matters over members of their respective communities.[95]

Several weeks passed before I was able to describe the purpose of the intercommunal talks in simple terms, and only then could I begin to appreciate their complexity and understand why there would be no early solutions.

On 3 February 1969, Clerides and Denktash held a joint press conference at which they reported that they had exchanged drafts on the future legislature, executive, judiciary, police force and local government. They expressed the belief that, if the prevailing calm atmosphere continued, patience, understanding and goodwill would lead to a just and workable solution being found. Denktash warned against over-optimism: it would not be surprising, he said, if the talks were to go on through the year.

Already it was clear that the general elections in Turkey, though not to be held until October, were having an effect on the pace of the talks. The Greek Ambassador told me that efforts had been made to persuade President Makarios to ensure some sign of progress in the talks by June so that Cyprus would not loom too large in the election campaign. The Turkish Chargé d'Affaires had a different view. Yavuzalp was pessimistic of the chances of any solution being reached in 1969 because, he sought to persuade me, the maximum Greek Cypriot concessions did not meet the minimum Turkish Cypriot demands.

The peacemakers spent a gloomy February because of the incidents in Omorphita and signs of increased divisions within the Greek Cypriot community. On 3 March, Osorio-Tafall convened a meeting of the United States Ambassador, Taylor G. ("Toby") Belcher, the British High Commissioner, Sir Norman Costar, and me to discuss the situation. It was the first time in his two years in Cyprus that Osorio-Tafall had turned to the three western diplomatic missions in this way. He was concerned that an impasse had been created by the erroneous belief of each side that time was on its side. He contended that the hawks were taking charge of both communities and that the positions of Clerides and Denktash were being eroded. The Turks, he argued, had recently shown a new obstinacy, encouraged by the growth in their Fighter organization while the National Guard of the Greeks was displaying signs of demoralization.

Osorio-Tafall advanced a proposal on local government which had been put privately to him by Denktash. This plan called for the grouping of the representatives of Turkish villages into central municipal councils large enough to deal with all aspects of municipal government. It was, in essence, a plan for symbolic rather than territorial separation. Osorio-Tafall commended the plan to us and asked for our support. Belcher, Costar and I examined the proposal in a discussion a week later and, while we decided not to endorse it, we agreed that we should support Osorio-Tafall generally in any peacemaking efforts.

On 20 March, at a dinner at my house, Rauf Denktash told me that Glafcos Clerides would be going to Athens at the end of the month to sound out the Greek Government on various proposals. This unexpected development was encouraging. Denktash said that he had first put forward his proposals on the grouping of the village representatives at the beginning of the talks in mid-1968 and had presented a paper on them in January. On the slow pace of the talks, Denktash admitted that for some weeks he and Clerides had marked time until Clerides could arrange his trip to Athens; they realized that this had given the impression that a stalemate existed. Denktash expressed confidence to me that real progress would be made after Clerides returned from Athens.

The following day, I saw Clerides at a luncheon given by Foreign Minister Kyprianou in honour of Norman Costar who was about to leave Cyprus. I startled Clerides by asking him when he was travelling. "How in God's name do you know about that", he asked anxiously and I told him that Denktash had been to dinner with me. Clerides said that he was going to Greece on 2 April. I remarked to him that some of us had regarded the press conferences that he and Denktash had given after their three meetings in March as over-optimistic and we had been preparing to apply pressure; we would not have to do so now that we knew what was up. Clerides responded that, after his return, "a little pushing in certain places" might be useful and added that he would let me know if he thought that I could help.[96]

Diplomatic pressure was in fact applied before the end of the month. The United States made *démarches* in Ankara and Athens in favour of a modified form of the Denktash plan for local government. The Turks were completely negative and said that the American initiative was unfortunate. The Greeks, however, welcomed it. At about the same time, an unrelated step was taken by the United Nations when Secretary-General U Thant handed an *aide-mémoire* to the Cypriot and Turkish ambassadors urging speed in the talks and expressing the misgivings of contributors to UNFICYP at the lack of progress.

On the first of April, a date celebrated as *EOKA* Day by the Greek Cypriots, Toby Belcher gave me an outline of the proposals which Clerides was taking to Athens the next day. Approved by the Council of Ministers, these provided for the grouping of villages into area councils on a geographical and non-ethnic basis as opposed to the ethnic and non-geographical basis proposed by Denktash. The power of district officers would be transferred to district and area councils, and one area council of every six in each district would be controlled by the Turks, even though the area might have a Greek minority. Belcher thought that the plan was encouraging and a big step forward, but I did not believe that it would wash with the Turkish Cypriots to whom communal control and communal security were all-important. That evening, I briefly outlined the plan to Denktash who declared that it represented a complete misunderstanding of the Turkish Cypriot position.

Clerides and Denktash met on 7 April when Clerides returned from Athens where, it was believed, heavy pressure had been put on him. Speaking to the press on the conclusion of the meeting, they said that two sub-committees would be established, one to deal with the electoral roll and the other with Turkish Cypriot participation in the central boards for electricity, water and telecommunications. However, it soon became obvious that Clerides had not revealed to Denktash the details of the proposals that he had brought back from Athens. On 10 April, the heads of the diplomatic missions of a half dozen countries — Britain, Canada, France, Germany, Soviet Union and United States — were called in separately by the Acting Foreign Minister, Nicos Dimitriou, to be presented with a paper on the Greek Cypriot counterproposals. Chris Veniamin, the director-general of the Foreign Ministry, was also present. After the interview I wrote:

> Dimitriou said that it had been decided to inform 'interested countries' of the Cyprus Government's counterproposals to the Turkish Cypriot ideas on local government. He described the proposals as 'generous' and representing major concessions by the Greek Cypriots. If the Turks rejected them out of hand, it would prove that they had no interest in a settlement. Warming to the subject, Dimitriou said that they could then try a military solution... if that is what they wanted. Veniamin made an interjection to the effect that the proposals represented the 'maximum' so I returned to Dimitriou's point that they were a negotiating position. He agreed, but his remark about the Turk military solution and Veniamin's interjection made me wonder whether the Cyprus Government had already decided that the Turk response would be completely negative.[97]

It was 21 April before the Greek counter-proposals were presented to the Turkish Cypriots who were angered by this insulting and unnecessary delay. Denktash was particularly upset that the proposals had been given to foreign countries before he saw them. But, as he told me later, he had to spin out the negotiations and hence had asked Clerides for "clarifications" in order to try to have the Greek Cypriots move beyond ideas on local government that were basically unacceptable to the Turkish side. From Clerides I learned that the request for clarification had come as a pleasant surprise, especially because all of the questions asked by Denktash were in areas where Clerides had negotiating flexibility.

The pace of the talks slowed once more in mid-summer because of the approaching general elections in Turkey, due in October: it was in the interest of all concerned with the Cyprus problem that it should not become an issue in the election. This circumstance seemed to rule out progress on the talks because the Turkish Government would hesitate to make any concessions for fear of providing ammunition to its opponents. At the UN office in Cyprus, vent was given to exasperation at the length of the period of inactivity which Osorio-Tafall had sought to avert in April by making a visit to Ankara to see Prime Minister Demirel. His reception had been cold, the Turks insisting that there be no UN interference in the political talks on the island — and no reduction in the size of UNFICYP.[98] The knowledge that Clerides and Denktash would take a long summer break from the intercommunal talks added to the gloom among the peacemakers for not only would the international community have to pay for the maintenance of UNFICYP during this period but there was the danger that the wilder elements on both sides of the cease-fire lines might use the hiatus to cause trouble.

Already the divisions within the Greek Cypriot community had resulted in the emergence of a number of underground organizations, most of them composed of former members of *EOKA*. Archbishop Makarios told me on 14 May that he would not permit the extremists to disrupt any possible progress towards a settlement. Terrorism had begun in April with the wounding of the commissioner of the Cyprus Police in an attempted assasination and the explosion of a bomb outside the house of the Minister of Justice. It was already apparent that Makarios could not control the dissident Greek Cypriots who were blamed for these incidents but, in our conversation, he discounted their importance. Others were less sanguine. During a call that I made on the Acting Foreign Minister two days later, he recollected that in 1955, when a solution seemed possible during the talks between Makarios and the British Colonial Secretary on the future of Cyprus, Colonel Grivas had scuttled an agreement by setting off bombs in Nicosia which Lennox-Boyd took as proof of the Archbishop's perfidy.

Pessimism prevailed during the hot month of June. The English-language daily of Nicosia, the *Cyprus Mail*, suggested editorially that despite the recess in the intercommunal talks, progress should be sought in other areas such as deconfrontation and freedom of access for Greeks into Turkish sectors. The newspaper added that the press and other onlookers should also stop criticizing those who were directly involved. The atmosphere improved somewhat at the end of the month when a United Nations seminar on human rights in developing countries was held in Nicosia. Turkey had protested to the UN at the holding of such a meeting in Cyprus and the Turkish Cypriots seemed ready to use the seminar to expose, in the words of Dr. Kuchuk, the violations and sufferings his community had been subjected to "so that the hosts might be seen in their true identity". On the eve of the conference, however, a compromise was reached under which two prominent Turkish Cypriots were included in the Cyprus delegation. Archbishop Makarios delivered a welcoming address which dripped with devotion to human rights. That evening at a reception for the seminarists, he came up to me and said that he had just had a chat with the head of the delegation of Turkey; "a very nice person", he added.

271

All was not sweetness and light during the seminar; the Turkish Cypriot propaganda machine, for example, conducted a campaign against earlier Greek Cypriot atrocities. In a report on the meeting, however, I had to admit that I and other doubters had been wrong with our gloomy predictions of how things would go.

Before the summer ended, there was an even more encouraging contact between the two communities. On 7 September, the opening session of the 22nd Assembly of the World Federation of United Nations Associations (WFUNA) took place at the Ledra Palace Hotel, hard by the Green Line in Nicosia. Dr. Kuchuk came accompanied by all of the Turkish Cypriots who had been cabinet ministers in the first years of independence; their cars flew the rarely-seen flag of Cyprus.[99] At the end of the formal opening ceremony, Makarios shook hands with Kuchuk for the first time since 1963 and the room exploded with applause. Next morning at the residence, our Greek Cypriot maid Soula brought the *Cyprus Mail* to the breakfast table. It carried a large photograph of the dramatic handshake which Soula pronounced the best picture she had seen in years.[100]

To the surprise of most observers, the intercommunal talks had been resumed on 11 August when I was away from Cyprus on leave. Denktash had presented a nine-page document containing the comments of the Turkish Cypriots on the proposals and counterproposals on local administration. It was advocated in the document that a Turkish Cypriot communal administration be established with executive and legislative authority over the Turkish population throughout the island. This proposal was rejected by the Greek Cypriot side. Denktash and Clerides told me later that their respective positions were too far apart to be bridged and that, once more, they had shifted their attention to less controversial issues to avoid the appearance of deadlock.

At the beginning of October, I noted that Osorio-Tafall had been unusually silent at a luncheon.[101] This I attributed to the failure of his initiatives to break the deadlock in the intercommunal talks and the parallel talks on deconfrontation, and to the increasing evidence of obduracy on both sides with the Turks determined to make no concessions and the Greeks pretty well decided to starve the Turks out. That evening at dinner at my residence, he was silent again, this time in the presence of Denktash and other Turkish Cypriots. The erstwhile Minister of Defence of Cyprus, Osman Orek, did most of the talking and was almost more objectionable than usual in his rejection of our tentative suggestions on the need for flexibility.

Osorio-Tafall's gloomy silence proved well-warranted. A few days later, pessimism deepened everywhere when the Archbishop reacted to a statement by the Turkish Foreign Minister that the Turkish Cypriots would not budge by declaring that neither would the Greek Cypriots. Makarios followed this up with an interview for press attachés of embassies at which he vowed that he had the patience of Job and would out-wait the Turkish Cypriots living on Turkish dole in miserable conditions within their enclaves. He appeared to rule out a negotiated settlement and to reject any "solution" that might be imposed by Greece and Turkey or any combination of foreign powers. As if to warn the Turks of the risks of an attempted military solution, Makarios made visits in the next week to three National Guard camps.

Osorio-Tafall was dejected by the pronouncements from the two sides and, at a meeting with me and my American and British colleagues on 8 October, he gave voice to his depression. He told us that he feared that the UNFICYP would go down in history as a failure and he as the author of that failure. UNFICYP, he felt, had steered the Cyprus situation towards deadlock by the protection that it had given to the Turkish Cypriots, thus enabling them to consolidate their *de facto* autonomy. Bibi's sympathetic audience was inclined to agree with his analysis but we were less inclined than him to accept the notion of the failure of UN peace-keeping. I suggested that fluidity could be reintroduced only by the United Nations: either the Secretary-General must take some vigorous initiative with all parties or effect a dramatic large-scale reduction of the Force to shake everyone out of the deadlock.

The Turkish general election took place on the same weekend as the arrival of orders from the Department of External Affairs in Ottawa instructing me to tell the Cypriots that we would close the Canadian High Commission in Nicosia. That order turned my attention away from the intercommunal talks — and every other element of the Cyprus situation. Fortunately, little was happening on the island and the conclusion of the long period of inactivity in the Clerides-Denktash negotiations attributable to the Turkish election was followed by another hiatus caused by the illness of Rauf Denktash. When the two men eventually resumed their talks on 1 December, after a nine-week recess, they announced that the local government issue would be taken off the agenda for the time being. The lid was put back on the Pandora's box, imprisoning hope, until months after the High Commission closed.

The intercommunal talks and the incidents that punctuated them during 1969 are only a short chapter in the story of the United Nations

Force which, after five years of existence, seemed mired in the intractable ethnic politics of Cyprus and in danger of remaining there forever. The future of UNFICYP was constantly on the minds of the UN and the participating countries, as well as the superpowers and the countries of the region, especially Greece and Turkey. Urged on by economy-minded members of the Security Council in New York and generally encouraged by western diplomats on the island, Osorio-Tafall and Martola were ever on the lookout for ways to reduce the size of the Force without diminishing its ability to carry out its role.

When I arrived on Cyprus, the Force consisted of just over 3500 military personnel in seven national contingents and 175 civilian police from four countries. The total of about 3700 was down substantially from the early days when there had been 6369 men in blue berets on the island. Over the years, every device had been used by the United Nations to create conditions in which the Force could be made smaller or converted from a military force to an observer/police force so as to reduce the debt which was being accumulated by the world organization. Incidents were defused and the intercommunal talks nurtured; deconfrontation was arranged, little by little, in villages and valleys and along stretches of ceasefire lines; the return to normal economic life was promoted; here and there, freedom of movement rendered barricades obsolete. UNFICYP became ingenious in its testing of the climate for reductions. In December 1968, a plan to cut down further on the number of manned observation posts was quietly put into effect. Overnight, 10 outposts were withdrawn from the active list and, when all went normally without them, a larger number of manned posts were deactivated in January, leaving only 72 by the middle of 1969 of the 155 that had existed a year earlier.

The outposts that were de-manned were generally in areas where mobile patrols offered an acceptable alternative or where the Greeks and Turks did not confront each other at close quarters. In places where the two sides were eyeball-to-eyeball, UNFICYP tried to persuade them to pull back and to demilitarize, i.e., to remove their fortifications. Among the closest and most dangerous such confrontations was that on Artemis Road, leading south from Larnaca. Immediately to the west of the road, strong Greek Cypriot National Guard positions overlooked the Turkish Cypriot Fighter positions across the road. The Fighters could not withdraw because there was little room between their forward line and the Turkish area of Larnaca, the village of Scala, itself a narrow band along the seafront. Along the road, the Swedish contingent had stationed three armoured personnel carriers at short intervals. General Martola regarded

Artemis Road as the key to deconfrontation: if the Greek Cypriots could be persuaded to pull back unilaterally at Artemis Road, progress could be achieved elsewhere.

During my first official call on President Makarios on 31 December 1968, he raised the question of Artemis Road to tell me that Osorio-Tafall had suggested that a unilateral withdrawal by the National Guard could be followed about two months later by a pull-back by the Fighters. Makarios said that "perhaps", after returning from the Commonwealth heads of government meeting in London early in January, he would agree to the proposal, despite the disapproval of the commander of the National Guard. As things transpired, it was the point of view of the Guard commander that prevailed when he employed the troubles in Omorphita to stymie the plan for disengagement on Artemis Road.

The views of the Cyprus Government and of the Turkish Cypriot administration were also of importance to the efforts to cut the size of UNFICYP. While Archbishop Makarios consistently took the position that the Force was welcome to stay, he was equally willing to see it reduced in numbers and also to contemplate its conversion to an observer/police force about a thousand strong. The Turkish Cypriots, possessing less military strength on the island than the Greek Cypriots, were not at all disposed to see UNFICYP weakened. Rauf Denktash told the visiting Canadian parliamentarians in March 1969 that an untimely withdrawal of the United Nations Force, or a reduction in its size, could be "fatal". With the possibility of a Canadian withdrawal immediately in mind, but in words more general in application, he said:

> I feel that we need an effective U.N. force in Cyprus until the very day of a settlement. It will be catastrophic to think otherwise and it may render valueless all your sacrifices so far if an untimely decision of withdrawal is made.[102]

The views of the two communities on the island were a fair reflection of the views of the "mainland" Greek and Turkish governments. Among others in the world who were directly concerned with the problem, there was general agreement that a smaller UNFICYP could perform an effective role. However, the British were nervous of any wholesale cut in the size of the Force because stability in Cyprus was important to the usefulness and the preservation of the Sovereign Base Areas. When, at a meeting of 20 May, Osorio-Tafall revealed a proposal for the reduction of the Force, the newly-arrived British High Commissioner, Peter Ramsbotham, was alone in his reticence.

It was Osorio-Tafall's plan that, during the preliminary discussions at the UN in New York leading to the renewal of the mandate of UNFICYP in June, the representatives of the contributing countries should ask the Secretary-General to call on General Martola for proposals for the reduction of the Force. Ramsbotham pressed the concept of a study by "efficiency experts" of the "cost effectiveness" of UNFICYP. Out of the elaboration of these ideas, and after U.N. Assistant Secretary-General Ralph Bunche had visited Cyprus, the Secretary-General appointed a mission of enquiry into means by which the Force could be reduced. Their visit took place in September and I wrote afterwards:

> They have come under obvious instructions, arising from Bunche's visit in August, to cut the UN Force to 3000 — apparently no more and no less. They appear to have adopted Ted's [Leslie] plan for the relocation of contingent boundaries without accepting his idea of a force of 2500. What will apparently happen is that their report will be blessed by the Secretary-General and will then become the basis of instructions to the new Indian commander of UNFICYP who will arrive in January to implement the reduction — and claim authorship.[103]

The Survey Team was to report as the "considered opinion of all concerned in UNFICYP" that a further overall reduction in the strength of the Force:

> ... should not be made unless there is a major reduction in the areas of direct confrontation between the two communities and a concurrent and considerable improvement in the political situation, including serious progress on basic issues in the intercommunal talks. At the present time the Force Commander estimates that the availability of approximately 2000 UNFICYP military personnel for operational tasks is a minimum requirement under the existing mandate and finds that the present strength barely meets this minimum.[104]

The report of 3 December 1969 of the Secretary-General to the Security Council, to which the Team's report was appended, reflected the pessimism that Osorio-Tafall felt about the situation. While recognizing the fact that contacts between the two communities had multiplied during the second half of the year, the report noted that solutions were still not in sight on the basic problems dividing the Greeks from the Turks. The National Guard and the Turkish Cypriot Fighters continued to stand in direct confrontation in sensitive areas and to maintain a high degree of military preparedness and vigilance and the intercommunal talks had yet to achieve any meaningful agreement on the fundamental political issues. UNFICYP's efforts to persuade the parties to agree to military disengagement, the report conceded, had achieved no tangible result. On the matter of freedom of movement, the report said gloomily, that there had been no major change:

> The Government has continued to express serious concern at the lack of free access by Greek Cypriots to Turkish Cypriot-controlled areas. Besides the Turkish Cypriot 'enclaves', a number of Turkish Cypriot villages and public trunk roads remain closed to Greek Cypriots although Turkish Cypriots have been moving freely throughout the Island for nearly two years except in militarily restricted areas.[105]

January was devoted to preparing to leave, which also meant paying farewell calls on cabinet ministers, government officials and colleagues in the diplomatic corps. New Year's Day had been spent attending a *Te Deum* at St. John's Church in the complex housing the Archbishopric. Makarios presided over the ceremony which was followed by a reception at the Presidential Palace where, one by one, cabinet ministers and heads of diplomatic missions were called to an ante-room to shake the President's hand and wish him a happy new year. Next morning, the Corps paraded again, lining up at the airport to wish Makarios godspeed as he left on official visits to Tanzania, Kenya and Zambia.

I noted in my diary for that day, my 48th birthday, that I had set our departure, "Ottawa willing", for the 18th and that our social calendar was filling up alarmingly. The farewell calls provided special insights into the Cyprus problem because those whom I saw were unusually frank in their comments on the future of the country. Perhaps they felt that they could speak openly to me because we were closing the mission — but a new element in the security situation provided the impulse for much of what was said.

On New Year's Eve, 10 armed men raided a mine near Limassol and stole 2500 sticks, a ton, of dynamite. The news was revealed to the council of ministers only after the Archbishop's departure for Africa and reported in the press the next morning. That day I called on the Acting Foreign Minister, Nicos Dimitriou, and Tassos Papadopoulas, the Minister of Labour and Health. Dimitriou foresaw great trouble ahead and put the Limassol incident down to the National Front which had re-emerged as a threat in 1969. Reflective as always, he remarked that in historical retrospect the *EOKA* campaign had been a serious mistake: it was unnecessary as Cyprus would have gained its independence anyway and it had left a heritage of bloodshed and distrust by training Cypriots in underground activities and splitting the two communities apart. Papadopoulos, an ex-*EOKA* fighter, was less worried. He said that he knew the leaders of the National Front, "stupid men with petty grievances". His *EOKA* experience suggested to him that the target of bombings would be police stations. Morale amongst the police, who had already suffered from National Front attacks, was low: their chief had lost control and the Minister of the Interior had not been in office long enough to command respect and discipline. Hence, Papadopoulos continued, no real investigations were taking place and the members of the National Front enjoyed immunity from criminal proceedings because British legal rules still applied. He said that he had suggested to the cabinet that he be given a free hand for a week to deal with the Front: a week would be all that he would need to subdue the organization.

As President of the House of Representatives, Glafcos Clerides was Acting President during the absence of His Beatitude from the country. When I called on him, he expressed confidence that the Government could easily round up the small men of the National Front but wanted to catch the leaders. Clerides said that he had all along wanted the imposition of emergency powers but "others" — which I took for the usual code for the Archbishop — were reluctant to invoke them. Meanwhile, Clerides went on, public confidence in the Government was waning because of its apparent impotence and police morale was dwindling. The slide had to stop: Clerides declared that, if one bomb went off while Makarios was away, he would not hesitate one instant before rounding up the Front leaders even if he could hold them only under the "normal times" rules of 24 hours before a court appearance and two remands each of eight days.

Chris Veniamin of the Foreign Ministry was extremely worried. Like Clerides, he favoured early and drastic action against the leaders. Above all, Veniamin was concerned that the Front leaders were mad enough to throw their next bombs across the Green Line, which would cause war. But even if the targets were the United Nation or even the British bases and the Government which had already been attacked, the stability of Cyprus would once again be called into question.

I tried out Veniamin's line on some of those whom I visited later. When I called on Constantinos Phanos, the Minister of Communications and Works, another raid had taken place. This time the target was an armoury in a village, where the raiders persuaded the *mukhtar* to hand over his "legally" held arms store of 15 weapons and then had the villagers gather in the local cafe to proclaim their allegiance to *Enosis*. Neither Phanos nor the Minister of Education, Constantinos Spyradakis, demurred when I remarked that there seemed to be a civil war brewing amongst Greek Cypriots and both agreed that the Government had to act quickly to suppress the National Front.

As it turned out, the decision to act had already been taken. That afternoon, when I returned from a drive to Famagusta, I came across a police roadblock at which vehicles from Nicosia were being stopped and searched. In the evening, the police began to collect the "legally-held" arms from villages. It was an operation which Dimitriou and Veniamin, with whom I dined, were pleased about just as they were delighted that the Greek Prime Minister had appeared in an interview on Cyprus Television to denounce the underground movement.[106] Komodromos, the Minister of the Interior, was also in a happy mood when I saw him the next morning and confided to me that the collection of arms from village armouries was to be followed by a request for the voluntary surrender of privately-held weapons. With Tassos Papadopoulos's comment on the effectiveness of the Minister of the Interior in mind, I asked Komodromous if he would prefer to be back in his home district of Paphos. The question touched a chord: "In Paphos, I was a King", he responded, and went on to complain that he found people in Nicosia dishonest: people whom he treated as friends, and whom he thought were friends, turned out to be enemies. Komodromous made it clear that he had something to grouse about.

Our farewell to the Turkish Cypriot community was given by the Turkish Chargé d'Affaires who included Rauf Denktash and Osman Orek, still recognized by us as the Minister of Defence of the island. The conversation centred on the disunity amongst the Greek Cypriots, Denktash stating his fear that Makarios might instigate a dispute with the Turks as a way of reuniting the Greeks. Orek demonstrated the touchiness of the Turkish side to any hint of the favouring of the Greeks by foreigners when he cornered me about a scholarship offer by the Canadian International Development Agency (CIDA) that had appeared the previous day in the Cyprus Government Gazette and nowhere else. Our attention had been drawn by a Turkish liaison officer to the notice and we had been no more amused by CIDA's gaffe than he was. As it happened, my telegram of outrage that CIDA should do this without our knowledge was the last classified message sent by the post; our cypher machinery was dismantled that day.[107] I could not refrain from commenting to Orek that the closing of the resident High Commission would result in contretemps of this sort in the future.

While Clerides stuck to his hard line, some were sceptical that the Archbishop would maintain it when he returned to Cyprus on 18 January, my departure day. One sceptic was Michael Triantfyllides, a Justice of the Supreme Court, who considered that a period of detention without trial of 30 days would suffice because if that period didn't see the bagging of all the extremists, the country would fall apart anyway.[108] The following day, we learned of more police successes against the National Front. A couple of hundred hand grenades had been found in a garden in Famagusta, apparently dumped there by someone who found them too hot to handle. Three arrests were made in Nicosia of men transporting arms to a pharmacy in Ledra Street. When I made a farewell call on Osorio-Tafall, I learned that the lead to the druggist had given clues to the top echelon of the Front.[109]

After I left Cyprus for London and a sabbatical year at the Imperial Defence College, the situation continued to be tense on the island. On 8 March 1970, the dissidents struck: as Makarios was leaving the Archbishopric in Nicosia, three men fired on his helicopter as it lifted off. Though seriously wounded, the pilot landed the aircraft safely. Makarios lived to rule for seven more years.

They were difficult years. Tensions in the area led, in 1974, to the invasion by Turkey, its seizure of the entire northern part of the island and the creation of a Turkish Cypriot republic. Makarios was deposed by the military dictatorship of Athens but later restored to the presidency of the diminished, all-Greek, south. The separation persists.

At the turn of the millennium, my time in Cyprus is evoked whenever I read of the continued tension between the two communities on the island — and the absence of talks between the respective presidents of the Greek and Turkish sides, Glafcos Clerides and Rauf Denktash, my friends and confidants of that final year of Canada's helpful diplomatic presence.

CHAPTER 16

CLOSING A MISSION

Just over a year after arriving in Cyprus, I closed the doors of the Canadian High Commission on instructions from Ottawa.[110]

Until 1969, few heads of Canadian diplomatic posts had had this unpleasant experience. For those who were required to close shop, the necessity had arisen at the outbreak of war, in enemy territory, with the rules of the game well defined by international custom. To pull up stakes in a friendly country is far more difficult because no rules exist. Diplomatic relations that have been entered into with solemn professions of mutual respect are terminated because the financial wizards of a country tell their government that it must economize and it is decided that the foreign ministry must join in the economy drive.

And, so, a mission or two or three are chosen for the axe. The country's diplomats then have to adduce reasons for closing those missions, reasons which often are transparent because a government cannot admit to being broke and cannot tell another country that it is of no consequence. So the rationale usually stretches the truth. And this makes the task even less agreeable. It was like that in Nicosia, Cyprus, in 1969.

Closing Nicosia had always been a possibility, because the Canadian High Commission had never been "established" in a formal sense as a post; all of its job positions had been borrowed from elsewhere in the Department of External Affairs when the post had been created in March 1964, a few days in advance of the arrival of the first Canadian troops. It was the understanding then that the post would remain as long as the troops were there: when I came to Nicosia, I knew that it was intended to close the post if the Canadian contingent in the United Nations Force in Cyprus (UNFICYP) were to be withdrawn.

When this would happen was a moot point. Some thought that it might be in two or three years, near the end of my tour of duty in Cyprus.

Others believed that it would be earlier. At the meeting of heads of European posts, in January 1969, I joked that my aim was to achieve the first post closing since that of the mission in St.John's, which became redundant when Newfoundland entered Confederation. I was quite prepared to work towards the termination of Canada's presence in Cyprus but, to ensure that I would look at that possibility objectively, I asked only that, if the post were closed, I be given another assignment abroad. This was readily agreed to by the departmental powers-that-were in November 1968, although the promise was to be lost in the confusion that surrounded the decision to close the mission and the way in which it was executed.

Pierre Elliott Trudeau was to have more impact on the Department of External Affairs than any of us suspected when he became Prime Minister in April 1968. Most of us welcomed the arrival in power of the first Canadian Prime Minister born in the 20th Century. We thought that he would bring fresh ideas to Canadian foreign policy and to the style in which we should conduct it. What we did not realize was that he had some antipathy toward senior members of the foreign service.

In ordering the review of foreign policy in 1968, Mr. Trudeau explained that there was no commitment to change but only to re-examine the premises on which policy was based. But it was soon apparent that membership in NATO was in jeopardy and that relations with Europe were regarded as unimportant when compared with those with China and the Soviet Union. While this alarmed senior officers of the Department, they failed to assess what the Prime Minister really wanted and to adjust to the new bench-marks that he set. There was also a failure to ensure that he understood the role of the Department. The first months of contact did nothing to establish the credibility of the foreign service in the eyes of the Prime Minister. As Bruce Thordarson was to write:

> If Mr. Trudeau was generally sceptical of civil servants, he was particularly critical of the Department of External Affairs. Other departments he viewed as excessively conservative: External he seemed to regard as largely irrelevant. He seemed to believe that the main function of Canada's diplomatic service was to collect and despatch information.[111]

The early stages of the review of policy towards Europe, an exercise known as "Stafeur", occupied the Department throughout the second half of 1968. The initial draft of the report was the central item on the agenda of the London meeting of heads of posts which coincided with the 1969 conference of Commonwealth Heads of Government; it was the first time that they — and we — were exposed to the new Canadian

Prime Minister. As Secretary of State for External Affairs, Mitchell Sharp was the chairman of the heads of post gathering; but during his frequent absences at the Commonwealth meeting his Parliamentary Secretary, Jean-Pierre Goyer, led the discussions.

Stafeur's draft report examined the bases of the Canadian relationship with Europe in great detail. It argued that the institutional framework of the relationship had served us well for almost two decades and should be continued, more or less unchanged. This was not what Trudeau and Goyer wanted to hear. They regarded the report as a rigid, conservative defence of the *status quo*, devoid of imaginative thinking. They found that the report gave no hint of any departmental feeling for a new approach to problems or awareness of the new ideas which Mr. Trudeau and the inner group of his cabinet and staff prided themselves on. These were serious flaws, but the Department's error was compounded by its failure, in the writing of the report, to observe the newly promulgated procedures for the presentation of material to the Prime Minister. Moreover, his predilection for "trendy" turns of phrase and a neo-Kennedy vocabulary had been ignored.

Mr. Trudeau thus became convinced that the foreign service was opposed to change of any kind. It must be admitted that the Department almost invited this criticism, even if it did not merit the punishment that the Prime Minister was to inflict.

I saw Mr. Trudeau in action for the first time at the London meeting when he spoke to the heads of post. There were about two dozen of us present, one woman and 23 men, whose responsibilities ranged from those exercised at the important capitals of London, Bonn and Paris to the comfortable sinecures of Berne, The Hague and Lisbon and down to my small hornets' nest at the eastern end of the Mediterranean.

The Prime Minister's opening words were condescending: foreign service officers were always considered an intelligent group of civil servants, he said, and it was a new experience for him to meet so many distinguished members of the service at one time. He remarked that he knew more first and second secretaries than ambassadors and he was concerned that the junior officers were excluded from policy-making. He wondered — "I am talking off the top of my head but I do know these people and what they are thinking" — whether ambassadors encouraged them to think about policy, the way he wanted his ministers to do. It was his impression that the brainpower of the juniors was not being employed, that the windows were closed. This ploy by the 49-year-old Prime Minister to associate himself with the younger group of the foreign service, did not sit well with an audience whose average age was only a few years beyond his, even though it included some of the most venerable and respected of Canada's ambassadors. Those of us who were younger were well aware of Mr. Trudeau's earlier years of "bumming" around Europe and dropping in on junior officers to "borrow" the price of a meal.

Mr. Trudeau continued by giving notice that the very basis of our policies had to be examined and that we had to determine what was best for Canada and why. Foreign policy had to reflect the geography of Canada, its size and economic strength and the existence of the two founding groups; policy remained to be defined in new conditions and with reference to new areas of technology. Meanwhile, he asked himself, were our diplomats doing the right things? Were they emphasizing only the traditional diplomatic role or did they know the young Canadian artists in their countries? Were they aware of the importance of multi-national corporations in limiting or influencing the foreign policies of countries? Were they following developments in cybernetics and electronics? Mr. Trudeau posed these and other like questions but neither invited comments nor stayed for answers. As he left his chair and neared the door he smiled broadly at the Deputy High Commissioner at Canada House, an old friend of his, and winked impishly as if to convey his amusement at having laid down the law to a roomful of "Excellencies".[112]

It was a most impressive performance. But it was disturbing. Only later did I learn that Jean-Pierre Goyer had helped to sharpen Mr. Trudeau's doubts about us. At the first meeting I had formed the impression that Goyer regarded the officers of the Department present as members of a professional establishment resentful of change. He had reported to the Prime Minister that the cream of Canadian diplomats had not come up with a single new idea during the meeting. In terms of the review of foreign policy, that meeting had been a failure; for the Department, the consequences were to be even more serious.

While relations with NATO were a principal target of the policy review, the very future of the armed forces was also at stake. If the forces were to be reduced, then the continued participation of Canada in the peacekeeping force in Cyprus was also in question. In addition to the Department, the Committee on External Affairs and National Defence of the House of Commons had been put to work on the review of foreign policy. On February 11, I learned that the Committee would visit Cyprus a month later as part of a swing through Europe to look into peacekeeping and NATO and to examine the options of disarmament (in Geneva) and neutrality (in Stockholm).

The visit took place on March 10–11 or, more precisely, for 25 hours from 4:30 p.m. on the 10th until 5:30 p.m. on the 11th. Ian Wahn, the chairman of the Committee, was the leader of the 30 members making up the group, which included many distinguished parliamentarians. They were briefed at the United Nations headquarters by General Martola and Dr. Osorio-Tafall. Then, at Camp Maple Leaf, leaders of the Greek and Turkish Cypriot sides made strong endorsements of the need for a Canadian military presence. General Leslie and I also made presentations.

My pitch was solidly in favour of continued Canadian participation in UNFICYP. After setting the scenario for peacekeeping in the long and involved history of the island, I spoke about the current intercommunal talks between Greeks and Turks and the part that had been played by the United Nations in bringing them together. I made the point that the possibility of renewed fighting must not be discounted; in these circumstances, the role of UNFICYP was perhaps even more important than it had been before the talks began.

The job of peace*keeping*, I argued, had to continue so that the more delicate enterprise of peace*making* might be undertaken. I went on to say:

> This enterprise involves the search for a reasonable and workable arrangement under which the Greek Cypriot majority and the Turkish Cypriot minority may live and work in peace. Such an arrangement must obviously provide the Turkish Cypriots with every assurance that their cultural, linguistic and religious individuality will be protected and enabled to flourish. It must also provide the one community with assurances that the other community will not obstruct the governing of the state or the development of the economy. These are difficult objectives but their attainment is made even harder by the need to satisfy Greece and Turkey that their national interests in Cyprus will be safeguarded. And going beyond that, the ultimate solution of the Cyprus problem must be viable enough — at the very least — to withstand scrutiny in the world at large and particularly at the United Nations. All of these factors make it seem unlikely that peacemaking will be a rapid process.[113]

Continuing, I said that I did not claim that the High Commission played a direct role in the task of peacemaking although the possibility that it might should not be ruled out. However, the High Commission did provide diplomatic support to the Canadian contingent and to the peacekeeping efforts of UNFICYP whose political heads consulted us frequently.

I felt that I had been speaking to the converted for many of the parliamentarians assured me before they left the next day that they were convinced of the need for continued Canadian participation in the peace-keeping force. They seemed, too, to take for granted the continued presence of a Canadian diplomatic mission as long as Canadian troops were on the island.

As spring progressed and I planned for a week of consultations in Ottawa in late May, I became more and more persuaded that a case existed for placing the High Commission in Nicosia on a permanent basis. I believed that a settlement of the island's problems would not be achieved in the immediate future and might take several years. Meanwhile, our office was doing much more than providing diplomatic support to the peacekeepers. Canadian trade with Cyprus was assuming some importance. Immigration to Canada had grown; consular work was increasing as more Canadians visited Cyprus and more Cypriots took up residence in our country. The post was a link between Canadian missions in Arab countries and the embassy in Israel. In a war in the Middle East, Cyprus would probably be a safe haven. Other considerations mattered: Cyprus was in the Commonwealth; its strategic position was important to the West. For these reasons, I was certain that we should establish the small High Commission on a permanent footing, giving that action a high priority and, if necessary, precedence over the setting up of new missions elsewhere.

My enthusiasm for this thesis was crushed within hours of my arrival in Ottawa on May 21. Those in the Department of External Affairs who dealt with Cyprus and Europe preferred that the question of Nicosia's permanence or impermanence should not be raised in days of defence cuts — days too, I learned, of the possible abolition of some other posts. Although the parliamentary committee had expressed support for peace-keeping, it seemed that there were elements within the cabinet who did not want us to stay in UNFICYP. The possibility of posts being closed came to mind the next day when I was told by a senior officer that we were not being given the money to run the foreign service at its current level, let alone paying for new posts and rising salaries and allowances. If we were not allowed the funds, he said, something would have to give. My informant remarked that budgetary problems were not the only ones for the Department in the Trudeau age: because of the new style of government, the Department had not made a policy recommendation for months. A friend at National Defence, which was about to be decimated, spoke bitterly about the centralization of power in the Prime Minister's office and, within the cabinet, in a few ministers. My friend opined that there was a direct parallel between the predicaments of National Defence and External Affairs. Military bases would be closing. Why not diplomatic posts too?

Throughout June and into July there was little word from Ottawa to suggest that the High Commission would not remain open. On July 17, with the Department's agreement, I renewed the lease on the official residence for another year and wrote in my diary: "I presume we will still be here: the Cyprus problem is certainly no closer to solution."

I was on leave on August 13 when I heard Prime Minister Trudeau's announcement that he would reduce the civil service by 25,000 over the following two years and freeze the budgets of government departments. It was all in the interest of fighting inflation, he said. My only reaction at the time was that the Ottawa merchants would be worried: the curbs on spending did not seem to have any direct relevance for me. When I returned to Nicosia, however, the austere wind from Ottawa was felt in a letter notifying us of a general cut of 10 percent in our allowances for representational activities.

About that time I also received a report from a Canadian newspaper on the austerity programme. In it, Mitchell Sharp was quoted as describing as speculative a rumour that the External Affairs budget would be chopped by two million dollars annually. The news article also quoted an "inside source" as claiming that the Department planned to cut or close eight embassies or consulates, including three in Latin America. A few days later, a military visitor from Ottawa told us that Nicosia had been listed in a newspaper story on posts which might be closed in the next year. The courier bringing our diplomatic bag from Ottawa that week also conveyed the rumour that we were on the short list for closing. I decided that the time had come to seek confirmation and, on 15 September, wrote to the head of the office dealing with political-military affairs in the Department, to ask what was up. Planning was necessary, I said, if we were to close: we had to try to minimize the harm to bilateral relations with Cyprus, overcome difficulties which the Canadian contingent would encounter without diplomatic support, and avoid undue hardship to personnel.

A few days later, the first official indication that something was amiss came in a telegram cancelling my secretary's impending posting and the move of her replacement. On the strength of this, I sent an "immediate" priority telegram to the Department, using the gist of the arguments in my letter to Ottawa and asking to be brought into the picture. Other posts must also have heard of the list of posts to be eliminated and made the same request for, on September 22, there came an unclassified telegram signed by Mitchell Sharp acknowledging the rumours. He deplored the speculation saying that "it cannot but cause largely unnecessary and certainly premature concern." He went on to tell us that the conclusions of the departmental study of savings would "shortly" be brought before the Cabinet. The message concluded:

> The interest and concern of departmental personnel are very much in our minds and will be taken fully into account, and I can assure you further that decisions when taken will be communicated to you as soon as possible.

September ended before we heard anything more definite than this. Meanwhile, Ted Leslie had communicated his views to the Chief of the Defence Staff in Ottawa on the need to maintain a High Commission as long as there was a Canadian contingent in UNFICYP. One of his arguments was that the diplomatic presence constituted a deterrent against the Cypriots making trouble for the Canadians, which prompted me to say to Ted that, as the deterrent was exercised by my occupying my chair, it might be called backside diplomacy.

Early in October, the reports that Nicosia would close became more solid. It was also learned that between 40 and 60 foreign service officers were being rusticated, about 20 of these by means of an early retirement scheme of doubtful legality. The gloom in the Department, we heard, was deep. There was a matching gloom in my small office. The circumstances hardly encouraged us to maintain routine reporting on the Cyprus situation or to cultivate contacts. Why, I asked myself, keep up our "presence" if we were going to pull out? The Department replied to my mid-September letter to confirm that Nicosia was on the list and that, while it would be premature to consider the post axed, we should think about "precautionary measures." I commented in my diary: "So much for consultation between the department and posts."

A day later — Sunday, October 12 — the orders of execution at last arrived. I was informed in a telegram that, on the 14th, it would be announced that the post in Nicosia would be closed along with six others: Berlin, Santo Domingo, Montevideo, Quito, Vientiane and Phnom Penh. This action was "essential" to achieving the government's intention "to combat inflation by containing federal government expenditures." I was instructed to pass immediately a message from Mitchell Sharp to the Cyprus Government.

The Minister's message began with the words: "As a result of a decision to effect significant economies in the Government's operations," it was necessary that the resident mission in Nicosia be withdrawn. Yet, the message went on, Canada attached the greatest importance to the continued development of relations with Cyprus in all fields and, above all, to the maintenance of ties as members of the Commonwealth. To prove that we would continue to care about the problems of the island republic, arrangements were proposed for Canadian representation by one of our diplomatic posts nearby.

The cold, peremptory communication contained not one suggestion, let alone expression, of regret. It was left for me to add that. I sent a reply to Ottawa to say that I would deliver the message the next day and followed this telegram up with a reminder that others besides the Cypriots, especially the United Nations Secretary-General, should know of our intentions.

I saw Nicos Dimitriou, the Acting Minister of Foreign Affairs, at noon on Monday, October 13, to deliver the message. As instructed, I explained how the closing was solely for "important reasons of economy" and that we placed great value on our continued relations with Cyprus. The instructions also required me to state that the action should not be interpreted as reflecting any abatement of our deep concern to see an early solution of the Cyprus problem or any lessening of our willingness to search for that solution. Nor, the script continued, did the action imply any decision with respect to the nature of Canada's participation in UNFICYP.

Mr. Dimitriou said that he was sorry to hear the news. He observed that, in its five years in Nicosia, the Canadian High Commission had done much for the development of relations between Canada and Cyprus. But he regretted more that, like the Canadian decision to pull troops out of Europe, this decision seemed to reflect a turn by Canada towards isolationism and a withdrawal from the role in world affairs that we had played so well for the past 25 years. He also made the cogent observation that foreign expenditures, such as those for an embassy, had little to do with domestic measures to fight inflation.

The instructions from Ottawa had said that a message from Prime Minister Trudeau to President Makarios would follow. I asked the Foreign Minister to arrange for me to call on the Archbishop and was given an appointment for the 15th. Overnight, however, messages arrived advising us that the public announcement of the closing of missions was postponed because Ottawa wished to be able to consider any representations that might be made by the governments concerned. The Department was anxious that our intentions be kept secret; in the event of a leakage, we were to say that no details would be announced until the governments concerned had made their views known. As it would have been untrue to assert that we had invited comments from the Cypriots, I phoned Chris Veniamin, the Director-General of the Foreign Ministry, to tell him that it seemed that Ottawa might be susceptible to pressure. He saw President Makarios and called me afterwards to express "His Beatitude's surprise and concern." The President, he said, believed that there should be a resident Canadian diplomatic mission because of the Canadian contingent, with which the High Commission worked so closely, thus making an effective contribution to peacekeeping, to the Commonwealth link and to Canada's place in the western world with which Cyprus needed close ties.

While all this was going on, the Department asked us to submit a plan for the closing of the High Commission. I proposed that we should remain operational until December 15 when the Security Council would have extended the UNFICYP mandate for another three to six months. Then, I suggested, we could run down our activity over a two-week period and spend January disposing of leases, furniture and files. We had been asked not to bother the Department with administrative questions, a request which I found ironic when the objective of the entire exercise was to save taxpayers' money.

A bizarre contribution to the mood of the day came on 15 October with the announcement by the Prime Minister of the establishment of a Canadian diplomatic mission to the Vatican and the appointment of Dr. John E. Robbins as its first head. The timing of the announcement disturbed me. Why was the Canadian Government adding salt to the wounds of the Cypriots and others by broadcasting the opening of the Vatican post at this time? And how could the Government be so callous as to appoint a 66-year-old from outside the service when there was talk of firing much younger career officers as part of the economy drive?

The Turkish-Cypriot leadership gave me their reaction to the notification of the post closing on October 17 in the form of a letter from Vice-President Kuchuk to Prime Minister Trudeau. The Canadian High Commission and the Canadian contingent, he said, had been instrumental in bringing peace to the island and their influence would be equally important in assisting with a final solution. The High Commission had been valuable to the people of Cyprus and particularly to the Turkish community. It was not a persuasive plea.

The next day — a Saturday — we received the long-awaited message from Mr. Trudeau to President Makarios. It was clear that it could no longer be delivered because its case had been overtaken by developments and so, in an immediate reply, I proposed some changes. Much later I was to learn that my telegram was not received by the departmental desk officer for a week. This communications breakdown seems, in retrospect, a normal event in a political and administrative snafu that was becoming messier by the day. Although we were under orders from headquarters to observe secrecy about the closing, we were being bombarded with uncoded telegrams on housekeeping matters. Messages arrived in clear language directing us to wind up our leases on the chancery at 15A Heroes Street and the residence at 8 Epaminondas Street, to count our china and pots and pans, to report the condition of vehicles and furniture, and so forth. Such was the Department's notion of secrecy.

Although pressure had been put on the Canadian Government in Washington, London, Athens and Ankara to keep the post in Nicosia open, Ottawa remained unmoved. In his press conference of October 15 on the opening of the mission to the Holy See, the Prime Minister had been downright cavalier. He said:

> We will have to close other embassies abroad. I suppose Mr. Sharp will be announcing them as part of his guideline application. I would not like to give the examples now. I believe certain countries have been contacted but until Mr. Sharp announces it and until they have agreed or resigned themselves to it, I don't want to give examples. But if you look at the lists of our diplomatic posts abroad there are some and perhaps several which are of very, very little importance to Canada. We think that the Vatican will give us much more grass roots information about the countries of the world than these particular posts which we will have to close. And that's the whole objective of the guidelines. It is not just to save money, it is in order that we use the money... more efficiently... We are closing some posts which are not giving us the results we need in the diplomatic area and we are opening others... We do not have posts to sort of flatter the other guy. We should have them in order to help Canadians, either travellers or the Government, to follow its policies and its international developments.[114]

"So much," I wrote in my diary, "for (1) the Cypriots (2) the Canadian contingent to UNFICYP and (3) peacekeeping. Let alone some of our friends." I added that I would like to think that a review of the usefulness of the Vatican post would be made within a year or two, but knew that it would not be.

The formal reply of Acting Foreign Minister Dimitriou to my note to him of October 13 was delivered on October 18. It contained no new arguments. "Surprise and deep concern" were once again expressed. Mr. Dimitriou wondered whether our decision might not be misconstrued at a stage when the Cyprus problem was turning to a new and critical phase. Our association in the Commonwealth was referred to as was Canada's exemplary record in UN peacekeeping. I felt that the note lacked bite.

Mitchell Sharp scheduled a press conference for October 21 at which it was intended that he would announce the names of the missions to be closed. In the event he confined himself to the fatuous remark that the posts were not in countries where Canadians visited. We were amused by this echo of Mr. Trudeau's reference to helping Canadian travellers because the Cypriots often called the UNFICYP troops "permanent tourists". We had 584 of them: multiplied by 365 days of the year, that amounted to a lot of Canadian tourism.

On October 23, we received a message stating that, although careful consideration had been given to the representations of the Cypriots, there would be no change in the decision. I was given discretion to tell the Archbishop and so I acknowledged the instructions and proposed the text of a note that I would deliver to him. This, I suggested, might be done early in the following week. The air had been cleared, I thought: we were indeed closing and had cut through the fog created by Ottawa.

I was wrong. That evening a highest priority ("flash") telegram asked that the Cypriots not be spoken to because it would be inconsistent with a remark made by Mitchell Sharp to the press to the effect that a public announcement of the closing of missions would need to be deferred to give an opportunity for the Government of Canada to consider representations from various quarters. So we were again back behind the smoke-screen.

The "flash" message had advised me that it was not thought that there would be any change in the plan to close Nicosia, but I would be told as soon as possible. It would have to be soon because, earlier in the day, we had learned that *The Times* of London had carried a story naming Nicosia as one of the posts to be closed. It was a clever article because it linked the Canadian withdrawal from the International Control Commission in Cambodia and Laos with that from peacemaking in Cyprus. It had the earmarks of a Foreign Office plant and I speculated to myself that it would force Ottawa's hand.

On October 24, I called on Foreign Minister Spyros Kyprianou, who had just returned from a visit to Washington and the United Nations General Assembly in New York. He said that he had learned with sorrow of the Canadian decision and could not believe that it was for economic reasons. He deplored the possibility that we would go because we and the British were the only Commonwealth countries with resident diplomatic missions in Nicosia and, moreover, the only UNFICYP contributors represented by envoys on the spot. Our withdrawal would leave Cyprus with only the British High Commission to turn to and the Cyprus Government did not relish that situation.

But what concerned Mr. Kyprianou most was that, when our decision became public, it would give rise to serious misunderstandings and misinterpretations. He said that the Archbishop had made this point to him that morning and expressed dismay at the probable public reaction to the move. Nobody would believe that Canada could not afford a resident diplomatic mission. Invidious comparisons, he continued, would be drawn between our closing in Nicosia and opening in the Vatican and several other places. Viewed against the background of the Cyprus problem, he said, our decision to pull out would be taken as proof that we regarded the problem as insoluble. It would also be conjectured that we would follow up by withdrawing from UNFICYP.

The Foreign Minister had marshalled his arguments better than anyone else I had heard from. He asked me to report his views and expressed the hope that the decision would be reversed.

On October 28, yet another telegram came from External Affairs to confirm the finality of the decision to close the High Commission. I was instructed to convey this to the President, while emphasizing our continued interest in the Cyprus problem and our willingness to contribute by any means at our disposal to the search for a satisfactory settlement. The message warned me that no public announcement had yet been made by the Secretary of State for External Affairs and it was hoped that the Cypriots would not comment publicly; it was especially hoped that there would be nothing along the lines that Foreign Minister Kyprianou had followed in his meeting with me. Clearly his home-truths had discombobulated the myth-makers at headquarters.

On October 31, I called on President Makarios to deliver a note on the "final" decision. Makarios was gentle, saying that he did not want to make comments that could be taken as interference in Canada's internal affairs. But he expressed concern about the Commonwealth aspect. He asked how much money we would save by closing the mission and, when I replied that it might be a quarter of a million dollars a year, he responded archly: "Not very much, is it?" — and asked about our economic problems. When I turned the conversation by relating that Mr. Trudeau had established priorities such as national unity, the President referred to the visit earlier in the week of the French Under-Secretary of State for Foreign Affairs, Count de Lipkowski, and came out with this:

Mr. Lipkowski told me that the position of French-Canadians is that of second-class citizens and that the recent Ottawa legislation doesn't change this.

Was Mr. Trudeau really French, the Archbishop asked. I tried to straighten him out on the Prime Minister's lineage and the important role of French-speaking Canada in our society and the federal government, especially within the Cabinet.

The President did me the honour that day of accompanying me from his office to my car. His last words to me were that he would "pound Mr. Trudeau very hard" about the post closing when they next met. That was not to be for some years, by which time — to paraphrase Mr. Trudeau — the Archbishop had resigned himself to the loss of the Canadian High Commission.

The English-language daily *Cyprus Mail* carried an account of the closing of the mission on November 4. It was triggered, we learned later, by the announcement of the post closings which had been made in the House of Commons by Mitchell Sharp the previous day. The Minister said of my post:

> We propose to close our resident High Commission in Nicosia. Our relations with Cyprus and any diplomatic assistance required by our forces there can be provided for effectively through dual accreditation of the Canadian representatives to a neighbouring country. There is no connection between this decision and the question of our continuing participation in UN peacekeeping forces on the island. Canada remains deeply concerned in the search for a solution of the Cyprus dispute and is willing to make whatever contribution it can to the settlement of the problem.

And, at long last, there was a hint of regret buried in this paragraph of cant:

> These actions have been taken with the utmost regret and after long and careful study. They are dictated by the need for economy and do not reflect any lessening of Canada's interest in the areas concerned or suggest that our relations with them have diminished in importance. The governments concerned have been notified.

Finality, it seemed. But it was not. A few days before, we had learned through a routine request for an aircraft clearance that Mitchell Sharp would spend an hour at Nicosia airport on Friday, November 14, en route from Tel Aviv to Cairo during a tour of the Middle East.[115] After checking with the Foreign Ministry, I sent a telegram pointing out that the Cypriots would want to extend courtesies and suggesting that

Mr. Sharp might wish to use the opportunity to reassure them on the closing of the mission. The Department replied that if courtesies were customary, they would have to be accepted — but no fanfare was wanted. I arranged to keep the stopover event small. The Cypriots, however, had every intention of using the occasion for one last attempt to have us maintain our office.

Those early November days were poignant for the small Canadian diplomatic community. I noted in my diary after a reception at the Ledra Palace Hotel:

> Many people spoke to me about the closing of our office. Nothing nasty whatever: they express sorrow, shock and surprise and ask with obvious bewilderment why we are doing this to them. I try to hide behind the simple answer that it is a domestic political decision and that we personally are also very sorry that it has been taken. Nobody believes that economy has anything to do with it.

Eleftheria, the principal Greek language newspaper, carried an editorial on November 9 speaking of its sorrow at the action. The editorial employed an argument that had not previously been used elsewhere, although hinted at by the Archbishop to me:

> Canada's diplomatic representation could also help the island in another way. Canada can understand our external problems perhaps better than any other country because the separatist tendencies of one of its provinces are causing trouble there too.

Concluding, *Eleftheria* once more regretted the decision and hoped that it would be rescinded "for the sake of mutual interests."

The brief visit of Mitchell Sharp to Cyprus took place during the lunch hour of November 14. Aboard the Cosmopolitan aircraft of the Canadian Armed Forces with the Minister were Marcel Cadieux, deputy head of External Affairs, some other officials and a number of Canadian journalists. The meeting with Foreign Minister Kyprianou took place in the VIP lounge of the airport terminal building. Besides Mr. Kyprianou, the Cypriot side included Chris Veniamin of the Foreign Ministry, and George Pelaghias, Chief of Protocol. Marcel Cadieux and I were with Mr. Sharp.

Mitchell Sharp began the exchange by telling Mr. Kyprianou that the decision to close Nicosia was dictated solely by economic considerations and had nothing to do with political factors. Mr. Kyprianou responded with the Cyprus Government's case why we should not close, using arguments that were familiar to me. He asked Mr. Sharp to reconsider the decision. Before replying to that point, my Minister observed that, although the External Affairs budget had been cut, that of the Canadian International Development Agency had not been touched and there was money available for aid. Mr. Kyprianou retorted that Cyprus wanted not aid but the support that a Canadian diplomatic mission would give it. Then, to my great surprise and to the consternation of Marcel Cadieux, Mr. Sharp undertook to have another look at the decision to close the High Commission.

After a very brief press conference, in which very little was said about the office, the two ministers walked to the aircraft. Although I had been instructed to avoid fanfare, I arranged for a piper of the Black Watch — the regiment which then made up the Canadian contingent and was also about to be axed in the economy drive — to play a lament as Mitchell Sharp boarded the aircraft.

Fuad Sami, a prominent Turkish Cypriot, visited me to convey his regret, "as an ordinary member" of his community, at our decision to close down. He declared that his community would greatly miss the Canadian voice because we were the most impartial diplomats in Cyprus and could understand the Turkish point of view better than others because we had two language groups in Canada. He said that he had wondered if we had decided to leave because of a tiff with the Greeks over the holding of a national day party on the Turkish side. This was a novel twist to me for by celebrating Dominion Day on both sides of the Green Line, I and my two predecessors had demonstrated Canada's neutrality and our disregard for whatever the Greek Cypriots might think of the practice. I told Mr. Sami about Mitchell Sharp's undertaking to Mr. Kyprianou to reconsider the decision and said that he could pass this on to Dr. Kuchuk. I added that if I were to pay a special visit to the Vice-President to convey this information, he might attach more significance to the undertaking than I felt was justified.

Although I had no illusions that Mr. Sharp's undertaking to the Cypriot Foreign Minister would make any difference, it was a disruptive factor for the remainder of the month. In the last week of November, I went to Ottawa for consultations and to learn about my own future. When I checked in at the hotel and phoned the young officer on the Cyprus desk, he exclaimed: "By the way, do you know why Nicosia is being closed? I don't!"[116]

During the first morning of my rounds in the Department, it was said to me that the decision had been a purely departmental one. But all this was now becoming of only academic interest to me. I learned that the

Minister had spoken to the Prime Minister "very briefly" about the closing of the post and that the answer was "no" to reconsideration. I had come to Ottawa with my own draft of a message to Foreign Minister Kyprianou conveying a negative response. A few days later, Ray Caldwell, the Acting High Commissioner in Nicosia, was instructed to see the Foreign Minister and tell him that, after a careful review, it had been concluded with great regret that it would be impossible to reverse the decision.

When I returned to Nicosia two weeks later, we proceeded quickly with the closing of our operations. We stopped reporting on the political situation and ceased, on the diplomatic level, to concern ourselves with the problems of peacekeeping and faced the problems of packing. Except for the Canadian Forces Adviser, the communicator and me, every Canadian in the office was being returned to Ottawa for duty. Happily, there were no rustications among us in consequence of the economy drive. The Cypriot staff were less fortunate: they were laid off with little to show for their service to Canada.

Orders came to send furniture from the office and residence to various embassies. Much of the residence furniture was to go to the newly-appointed ambassador to the Vatican. When it arrived, it was cast off to staff quarters because a completely new set of furniture had been sent from hard-up External Affairs to the new ambassador. The official car in Nicosia was directed by Ottawa on a journey around the Cape of Good Hope and up to Kenya where it was wrecked by the local chauffeur within days of arrival. Its fate epitomized the wasteful side of the closing operation.

On the last day of 1969 I paid my farewell call on President Makarios. He was on the eve of a trip to Zambia and Tanzania and our conversation turned to Kaunda's doctrine of humanism and the question of Rhodesia. Africa was an appropriate subject on which to end the call — and the 1960s, which had begun for me on that continent.

I returned from the presidential palace to the High Commission where I invited the Canadian staff and Helen Pandelas, our local receptionist, into my office to thank them for their collaboration. I asked one of the security guards if, with all of us present, he would lower the Canadian flag that flew on the roof. When this was done, I wondered what we should do with the flag and someone suggested "Give it to Helen." So that is what we did and Helen, very moved, promised that when she was a grandmother she would still have the flag and think of it flying over 15A Heroes Street.

NOTES

1. I had known Ross Francis since he joined External Affairs in the mid-1950s, fresh from Oxford where he had been a Rhodes Scholar. His wife, Ardath, had also been a promising foreign service officer but had been required to resign on marriage, as was the rule in those days.

2. *Cape Argus*, 5 August 1958.

3. Johannes Gerhardus Strijdom had been Prime Minister since November 1954 when he succeeded Dr. Daniel F. Malan, who had won power for the National Party in 1948.

4. In 1959 the thesis was the principal publication of the *Archives Year Book for South African History* of that year.

5. Letter to T.W.L. MacDermot, High Commissioner of Canada in Australia, who had previously held that position in South Africa.

6. JCGB diary entry 2 April 1959.

7. First published in 1952 (London, Oxford University Press), *The Peoples and Policies of South Africa* was to appear in a second edition in 1960.

8. JCGB diary entry 6 May 1959.

9. Ibid: 7 May 1959.

10. Ibid: 14 May 1959.

11. The Broederbond or "Band of Brothers" was created in 1920 and became a secret society two years later to further the cause of "true" Afrikanerdom. Most, if not all, members of National Party governments from 1948 on were "brothers", as were senior civil servants.

12. Although Professor Fourie had broken with the Progressive Party, it was joined by Walter P. Stanford, a sitting MP of the Liberal Party.

13. House of Assembly Hansard, 9 March 1960, quoted in *A Survey of Race Relations: 1959–60* (South African Institute of Race Relations, Johannesburg, 1961).

14. *The Peoples and Policies of South Africa* (Cape Town, Oxford University Press, second edition, 1960) p. 176.

15. In his autobiography, *My First Seventy-Five Years* (Toronto, MacMillan, 1967) p. 371, Lower made four points in his brief reference to his post-retirement tour of 1959–60. The final one was "to register the extraordinary parallel afforded by Afrikaner and English in South Africa to French and English in Canada". It is a pity that he did not describe the parallel which has never seemed close to me.

16. "From my Political Pen" by "Dawie", *Die Burger*, 13 February 1960.

17. Letter of 19 June 1960: Professor A.R.M. Lower to JCGB.

18. House of Assembly Hansard, 28 March 1960.

19. I had met Phillips earlier that week when he came to the office. I took him to lunch with Waldo Campbell of the U.S. Embassy and afterwards to the gallery of the House of Assembly when the debate on the banning of the ANC and PAC was in progress.

20. J.S.F. Botha, then assistant secretary for International Organizations and United Nations Affairs, was one of few officials of the Department of External Affairs to come to Cape Town for the parliamentary session. He had served in Ottawa and was married to a former member of the Canadian foreign service.

21. Section 4 dealt with the "arrest and detention of persons" and empowered the Minister of Justice to do so with or without a warrant if this was deemed desirable in the interest of public order or safety, and to hold any person "for such period as the Minister may determine...". The regulations provided for the deportation of non-South Africans on release.

22. This remark did not square with Louw's statement in the House of Assembly on 21 April 1960 that he had been consulted by the Minister of Justice before the arrest because it was a matter affecting

a foreigner and it was expected that Mr. Phillips's detention might evoke a protest from the Canadian Government.

23. The assailant was an English-speaking farmer, David Pratt, who was conveniently found to be mentally disordered when he appeared in court.

24. Unclassified telegram G34 of 9 April 1960 from Secretary of State for External Affairs (SSEA), Ottawa, to the High Commissioner, Cape Town.

25. Norman Phillips: *The Tragedy of Apartheid* (Toronto, Longmans Green and Company, 1960) p. 200.

26. JCGB diary entry 20 April 1960.

27. The final result was: For — 849,958 (52.3 percent); Against — 775,878 (47.7 percent); Majority — 74,080. In only one constituency that had gone to the opposition United Party in 1958 was there a majority in favour of a republic.

28. Despatch of 19 October 1960, Pretoria to SSEA, Ottawa.

29. JCGB diary entry 1 February 1961. See also *Diefenbaker's World* by H. Basil Robinson (University of Toronto Press, 1989) p. 177:

    As the year ended there was no sign that the Prime Minister was closer to deciding what his tactics should be. If anything, he seemed particularly determined to avoid being held responsible for South Africa's expulsion, and this tendency was reinforced by a meeting he held on 20 December with Sir de Villiers Graaff, the leader of the United Party, the main opposition party in the South African parliament. 'A very thoughtful man', was Diefenbaker's judgment, given in a memorandum in which he recorded the arguments de Villiers Graaff had raised against a failure by the Commonwealth to accept South Africa's application for continuing membership.

30. JCGB diary entry 2 February 1961.

31. JCGB diary entry 12 March 1961.

32. Albert J. Luthuli, *Let My People Go* (London, Fontana, 1962) pp. 204–5.

33. H. Basil Robinson, op. cit. p. 188.

34. Molly Wilson had been on the African Endeavor with us on the

voyage from New York to Cape Town in 1958. Stanley was head of Mobil Oil's southern African area.

35. My diary entry for 6 March 1961 noted that my income had passed into five digits with salary providing Cdn $9453 and the rental of our house in Ottawa $657.

36. JCGB diary entry 1 September 1963.

37. See *Toward a World Policy for South Africa* by Patrick Duncan (Foreign Affairs, Vol. 42 No. I, October 1963) pp. 38–48.

38. JCGB diary entry 11 February 1960.

39. London, Pall Mall Press, 1958.

40. The three churches were the Nederduitse Gereformeerde Kerk (N.G. Kerk) of the Transvaal, the N.G. Kerk of the Cape, and the Nederduitse Hervormde Kerk of South Africa (N.H. Kerk).

41. JCGB diary entry 14 November 1961.

42. Anthony Delius: *The Day Natal Took Off* (Cape Town, Insight, 1963).

43. JCGB diary entry 12 February 1962.

44. Police in the USSR were called "militiamen". Those stationed at the Embassy gate were probably KGB personnel in Militia disguise.

45. Puntulis was never extradited. He died in Toronto just days after the Canadian weekend magazine *Today* carried an emotive article about him entitled "War Criminal".

46. *Looking for Trouble* (Toronto, Key Porter Books, 1984) p. 286.

47. My search, on trips abroad, for the English-language edition of the 1914 Russia led me to form a large collection of Baedekers which, in 1995, I donated to the rare books library of the University of Alberta in Edmonton.

48. During the U.S. presidential election campaign of 2000, George W. Bush scored heavily against himself by calling Clymer, then of *The New York Times* and critical of Bush, "a big league asshole".

49. Upidika was the acronym for *Upravleniye Po Obsluzhivaniyu Diplomatichestova Korpus* (Office for the Servicing of the Diplomatic Corps). It was also known by the initials UPDK. Officially an agency of the Foreign Ministry, Upidika worked

closely with the KGB. Upidika dealt with everything that a diplomatic mission and its personnel might require, including apartment rentals, building maintenance and construction, kindergarten enrolments, Russian-language tuition, food, motor oil, car repairs, the provision of local staff, interpreters, domestic staff and drivers, hotel accommodation, air and rail tickets. Most large diplomatic missions brought in their own technicians to avoid the invasion of their premises by KGB agents disguised as car mechanics, painters, plumbers and electricians. But it was impossible to by-pass Upidika on most matters.

50. The Soviets in Ottawa were permitted to travel freely up to 120 km from the capital, three times farther than the Canadians in Moscow — and within a vastly larger area.

51. Two months later, the Soviet Ambassador in Ottawa remarked to a senior official of the Department of External Affairs that the Canadian Embassy would have less difficulty in "registering" (i.e., obtaining permission for) trips in the USSR if we did not travel with Americans. The remark was clearly a ploy to weaken the co-operation that took place among all NATO missions in gathering intelligence inside the Soviet Union.

52. That afternoon, I signed a letter to the head of Upidika returning his note for its "unacceptable allegation" and stating that the damage had been done by a person — "apparently a Soviet citizen under the influence of alcohol" — to whom the bill should be redirected.

53. Founded in 1340 AD, the monastery, or convent, just outside Zagorsk (formerly Sergiyevo), was the richest and most distinguished surviving religious centre in Soviet Russia, as well as being the most important historically. The tomb of Boris Gudunov was located there.

54. Notwithstanding the fulsome praise from the Toronto visitors when they left Moscow, a member of the group took it upon himself to forward an anonymous "report" — with which he said he agreed — to the SSEA, the Honourable Paul Martin. The report criticized the Ambassador's briefing, alleged that the Embassy staff liked living apart from the Russians, towards whom they were "smart-assed": in sum, the staff were not doing a good job for Canada. Ford responded with a letter to Mr. John Taylor, the head of the delegation, to tell him that he did not accept the rebukes and to point out that we lived apart from the Russians because that was decreed by their government.

55. Maliciously perhaps, we took "hon" as the abbreviation for "honourable", but it was more likely a coding corruption for something else.

56. Khrushchev died on 11 September 1971. His life and times were reviewed extensively in the world press the next day but the Soviet media did not report the event until the 13th when *Pravda* and *Izvestiya* announced in one sentence the death of "pensioner Nikita Sergeyvich Khrushchev" — period. He had spent the seven years since the coup in obscurity.

57. Robert Ford relates the stories of the Shirley Temple and Smallwood-Nixon visits on pp. 64–65 of his autobiography *Our Man in Moscow* (1988) saying: "I was asked to help the two important visitors to see him [Khrushchev]: Shirley Temple Black and Richard Nixon." This is inaccurate: Ford was not directly involved in either of the incidents and, indeed, was absent from Moscow for the second.

58. Letter of 23 June 1965 from the Honourable Arthur Laing to JCGB. It was to amuse us that the help that my wife and the administrative officer, Edith Laidman, provided on the evening of 7 June led to a rebuke from the Ambassador, on his return to Moscow, for our having used the residence for the comfort of Minister Laing and some of his delegation. I was constrained to remind Ford that his residence was furnished by the Canadian Government.

59. The Belgian names of several Congolese cities were dropped on 30 June 1966. Leopoldville became Kinshasa, Stanleyville was changed to Kisangani and Elizabethville was replaced by Lubumbashi. The country's name — and that of the great river after which it had been called — remained the Congo until late October 1971 when it became Zaire, a Kikongo word meaning "river". The old and new names are used in these memoirs for the periods when they, respectively, were contemporaneous.

60. Letter of 23 July 1965 from R.A.D. Ford to JCGB.

61. On a trip to Ottawa in the late summer, Lumumba and his entourage ran up a very large bill at the Chateau Laurier hotel which the Canadian Government eventually had to pay. His high-handedness left him few friends either in Ottawa or at the UN in New York.

62. The United States had fielded a strong team in Leopoldville which was led by Ambassador G. MacMurtie Godley and the Central Intelligence Agency station chief, Larry Devlin. Godley's forceful

personality and Devlin's six-year cultivation of Mobutu in Brussels and Leopoldville were important elements in the American position of dominance in the Congo. Another telling factor was the placing of an American, Dr. William T. Close, as personal physician to Mobutu.

63. Senior officers of the *Societé Générale* whom I saw in Brussels on 12 November 1965 were confident that Tshombé would win the election.

64. Osakwe and I had an extraordinary encounter in London in early 1970 when I was a student at the Imperial Defence College. One morning I was about to board a bus in Swiss Cottage, books under my arm, when Osakwe descended from the bus, books under his arm. After expressing pleasure at seeing him alive, I exclaimed, pointing to his books, "But, Albert, what are you doing here!" He looked at my books and retorted: "What are you doing here?" I quickly gave him my phone number and invited him to visit us, but never heard from him again.

65. The Nigerian Police Contingent of about 400 was the last UN contingent in the Congo, staying 18 months after the rest of the Force.

66. The C-130, produced by Lockheed at Marietta, Georgia, was first flown in 1955. The RCAF acquired 24 C-130s in the early 1960s and the aircraft remained the workhorse of the Canadian Armed Forces beyond the 1990s. In December 1965, the British had not yet taken delivery of the 66 transports which they had ordered from Lockheed. Most of Lockheed's production of C-130s was engaged elsewhere, in the war in Vietnam.

67. Western International Ground Maintenance Organization. Registered in Monaco and assumed to be CIA-sponsored, WIGMO provided anti-Castro Cuban pilots to the Congolese Air Force as well as maintaining its aircraft.

68. The copper was a Zambian penny. Jim Nutt later told me that he had given it the the desk officer on the airlift "for a job well done".

69. Derek Arnould, a first secretary in Accra, had been assigned to Leopoldville on temporary duty to help out with the extraordinary workload.

70. Cooling replaced Webb as Operation Nimble commander in February.

71. Ironically, the tankards were made in Rhodesia.

72. My last visit to Zambia as a member of the foreign service was in 1976 when I inspected the Canadian mission and was taken to an official Zambian event by the High Commissioner. I was introduced by name to President Kaunda who exclaimed "Welcome back, Mr. Airlift!"

73. Kimbanguism — formally "The Church of Christ on Earth by the Prophet Simon Kimbanga" — was an early manifestation of opposition to colonial rule which was banned by the Belgians. The sect sought to reconcile traditional beliefs and rituals with Christianity, and achieved a large following. In 1969, the church was admitted to the World Council of Churches.

74. The Free University perpetuated the old Stanleyville College which, in 1966, had only a few students and was located in Leopoldville.

75. Dr. Close was widely believed to be connected to the U.S. Central Intelligence Agency.

76. H. Basil Robinson was then Acting Under Secretary of State for External Affairs.

77. JCGB diary entry 29 December 1966.

78. In November 1966 in a conversation with a Belgian businessman in Kinshasa, I had related this story to illustrate the difficulty of getting word to the President about our programme of aid to the Congo. The businessman spoke to Mobutu's Belgian major-domo, Commandant Powys, who expressed shock. Powys was even more shocked to hear that I had been so put off by the circumstances that I had asked Ottawa to hold back on other aid until the Congolese acted in a more receptive manner. Perhaps it was this conversation that resulted in my obtaining the Christmas Eve audience.

79. At independence in 1960, the Binza Group represented the union of civilian and military sources of power.

80. The red and white flag was first flown on 15 February 1965 and the Order of Canada inaugurated on 1 July 1967 as a central feature of the centennial year.

81. Vanier died on 5 March 1967. He was succeeded by Roland Michener. Both had served as heads of Canadian diplomatic missions.

82. *Toronto Star*, 20 June 1967. In March 1968 I learned that Pierre Mbale had been jailed for his misdeeds but was then being "rehabilitated" in the Congolese foreign ministry.

83. We were to learn later that this was the third private meeting of the day between Johnson and Kayibanda which suggests that the Rwandan did not give in easily to the Quebec agenda.

84. The total population was estimated in 1968 at 614,000 of whom 78 percent were Greek, 18 percent Turkish and four percent "others", mainly Armenian and Maronite, but including a number of British expatriates. Nicosia's population was about 100,000 of whom a quarter were Turkish. The island's major ports, Limassol and Famagusta, each had less than 50,000.

85. For this explanation of the background of the Cyprus problem, I have drawn on my statement in Nicosia on 10 March 1969 to a visiting Canadian parliamentary committee. (See: House of Commons, First Session, 28th Parliament, Standing Committee on External Affairs and National Defence: Journal, No. 50, pp. 1777–79.)

86. *EOKA* — *Ethniki Organosis Kyprion Agoniston*: National Organization of Cypriot Fighters — began its guerilla warfare against the British in Cyprus on 31 March 1955 and the campaign continued until a ceasefire was ordered after the signing of the Zurich Agreements of February 1959. Grivas bitterly resented the agreements, especially the setting up of the Sovereign Base Areas. He left Cyprus at independence but returned as a General in 1964 to assume command of the legal and illegal Greek forces on the island. In 1967, he launched an offensive that failed and paid the price by being removed from the island. He died in 1974 at age 76.

87. Polykarpos Georghadjis, who had been forced from the Cabinet in December 1968 after allegations that he had plotted to kill Greek Prime Minister Papadopoulos, was implicated in the attack on the Archbishop's helicopter on 8 March 1970. Five days later, he was prevented from leaving Cyprus on a plane to Beirut and on 15 March was himself assassinated.

88. Nancy Crawshaw: *The Cyprus Revolt* (London, Allen and Unwin, 1978). Crawshaw has used a "K" in transliterating the first letter of Clerides name. Clerides himself used a "C".

89. Clerides was born in 1919 and Denktash in 1924.

90. Born in 1896, Lieutenant-General I.A.E. Martola had been appointed to command UNFICYP in May 1966 and was to remain in the post until 19 December 1969 when he handed over to Lieutenant-General Prem Chand of India. During the Second World War, Martola had commanded a Finnish Army Corps fighting against the Soviet Union.

91. Dr. Bibiano Osorio-Tafall was born in Spain in 1903 and trained as a marine biologist. In the last days of the Spanish Republic, he served as a cabinet minister and, when the Civil War ended, moved in exile to university posts in Mexico and became a Mexican citizen. In 1949 he joined the Food and Agriculture Organization, subsequently serving in several countries as the head of UN technical assistance and development programme missions. He was appointed to Cyprus as the special representative of the Secretary-General on 26 January 1967.

92. In 1969 Cyprus had only eight missions abroad, in the UK, USA, Greece, Turkey, Germany, United Arab Republic (Egypt), USSR and to the United Nations in New York.

93. Before the visit of Lipkowski, the *Economist* of 25 October 1969 carried an article entitled "En garde, Makarios!" which concluded:

    M. Makarios appears to have relapsed into the position that General de Gaulle stated most forcefully, a year ago, when he included Canada in his denunciation of federations in which he said, different peoples were unwillingly brought together and 'one ethnic element imposes its authority on the others'. On that occasion, the general bracketed Canada with Cyprus. Next Monday, M. de Lipkowski begins a visit to Cyprus.

    Chris Veniamin, the Director-General of the Cypriot Foreign Ministry, told me later that Makarios had not been briefed on an earlier visit of Lipkowski to Canada which had led to his being rebuked by Ottawa: though a brief had been prepared, Chris had failed to pass it up to the Archbishop. (JCGB diary entry of 4 November 1969.)

94. UN Security Council document S/9233 of 3 June 1969, "Report by the Secretary-General on the United Nations Operation in Cyprus".

95. Speech by Glafcos Clerides to Lions Club, Nicosia, 17 November 1969.

96. JCGB diary entry 21 March 1969.

97. JCGB diary entry 10 April 1969.

98. Osorio-Tafall confided to me that he had been lectured to by the Canadian Ambassador in Ankara, Klaus Goldschlag, and told me, with a grin, that Goldschlag had written me off as "pro-Greek".

99. The Cyprus flag featured an outline of the island in yellow on a field of white; it was seldom flown after the outbreak of the inter-communal troubles. In its stead, the Greek Cypriots used the blue-and-white Hellenic cross of Greece and the Turkish Cypriots the red standard of Turkey with its star and crescent.

100. At dinner at Osorio-Tafall's on 19 September, I sat next to Brian Urquhart, a long-time British official of the UN Security Council, who was in Cyprus to study how to effect economies in UNFICYP. I commented to him that the recent Human Rights Seminar and WFUNA meetings in Nicosia had made a positive contribution to the renewal of intercommunal talks. Urquhart remarked to his American colleague on the study team that perhaps the UN should flood the island with minor conferences.

101. JCGB diary entry 2 October 1969.

102. House of Commons, First Session, 28th Parliament, Standing Committee on External Affairs and National Defence: Evidence, No. 50: Statement by Rauf Denktash.

103. JCGB diary entry 22 September 1969.

104. UN Security Council Document S/9521 of 3 December 1969, Appendix I, Paragraph 11. The Survey Team's scenario was adopted and, in February–March 1970, the military force was reduced to 2969 while UNCIVPOL remained at the 175 level.

105. UN Security Council Document S/9521, para 54. In paragraph 6 of the appendix, the Survey Team referred to the expense to UNFICYP of operating two convoys a day in each direction between Nicosia and Kyrenia to make it possible for Greek Cypriots to use this important road.

106. On the first leg of his trip to Africa, Presdident Makarios stopped in Athens to enlist the aid of Prime Minister Papadopoulos against the National Front. The interview was a result of the appeal for help.

107. JCGB diary entry 7 January 1970.

108. JCGB diary entry 14 January 1970. Triantafyllides was often unflattering in his remarks about the Archbishop.

109. Bibiano Osorio-Tafall and I had been in the Congo together. His parting shot as I left him at the end of my farewell call on 15 January 1970 in Nicosia was: "Well, Gordon, we have known each other in the Congo and in Cyprus. The next hot spot where we meet will be Hell!" I never saw him again. He died in Mexico in 1989.

110. Chapter 16 was published (with minor differences) in *Special Trust and Confidence — Envoy Essays in Canadian Diplomacy* edited by David Reece (Ottawa, Carleton University Press, 1996) pp. 49–67.

111. Bruce Thordarson, *Trudeau and Foreign Policy* (Toronto, Oxford University Press, 1972) p. 71.

112. For another account of the London meeting, see Arthur Andrew: *The Rise and Fall of Canadian Diplomacy* (Toronto, Lorimer, 1993) p. 86.

113. Canada, House of Commons, Standing Committee on External Affairs and National Defence, Evidence No. 50, March 8–22, 1969, p. 1779.

114. Telegram PST 53 of 17 October 1969 from External Affairs to Nicosia and other posts transmitting extracts from Prime Minister Trudeau's press conference of 15 October relating to the opening of the Vatican embassy and "the possible closing of posts".

115. The stop-over in Cyprus by members and representatives of foreign governments travelling to Israel from an Arab country — or vice versa — had been standard practice for many years to avoid requests for air clearances for direct flights to or from Israel which would have been refused by the Arab States. Double passports — one for Israel and the other for the rest of the world — were also employed by official travellers in the area.

116. In March 1970, Ray Caldwell wrote to me in London from Ottawa to tell me that he had established that it was the Commonwealth Division of External Affairs that had been responsible for the inclusion of Nicosia in the list of posts to be closed. As an "area" division, Commonwealth proposed Cyprus, with which it had little to do, so avoiding hard decisions about the Commonwealth posts for which it had a mandate. Though in the Commonwealth, Cyprus was under the supervision of the Defence Liaison (I) Division which was responsible for military matters and peacekeeping. Though these were the main Canadian interests, Defence Liaison was not consulted by senior management about the closing of the Nicosia post.

INDEX

ISBN 155212524-6